The Augustans

VOLUME ONE · THE AGE OF CHAUCER

VOLUME TWO · ELIZABETHAN DRAMA

VOLUME THREE · RENAISSANCE POETRY

VOLUME FOUR · MILTON

VOLUME FIVE · THE AUGUSTANS

VOLUME SIX · ROMANTIC AND VICTORIAN POETRY

VOLUME SEVEN · MODERN POETRY

ENGLISH MASTERPIECES · AN ANTHOLOGY OF
IMAGINATIVE LITERATURE FROM CHAUCER TO
T. S. ELIOT · UNDER THE GENERAL EDITOR-
SHIP OF MAYNARD MACK, YALE UNIVERSITY

The Augustans

edited by

MAYNARD MACK

Professor of English, and Fellow of Davenport College
Yale University

1950

NEW YORK · PRENTICE-HALL, INC.

TO THE READER

These volumes present a carefully proportioned collection of writings in English, from Chaucer to the present, which are primarily valuable as literary works of art. Writings in the less imaginative modes have been almost entirely excluded, and complete works have been preferred to excerpts. Where cutting or selection was necessary, an effort has been made to preserve what is crucial for an understanding of the artistic value of the whole piece. Since novels cannot be condensed or excerpted satisfactorily, they have been omitted. Separate reprints of prose fiction may be used to supplement the last three volumes of this set. The introductions try to focus the reader's attention on what is imaginatively interesting and valuable in the various selections. If they succeed, they will at the same time provide the justification for this anthology and distinguish it from the many other anthologies that are available.

For

F. B. M.

noli equi dentes inspicere donati

Contents

Introduction   1

JOHN DRYDEN

Mac Flecknoe   35
Absalom and Achitophel   42

JONATHAN SWIFT

An Argument against Abolishing Christianity   71
A Modest Proposal for Preventing the Children of Ireland
    from Being a Burden to Their Parents or Country   82
Gulliver's Travels   90

JOHN GAY

The Beggar's Opera   173

ALEXANDER POPE

An Essay on Criticism   229
The Rape of the Lock   250
An Essay on Man   272
Epistle to a Lady   311
Epistle to Dr. Arbuthnot   319
Epilogue to the Satires   332

Biographical and Bibliographical References   339

Introduction

BACKGROUND

The authors represented in this volume used to be thought of as occupying a sort of placid back-water in the history of English literature known as the Augustan Age. It was, so the story went, an excessively well tamed and tended period, cool, polite, superficial, an Age of Reason, an Age of Prose, supremely self-satisfied with what it was, and somehow a little remote from the main literary traditions, which ran from a Renaissance conceived as a nest of singing birds to a nineteenth century inhabited by great solitary thrushes, larks, and nightingales.

We know now that this picture of an age in which the theme of most of the significant men of letters was regeneration of some sort, and in which Swift in *Gulliver* and Pope in the *Dunciad* wrote two of the most searching comments on human frailty in the English language, was naive. What had been missed, it seems, was that there are at least two Augustan Ages (as there can be multiple views of any period), depending on where one looks. Among Augustan philosophers, minor essayists, miscellany poets, early scientists, popular preachers, it is possible to pile up evidence in support of the description given above. But the story alters when one looks at the great imaginative artists of the time—Dryden, Swift, Pope, and even Gay— and especially when one looks at their greatest works. There we can see that these men were challengers of complacency, that their analysis of the human situation was not superficial but profound, and that, far from being remote from the main traditions of English literature, their writing is notable for having assimilated these traditions and carried them alive to our own day.

This literature has, however, like that which preceded it, and that which followed, its own particular ways of coming to grips with life: ways that for the reader tuned to nineteenth-century lyricism require some familiarization. And since it is foolish to demand of authors what they have not to give—still more foolish to miss what they afford—this is the place to notice briefly some of the salient qualities of Augustan writing before going on to examine particular works.

The subject of Augustan literature is predominantly man in his public aspects—general human nature—the permanent relations of human beings in society. Concerned with such matters, it would have occurred to no Augustan writer to give an account of the growth of a poet's mind, as Wordsworth does in *The Prelude,* since it would never have occurred to him that a poet's mind was in any way peculiar or that an individual poet's mind was a fit object for public contemplation. It is significant that the Augustan works which roughly—very roughly—correspond to *The Prelude* have generic titles like *An Essay on Man* and *The Pleasures of Imagination.* For the same reasons, Augustan literature is never intimate. When it turns to subjects like religion, or any of the great sources of human emotion, it tends to treat them in their public aspects: philosophical, social, moral; it does not record, like Donne's or Herbert's religious poems, the devotional act itself; or like much romantic poetry, the contours of individual feeling.

Closely related to the public character of Augustan literature is its concern with the here and now. Perhaps the most characteristic mood of nineteenth-century poetry is one which looks before and after, and pines for what is not. Its gaze is typically elsewhere—on the future, with "something ever more about to be" or on the spring that if winter comes cannot be far behind; or perhaps it is on some other mode of existence: "Away! away! for I will fly to thee"—"Ah, happy happy boughs! That cannot shed Your leaves"; or else it is on the past, where "ages long ago These lovers fled away into the storm," and where idle tears arise "In looking on the happy autumn-fields, And thinking of the days that are no more." The tendency of this poetry is to extract itself as far as possible out of "The weariness, the fever, and the fret Here, where men sit and hear each other groan." By contrast, this is precisely the material in which Augustan literature is immersed. (Swift sends Gulliver on distant voyages, but only to bring him closer to the present state of man.) And one result is that Augustan writing swarms with allusions to the contemporary scene, some of them at first slightly baffling to a modern reader. Their importance, however, should not be exaggerated. To appreciate them fully in a historical sense calls for an intimate knowledge of the period; to appreciate them as elements of meaning seldom calls for more than a careful reading. Shimei, for instance, in Dryden's *Absalom and Achitophel,* was a Whig sheriff in London, about whom, historically, a great deal could be written; but his meaning *in the poem* is amply clear from the terms in which he is described.

Dryden's treatment of Shimei points to a third characteristic of the writers represented in this volume. They are all, in a profound sense, conservative of a system of values that they saw increasingly threatened by shifts of thought and value which we now associate with the formation of the modern outlook. What all these shifts were eventually to effect was a disengagement of human life and culture from the religious context in which Chaucer, Shakespeare, Milton, and all the older poets had viewed them. Politically, the conception of society as a divinely constituted *order*—reflecting a larger cosmic order in its hierarchical structure and in its classes circulating planet-like around a focal monarch—was slowly changing toward, though not yet to, a conception of society as an *aggregate of interests*. Economically, the acquisitive impulses, which throughout the Middle Ages had been restrained both by man's inability to master the environment and the theological teaching that usury was unnatural, were expanding as fast as the new conquests of the physical universe permitted. By the latter part of the seventeenth century, they were already approaching the point at which, in the words of a recent historian, economic ethics would be severed "from control by any comprehensive conception of the ultimate purpose of human, not to say Christian, living."

Meantime, there had been equivalent shifts in the philosophical view of man. The old pattern of Grace, embracing the Fall, the Atonement, and the Last Judgment, had commenced for many minds to lose its priority as truth. It was still there, to be accepted by many, deferred to by most; but its supernatural explanations were being progressively dislodged by natural ones. For example, one of the truths implicit in the Fall story—that man is a depraved, limited, but somehow redeemable creature—reappears in Hobbes and Locke. Man, in Hobbes's view, is as fallen a creature as anyone could ask, but the explanation given for this is psychological, not theological, and the ideal community is not achieved through grace, but imposed by a totalitarian state. Human understanding, for Locke, is similarly imperfect, but this is again referred to psychology instead of the Fall; and, in any case, human understanding is claimed to be quite adequate for human purposes.

To some extent, the writers we are about to study shared in this change of mind. Except for Dryden, the scheme of grace appears only rarely and never centrally in their work. Pope in the *Essay on Man,* and Swift in *Gulliver's Travels,* give an interpretation of man fallen and man potentially regenerate, entirely in non-Christian terms. Nevertheless, all these writers may be correctly said to have waged war unceasingly on secularism, if we mean by secularism the tendencies of thought that deny to man and his activities a universal spiritual and moral context. It is the corruption of a society where everything is for sale that Gay makes the subject of his satire in *The Beggar's Opera*. It is the hypocrisy of that same society in paying lip-service to higher values that Swift uncovers in *An Argument against Abolishing Christianity* and *A Modest Proposal*. It is the danger in regarding political relationships as simply relationships of interest or convenience that Dryden analyzes in *Absalom and Achitophel*. Wherever one turns in the writings of these men, one finds them engaged in the work by which the great writers of every age are known: engaged in making men conscious of the responsibilities of being human.

Yet, and this is equally important, the best Augustan writing is never solemn about itself. It is serious writing, but serious through its wit—like that of the metaphysicals, which it has absorbed. And because the Augustan ideal, in writing as well as life, was graceful negligence, it has a simplicity of surface by which one cannot afford to be deceived. This is true not merely of the prose, which may profitably be contrasted for ease and grace with Milton's (Milton's is of course superior in pomp and circumstance), but also, and particularly, of the poetry. Augustan poetry calls less attention to itself as "witty" than metaphysical poetry, and less attention to itself as "poetry" than romantic poetry. No one can miss the wit of Donne's direct comparison of lovers to a pair of compasses, but it is easy to read over the equally startling and witty—*implied*—comparisons in lines like these: "Or stain her honour or her new brocade"; "And sometimes counsel take—and sometimes Tea"; "Now lap-dogs give themselves the rousing shake, And sleepless lovers, just at twelve, awake"; "Dried butterflies, and tomes of casuistry." The tone with which the correspondences are suggested—between Belinda's attitudes to chastity and brocade, between Queen Anne's and her society's to politics and tea, between lap-dogs and lovers, ethics and Lepidoptera—is wry, reticent, casual. And this very casualness, it should be noticed, is usually an important element in the meaning, as the following couplet shows: "The hungry Judges soon the sentence sign, And wretches hang that jury-men may dine." The literal meaning is simply that everybody was in a hurry to get home to dinner; but the chasm between the savage *content* and the offhand *manner* stresses unforgettably the moral chasm between man's practice and his pretenses. This is the witty seriousness for which the reader of Augustan literature must keep his eye alert.

❧

DRYDEN

Mac Flecknoe

Mac Flecknoe is a good example of Augustan wit in both its humorous and serious aspects. The heart of the joke, of course, is mock-heroic: it lies in taking a bad writer at his own evaluation as an eminent figure and showing where he is really eminent: "Thro' all the realms of *Nonsense,* absolute." Flecknoe himself, an Irish Catholic priest with whom Dryden is not known to have had any personal relation, is simply used as a type of the bad versifier. Growing old (his death in 1678 was possibly the occasion of the poem), he begins to consider the problem of succession and chooses Shadwell, a playwright of some merit but an execrable poet, for his heir. Shadwell alone among his sons has earned the right to bear the royal patronymic—Mac, son of Flecknoe. He only has shown the necessary precocity in government: "Mature in dulness from his tender years." He only has been "confirmed" in the true church of "full stupidity." And further, he is destined to be the ripest fruit of the royal line; earlier poetasters, like Heywood and Shirley, were but his prefigurations—"types"—as the prophets of the Old Testament prefigured Christ. Even Flecknoe himself is only a John the Baptist to this Messiah (31-4).

From this point on, the poem jests specifically at some of Shadwell's ludicrous performances, while "father Flecknoe" reaches the conclusion that "All arguments, but most his plays, persuade, That for anointed dulness he was made" (63). Then the scene turns to a disreputable section of London, the seat of dulness, where the actual coronation is to take place. Flecknoe's permanent consort—the Virgilian and Chaucerian Fame, or rumor—spreads the good news, and the imperial populace gathers, unrolling before its new master a royal drugget composed of the unsold pages of dull books, including his own: "Much Heywood, Shirley, Ogleby there lay, But loads of Sh——— almost choked the way" (101-2). We are then given a view of the old and new emperors on their thrones, with the symbols of their *imperium*—ale, bad writings, soporific poppies—and an omen of their continuing prosperity: "twelve reverend owls" (129). Then Flecknoe concludes the poem with an address from the throne, invoking the spread of empire "Still in new impudence, new ignorance" (146); offering advice on ministers of state: "Let 'em be all by thy own model made" (157); warning against a rival lineage: "Thou art my blood, where Jonson has no part" (175); and counseling, in view of Mac Flecknoe's peculiar talents, a quiet reign: "Some peaceful province

in acrostic land" (206)—in preference to a militant one: "Thy inoffensive satires never bite" (200).

Dryden and Shadwell had been on reasonably good terms in the
1670's, and *Mac Flecknoe* undoubtedly points to some break in their
relations. To this extent, it is a personal poem. It is important to
realize, however, that it points equally to the universal war in every
age between the first- and second-rate; and to the Augustan writer's
characteristic insight that on the health of literature depends, in part,
the health of society as a whole. Shadwell is represented as simply the
newest champion in dulness's "immortal war with wit" (12). His coronation oath is to be that he will never "have peace with wit, nor truce
with sense" (117). His glorification is set in an environment of brothel
houses and infant punks, not only to disparage him, but because there
is a connection between moral shoddiness and literary shoddiness. He
becomes "sworn foe to Rome" (113) only partly because he is for the
moment compared to Hannibal; as an irresponsible writer, his work
denies the disciplined tradition in arts, morals, government that
Rome embodies; for the same reason, he stands apart from Jonson's
lineage. Most important of all, he can be both wittily and seriously
depicted as a monarch, because, as Dryden well knew (and the best-
seller lists still show), the widest audience is always readier to acclaim
a new literary *Führer* than to undergo the pains of moral and
artistic discrimination: "He paused, and all the people cried, 'Amen.' "

Absalom and Achitophel

Dryden's greatest satire, *Absalom and Achitophel,* grew out of the
political uproar of the years 1678-81. In 1678 a disreputable Londoner
named Titus Oates came forward with an alleged "discovery" of a
plot by English Roman Catholics to fire the city of London, kill the
king, massacre the Protestants, and bring the country back to the
papal fold. With the memory of the Gunpowder Plot against James I
and Parliament only three generations old, the news naturally threw
all England into a panic, which only grew more excited when in
October of the same year a justice of the peace (in whose care a
copy of the charges had been placed) was murdered—by persons
unknown. The murder was of course attributed to the Catholic
party, and when it was found in the resulting investigations that the
secretary of James, Charles's brother and presumptive heir, had been
corresponding with the court of Louis XIV about restoring Catholicism to England, it was agreed by many Protestants that James must
be excluded from the throne.

On this issue of exclusion, the nation divided into two factions, eventually to be known as the Whigs and Tories. The Tories, or more conservative group, to which Dryden belonged, felt that no threat from the Catholics could be as dangerous as upsetting the constitutional succession, and many of them were inclined to suspect that the plot was largely spurious—as indeed it was. The Whigs, on the other hand, under the leadership of the Earl of Shaftesbury (Dryden's Achitophel) and the Duke of Buckingham (Zimri), whipped up the antagonism roused by James in the bosoms of the extremer Protestants —for instance, the various sects of Puritans who constituted much of the London business class—and cast about for a substitute heir to the throne. The man they chose was the Duke of Monmouth (Absalom), an illegitimate son of Charles. He was physically an attractive person and a favorite with his father (which is doubtless the reason Dryden's poem is not overtly hostile to him), but a man of worthless character.

Between 1679 and 1681, while feeling about the "Popish plot" was at its height, the Whigs three times introduced in Parliament a bill for the exclusion of James. During the same period (in 1680) they sent the Duke of Monmouth on a quasi-royal progress through parts of England to stir up popular support. On its second presentation, the Exclusion Bill very nearly passed, and on its third probably would have, if Charles had not abruptly dissolved that Parliament and ridden to Windsor, surrounded with his troops. Convinced by this strategic action that exclusion could easily lead to civil war, the soberer sentiment of the nation, particularly that of the country districts, rallied strongly round Charles. By midsummer of 1681, Charles felt himself secure enough to move against the Whigs and indict their leader Shaftesbury of high treason, and at about this time Dryden seems to have composed the poem. As its close suggests, the king has revealed himself in his full authority. Nothing, politically speaking, has been settled in the poem, for the reason that nothing had yet been settled in the historical situation. But with respect to values, which are the poem's underlying theme, everything has been settled: the king has been translated from the David of the opening lines, a monarch whose ethics are no better than they should be, to an image of the God whose vicegerent he is, desiring to exercise his attribute of mercy, but willing, if compelled, to use his attribute of justice.

Dryden's strategy in effecting this translation is subtle. One aspect of it is the basic metaphor of the poem, a comparison between the situation in England and a famous episode of Old Testament history. This enables Dryden (through analogy with King David) to palliate Charles's faults, and particularly his notorious sexual promiscuity, while at the same time taking frank cognizance of these faults in such a way as to indicate that they are beside the point: the question of loyalty, and thereby of the succession, concerns Charles as symbol, as God's anointed representative, not as man.

Within this general Biblical metaphor, Dryden places his gallery of trenchant portraits. On the king's side, Barzillai, Zadoc, Adriel, Jothan, Hushai, Amiel; on the rebel side, Achitophel, Absalom, Zimri, Jonas, Shimei, Corah. Several of these portraits, especially those of Achitophel and Zimri, have become justly famous, but their brilliance should not divert attention from what Dryden is doing with them. This is a confrontation of forces, executed—since the historical situation allows no decisive action in the poem—as an analysis of value, and especially of the kind of value that can envisage rebellion against an anointed king.

The character of this aggressive value has several facets, of which the two chief are epitomized in Shimei and Achitophel. Dryden's description of Shimei (583 ff.) is constructed in terms of a perversion of religious values by price values. The sacramental view of human loyalties has been in Shimei's case replaced by (though it is still the cloak for) a wholly secular philosophy based on gain. This was a charge to which the Puritan and dissenting movement was in certain of its aspects liable, and Dryden's criticism here anticipates by about two and a half centuries several modern studies of the relation between early capitalism and Puritanism. All through the portrait, these competing values are juxtaposed. Shimei's evaluation of sins depends on how much they cost. His Puritanical keeping of the Sabbath may be interrupted if in the interests of profit. He is strict about profanity (a pun on the two senses of both *oaths* and *curse*), except when directed against the government, which interferes with his prosperity. For as he says when he turns to pamphleteering, kings are "useless" (a further pun on use, meaning return on money) and "a clog to trade." Significantly, Shimei's neck, like the justice he is supposed (as sheriff) to administer impartially, is "loaded with a chain of gold"; and the atmosphere which Dryden causes to enclose him is one made up of Scriptural and Prayer Book phrases, all corrupted from their proper sense: "Yet loved his wicked neighbor as himself"; "When two or three were gathered to declaim"; "With spiritual food he fed his servants well."

Shimei's materialism is not confined to his own sort. It taints, as Dryden carefully points out (491 ff.), almost all those to whom Shaftesbury is able to appeal, involving their thinking in the same contradictory terms as Shimei's—"property" *vs.* "government," "interest" *vs.* "the State," "duty" *vs.* "a dearer rate," "markets" *vs.* "the throne," "spoils" excused by "inspiration," "dominion" founded in "grace."

And it also taints the whole religious controversy. For the fact is, Dryden reminds us (85 ff.), might is always threatening to mistake itself for right. The "right," when the English were still a Catholic nation, was with the Jebusites—"But when the chosen people grew more strong, / The rightful cause at length became the wrong." Though Dryden himself belonged, at this time, to the numerically superior Protestants, his whole poem is a protest against the identification of right with strength, whether that strength be numerical or (as in Shimei and his kind) financial.

The other half of Dryden's analysis of value is exhibited in Achitophel. The poet indicates very early in the poem that Charles as God's vicegerent (though not necessarily as man) is the focus of the same kinds of value as attend on God. He is, in other words, more than a political convenience: he is the symbol and center of loyalties that go beyond materialism. Hence even in the humorous opening lines, he is depicted as using (and abusing) the creative power associated with Deity; while, later on, his subjects' disobedience is likened to Adam's disobedience to God (51), and their desire to change him, to the Hebrews' desire to substitute for Jehovah the golden calf (66). Against this background, Dryden presents Achitophel's temptation of Charles's son, partly in terms of Satan's temptation of Adam in the Garden, and partly in terms of Satan's temptation of the Messiah to deny his Father in favor of the kingdoms of this world. These comparisons are never made explicit, because they could not be without damaging Monmouth more than Charles would have been willing to allow; but the references are kept floating behind the surface. Shaftesbury's portrait is commenced only a few lines after an allusion to the rebellion of the angels: "Some had in courts been great, and thrown from hence, Like fiends were hardened in impenitence" (145). He has, like Satan, "a name to all succeeding ages curst" (later, he is "hell's dire agent," 373). When he speaks to Absalom, he sheds his "venom" (229). And his temptation of the young man, like Satan's of Christ, consists in an effort to persuade him to declare himself Messiah: indicated in the allusion to the star of Bethlehem (230), the allusion to the Old Testament prophets prefiguring him (236), the exploitation of the ambiguity in "Savior" (240), the covert reference to the Tree of Jesse (262).

It is because of the establishment of this kind of value—or rather, disvalue—around his central episode that Dryden is able to represent the king in the closing address of the poem as so easily and completely victorious. For the historical situation itself, no such clear-cut outcome was likely; at any rate, no such outcome had yet appeared. But for the confrontation of values that the poem dramatizes, this was the appropriate conclusion. Charles the actual king of England might grow still stronger than he was in the summer of 1681, and this no doubt was Dryden's wish. But Charles the vicegerent, and also the metaphor, for Omnipotence—the godlike David whose son could be tempted to declare himself Messiah—the emblem of a sacramental view of human loyalties: *that* Charles had always been omnipotent, as value, from the start. Dryden's magnificent achievement in the poem is to have translated the historical Charles II, and along with him a forgotten fragment of English history, into this theme of universal scope.

❧

SWIFT

An Argument against Abolishing Christianity

Writers whose theme is conduct, like those of the Augustan Age, are bound to be ironists and masters of the oblique attack. The primary reason for this, of course, is that moral truth, always tending to degenerate into platitude, can only be brought alive to men's business and bosoms when stripped of its corrosive familiarity. Irony and indirection are effective tools for this task because they compel the reader to participate in it. Swift states the case in one of his poems:

> I find it by experiment,
> Scolding moves you less than merriment.
> I may storm and rage in vain;
> It but stupefies your brain.
> But by raillery to nettle
> Sets your thoughts upon their mettle;
> Gives imagination scope;
> Never lets your mind elope;
> Drives out brangling and contention,
> Brings in reason and invention.

The function of irony is to "bring in" the reader's reason and invention.

How this works out in practice may be seen in Swift's *Argument against Abolishing Christianity*. The direct attack in this instance (to borrow Swift's own description of it from the essay) is for the preacher "to bawl one day in seven against the lawfulness of those methods most in use toward the pursuit of greatness, riches, and pleasure, which are the constant practice of all men alive on the other six." To this kind of appeal, as we all know from experience, the audience nods piously, and goes home happy that the eternal verities have been taken care of for another week. But under the indirect strategy of the *Argument,* no such simple response is possible. The *Argument* studiedly constructs a fictitious audience—wholly naturalistic in its outlook—which can be counted on to consider a drop of one point in the stock market more calamitous than a condition of perpetual hypocrisy. For such an audience it is unthinkable (as Swift's speaker in the essay hastens to assume) that Christianity should be restored as an influence on practice—"It would be to dig up foundations; to destroy at one blow all the wit, and half the learning of the kingdom; to break the entire frame and constitution of things, to ruin trade, extinguish arts and sciences with the professors of them; . . . to turn our courts, exchanges, and shops into deserts." It would be, in short, in the words of the New Testament, to "take up your cross, and follow me."

Since this program is too depressing even to contemplate, what—the essay asks—are the alternatives? One is to accept the program of the materialists—free-thinkers, as Swift calls them (Marxists, he might say today). Their plan will save the money now wasted on the upkeep of churches, extend the work-week by a day, produce a sectless and classless state from which all kinds of controversy have been removed, and eradicate the prejudices contracted from a religious education, "which, under the names of virtue, conscience, honour, justice, and the like are . . . apt to disturb the peace of human minds." The only other alternative is to go along with the writer of the essay, who has some equally appealing arguments of his own: that a nominal faith is no disadvantage in the pursuit of any employment; that Sundays, far from hindering, provide the best possible occasions for erotic and business affairs; that the existence of a low-salaried clergy ensures the presence in society of one group undebauched by diseases; that the prejudices of a religious education, such as virtue and honour, have already been effectively removed from the contemporary world; and that the abolishing of Christianity might bring in popery or Presbyterianism in its stead. (The last is Swift's gibe as a Church of England man at Puritans and Catholics.)

While all this has been going on, Swift's actual reader—the ordinary well-intentioned but complacent citizen as distinguished from the thoroughgoing materialist of the fictive audience—has been shocked into acknowledging a real dilemma. He has been compelled to see that the platform of the free-thinker (or Marxist, to translate again into modern terms) is only the platform of his own materialist society carried out to its logical conclusions. He is not happy to declare himself a part of this. On the other hand, if he goes along with the writer of the essay, he finds himself identified with blatant hypocrisy in addition to materialism—an atheist and immoralist defending religion in the name of its convenience. This is not a happy choice either. Meantime, there is always the implied third alternative, a genuine Christianity. Ought not one (so Swift's strategy implies) reflect on that again?

This is not to say, of course, that the reader rises from the *Argument against Abolishing Christianity* a regenerate man. It is rather that Swift has made it hard for him to rise from it without being a wiser one.

A Modest Proposal

Swift's irony always presupposes, in addition to the fictitious audience discussed above, a fictitious writer—what we shall call an assumed identity, a *persona*, a mask. The assumed identity was a specialty of the Augustan Age, as we can readily see by remembering the titles of the popular journals of the time (*The Tatler, The Spectator, The Guardian,* etc.); and even a philosophical work like Locke's *Essay on Human Understanding* was written "in the character of a plain man, applying the methods of common sense." It is necessary to emphasize this fact about Augustan literature because, while all literature is dramatic in the sense that it implies a person speaking in a particularized situation, it is not necessarily fatal to identify the speaker of the "Ode on Intimations of Immortality" with its author Wordsworth, or the speaker of Andrew Marvell's "Horatian Ode" with Marvell. On the other hand, in Augustan writing, this identification is very often fatal.

The reader will already have noticed that the *persona* of the *Argument against Abolishing Christianity* was not Swift. He was a person either so bland or so blind that he could embrace contradictions, and while embracing them make the reader perceive them. The *persona* of *A Modest Proposal* has the same function. He has been moved by Christian and humane benevolence to bring forward a proposal for alleviating the miseries that he sees all about him in his native land; but the proposal to which he has been moved is so horrifyingly un-Christian and inhuman that one would suppose only the profoundest malevolence could have invented it. This is Swift's way of making us realize imaginatively the ordinary citizen's (in short, our own) capacity for being viciously self-deceived. For there is nothing intentionally malevolent whatever about the projector of the modest proposal: he is a man intoxicated with his own good intentions; his mouth is filled with pious *clichés:* "that horrid practice of women," "sacrificing the poor innocent babes," "the sincerity of my heart," "the public good of my country." Moreover, and this a contemporary would have grasped at once, his plan with all its horrors is not very different from the implications of many an actual proposal that was at this time being made about Ireland's wretched condition. For the assumption of all such proposals, like the assumption Swift carefully signalizes in this one, was that England's economy must be in no way modified to improve Ireland's. Swift thus lays bare (for our time as well as his) the unconscious gross brutality of mankind, who commonly regard the "standard of living" of their own country as more important than whether *human* lives can be lived at all in another.

Despite the *persona's* manifestly good intentions, we are gradually allowed to realize the values to which his unquestioning acceptance of an economic standard has brought him. A hint of this is let fall when he speaks of a child "just dropt from its dam"; human beings are here referred to as if they were animals. The hint expands when the *persona* meets other proposals for amelioration—such as training the children to live by thievery, or selling them into slavery—not with moral but with practical objections. Then the rim of the horror slides into full view as he announces that a friend of his in America (in Swift's time supposed to be inhabited partly by cannibals) had assured him of the succulence of a yearling child; and from here on it is simply a question of revealing, through the *symbol* of the butchered child, facet after facet of modern economic materialism: "and when the family dines alone, the fore or hind quarter will make a reasonable dish, and seasoned with a little pepper or salt will be very good boiled on the fourth day, especially in winter"—"the skin . . . artificially dressed, will make admirable gloves for ladies, and summer boots for fine gentlemen." As for the older folk, "I am not in the least pain upon that matter, because it is very well known that they are every day dying, and rotting, by cold, and famine, and filth, and vermin, as fast as can be reasonably expected."

As these sentences illustrate, the power of *A Modest Proposal* comes from an immense disproportion set up between the offhand casual tone and the grim savagery of its content. This is again the value of using a mask. Swift in his own person could not write in this way without forfeiting all our respect for him as a human being. Through the *persona,* however, he can open up a chasm between manner and matter (like that noted earlier in the couplet from the *Rape of the Lock*) that images the chasm between the pretensions of our Christian societies and their actual behavior. And the cause, as Swift is always at pains to remind us, is not primarily men's malice but their blindness, their capacity for self-delusion. The nub of his whole indictment is exhibited in the final sentence, where the proposer, substantiating his selflessness by remarking that the plan will not benefit him since he has no young children, reveals the instinctive and apparently unconscious selfishness with which he has evolved just the plan that will not damage him.

Gulliver's Travels

It is a misfortune that Swift's greatest satire, *Gulliver's Travels*, cannot be presented complete in an anthology. Nevertheless, its main outlines can be preserved (as they have been here), and one can see that the reason it is sometimes relegated to the nursery is that most adults are unwilling to face the truth about themselves.

Gulliver, who is Swift's *persona* in this work, is more complex and more complexly used than the assumed identities we have met in the *Argument* and the *Modest Proposal*. He is, first of all, a stolid, unemotional, but candid and reliable observer. In this respect, his account has been made to resemble those of the authentic voyagers of Swift's time, whose narratives of distant lands (it was the last great age of exploration) were devoured by Augustan readers. Voyages, both authentic and imaginary, were in fact one of the prominent literary genres. The intent of the imaginary voyage was almost always to satirize the existing European order, and it did so by playing up the innocence, manliness, and high ethical standards of the untutored peoples whom the voyager claimed to have met. But the real voyages also, even those recounted by missionaries and priests, pointed to the same conclusion. Reflecting, without realizing it, the general modern rehabilitation of "nature" (in contrast to the older view of nature as fallen and in need of redemption), all these voyages tended alike to stress the goodness of unspoiled primitive man. The human nature presented in such accounts (and in a substantial tradition of other writings ranging from Montaigne to Rousseau) did not appear to be morally unreliable, or controllable only by the disciplines of civilization. On the contrary, it was evidently instinctively good, and had been corrupted by civilization; if these corrupting influences could be removed, there was practically no limit to its perfectibility.

Swift, whose aim in *Gulliver* is (among other things) to show the fatuity of this creed, deliberately adopts the voyage genre of the enemy and turns it to his own ends. Wherever Gulliver goes among his fantastic aborigines, he is always encountering, instead of handsome and noble savages, aspects of man as he perennially is, whether in civilized society or in nature. Among the Lilliputians, it is human pettiness, especially moral pettiness, and the triviality of many of the forms, titles, customs, pretenses, and "points of honour" by which men assert their dignity and about which they conduct their quarrels. Characteristically, the devices Gulliver meets with in this country are those of little men: pomposity, intrigue, and malice. Among the Brobdingnagians, on the other hand, it is the physical grossness of the human species, its callous indifference to what it flings aside or tramples underfoot: "For I apprehended every moment that he would dash me against the ground, as we usually do any hateful little animal which we have in mind to destroy." In this country, Gulliver is constantly being appalled by circumstances of coarseness: the nurse's monstrous breast, the linen "coarser than sackcloth," the Queen crunching "the wing of a lark, bones and all, between her teeth," and drinking "above a hogshead at a draught"—or else of callused contempt: the schoolboy's hazelnut, the farmer's indifference to Gulliver's fatigue, the pet lamb promised to Glumdalclitch but casually dispatched to the butcher. At the same time (for in this voyage the satire cuts two ways), Gulliver's conversations with the King throw a frightful light on man as civilized European.

The fourth voyage brings us the Yahoos and the animal nastiness that is also one aspect of the human situation. The Yahoos are Swift's climactic answer to the contemporary infatuation with noble "natural" men; and the language used of them becomes especially vulgar and anatomical to indicate the repulsiveness of "unspoiled" nature, either physical or moral. But the Yahoos are also something more. We may see embodied in them that extreme view of man as hopelessly irrational, decadent, and depraved, which extreme Puritanism fostered in religious terms, and which had been exemplified in nonreligious terms by Hobbes's portrait of life in a state of nature as "nasty, brutish, and short." This view, it will be observed, Swift embodies in the Yahoos only to reject it. Though Gulliver makes the error of identifying himself and other human beings completely with the Yahoos, we and Swift do not. Nor do we take the ideal life for man, as Gulliver does, to be the tepid rationality of the horses. Reacting against the Yahoos because he mistakes the animal part of human nature which they represent for the whole, Gulliver goes to the other extreme and worships pure rationality in the Houyhnhnms, which is likewise only a part of the whole. Neither extreme answers to the actual human situation, and Swift, despite the persistence with which this voyage has been misinterpreted, is careful to show us this. That Gulliver's self-identification with the Yahoos is mistaken, we realize (if we have not realized it long before) as soon as we see Gulliver insisting that his wife and children are Yahoos, and preferring to live in the stable.

Similarly, we see the mistakenness of his desire to be like the Houyhnhnms as soon as we pause to reflect that they are horses: Swift has used *animals* as his symbols here in order to make it quite plain that pure rationality is not available to *man*—would make us as absurd, monstrous, and tedious as the Houyhnhnms. For the truth, as we are meant to realize, is that man is neither irrational physicality like the Yahoos nor passionless rationality like the Houyhnhnms; neither (to paraphrase Swift's own terms in a famous letter to Pope) *animal implume bipes* nor *animal rationale,* but *animal rationis capax.*

And now, if we look back again at the voyages, we can see that this middle view has been the theme from the very beginning. In Lilliput, the vices and trivialities of the little people are seen against the normal humanity and benevolence of Gulliver. In Brobdingnag, over against Gulliver's unconscious brutality in recommending gunpowder and the description of Europeans as "the most pernicious race of little odious vermin that nature ever suffered to crawl upon the face of the earth," Swift shows us the magnanimity of the King and the tenderness of Glumdalclitch. Even in the last and darkest voyage, we are never allowed to suppose (witness the Portuguese sea-captain) that real human beings are the detestable creatures Gulliver supposes them. Man is fallen so far as Swift is concerned, and the new notions of natural goodness and infinite perfectibility are nonsense; but man is also—to put it in the nonreligious terms that Swift has chosen for his parable—capable of regeneration: *rationis capax.*

Swift's instrument in this blending of light and shadow is the assumed identity, Gulliver. Through Gulliver, Swift is able to deliver the most powerful indictment of man's inhumanity ever written in prose, and at the same time to distinguish his own realistic view of man's nature from the misanthropy of which he has sometimes been accused. While Gulliver is still naive, mainly in the first two voyages, satire can be uttered through him, he himself remaining unaware of it. Later, when he begins to fall into misanthropy, still more corrosive satire can be uttered by him. But in the end, satire is uttered of him, and we see his mistake. For we discover, if we look closely, that all through the fourth voyage Gulliver is represented as becoming more and more like a horse—learning to neigh, to walk with an equine gait, to cherish the ammoniac smell. He is represented, in other words, as isolating himself from mankind, and it is only this isolation in its climactic form that we see in his treatment of his family and his residence in the stables at the close. To suppose, as many careless critics have done, that Swift is recommending *this* as an ideal for man is the consequence of the fatal error mentioned earlier—of identifying the author of an Augustan work with its *persona.*

GAY

The Beggar's Opera

Though John Gay was otherwise a minor author, he produced in *The Beggar's Opera* one of the wittiest and most searching works of his age. In form, as its name implies, it is a mock-opera, and the reader who is familiar with serious opera will notice in it many an amusing parody of operatic conventions—for instance, in II xiii, a parody recitative built out of song fragments. Gay intended this work, in part, to dispel, or at least make ridiculous, the vogue of the Italian operas of the day, which seemed to him and many others to be corrupting English taste. And its popular success was in fact sufficient to effect both these ends for a short time.

The satire of *The Beggar's Opera* looks in other directions too. Sir Robert Walpole, prime minister under George II, was reputed to have said, with reference to the scheme of systematic bribery by which he kept himself in power and England on an even keel, "Every man has his price." *The Beggar's Opera* takes account of this, and everyone in the contemporary audience knew that Gay's allusions to "Robin of Bagshot, alias Gorgon, alias Bluff Bob, alias Carbuncle, alias Bob Booty" (I iii)—along with a good many other allusions to political cheats and ministers of state—were glances at a corrupt administration. On this account, Gay's second opera, *Polly,* was forbidden to be played.

A further element of parody in the *Opera* is literary. It will be noticed that the Lucy-Polly episodes are a mock rendering of the stock dramatic revenge theme, and that the affair of Macheath and Polly offers a burlesque version of the standard stage conflict of love and duty. Moreover, the plot laughingly suggests in its main outlines the pattern of Aristotelian tragedy, which calls for a great man's fall through a tragic weakness. To this end, Macheath is set somewhat apart from the other characters as a "great man" (this was also contemporary slang for Walpole); tag ends from Shakespeare are put in his mouth; and he is supplied with a tragi-comic flaw in the form of a weakness for women. As the play progresses, however, we begin to realize that this parody of tragic pattern is not simply a lighthearted joke, but the focus of the play's most serious implications. For Macheath's weakness for women proves to be a way of dramatizing a more paradoxical flaw in this "hero": the error of supposing that the society he moves in honors any values except money. The satire of Macheath, in short, turns into satire of a world where everything is for sale.

Gay builds up this world in a brilliant variety of ways. We are introduced at the very beginning to Peachum going over his account book—the basic symbol of a price-society. As he and his wife and his servant Filch speak, we notice the persistence of the language of business: "property," "profit," "employment," "customer," "interest," "credit," "bank-notes." We notice too the prevalence of what Gay's age called cant: a hollow jargon of piety, associated mainly (as also by Falstaff in I Henry IV) with the Puritans, who composed in large part the trading middle classes. So Peachum loves to make his friends "easy" (I ii). Filch asserts the pleasure of being "the messenger of comfort to friends in affliction" (I ii). Mrs. Peachum acknowledges the "frailty of an over-scrupulous conscience" (I iv) (in shrinking from murder). She dispatches Filch—"since you have nothing better to do" (I iv)—to learn his catechism, and urges him not to lie because she hates a liar. In the same way, she is respectably upset by her daughter's "ruin" (I viii).

This middle-class price taint is not confined to the Peachums. Lockit shows it equally, and both Peachum and Lockit constantly reach out in their observations to identify their standards with those of the whole society: "We and the surgeons are more beholden to women than all the professions besides"; "What business hath he to keep company with lords and gentlemen? he should leave them to prey upon one another"; "My daughter to me should be, like a court lady to a minister of state, a key to the whole gang" (I iv); "A lawyer is an honest employment; so is mine" (I i). Even the highwaymen make their contribution to this picture: "Why are the laws leveled at us? Are we more dishonest than the rest of mankind?" "The world is avaricious, and I hate avarice" (II i).

Dramatically, this standard of price serves the purpose of discriminating between the characters. Peachum and Lockit are wholly infected, and accept their world quite frankly on its own terms. The thieves, ironically, are somewhat less tainted, mitigating the price standard with ideals of courage, magnanimity, and (for a time) loyalty. They take pride in the fact that they would not betray a friend, that they are freehearted in the use of money, and that "what we win, gentlemen, is our own by the law of arms and the right of conquest" (II i). The latter is Gay's application of a familiar imperialistic *cliché* to a context which reveals its hollowness; but as compared with Peachum and Lockit, we can see that the thieves have a slight moral edge: they are not miserly, they risk their lives for their winnings, and all but one of them proves to be loyal. Macheath is still less tainted than the other thieves. Competing with love of money in his case are an aristocratic consciousness of "honor"—"These are the tools of men of honor. Cards and dice are only fit for cowardly cheats" (II iv)—and a romantic interest in "love"—"I must have women. . . . Money is not so strong a cordial for the time" (II iii). We must not forget that Macheath is always a comic character, only a parody hero; but we must not overlook, either, the various associations with which Gay surrounds him: Mrs. Trapes's Pilate-like washing of hands (III vi); Jenny's Judas-kiss of betrayal (II iv); the fact that he, unlike anyone else in the play, reacts with moral anger at this evidence of the ways of the world; that he is associated, by Peachum, even though comically, with "the greatest heroes"; that he freely proffers his purse to his colleagues; and that he is really surprised when one of his own gang peaches him—an unwelcome "proof that the world is all alike."

The chief purpose of the price standard, however, is to provide the environment with which those who are not wholly infected by it struggle, and before which they all have to admit defeat. Thus Macheath is twice betrayed for his error in supposing that "love" (Jenny Diver) or loyalty (Jemmy Twitcher) might be above price. Polly likewise (a parody of romantic ideals as Macheath is of heroic ones) sins before the *mores* of her world in refusing to be a prostitute: she seems dangerous and dishonest to the Peachums because she proposes to be honest. Even the standard above money by which she and Lucy are motivated in their passion for Macheath proves, in this environment, to have a large infusion of self-interest. Their quarrel over him, and Lucy's design to poison Polly, simply enact at another level the cut-throat competition that everywhere prevails.

And in the end, this society requires even the beggar poet who (professedly) has composed the play to put his integrity on sale. He had intended, he tells us (III xvi), to exhibit Macheath and all the other personages of the drama either hanged or transported; but "the taste of the town" will not permit this. Blind to the catastrophe of a culture rotted through with "business" values, the audience is hypersensitive to the "catastrophe" in plays. And the artist (naturally in a society like this a *beggar*-poet), though he knows that moral values ought to prevail, has no recourse but to discard them and bring literature into line with life. This is the "down-right deep Tragedy," profoundly serious as well as comical, of *The Beggar's Opera*.

POPE

An Essay on Criticism

Augustan literature, especially the poetry of Pope, is marked by a warm concern for corporateness: for the relation of the individual, whether a man, an idea, a work of art, or a critical term, to a community, a One. In the *Essay on Criticism* (much of what follows could be applied also to the *Essay on Man*), this corporateness expresses itself in several striking ways—which turn out also to be the striking characteristics of the work. One is the poet's studied depersonalization of himself. Another is the poem's broadly assimilative treatment of critical doctrine. A third is the remarkably inclusive nature of the *Essay* as an imaginative whole.

With respect to depersonalization, every reader has noticed that the poem teems with classical reminiscences. From Aristotle, Horace, Quintilian, Longinus, to name the chief ancient sources. From at least one Italian Renaissance critic and poet, Vida. From several French writers of the great age of Louis XIV, especially Boileau and Rapin. And in the English past, besides a multitude of minor authors, from Ben Jonson and Dryden. Not every reader, however, has rightly understood the meaning of this characteristic of the poem. Pope was not interested in plagiarizing—a term that, applied to criticism, he would hardly have understood; on the contrary, he relied on his audience to recognize the traditional sources of his views, and to make sure there was no mistake about this he indicated a reasonable number of them in notes. Still less was Pope interested in airing what De Quincy later called "mouldy commonplaces." Commonplaces, in criticism as elsewhere, are not mouldy so long as they remain the vehicle of live values, and for Pope and Pope's time the classical values were very much alive. It was precisely to express this fact that he so emphasized his precedents. To keep the great voices echoing beneath his own was a way of identifying his poem with the collective classical tradition, and thus with the sensibility of the society formed by that tradition, whose spokesman in this work he was offering to become. Moreover, it was a way of practicing the critical philosophy that the poem preached: of acknowledging that the idiosyncracies of individual intelligence and taste must be tried, and normalized, against those of educated men everywhere in all times: the cumulative wisdom of the corporate whole.

This is the point that the poem also makes in its assimilation of critical terms and doctrine. In Part I, the theoretical portion of the *Essay*, two questions are asked and answered which go to the root of the critical problem in Pope's time or any other. One is, how can literature and criticism meet? That is to say, how can anything as subjective as "wit" (meaning by wit the creative imagination of the individual artist, or its result, the work of art) ever mesh except fortuitously with anything as subjective as the judgment, the taste, of the individual critic or reader? What is the common denominator that enables literature to communicate, criticism to be practiced? The answer in Pope's day was always "Nature." Nature for the Augustans was a peculiarly honorific term and concept, used to carry a multitude of related meanings, but always tending to imply the creative operations of a (quasi-divine) principle or agency which made for order, universality, permanence—alike in man, in art, and in the cosmos. Literature and criticism have therefore a common ground, the poem says, not only because each of these activities is ultimately underlain by the same two powers in the human mind (wit and judgment), but because the *characteristic* power expressed in each activity (wit in art, judgment in criticism) derives from a common source—"Unerring Nature," by which it may be normalized as one normalizes one's watch (9-10) by the true time of the sun (13,68 ff.).

The method of achieving normalization constitutes the second basic question of Part I. How may we reconcile (to give the issue a twentieth-century coloring) modern Reason with ancient Authority, current artistic insights with past ones, the individual talent with tradition? Again the poem points to a resolution in terms of the mercurial concept Nature. "Reason" for the Augustans being simply the name of the universal and permanent when considered in its intellectual aspect, it was (by definition) one of Nature's manifestations. So was Authority. For since the ancients had obviously as human beings possessed this universal and permanent Reason and had left behind them works whose permanent and universal character many centuries had proved, ancient literature had to be considered likewise one of Nature's manifestations: "Nature and Homer were . . . the same" (135). This in turn meant that the so-called Rules—the principles of effective writing which a long line of critics had derived from Homer and other poets—were by no means impositions of a dead hand upon the present: they were "Nature still, but Nature methodized" (89). And it meant also that the surest way to a sound art and criticism was the study of these authors and these Rules: "To copy nature is to copy them" (140).

Pope does not intend by this a theory of servile imitation. He means rather that every new age must strive to assimilate the art of those whose success in rendering our common humanity ("Nature"), time has demonstrated unquestionably; the individual talent must steep itself in the tradition; and in Pope's day, when the only internationally accepted literature was still that of Greece and Rome (and when serious poets were as agreed on the primacy of the epic poem as they are nowadays on the primacy of the verse play), Homer and Virgil naturally comprised the heart of this tradition. Pope knows, of course, that criticism cannot afford to let a tradition deteriorate into formulae, dictating "dull receipts how poems may be made" (115); or lose the contemporary sensitivity (the "wit" in judging) that alone enables it to discern and applaud the "beauties . . . no Precepts can declare" (141). But he knows even more firmly that the individual author's imagination must be guided by his judgment, reflecting the collective objectivity incorporated in the Rules (84 ff.); and that true wit, to quote the best remembered line in the poem, is always "Nature to advantage dressed" (297)—i.e., the universal in experience (rather than the idiosyncratic) so rendered that its universality comes home.

In the *Essay* as a whole, this ideal of corporateness, of subjective "time" constantly regulated against universal "time," becomes the major theme. One aspect of it can be seen in the evolution of the poem's argument, as it marches from what a critic is supposed to *know:* Part I, concluding significantly with a celebration of the great creative tradition—to what he is supposed to *do:* Part III, in which the ideal critic is described and the great practitioners of criticism are reviewed. This is a development extending theory into practice, and esthetics to ethics, which by its climactic emphasis on good manners in criticism underscores again the social and corporate ideal. Another aspect of the theme is not far to seek in Part II. As the opening simile of the Alps suggests, followed by the anecdote of Don Quixote, the positives behind the satire in this section are humility in the presence of what is greater than ourselves and intelligence to rectify our personal vision by collective wisdom. All the ways of straying in criticism (and poetry) which constitute this portion of the poem arise from indifference to corporateness, "love to parts" (288), individualism and sectarianism—in short, a self-confidence about windmills of which Don Quixote (267 ff.) is the proper symbol.

The poem's final extensions of this theme are carried by the imagery. One pattern, involving especially images which are physiological or institutional, widens the specific relation of part to whole that the poem declares to be necessary for a healthy criticism into the more generic relation of part and whole that in man is called health and in societies a healthy social order. Literary norms, these images suggest, are not ultimately dissociable from greater norms. A perverse criticism and a corrupt art are equivalent in their own way to other symptoms and symbols of deterioration: tyranny in the state; bigotry and schism in the church; impotence, nausea, flatulence, jaundice, in the individual organism. Simultaneously, another pattern of images gathers up all these separate instances of whole-and-part and subsumes them under the universal concept of the One and Many. The crucial image in this pattern is that of the light (or "creative fire") emanating from the sun, which in turn is identified with the light (and creative fire) emanating from "Nature," and these in turn are associated, by implication, with something very closely resembling Grace—emanating from a Logos, a Universal Light. This last analogy must not be pushed too far; Pope's language never wholly leaves a naturalistic base. Yet in the recurrent references to the great light by which men's little lights are fed; or in the presentation of the ancients as altars burning with celestial fire (181, 195)—men who have talked with Heaven and brought back commandments (98-9)—beings in whom "Nature" was fully incarnate and may still be known (135, 140); or in the stress on pride as cause of the falling-off from critical "grace" recorded in Part II; or in the likeness of Part III to a catalogue of the saved; or in the progress of the poem's whole argument from self-will to submission before corporate Truth—in all these respects Pope extends his literary ideal to its profoundest implications, and, as it were, derives and tests (following his own precepts) his individual vision from and by a corporate vision, a Universal Light—"at once the source and end and test" (73) of the poem he has made.

The Rape of the Lock

With *The Rape of the Lock,* we come to a more comprehensive instance than *Mac Flecknoe* of what was perhaps the Augustan writer's favorite literary form—the mock-epic or mock-heroic. Heroic poems, as we saw in Volume IV, are poems like the *Odyssey,* the *Aeneid,* and *Paradise Lost,* dealing with man in his exalted aspects. Their action is weighty, their personages are dignified, and their style is elevated. Mock-heroic writings imitate this style, and by applying it to situations that are not at all exalted, secure a ludicrous effect. One purpose of this, we must never forget, is wit and pleasure. The other is the criticism that comes from comparing what man has been or can be with what he usually is.

In the *Rape of the Lock,* Pope applies his high style, and along with it a complete set of epic conventions, to the world of contemporary fashion. The poem originated from an incident that actually occurred in Pope's circle of acquaintance, when Robert, Lord Petre (the Baron), cut a lock of hair from the pretty head of Arabella Fermor (Belinda), and Pope was asked by a mutual friend of the Petre and Fermor families to toss off a jesting poem that would heal the resulting rancor. Pope did so; but the poem, as his imagination worked over it, expanded from a jest into a witty and tender analysis of the perennial war of the sexes (compare the theme of James Thurber), executed against a shimmering background of upper-class decorums.

The parodies of epic convention in the poem are too numerous to be itemized, but among them may be singled out these: the dream message from the gods and the arming of the champion (I 23 ff., 121 ff.); the sacrifice to the gods and the "charge" to the troops (II 35 ff., 73 ff.); the single combat at *Ombre*, and the epic feast (III 25 ff., 105 ff.); the journey to the underworld (IV 11 ff.); the general combat, divine intervention, and the apotheosis of the lock (V 35 ff., 71 ff., 113 ff.). The reader familiar with *Paradise Lost* will notice a particularly large number of mock-parallels with that poem—for example, between the situation of the fallen angels at the opening of Milton's first book and the punishments promised by Pope's Ariel to careless sylphs (II 125 ff.). As for the sylphs themselves, they are a splendid re-creation in social terms of the divine powers who watch over the fortunes of epic heroes. And they are also Pope's way of rendering—in their luminosity, fragility, and grace—the womanliness of woman.

The "action" of the *Rape of the Lock* has many layers of complexity. The surface level is simply a narrative of Belinda's day: how she awakes, dresses for conquest, is conveyed down the Thames to Hampton Court, bests the Baron at *Ombre*, exults too proudly and therefore suffers an Aristotelian reversal of fortune in the loss of her lock, screams, collapses in a tantrum, receives good advice from Clarissa but refuses to take it, and finally participates in the general huffing and puffing of polite indignation with which the poem ends. The progress of Belinda's day is denoted by successive references to the sun, the last of them (V 147) suggesting an implicit relation between the pattern of her day and the pattern of human life.

A second level in the action takes up the war between the sexes. Here we recognize that Pope's title has a possible literal as well as figurative significance, and that the poem is concerned with the elaborate forms that surround the courtship of man and woman. Belinda arms her beauty for an encounter the object of which is not to defeat the enemy but to yield to him—on the proper terms. By using force, the Baron violates the rules of the game. But on the other hand, as Clarissa wisely points out, Belinda should not profess to be ignorant of or outraged by the game's objective: "she who scorns a man, must die a maid."

On a third level, the movement of the poem is psychological. We first see Belinda fancy-free, i.e., surrounded with the influence of the sylphs (her own maidenly coquetries), whose protective power depends on her remaining fancy-free. At the critical moment, however, the sylphs are helpless to save the lock because Belinda's affections have become engaged: an earthly lover lurks at her heart, and as a consequence the lock of maidenliness is forfeit. This is the purpose for which the rituals of courtship exist, and it is therefore prudish in Belinda to affect such horror at the event. To represent this, Ariel the sylph is now replaced by Umbriel the gnome—for the gnomes are reincarnations of women who were prudes. Hence it is Umbriel who penetrates down into that dusky cavern of neuroses, the Cave of Spleen, returns thence with rages which are largely affectation, and presides "on a sconce's height" over the fracas of the last canto, which affectation has precipitated. The nature of the affectation is made clear in Thalestris's speech (IV 95 ff.), where we see that the pose of outraged innocence she urges Belinda to adopt rests on a confusion of values. "Honour," in Thalestris's vocabulary, does not mean the reality of chastity, but the reputation; and in the interest of the reputation, she is prepared, if necessary, to sacrifice the reality itself: "Honour forbid! at whose unrivalled shrine Ease, pleasure, *virtue, all,* our sex resign." Belinda's final couplet in this canto shows that she too has started putting appearance first.

The final level of meaning takes us to the general social criticism which forms the background of the poem. Here confusion of values is again the theme, but on a broader scale. Pope presents the absurdities of the fashionable world with affection, and with an eye to the delicate beauties that its best graces unfold. But he never allows us to forget that it is also a world whose ethical judgments are in sad disarray. Hearts and necklaces, lap-dogs and lovers, statesmanship and tea, queens and Indian screens, the hunger of jurymen and justice, Bibles and billets-doux: the verse of the poem entangles these trifles and values together in order to reflect a similar entanglement in this society's mind. And it is just here, in the presentation of a moral muddle, that the mock-heroic structure proves itself invaluable. By juxtaposing the contemporary with the heroic, the poet can emphasize both the epic proportions to which this society has magnified its trifles (like the estrangement of families over a lock of hair) and also their real triviality. Furthermore, by the contrast between the social ephemera that his verse licks up as it flows along—watches, sedan chairs, coaches, cosmetics, curling irons, men, monkeys, lap-dogs, parrots, snuff boxes, bodkins—and the quite different world of heroic activity invoked through the epic parodies and the style, he can remind us of the inexorable conditions of life, death, and self-giving that not even the most glittering civilization can afford to ignore.

An Essay on Man*

The *Essay on Man* presents, with very little fiction or indirection, the affirmations—in other words, the positives—that underlie and motivate the Augustan writer's satiric criticism of his age. Some of these affirmations are so memorably phrased in the poem (a school-boy once said that it seemed to be composed entirely of quotations) that it has become habitual to read them out of context and so to misinterpret the meaning of the whole. Those who have misinter-preted it usually claim that the *Essay* is shallow as thought, structure-less as poetry. Neither charge is true.

In its "thought," the poem is concerned like *Paradise Lost* with two problems. The metaphysical problem of accounting for the pres-ence of evil in a divinely administered universe; the ethical problem of how man should conduct himself in the manifold contexts in which he has been placed—the context of the universe as a whole, of his own psychological nature, of his fellow creatures, of happiness. These problems are intimately related, because, as both Pope and Milton see it, if man is to get on with his ethical job, he must have a firm faith in the fundamental justice of the universe he lives in. The soldier who fights best, they would argue, is the one who believes that he will be spared *unnecessary* sufferings, not the one who thinks the High Command is wasteful, or indifferent to him, or that there is no High Command.

The evils that afflict men must therefore be shown to have a point, a meaning, and to this purpose Pope devotes his first epistle. He accepts the traditional division of evils into three kinds: those caused by natural forces (earthquake, plagues); those caused by man's posi-tion in the ladder of beings (i.e., he is not an angel or a brute and so lacks their particular powers); and those caused by his own moral failures (poverty, war, the crimes of a Borgia or a Catiline, etc.). Though there is not space to discuss the arguments brought forward

---

*This discussion of the *Essay on Man* is derived in part from certain pages in my introduction to the poem, to be published in The Twickenham Edition of the Poems of Alexander Pope (Volume III, Part 1), by Methuen and Company, London.

to account for these, one point must be insisted on. Pope's explanations all belong to an orthodox tradition stretching back through Aquinas to St. Augustine, the Stoics, and Plato. In other words, Pope is not giving his own impressions, but reflecting the accumulated wisdom of the race. If we no longer choose to accept his reasonings, it is not because, given the premise of a divinely administered universe, we have reached better ones of our own. The problem of evil remains insoluble, and one of the virtues of Pope's traditional arguments is that, for all their show of rationality, they frankly say so. They assert firmly that the universe is rational, has a meaning: "Whatever is, is right." They do not assert that it is fully intelligible to men.

Having established a background of faith as the condition of ethical endeavor, Pope goes on to show, in Epistle II, what man's moral task is, psychologically speaking. Briefly, it is the task of coming to terms with the whole of his nature—with the appetitive instincts or passions, which link him with the animal creation, as well as with his reason, which he shares with the angels. His problem is to unite both these elements in the peculiar synthesis that constitutes the art of being human. Here the ruling passion plays its role as a kind of focus around which all the other elements of the personality must be organized if any lasting consistency of character is to be achieved; for it is obvious from the imagery in this epistle that Pope thinks of human character as a creative achievement, an artistic result, something built out of chaos as God built the world. It is obvious also that Pope expounds in this epistle a double view of human character when considered "in itself." Man is the world's glory, but also its jest and riddle. Reason is a god within the mind, but also a deluded queen. The ruling passion is divine, but also a troublesome disease. What Pope means by all this is simply what many ethical systems have taught: that there is a sense in which man as he is and the worldly objects he pursues have a reality and validity in their own right—"To these we owe true friendship, love sincere, Each home-felt joy that life inherits here" (II 255-6)—and another sense in which, standing off from them, man realizes that his real home is elsewhere, his real values different. Seen from this other plane, the home-felt joys dwindle to bubbles laughing in Folly's cup, and painfully won successes at the naturalistic level become simply another stage to be transcended. Man must lose his soul to find it.

In the third and fourth epistles, Pope shows man finding it. The gist of the third is that man's instinctive urge to self-fulfilment—the self-love of Epistle II, from which all the human desires spring—is the means to loss of self in something larger. Through self-interest in this sense, man is led into wedlock, family, political societies; when abused, self-fulfilment produces despotism in government and super- stition in religion; but when restrained, true religion and government by law. What the fourth epistle adds to this is a brilliant account of the preëminence of inward happiness—Milton's "Paradise within thee, happier far"—over external goods, partly by way of vindicating Provi- dence for the unequal distribution of such goods, partly by way of showing where true ethical objectives lie.

The poetic theme which is gradually developed around this struc- ture of ideas closely resembles that of *Paradise Lost;* it presents a divine order, a tendency to rebellion, and a way of salvation. Each of the epistles asserts the divine order in a different aspect: cosmic, psy- chological, social, ethical; and each shows man's inclination through his pride to repudiate it. In the first epistle, he is seen revolting against his middle rank in the cosmic chain of beings; in the second, against his condition as a dual creature compounded of passion as well as reason; in the third, against his several relationships in the total fellowship of created things; and in the last, against the ethical order which makes virtue the only stable source of happiness.

But each epistle also suggests the means of reconciliation: at the close of each comes a picture of man reunited with the divine order, and there is an unmistakable progression in these pictures. In the first, the order dwarfs him. He is embraced in it, but mainly as a "vile worm" contrasted with the highest of angelic beings, the seraph. Unlike the seraph, man lacks the beatific vision, is vile, and mourns. In the second, man has traveled a certain distance. Compared with Providence, he is a poor thing, a fool where God is wise, an indi- vidualist pursuing his own ends, which are only to be reconciled with the larger scheme by divine power. But he is now squarely in the center of the picture, he is capable of virtues, and if his ways of fulfilling himself seem, when looked at from a higher plane, partly illusory, they are after all an aspect of man's reality with which the higher view must come to terms: *grandeur,* but not without *misère.* This is Pope's portrait of man the eternal child.

In the picture of reunion with which the third epistle closes, man is no longer diminished or even deluded; he is a creative agent re- producing in his society the harmonies of God's, living "supported" by the Whole, but nevertheless contributing to it. And in the cor- responding passage of the fourth (which brings together the lead- ing themes of all: acceptance, self-love, sociality, happiness) man be- comes regenerate. For when he has thrown an ever-widening circle round the universe as a whole—extending his spiritual embrace to include his neighbors, enemies, and every created thing—self-love disappears in charity, and man reflects to heaven an inclusiveness of love that is the mirror image of the love of God. "And Heaven beholds its image in his breast."

In short, the controlling theme of the *Essay on Man* as a poem is a theme of constructive renunciation. By renouncing the exterior false Paradises, man finds the true one within. By acknowledging his weaknesses, he learns his strengths. By subordinating himself to the whole, he finds his real importance in it.

THE FORMAL VERSE SATIRES

The twentieth century is gradually rediscovering the art of reading satire. Many nineteenth-century readers, taught to see in literature the spiritual biography of the author, took satire to be the product of a vindictive spirit and recoiled from it. Knowing, for instance, that the ultimate occasion for Pope's portrait of Atticus was a quarrel with Addison, they tended to substitute an interest in the quarrel for the poetry itself. Today, we have begun to grasp that the genesis of a poem is not to be confused with the poem as a work of art, which can be enjoyed apart from any knowledge of its biographical origins. However exactly Pope's description of Atticus may fit Addison, the portrait remains, we now realize (like those of Chaucer or Shakespeare, which may have had real-life originals too), the realization of a universal type.

For we have become aware, through renewed interest in the classical rhetorical traditions, that satire is simply a special literary way of dealing with experience, like tragedy or comedy or a lyric or an epic. To put it more specifically, satire belongs to the rhetorical category of praise and blame. It aims like all poetry, in Sir Philip Sidney's phrase, at "that delightful teaching" which is "the right describing note to know a poet by." But it has its own characteristic means to this, prominent among which is the *exemplum*—the concrete illustration like Pope's "Atticus." And it uses a characteristic style—the middle style, which calls for conversational speech (rather than passion or grandiloquence), along with aphoristic phrasings, witty turns, and ironical indirection.

Of the Characters of Women

One of Pope's most brilliant series of *exempla,* and perhaps the most brilliant *series* of this kind in English, occurs in his second *Moral Essay,* entitled *Of the Characters of Women.* When Pope quotes at the beginning of the essay, "Most Women have no Characters at all," it is important to observe that he is not disparaging women: he is simply speaking in classical rhetorical terms, according to which feeling or sensibility is the term applicable to women, consistency or "character" (*ethos*), the term applicable to men. He then goes on to sketch—or in terms of his own painting metaphor, to paint, like the fashionable painters of fashionable women—a variety of *exempla* illustrating the rainbow evanescence of female sensibility. "Choose a firm Cloud, before it fall, and in it / Catch, ere she change, the Cynthia of this minute." Cloud, fall, catch, change, Cynthia (a name recalling the shifting moon), and minute: one can see how all the terms conspire to underscore the theme of transience.

The metaphor of the painter is kept alive throughout most of the poem because it also underscores this theme. The reason these portraits are hard to paint, the poet admits, is that their subjects change so fast; and their changeableness of mood is only a reflection of a deeper law of change: "Still round and round the Ghosts of Beauty glide." "Painting," therefore, gradually deepens in the poem from a pleasant way of imaging the delicate variegations of female temperaments to a very profound image for what is the matter with this world: it lives like painting—like the symbolic woman of the opening lines who is merely a succession of "paintings"—in appearances, in surfaces, in pose. For this reason, when the poet comes to speak of the ideal woman, he drops the painting figure and turns aside from the imaginary gallery to the living woman beside him with whom he has been discussing it. In *her* he can depict the ideal because she is *real:* she does not live in a world of surfaces—and so is not a creation of canvas and paint.

An Epistle to Dr. Arbuthnot

The portraits in *Of the Characters of Women* define the entire structure of the poem. In the *Epistle to Dr. Arbuthnot,* the portraits define the character of the speaker. This speaker must not be taken as identical with the historical Alexander Pope. Pope reveals himself through the speaker, but the latter is partly a *persona:* he is "the plain good man driven to write satire."

Classical rhetoric divides the persuasive elements in any communication from one man to another into three sorts: the force of the actual arguments employed, the appeal to the interests and emotions of the hearer, and the weight of authority that comes from the hearer's judgment of the speaker's character or *ethos*. For the satirist, the latter is an especially important point. If he is to be successful in "that delightful teaching," he must be accepted by his audience as a fundamentally honest, tolerant, and courageous man, who challenges the doings of other men, not whenever he happens to feel vindictive, but because he has the decent citizen's right to do so. The *Epistle to Dr. Arbuthnot* is a poem *establishing,* through the *persona* of a plain-good-man, a persuasive *ethos* for Pope as a satirist and moral critic.

The three portraits in the *Epistle*—Atticus, Bufo, and Sporus—signalize three aspects of this *ethos.* Pope is developing throughout his poem the picture of an author harassed past all reasonable patience by persons who, though individually insignificant—they are like a cloud of stinging gnats: hence the abundance of insect references—have become collectively unbearable. (The mood appears even in the staccato movement of the opening lines: "Shut, shut the door, good John! fatigued, I said.") These persons are impossible to pacify because they are morally and intellectually dishonest; they not only seek flattery—"how wretched I! Who can't be silent, and who will not lie"—but in order to obtain it are willing to give it too—"It is the slaver kills, and not the bite." The poet, for his part, has paid their dishonesty with honesty, thus maddening them further—and it is just here, appropriately, that the portrait of Atticus appears (193 ff.). For the character of Atticus brings out by contrast the speaker's own straightforwardness, and the tone of the passage exemplifies it. It lets us see a poet judicial enough to recognize the virtues of an opponent: "Blest with each talent, and each art to please," and dispassionate enough to mirror in his very language—in its subjunctives, antitheses, hesitations, and the way it hangs the portrait over the man without quite identifying it with him—the tentative, insinuating, uncommitted hollowness that he is criticizing.

Next come the satirist's expressions of indifference to the adulation showered on him (likewise knit up in a contrasting symbol, Bufo, 231 ff.), which assure us that the poet as a teacher in the rhetorical modes of praise and blame is not himself corruptible by love of praise. And following this, after a discussion of various sorts of duplicity, the portrait of Sporus (309 ff.). This is the strongest *exemplum,* reserved to the last because it gives us the poet-satirist in his most important aspects—in his detestation of evil and his courage to attack it. Sporus is made detestable because evil is detestable and because the poet with a proper *ethos* must show his fellows that he knows it. Hence, if we take this portrait, as has sometimes been done, for evidence of Pope's capacity for malice, we miss the point entirely: we turn the effectiveness of Pope the artist into a denigration of Pope the man, just as if we cited Shakespeare's Goneril and Regan as evidence of a vicious mind. What we ought to see instead in Sporus—carefully pointed up by the association with Satan—is a concrete realization of the fundamental attributes of Evil. Its specious attractiveness, as a butterfly, a painted child, a dimpling stream. Its nastiness, as a bug, a creature generated out of dirt, a thing that stinks and stings, a toad spitting froth and venom. Its essential negativism and lack of positive potency (we have already noticed this aspect of evil in *Paradise Lost*), as a mumbling spaniel, a shallow stream, a puppet, an hermaphrodite. Yet its menace as temptation, always lurking to usurp the potency of virtue "at the ear of Eve"; and its destructive capacity, when it has succeeded, to pervert what should be goods—for instance, an angelic face, or beauty, or intellectual gifts, or wit, or self-reliance.

It is against this *exemplum* of radical Evil that Pope consolidates the *ethos* which he has developed throughout the poem. This *exemplum* shows us the poet-satirist no longer patient but aroused, touching with the spear of satire, like another guardian in an earlier garden (*Paradise Lost,* IV 810-11), the eternal masquerading toad and revealing him for what he is. Such, Pope implies, is the function of every "plain good man driven to write satire."

Epilogue to the Satires, Dialogue I

It is frequently said of Pope's formal satires that while they swarm with brilliant passages, they have no underlying unity of theme. Such statements arise from careless reading. The fact is that each of these poems has a distinctive unifying pattern—usually asserted by a reference or a description or a word, very near the beginning, like the "posed" woman in *Of the Characters of Women.* For a typical illustration of such a pattern and its evolution, we may take a satire that at first glance looks entirely casual and disjointed: the first dialogue of the *Epilogue to the Satires.*

The theme of this poem is hinted in the first line with the word "appear"—significantly balanced against the word "see," which follows. The friend with whom the dialogue is conducted establishes himself at once as a man of questionable values, associating "appearance" with the poet and "seeing" with the court; for what he wants the poet to do, as his subsequent advice makes clear, is to become the champion rather than the critic of an appearance world. Instead of calling knaveries by their right names, the satirist (he urges) should accept the politer euphemisms (a further instance of the appearance theme); should, in fact, function in his society as a kind of "screen" (22)—like Walpole, who always blocked Parliamentary inquiries into public frauds. To this the poet replies with a distinction between two sides of Walpole, again stressing the difference between reality and appearance—the man's sincere private smile set against his ministerial smile which cloaks ulterior motives; and his real personal winningness, against his political victories won by covert bribes. The friend's response confirms the clash of values which we have sensed developing here, and which the dialogue form is being used to dramatize. Scripture, principle, patriotism, and virtue: all these, the friend implies, are show, to be associated with wigs, stages, fashions, clothes (37 ff.). Accordingly, he goes on to suggest that moral discrimination should be left out of satire altogether. Let the poet attack the good— they won't mind; it is attacking the guilty that gets him into trouble. "Impartial men," he observes—and the term reveals once more a vice masquerading as a virtue—sneer at everything (59).

The poet now affects to take the friend's advice seriously, illustrating its implications by pretending to adopt an "appearance" of his own. He will cease to write like himself, he says; he will assume the style of others and play the hypocrite in praise of the *status quo:* "So—Satire is no more—I feel it die" (83). But satire need not die, the friend retorts; it can still be used against those whom merit has forsaken—merit, in the friend's vocabulary, proving again to be simply an appearance: what a man has so long as he is in favor with the court. The picture which follows this, in its blasphemous comparison of King George's court to God's court and of the beatitude of the saints to the cynical indifference of courtiers, drives home the thoroughgoing idolatry of appearances for which the friend stands (91 ff.).

The rest of the poem extends the appearance theme in various ways —mainly (with a masterly irony) in terms of the lower classes' impudence in adopting the vices of their betters. The subtlety of the presentation lies in the fact that Pope here (ostensibly) follows his friend's advice, and instead of directing his attack against the real root of the evil in the aristocratic classes, seems to be directing it against those who lack the appearances of wealth, birth, and position to screen them. The result is a crescendo of scathing irony that culminates in the great portrait of Vice (141 ff.), probably the greatest satiric portrait ever written. It not only consummates, in a vivid final symbol, the deification of appearances together with the repudiation of true values which has been the poet's subject from the start, but by invoking around this subject a powerful religious context unfolds its true significance: the fall of man and angels, the triumphal procession of the Whore of Babylon, the ugliness of human sacrifice, before the idol Mammon ("And offer Country, Parent, Wife, or Son"), the black trumpet announcing Victory and Last Judgment—but not of God: of Anti-Christ.

∾

A Note on the Texts

The texts presented in this volume are based on the following original editions: *Mac Flecknoe,* on the revised second edition (1684); *Absalom and Achitophel,* on the revised second edition (1681); *An Argument against Abolishing Christianity,* on the edition in Swift's *Miscellanies* (1711); *A Modest Proposal,* on the first edition (1729); *Gulliver's Travels,* on Faulkner's Dublin edition (1735); *The Beggar's Opera,* on the corrected quarto edition (1729); and Pope's poems, on Warburton's edition (1751).

Spelling, punctuation, and capitalization (to a large extent) have been modernized.

John Dryden

Mac Flecknoe

or, A Satire upon the True-blue-Protestant Poet
T. S.
(1682?)

All human things are subject to decay,
And when Fate summons, monarchs must obey.
This Flecknoe found, who, like Augustus, young
Was called to empire, and had governed long:
In prose and verse, was owned, without dispute,   5
Thro' all the realms of *Nonsense,* absolute.
This agèd prince, now flourishing in peace,
And blest with issue of a large increase,
Worn out with business, did at length debate
To settle the succession of the State;   10
And, pondering which of all his sons was fit
To reign, and wage immortal war with wit,
Cried: " 'Tis resolved; for Nature pleads, that he
Should only rule, who most resembles me.
Sh—— alone my perfect image bears,   15
Mature in dulness from his tender years:
Sh—— alone of all my sons is he
Who stands confirmed in full stupidity.
The rest to some faint meaning make pretence,
But Sh—— never deviates into sense.   20
Some beams of wit on other souls may fall,
Strike thro', and make a lucid interval;

8. *with . . . increase:* with many heirs.

35

But Sh————'s genuine night admits no ray,
His rising fogs prevail upon the day.
Besides, his goodly fabric fills the eye,   25
And seems designed for thoughtless majesty:
Thoughtless as monarch oaks that shade the plain,
And, spread in solemn state, supinely reign.
Heywood and Shirley were but types of thee,
Thou last great prophet of tautology.   30
Ev'n I, a dunce of more renown than they,
Was sent before but to prepare thy way:
And coarsely clad in Norwich drugget came
To teach the nations in thy greater name.

    "My warbling lute, the lute I whilom strung,   35
When to King John of Portugal I sung,
Was but the prelude to that glorious day,
When thou on silver Thames didst cut thy way,
With well-timed oars before the royal barge,
Swelled with the pride of thy celestial charge;   40
And big with hymn, commander of a host,
The like was ne'er in Epsom blankets tossed.
Methinks I see the new Arion sail,
The lute still trembling underneath thy nail.
At thy well-sharpened thumb, from shore to shore   45
The treble squeaks for fear, the basses roar;
Echoes from Pissing Alley Sh———— call,
And Sh———— they resound from Aston Hall.
About thy boat the little fishes throng,
As at the morning toast that floats along.   50

---

25. *fabric:* "build"; Shadwell was corpulent. 26. *thoughtless:* (1) carefree,
(2) stupid. 29. *Heywood, Shirley:* Thomas Heywood (d. 1650?) and James
Shirley (1596-1668)—two Elizabethan dramatists of little standing in
Dryden's time. On *types,* see the Introduction, page 5. 30. *tautology:*
wordiness. 33. *Norwich drugget:* coarse woolen. So John the Baptist, a
type of Christ, was coarsely clad (Mark 1:6). 34. *thy . . . name:* with
reference to John the Baptist's words, "There cometh one mightier than I
after me." (Mark 1:7). 35. *whilom:* formerly. 36. Flecknoe had visited
the court of Portugal. 38-52. An allusion to some now unidentified water
pageant in which Shadwell apparently had part. 42. *Epsom blankets:*
Referring to the title of Shadwell's play *Epsom Wells* and the "blanketing"
of a character in his play, *The Virtuoso.* 43. *Arion:* legendary Greek musician, carried safe to shore by music-loving dolphins when he was thrown
into the sea by pirates. 46. *squeaks, roar:* i.e., as if in pain from Shadwell's
handling. 47-8. Dryden gives the echoes disreputable sites of origin. 50.
toast: feces.

Sometimes, as prince of thy harmonious band,
Thou wield'st thy papers in thy threshing hand.
St. André's feet ne'er kept more equal time,
Not ev'n the feet of thy own *Psyche's* rhyme:
Tho' they in number as in sense excel,   55
So just, so like tautology, they fell,
That, pale with envy, Singleton forswore
The lute and sword, which he in triumph bore,
And vowed he ne'er would act Villerius more."
Here stopped the good old sire, and wept for joy   60
In silent raptures of the hopeful boy.
All arguments, but most his plays, persuade,
That for anointed dulness he was made.

    Close to the walls which fair Augusta bind,
(The fair Augusta much to fears inclined)   65
An ancient fabric raised t' inform the sight,
There stood of yore, and Barbican it hight:
A watchtower once; but now, so fate ordains,
Of all the pile an empty name remains.
From its old ruins brothel-houses rise,   70
Scenes of lewd loves, and of polluted joys,
Where their vast courts the mother-strumpets keep,
And, undisturbed by watch, in silence sleep.
Near these a Nursery erects its head,
Where queens are formed, and future heroes bred;   75
Where unfledged actors learn to laugh and cry,
Where infant punks their tender voices try,
And little Maximins the gods defy.
Great Fletcher never treads in buskins here,
Nor greater Jonson dares in socks appear;   80
But gentle Simkin just reception finds
Amidst this monument of vanished minds:

---

53. *St. André:* The name of a dancing master. 54. *Psyche:* a rhymed opera
by Shadwell. 57. *Singleton:* an operatic performer. 59. *Villerius:* i.e., one
of the leading roles in William Davenant's operatic drama *The Siege of
Rhodes.* 64. *Augusta:* London. 65. *fears:* referring to the terrors excited by
the Popish plot: cf. the Introduction, page 6. 67. *Barbican . . . hight:*
i.e., it is called Barbican (a watchtower). 69. *pile:* structure. 73. *watch:*
police. 74. *Nursery:* a theatre (founded 1664) to train children for the stage.
77. *punks:* harlots. 78. *Maximins:* Maximin is the ranting hero of Dryden's
own early play *Tyrannic Love.* 79-80. *Fletcher, Jonson:* the two Elizabethan
playwrights that (along with Shakespeare) Dryden's age most admired—
Fletcher for tragedy (the buskin), Jonson for comedy (the sock). 81.
Simkin: i.e., any simpleton: there was no actual playwright of that name.

Pure clinches the suburbian Muse affords,
And Panton waging harmless war with words.
Here Flecknoe, as a place to fame well known,   85
Ambitiously designed his Sh——'s throne;
For ancient Dekker prophesied long since,   ⎫
That in this pile should reign a mighty prince,   ⎬
Born for a scourge of wit, and flail of sense,   ⎭
To whom true dulness should some *Psyches* owe,   90
But worlds of *Misers* from his pen should flow;
Humorists and hypocrites it should produce,
Whole Raymond families, and tribes of Bruce.

　　Now Empress Fame had published the renown
Of Sh——'s coronation thro' the town.   95
Roused by report of Fame, the nations meet,
From near Bunhill, and distant Watling Street.
No Persian carpets spread th' imperial way,
But scattered limbs of mangled poets lay;
From dusty shops neglected authors come,   100
Martyrs of pies, and relics of the bum.
Much Heywood, Shirley, Ogleby there lay,
But loads of Sh—— almost choked the way.
Bilked stationers for yeomen stood prepared,
And Herringman was captain of the guard.   105
The hoary prince in majesty appeared,
High on a throne of his own labors reared.
At his right hand our young Ascanius sat,
Rome's other hope, and pillar of the State.
His brows thick fogs, instead of glories, grace,   110
And lambent dulness played around his face.
As Hannibal did to the altars come,
Sworn by his sire a mortal foe to Rome;

---

83. *clinches*: puns. *suburbian*: suburban. 84. *Panton*: a contemporary
punster. 87. *Dekker*: Thomas Dekker, Elizabethan playwright, given a
place among the "types" of Shadwell possibly because Jonson had ridiculed
him in *The Poetaster*. 91-3. *The Miser* and *The Humorists* are plays by
Shadwell; Raymond is a character in *The Humorists;* Bruce appears in a
third Shadwell play, *The Virtuoso*. 101. i.e., destined to be used up in
cookshops (for wrapping pies) and in privies. 102. *Ogleby*: hack writer and
translator. 104. *Bilked stationers*: cheated booksellers. 105. *Herringman*:
well-known Restoration publisher. 107. *labors*: i.e., a throne built of his own
books. 108. *Ascanius*: Aeneas's son and hence *Rome's other hope* (in this
case, Shadwell). 112-13. Hannibal was said to have been sworn by his father
to eternal enmity against Rome, while he was still a child.

So Sh——— swore, nor should his vow be vain,
That he till death true dulness would maintain;   115
And, in his father's right, and realm's defense,
Ne'er to have peace with wit, nor truce with sense.

    The king himself the sacred unction made,
As king by office, and as priest by trade.
In his sinister hand, instead of ball,   120
He placed a mighty mug of potent ale;
Love's Kingdom to his right he did convey,
At once his scepter, and his rule of sway;
Whose righteous lore the prince had practiced young
And from whose loins recorded *Psyche* sprung.   125
His temples, last, with poppies were o'erspread,
That nodding seemed to consecrate his head:
Just at that point of time, if fame not lie,
On his left hand twelve reverend owls did fly.
So Romulus, 'tis sung, by Tiber's brook,   130
Presage of sway from twice six vultures took.
Th' admiring throng loud acclamations make,
And omens of his future empire take.
The sire then shook the honors of his head,
And from his brows damps of oblivion shed   135
Full on the filial dulness: long he stood,⎫
Repelling from his breast the raging god; ⎬
At length burst out in this prophetic mood:⎭
    "Heavens bless my son, from Ireland let him reign
To far Barbadoes on the western main;   140
Of his dominion may no end be known,
And greater than his father's be his throne;
Beyond *Love's Kingdom* let him stretch his pen!"
He paused, and all the people cried, "Amen."

————————

118. *sacred unction:* holy oil (for anointing the new king). 119. *priest:*
Flecknoe was a Roman Catholic priest. 120. *sinister:* (1) left, (2) deadly
(to the arts). *ball:* emblem of power. 122. *Love's Kingdom:* a bad play by
Flecknoe. 125. i.e., Shadwell's bad opera was a direct descendant of Flecknoe's bad play. 126. *poppies:* with reference to Shadwell's use of opium as
well as the soporific power of his works. 131. *Presage of sway:* prediction of
empire (i.e., when he founded Rome). 134. *honors:* epic term for hair.
136-7. *And . . . dulness:* parody of *Par. Lost,* VI 719-22, where the Father
"on his Son direct shone full," and the Son "all his Father full expressed."
137. An epic manner of speech, describing the seer or prophet as possessed
by the god. 139. *Ireland:* regularly thought of in this period as uncultured
(like Barbadoes, 140), and hence a stronghold of dulness.

Then thus continued he: "My son, advance   145
Still in new impudence, new ignorance.
Success let others teach, learn thou from me
Pangs without birth, and fruitless industry.
Let *Virtuosos* in five years be writ;
Yet not one thought accuse thy toil of wit.   150
Let gentle George in triumph tread the stage,
Make Dorimant betray, and Loveit rage;
Let Cully, Cockwood, Fopling, charm the pit,
And in their folly shew the writer's wit.
Yet still thy fools shall stand in thy defense   155
And justify their author's want of sense.
Let 'em be all by thy own model made
Of dulness, and desire no foreign aid,
That they to future ages may be known,
Not copies drawn, but issue of thy own.   160
Nay, let thy men of wit too be the same,
All full of thee, and differing but in name.
But let no alien S—dl—y interpose,
To lard with wit thy hungry *Epsom* prose.
And when false flowers of rhetoric thou wouldst cull,   165
Trust nature, do not labor to be dull;
But write thy best, and top; and, in each line,
Sir Formal's oratory will be thine:
Sir Formal, tho' unsought, attends thy quill,
And does thy northern dedications fill.   170
     "Nor let false friends seduce thy mind to fame,
By arrogating Jonson's hostile name.
Let father Flecknoe fire thy mind with praise,
And uncle Ogleby thy envy raise.
Thou art my blood, where Jonson has no part: 175
What share have we in nature, or in art?

151-3. *George* is George Etherege, often called the founder of Restoration
comedy; the other names refer to characters in his plays. 160. *issue:* off-
spring. 161. i.e., let the witty people in thy comedies be indistinguishable
from the fools. 163-4. Dryden hints that Charles Sedley, a noted wit who
had contributed a prologue to Shadwell's play, *Epsom Wells,* had contributed something more. 165. *flowers of rhetoric:* figures of speech. 168.
Sir Formal Trifle's speech in *The Virtuoso* is full of affectation. 170. *northern dedications:* i.e., dedications of his books to the Duke of Newcastle,
whose family seat was in the north of England. 176. *nature, art:* the two
realms of which (in traditional dramatic theory) a good playwright must be
master—holding a mirror up to reality (nature) by means of art.

Where did his wit on learning fix a brand,
And rail at arts he did not understand?
Where made he love in Prince Nicander's vein,
Or swept the dust in *Psyche's* humble strain?   180
Where sold he bargains, 'whip-stitch, kiss my arse,'
Promised a play and dwindled to a farce?
When did his Muse from Fletcher scenes purloin,
As thou whole Eth'rege dost transfuse to thine?
But so transfused, as oil on water's flow,   185
His always floats above, thine sinks below.
This is thy province, this thy wondrous way,
New humours to invent for each new play:
This is that boasted bias of thy mind,
By which one way, to dulness, 'tis inclined,   190
Which makes thy writings lean on one side still,
And, in all changes, that way bends thy will.
Nor let thy mountain-belly make pretense
Of likeness; thine's a tympany of sense.
A tun of man in thy large bulk is writ,   195
But sure thou'rt but a kilderkin of wit.
Like mine, thy gentle numbers feebly creep;
Thy tragic Muse gives smiles, thy comic, sleep.
With whate'er gall thou sett'st thyself to write,
Thy inoffensive satires never bite.   200
In thy felonious heart tho' venom lies,
It does but touch thy Irish pen, and dies.
Thy genius calls thee not to purchase fame
In keen iambics, but mild anagram.

177-8. Probably a reference to the satire on the scientific interests of the
Royal Society in Shadwell's *Virtuoso*. 179. *Nicander:* a character in *Psyche*.
181. *sold . . . bargains:* "Selling bargains" was a game in which coarse
phrases like the one in this line were featured. 182. *Promised a play:* i.e.,
as Shadwell did in the preface to *The Virtuoso*. 188. *humours:* i.e., characters based on a distinguishing eccentricity or *bias of mind* (189). Shadwell
boasts of his *new humours* in the preface to *The Virtuoso*. 189. Dryden
puns on *bias* meaning the oblique curve of a bowl (in English bowling)
caused by its extra weighting on one side. 194. *likeness:* i.e., to Jonson,
who was also corpulent. 194. *a tympany:* i.e., a drum (which is hollow).
195-6. *tun, kilderkin:* large and small wine casks. 199. *gall:* "edge," sharp-
ness. 202. Referring to the legend that Ireland has no snakes: as serpent
venom cannot survive in Ireland, so satirical "venom" cannot survive
transmission through Shadwell's "Irish" (i.e., uncultivated) pen. 204.
iambics: i.e., satire (from the metre in which the Greeks wrote it).

Leave writing plays, and choose for thy command   205
Some peaceful province in acrostic land.
There thou may'st wings display, and altars raise,
And torture one poor word ten thousand ways;
Or, if thou wouldst thy different talents suit,
Set thy own songs, and sing them to thy lute."   210
   He said: but his last words were scarcely heard,⎫
For Bruce and Longvil had a trap prepared,   ⎬
And down they sent the yet declaiming bard.   ⎭
Sinking he left his drugget robe behind,
Borne upwards by a subterranean wind.   215
The mantle fell to the young prophet's part,
With double portion of his father's art.

❦

Absalom and Achitophel

(1681)

*I*N PIOUS times, ere priestcraft did begin,
Before polygamy was made a sin;
When man on many multiplied his kind,
Ere one to one was cursèdly confined;
When nature prompted, and no law denied   5
Promiscuous use of concubine and bride;
Then Israel's monarch after Heaven's own heart,
His vigorous warmth did, variously, impart
To wives and slaves; and, wide as his command,
Scattered his Maker's image thro' the land.   10
Michal, of royal blood, the crown did wear,
A soil ungrateful to the tiller's care:

205-8. Poems containing anagrams and acrostics, or shaped through varying lengths of lines to look like altars and wings, or composed by using only the letters in a given word *ten thousand ways,* were the pastime of poetasters, and to this pastime Flecknoe urges Mac Flecknoe to confine himself. 210. *set:* set to music. 211-17. This passage applies to Flecknoe the trick played in *The Virtuoso* to Sir Formal Trifle. 212. *trap:* trap-door.

   ABSALOM AND ACHITOPHEL: 7. *Israel's monarch:* On the general comparison of Charles II and his contemporaries to King David and other Old Testament figures, see the Introduction, pp. 7-8. To save space, the Biblical identifications have been omitted from these notes. 11. *Michal:* Charles's queen, Catherine of Portugal.

Not so the rest; for several mothers bore
To godlike David several sons before.
But since like slaves his bed they did ascend,   15
No true succession could their seed attend.
  Of all this numerous progeny was none
So beautiful, so brave, as Absalon:
Whether, inspired by some diviner lust,
His father got him with a greater gust,   20
Or that his conscious destiny made way,
By manly beauty, to imperial sway.
Early in foreign fields he won renown,
With kings and states allied to Israel's crown:
In peace the thoughts of war he could remove,   25
And seemed as he were only born for love.
Whate'er he did, was done with so much ease,
In him alone 't was natural to please;
His motions all accompanied with grace;
And paradise was opened in his face.   30
With secret joy indulgent David viewed
His youthful image in his son renewed:
To all his wishes nothing he denied;
And made the charming Annabel his bride.
What faults he had (for who from faults is free?)   35
His father could not, or he would not see.
Some warm excesses which the law forbore,
Were cónstrued youth that purged by boiling o'er:
And Amnon's murther, by a specious name,
Was called a just revenge for injured fame.   40
Thus praised and loved the noble youth remained,
While David, undisturbed, in Sion reigned.
  But life can never be sincerely blest:
Heaven punishes the bad, and proves the best.
The Jews, a headstrong, moody, murmuring race,   45
As ever tried th' extent and stretch of grace;
God's pampered people, whom, debauched with ease,
No king could govern, nor no God could please;
(Gods they had tried of every shape and size,
That god-smiths could produce, or priests devise:)   50

---

18. *Absalom:* See the Introduction, page 7. 20. *gust:* gusto. 24. i.e., with Holland and France. 34. *Annabel:* Anne Scott, Countess of Buccleuch. 38. i.e., were excused as "wild oats." 39. *Amnon:* still unidentified. *A . . . name:* i.e., a euphemism. 44. *proves:* puts to proof. 45. *the Jews:* the English.

These Adam-wits, too fortunately free,
Began to dream they wanted liberty;
And when no rule, no precedent was found,
Of men by laws less circumscribed and bound;
They led their wild desires to woods and caves,   55
And thought that all but savages were slaves.
They who, when Saul was dead, without a blow,
Made foolish Ishbosheth the crown forego;
Who banished David did from Hebron bring,
And with a general shout proclaimed him king: 60
Those very Jews, who, at their very best,
Their humor more than loyalty expressed,
Now wondered why so long they had obeyed
An idol monarch, which their hands had made;
Thought they might ruin him they could create,   65
Or melt him to that golden calf, a State.
But these were random bolts: no formed design,
Nor interest made the factious crowd to join:
The sober part of Israel, free from stain,
Well knew the value of a peaceful reign;   70
And, looking backward with a wise affright,
Saw seams of wounds, dishonest to the sight:
In contemplation of whose ugly scars
They cursed the memory of civil wars.
The moderate sort of men, thus qualified,   75
Inclined the balance to the better side;
And David's mildness managed it so well,
The bad found no occasion to rebel.
But when to sin our biased nature leans,
The careful Devil is still at hand with means;   80
And providently pimps for ill desires;
The Good Old Cause revived, a plot requires:
Plots, true or false, are necessary things,
To raise up commonwealths, and ruin kings.

---

51. *Adam-wits:* i.e., "well off if they had only had the sense to realize it" (like Adam in Eden before the Fall). 55. i.e., they pointed to the "liberty" of wild beasts as a precedent. *Savages* in 56 means wild beasts. 57. *Saul:* Cromwell. 58. *Ishbosheth:* Cromwell's son Richard. 59. *Hebron:* Scotland, where Charles II was crowned several months before his coronation in England. 64. *idol:* pun on "idle." Charles was well known for idleness. 66. *State:* i.e., a republic. 80. *Devil:* often a monosyllable (as here). 82. *Good Old Cause:* i.e., the Commonwealth or republican government which ruled England from the execution of Charles I (1649) till Cromwell's assumption of power (1653).

Medical College Admissions
Test
Educational Testing Service
P. O. Box 592, Princeton, N. J.

Purdue

ARMY

N.C.S.

Navey

x

Ga Tect

U.N.C.

Th' inhabitants of old Jerusalem   85
Were Jebusites; the town so called from them;
And theirs the native right ——
But when the chosen people grew more strong,
The rightful cause at length became the wrong;
And every loss the men of Jebus bore,   90
They still were thought God's enemies the more.
Thus worn and weakened, well or ill content,
Submit they must to David's government:
Impoverished and deprived of all command,
Their taxes doubled as they lost their land;   95
And, what was harder yet to flesh and blood,
Their gods disgraced, and burnt like common wood.
This set the heathen priesthood in a flame;
For priests of all religions are the same:
Of whatsoe'er descent their godhead be,   100
Stock, stone, or other homely pedigree,
In his defense his servants are as bold,
As if he had been born of beaten gold.
The Jewish rabbins, tho' their enemies,
In this conclude them honest men and wise: 105
For 't was their duty, all the learnèd think,
T' espouse his cause, by whom they eat and drink.
    From hence began that Plot, the nation's curse,
Bad in itself, but represented worse,
Raised in extremes, and in extremes decried,   110
With oaths affirmed, with dying vows denied,
Not weighed or winnowed by the multitude,
But swallow'd in the mass, unchewed, and crude.
Some truth there was, but dashed and brewed with lies,
To please the fools, and puzzle all the wise.   115
Succeeding times did equal folly call
Believing nothing, or believing all.
Th' Egyptian rites the Jebusites embraced,
Where gods were recommended by their taste.

---

85. *Jerusalem:* London. 86. *Jebusites:* Roman Catholics. 88. *the chosen
people:* the Protestants. 94-7. An accurate account of the harsh treatment
of Roman Catholics in Dryden's and Pope's England. 98. *heathen priesthood:* Roman Catholic priests. 104. *Jewish rabbins:* Church of England
priests. 108. *Plot:* See the Introduction, pp. 6-7. 112. *winnowed:* sifted.
118. *Egyptian:* French, i.e., Roman Catholic: Dryden calls them Egyptian
with reference to the tradition that in Egyptian cults even edibles like the
leek and onion were held sacred. To this he compares the Roman Catholic
doctrine of transsubstantiation. Cf. *taste, savory, food* in the following
lines.

Such savory deities must needs be good,   120
As served at once for worship and for food.
By force they could not introduce these gods,
For ten to one in former days was odds;
So fraud was used (the sacrificer's trade):
Fools are more hard to conquer than persuade.   125
Their busy teachers mingled with the Jews,
And raked for converts ev'n the court and stews:
Which Hebrew priests the more unkindly took,
Because the fleece accompanies the flock.
Some thought they God's anointed meant to slay   130
By guns, invented since full many a day:
Our author swears it not; but who can know
How far the Devil and Jebusites may go?
This Plot, which failed for want of common sense,
Had yet a deep and dangerous consequence: 135
For, as when raging fevers boil the blood,
The standing lake soon floats into a flood,
And every hostile humour, which before
Slept quiet in its channels, bubbles o'er;
So several factions from this first ferment   140
Work up to foam, and threat the government.
Some by their friends, more by themselves thought wise,
Opposed the power to which they could not rise.
Some had in courts been great, and thrown from thence,
Like fiends were hardened in impenitence.   145
Some, by their monarch's fatal mercy, grown
From pardoned rebels, kinsmen to the throne,
Were raised in power and public office high;
Strong bands, if bands ungrateful men could tie.

Of these the false Achitophel was first;   150
A name to all succeeding ages curst:
For close designs and crookèd counsels fit,
Sagacious, bold, and turbulent of wit,
Restless, unfixed in principles and place,
In power unpleased, impatient of disgrace;   155
A fiery soul, which, working out its way, ⎫
Fretted the pigmy body to decay: ⎬
And o'er-informed the tenement of clay. ⎭

---

123. *ten to one:* Dryden's estimate of the ratio of Protestants to Catholics.
124. *sacrificer's:* priest's. 127. *stews:* brothels. 128. *Hebrew priests:* Cf. 104n.
129. *fleece:* i.e., income. 138. *hostile:* malign (because excessive). 150.
Achitophel: See the Introduction, page 9. 157. *Fretted:* eroded. 158. *o'er-informed:* filled too full.

A daring pilot in extremity;
Pleased with the danger, when the waves went high,   160
He sought the storms; but, for a calm unfit,
Would steer too nigh the sands, to boast his wit.
Great wits are sure to madness near allied,
And thin partitions do their bounds divide;
Else why should he, with wealth and honour blest,   165
Refuse his age the needful hours of rest?
Punish a body which he could not please,
Bankrupt of life, yet prodigal of ease?
And all to leave what with his toil he won,
To that unfeathered two-legged thing, a son: 170
Got, while his soul did huddled notions try;
And born a shapeless lump, like anarchy.
In friendship false, implacable in hate,
Resolved to ruin or to rule the State;
To compass this the triple bond he broke; ⎫   175
The pillars of the public safety shook,   ⎬
And fitted Israel for a foreign yoke: ⎭
Then seized with fear, yet still affecting fame,
Usurped a Patriot's all-atoning name.
So easy still it proves in factious times   180
With public zeal to cancel private crimes.
How safe is treason, and how sacred ill,
Where none can sin against the People's Will!
Where crowds can wink, and no offense be known,
Since in another's guilt they find their own!   185
Yet, fame deserved, no enemy can grudge;
The statesman we abhor, but praise the judge.
In Israel's courts ne'er sat an Abbethdin
With more discerning eyes or hands more clean,
Unbribed, unsought, the wretched to redress;   190
Swift of dispatch, and easy of access.
O, had he been content to serve the crown,
With virtues only proper to the gown,

---

164. *bounds:* i.e., those of genius (wit) and madness. 172. Dryden dis-
misses Shaftesbury's son (a man of no talents) with the phrase often
applied to man in general: *implume bipes* (featherless biped). 175. *triple
bond:* the triple alliance of Holland, France, and England, which Shaftesbury helped break. 179. *Patriot's . . . name:* the name taken by those who
wanted the exclusion bill passed: see the Introduction, page 7. 188.
Abbethdin: officer of justice: Shaftesbury was Lord Chancellor and also
chief judge in the Court of Chancery. 193. *gown:* judge's gown.

Or had the rankness of the soil been freed
From cockle, that oppressed the noble seed,   195
David for him his tuneful harp had strung,
And Heaven had wanted one immortal song.
But wild Ambition loves to slide, not stand,
And Fortune's ice prefers to Virtue's land.
Achitophel, grown weary to possess   200
A lawful fame, and lazy happiness,
Disdained the golden fruit to gather free
And lent the crowd his arm to shake the tree.
Now, manifest of crimes contrived long since,
He stood at bold defiance with his prince: 205
Held up the buckler of the people's cause
Against the crown; and skulked behind the laws.
The wished occasion of the Plot he takes;
Some circumstances finds, but more he makes.
By buzzing emissaries, fills the ears   210
Of listening crowds with jealousies and fears
Of arbitrary counsels brought to light,
And proves the king himself a Jebusite.
Weak arguments! which yet he knew full well
Were strong with people easy to rebel.   215
For, governed by the moon, the giddy Jews
Tread the same track when she the prime renews:
And once in twenty years, their scribes record,
By natural instinct they change their lord.
Achitophel still wants a chief, and none   220
Was found so fit as warlike Absalon:
Not that he wished his greatness to create,
(For politicians neither love nor hate,)
But, for he knew his title not allowed,
Would keep him still depending on the crowd,   225
That kingly power, thus ebbing out, might be
Drawn to the dregs of a democracy.
Him he attempts with studied arts to please,
And sheds his venom in such words as these:
    "Auspicious prince, at whose nativity   230
Some royal planet ruled the southern sky;

---

197. *one . . . song:* possibly David's song of lament for Absalom's death
(2 Samuel 18:33)—which, if Achitophel had been dutiful, David would
never need to have written, and so Heaven would have lacked (*wanted*) it.
202. *golden fruit:* i.e., of Charles's favor. 204. *manifest of:* revealing openly.
217. *prime:* first appearance of the new moon. 230 ff. Achitophel tempts
Absalom in terms better applicable to Christ: see the Introduction, page 9.

Thy longing country's darling and desire,
Their cloudy pillar and their guardian fire,
Their second Moses, whose extended wand
Divides the seas, and shews the promised land, 235
Whose dawning day in every distant age
Has exercised the sacred prophets' rage,
The people's prayer, the glad diviners' theme,
The young men's vision, and the old men's dream!
Thee, Savior, thee, the nation's vows confess; 240
And, never satisfied with seeing, bless:
Swift unbespoken pomps, thy steps proclaim,
And stammering babes are taught to lisp thy name.
How long wilt thou the general joy detain,
Starve, and defraud the people of thy reign? 245
Content ingloriously to pass thy days
Like one of Virtue's fools that feeds on praise;
Till thy fresh glories, which now shine so bright,
Grow stale and tarnish with our daily sight.
Believe me, royal youth, thy fruit must be 250
Or gathered ripe, or rot upon the tree.
Heaven has to all allotted, soon or late,
Some lucky revolution of their fate:
Whose motions if we watch and guide with skill,
(For human good depends on human will,) 255
Our Fortune rolls as from a smooth descent,
And from the first impression takes the bent:
But, if unseized, she glides away like wind,
And leaves repenting Folly far behind.
Now, now she meets you with a glorious prize, 260
And spreads her locks before her as she flies.
Had thus old David, from whose loins you spring,
Not dared, when Fortune called him, to be king,
At Gath an exile he might still remain,
And Heaven's anointing oil had been in vain. 265
Let his successful youth your hopes engage,
But shun th' example of declining age:
Behold him setting in his western skies,
The shadows lengthening as the vapors rise.

---

239. Joel 2:28: "Your old men shall dream dreams, your young men shall
see visions." This passage was interpreted as a prophecy of Christ's reign.
242. i.e., wherever Monmouth goes he is honored spontaneously. 247. *feeds
on praise:* is content with praise (instead of *solid power:* cf. 298). 264.
Gath: Brussels, where Charles had spent much of his exile.

He is not now, as when on Jordan's sand   270
The joyful people thronged to see him land,
Covering the beach, and blackening all the strand:
But, like the Prince of Angels, from his height
Comes tumbling downward with diminished light:
Betrayed by one poor plot to public scorn,   275
(Our only blessing since his curst return)
Those heaps of people which one sheaf did bind,
Blown off and scattered by a puff of wind.
What strength can he to your designs oppose,
Naked of friends, and round beset with foes?   280
If Pharaoh's doubtful succour he should use,
A foreign aid would more incense the Jews:
Proud Egypt would dissembled friendship bring;
Foment the war, but not support the king:
Nor would the royal party e'er unite   285
With Pharaoh's arms t' assist the Jebusite;
Or if they should, their interest soon would break,
And with such odious aid make David weak.
All sorts of men by my successful arts,
Abhorring kings, estrange their altered hearts   290
From David's rule: and 'tis the general cry,
'Religion, commonwealth, and liberty.'
If you, as champion of the public good,
Add to their arms a chief of royal blood,
What may not Israel hope, and what applause   295
Might such a general gain by such a cause?
Not barren praise alone, that gaudy flower
Fair only to the sight, but solid power:
And nobler is a limited command,
Given by the love of all your native land,   300
Than a successive title, long and dark,
Drawn from the moldy rolls of Noah's ark."
   What cannot praise effect in mighty minds,
When flattery soothes, and when ambition blinds!
Desire of power, on earth a vicious weed,   305
Yet, sprung from high, is of celestial seed;
In God 'tis glory: and when men aspire,
'Tis but a spark too much of heavenly fire.
Th' ambitious youth, too covetous of fame,

---

270. *on . . . sand:* i.e., at Dover where Charles was greeted on his Restoration. 273. *Prince of Angels:* Satan. 281. *Pharaoh:* Louis XIV of France.

Too full of angels' metal in his frame, 310
Unwarily was led from virtue's ways,
Made drunk with honor, and debauched with praise.
Half loath, and half consenting to the ill,
(For loyal blood within him struggled still,)
He thus replied: "And what pretense have I 315
To take up arms for public liberty?
My father governs with unquestioned right;
The faith's defender, and mankind's delight,
Good, gracious, just, observant of the laws,
And Heaven by wonders has espoused his cause. 320
Whom has he wronged in all his peaceful reign?
Who sues for justice to his throne in vain?
What millions has he pardoned of his foes
Whom just revenge did to his wrath expose?
Mild, easy, humble, studious of our good, 325
Inclined to mercy, and averse from blood;
If mildness ill with stubborn Israel suit,
His crime is God's belovèd attribute.
What could he gain, his people to betray,
Or change his right for arbitrary sway? 330
Let haughty Pharaoh curse with such a reign
His fruitful Nile, and yoke a servile train.
If David's rule Jerusalem displease,
The Dog-star heats their brains to this disease.
Why then should I, encouraging the bad, 335
Turn rebel and run popularly mad?
Were he a tyrant, who, by lawless might
Oppressed the Jews, and raised the Jebusite,
Well might I mourn; but Nature's holy bands
Would curb my spirits and restrain my hands; 340
The people might assert their liberty;
But what was right in them, were crime in me.
His favor leaves me nothing to require,
Prevents my wishes, and outruns desire.
What more can I expect while David lives? 345
All but his kingly diadem he gives:
And that"—But there he paused; then sighing, said—

---

310. *angels' metal:* i.e., the spirit of ambition that led the angels to rebel.
323-4. i.e., on his return from exile. 328. *crime:* his "crime" of mildness.
334. *Dog-star:* Sirius, always associated with summer heat and madness.

"Is justly destined for a worthier head.
For when my father from his toils shall rest
And late augment the number of the blest,   350
His lawful issue shall the throne ascend,
Or the *collateral* line, where that shall end.
His brother, tho' oppressed with vulgar spite,
Yet dauntless, and secure of native right,
Of every royal virtue stands possessed;   355
Still dear to all the bravest and the best.
His courage foes, his friends his truth proclaim;
His loyalty the king, the world his fame.
His mercy even th' offending crowd will find,
For sure he comes of a forgiving kind.   360
Why should I then repine at Heaven's decree
Which gives me no pretense to royalty?
Yet O that fate, propitiously inclined,
Had raised my birth, or had debased my mind;
To my large soul not all her treasure lent,   365
And then betrayed it to a mean descent!
I find, I find my mounting spirits bold,
And David's part disdains my mother's mold.
Why am I scanted by a niggard birth?
My soul disclaims the kindred of her earth;   370
And, made for empire, whispers me within,
'Desire of greatness is a godlike sin.'"
    Him staggering so when Hell's dire agent found,
While fainting Virtue scarce maintained her ground,
He pours fresh forces in, and thus replies: 375
    "Th' eternal God, supremely good and wise,
Imparts not these prodigious gifts in vain;
What wonders are reserved to bless your reign!
Against your will, your arguments have shown,
Such virtue's only given to guide a throne.   380
Not that your father's mildness I contemn,
But manly force becomes the diadem.
'Tis true he grants the people all they crave;
And more, perhaps, than subjects ought to have:
For lavish grants suppose a monarch tame   385
And more his goodness than his wit proclaim.

---

348. *worthier head:* i.e., that of a legitimate heir. 353. *brother . . . spite:*
James, Duke of York, hated for his Catholicism. 360. *kind:* family. 368.
mother: Monmouth's mother was Lucy Walters, of good but not noble
family. 373. *agent:* Achitophel (compared, as usual, to Satan).

But when should people strive their bonds to break
If not when kings are negligent or weak?
Let him give on till he can give no more,
The thrifty Sanhedrin shall keep him poor;   390
And every shekel which he can receive
Shall cost a limb of his prerogative.
To ply him with new plots shall be my care;
Or plunge him deep in some expensive war;
Which, when his treasure can no more supply,   395
He must, with the remains of kingship, buy.
His faithful friends, our jealousies and fears
Call Jebusites, and Pharaoh's pensioners;
Whom when our fury from his aid has torn,
He shall be naked left to public scorn.   400
The next successor, whom I fear and hate,
My arts have made obnoxious to the State;
Turned all his virtues to his overthrow,
And gained our elders to pronounce a foe.
His right, for sums of necessary gold,   405
Shall first be pawned, and afterwards be sold;
Till time shall ever-wanting David draw,
To pass your doubtful title into law.
If not, the people have a right supreme
To make their kings; for kings are made for them.   410
All empire is no more than power in trust,
Which, when resumed, can be no longer just.
Succession, for the general good designed,
In its own wrong a nation cannot bind:
If altering that the people can relieve,   415
Better one suffer, than a nation grieve.
The Jews well know their power: ere Saul they chose,
God was their king, and God they durst depose.
Urge now your piety, your filial name,
A father's right, and fear of future fame;   420
The public good, that universal call,
To which even Heaven submitted, answers all.

---

390. *Sanhedrin:* Parliament (which controlled the purse). 392. *prerogative:*
i.e., a body of rights and privileges attached to the kingship, which Parliament repeatedly sought to force the king to yield through its power
over the purse. 398. *Pharaoh's pensioners:* It was charged (correctly,
though no one knew it till later) that the court was receiving sums from
France. 401. *successor:* James. 408. *your:* Monmouth's. 417-8. *ere . . .
king:* an allusion to the kingless Commonwealth as a theocracy; but perhaps also an allusion to Charles I, the "royal martyr."

Nor let his love enchant your generous mind;
'Tis Nature's trick to propagate her kind.
Our fond begetters, who would never die,   425
Love but themselves in their posterity.
Or let his kindness by th' effects be tried
Or let him lay his vain pretense aside.
God said he loved your father; could he bring
A better proof than to anoint him king?   430
It surely shewed he loved the shepherd well,
Who gave so fair a flock as Israel.
Would David have you thought his darling son?
What means he, then, to alienate the crown?
The name of godly he may blush to bear: 435
'Tis after God's own heart to cheat his heir.
He to his brother gives supreme command;
To you a legacy of barren land:
Perhaps th' old harp, on which he thrums his lays:
Or some dull Hebrew ballad in your praise.   440
    "Then the next heir, a prince severe and wise,
Already looks on you with jealous eyes,
Sees thro' the thin disguises of your arts,
And marks your progress in the people's hearts.
Tho' now his mighty soul its grief contains,   445
He meditates revenge who least complains;
And, like a lion, slumbering in the way,
Or sleep dissembling, while he waits his prey,
His fearless foes within his distance draws,
Constrains his roaring, and contracts his paws;   450
Till at the last, his time for fury found,
He shoots with sudden vengeance from the ground:
The prostrate vulgar passes o'er and spares,
But with a lordly rage his hunters tears.
Your case no tame expedients will afford: 455
Resolve on death, or conquest by the sword,
Which for no less a stake than life you draw,
And self-defense is Nature's eldest law.
Leave the warm people no considering time;
For then rebellion may be thought a crime.   460
Prevail yourself of what occasion gives,
But try your title while your father lives;

---

429. *God . . . father:* David (cf. 436) was "the man after [God's] own heart" (I Samuel 13). 449. *distance:* range. 459. *warm:* excited.

And that your arms may have a fair pretense,
Proclaim you take them in the king's defense;
Whose sacred life each minute would expose   465
To plots, from seeming friends, and secret foes.
And who can sound the depth of David's soul?
Perhaps his fear his kindness may control.
He fears his brother, tho' he loves his son,
For plighted vows too late to be undone.   470
If so, by force he wishes to be gained,
Like women's lechery, to seem constrained.
Doubt not; but, when he most affects the frown,
Commit a pleasing rape upon the crown.
Secure his person to secure your cause;   475
They who possess the prince, possess the laws."
    He said, and this advice above the rest,
With Absalom's mild nature suited best;
Unblamed of life (ambition set aside)
Not stained with cruelty, nor puffed with pride;   480
How happy had he been, if destiny
Had higher placed his birth, or not so high!
His kingly virtues might have claimed a throne
And blest all other countries but his own.
But charming greatness since so few refuse,   485
'Tis juster to lament him, than accuse.
Strong were his hopes a rival to remove,
With blandishments to gain the public love,
To head the faction while their zeal was hot,
And popularly prosecute the Plot.   490
To farther this, Achitophel unites
The malcontents of all the Israelites:
Whose differing parties he could wisely join,
For several ends, to serve the same design:
The best, and of the princes some were such,   495
Who thought the power of monarchy too much;
Mistaken men, and patriots in their hearts;
Not wicked, but seduced by impious arts.
By these the springs of property were bent,
And wound so high, they cracked the government.   500
The next for interest sought t' embroil the State,
To sell their duty at a dearer rate;
And make their Jewish markets of the throne,

---

495 ff. See the Introduction, pp. 8-9.

Pretending public good, to serve their own.
Others thought kings an useless heavy load,   505
Who cost too much, and did too little good.
These were for laying honest David by,
On principles of pure good husbandry.
With them joined all th' haranguers of the throng
That thought to get preferment by the tongue.   510
Who follow next, a double danger bring,
Not only hating David, but the king:
The Solymæan rout; well-versed of old
In godly faction, and in treason bold;
Cowering and quaking at a conqueror's sword,   515
But lofty to a lawful prince restored;
Saw with disdain an Ethnic plot begun
And scorned by Jebusites to be outdone.
Hot Levites headed these; who, pulled before
From th' ark, which in the Judges' days they bore,   520
Resumed their cant, and with a zealous cry
Pursued their old beloved Theocracy:
Where Sanhedrin and priest enslaved the nation,
And justified their spoils by inspiration:
For who so fit for reign as Aaron's race,   525
If once dominion they could found in grace?
These led the pack; tho' not of surest scent,
Yet deepest mouthed against the government.
A numerous host of dreaming saints succeed,
Of the true old Enthusiastic breed: 530
'Gainst form and order they their power employ,
Nothing to build, and all things to destroy.
But far more numerous was the herd of such,
Who think too little, and who talk too much.
These, out of mere instinct, they knew not why,   535
Adored their fathers' God and property:
And, by the same blind benefit of fate,
The Devil and the Jebusite did hate:

---

513. *Solymaean rout:* London rabble. 517. *Ethnic plot:* the popish (lit.,
Gentile) plot. 519. *Levites:* i.e., the Presbyterians, who in 1662 had been
excluded from the national church (*th' ark*), which during the Commonwealth (*Judges' days*) they ruled (*bore*). 521. *cant:* hypocritical jargon.
525. *Aaron's race:* the priesthood. 529-30. Dryden refers to the Puritan
ideal of a community of saints (such as Milton sketches in *Areopagitica*).
Because of their claim to individual *inspiration* by God (524), the Puritans
were called *Enthusiastic* (i.e., God-possessed).

Born to be saved, even in their own despite,
Because they could not help believing right. 540
Such were the tools; but a whole Hydra more
Remains, of sprouting heads too long to score.
Some of their chiefs were princes of the land;
In the first rank of these did Zimri stand:
A man so various, that he seemed to be 545
Not one, but all mankind's epitome:
Stiff in opinions, always in the wrong;
Was everything by starts, and nothing long;
But, in the course of one revolving moon,
Was chymist, fiddler, statesman, and buffoon: 550
Then all for women, painting, rhyming, drinking,
Besides ten thousand freaks that died in thinking.
Blest madman, who could every hour employ,
With something new to wish, or to enjoy!
Railing and praising were his usual themes; 555
And both (to show his judgment) in extremes:
So over-violent, or over-civil,
That every man, with him, was God or Devil.
In squandering wealth was his peculiar art:
Nothing went unrewarded, but desert. 560
Beggared by fools, whom still he found too late:
He had his jest, and they had his estate.
He laughed himself from court; then sought relief
By forming parties, but could ne'er be chief:
For, spite of him, the weight of business fell 565
On Absalom and wise Achitophel:
Thus wicked but in will, of means bereft,
He left not faction, but of that was left.
  Titles and names 't were tedious to rehearse
Of lords, below the dignity of verse. 570
Wits, warriors, Commonwéalth's-men, were the best:
Kind husbands, and mere nobles, all the rest.
And therefore, in the name of dulness, be
The well-hung Balaam and cold Caleb, free;
And canting Nadab let oblivion damn, 575

---

539. *Born . . . saved*: a scornful reference to the Puritan doctrine of election. Cf. Vol. IV: *Par. Lost* III 173 ff. n. 541. *Hydra*: the fabulous monster that grew new heads as fast as they were cut off. 544. *Zimri*: George Villiers, Duke of Buckingham, strong believer in the Popish plot. 574-5. *Balaam, Caleb, Nadab*: Theophilus Hastings, Earl of Huntingdon; Lord Grey; and William, Lord Howard of Escrick—three supporters of Monmouth.

Who made new porridge for the paschal lamb.
Let friendship's holy band some names assure,
Some their own worth, and some let scorn secure.
Nor shall the rascal rabble here have place,
Whom kings no titles gave, and God no grace: 580
Not bull-faced Jonas, who could statutes draw
To mean rebellion, and make treason law.
But he, tho' bad, is followed by a worse,
The wretch who Heaven's anointed dared to curse:
Shimei, whose youth did early promise bring   585
Of zeal to God, and hatred to his king,
Did wisely from expensive sins refrain,
And never broke the Sabbath, but for gain;
Nor ever was he known an oath to vent,
Or curse, unless against the government.   590
Thus, heaping wealth, by the most ready way
Among the Jews, which was to cheat and pray,
The city, to reward his pious hate
Against his master, chose him magistrate:
His hand a vare of justice did uphold;   595
His neck was loaded with a chain of gold.
During his office, treason was no crime;
The sons of Belial had a glorious time:
For Shimei, tho' not prodigal of pelf,
Yet loved his wicked neighbor as himself.   600
When two or three were gathered to declaim ⎫
Against the monarch of Jerusalem,   ⎬
Shimei was always in the midst of them;   ⎭
And if they cursed the king when he was by,
Would rather curse than break good company.   605
If any durst his factious friends accuse,
He packed a jury of dissenting Jews;

---

576. He was said to have profaned the Eucharist by taking it in a dish called "lamb's wool"—ale poured over cooked apples and sugar. 581. *Jonas:* Sir William Jones, chief prosecutor of those indicted in the Popish plot; if he also had a hand in drawing up the Exclusion Bill, it would explain Dryden's description of him here. 585. *Shimei:* Slingsby Bethel, Sheriff of London, and zealous republican. Cf. the Introduction, page 8. 595. *vare:* staff. 598. *Sons of Belial:* Biblical phrase, used of men who have broken God's laws without compunction. 599. He was renowned for his miserliness. 600. Cf. Matthew 22:39. 601. Cf. the Prayer-Book's phrasing, ". . . and dost promise that when two or three are gathered together in thy Name, thou wilt grant their requests."

Whose fellow-feeling in the godly cause
Would free the suffering saint from human laws.
For laws are only made to punish those   610
Who serve the king, and to protect his foes.
If any leisure time he had from power,
(Because 'tis sin to misemploy an hour,)
His business was, by writing, to persuade
That kings were useless, and a clog to trade: 615
And, that his noble style he might refine,
No Rechabite more shunned the fumes of wine.
Chaste were his cellars; and his shrieval board
The grossness of a city feast abhorred:
His cooks, with long disuse, their trade forgot;   620
Cool was his kitchen, tho' his brains were hot.
Such frugal virtue malice may accuse,
But sure 'twas necessary to the Jews:
For towns once burnt such magistrates require
As dare not tempt God's providence by fire.   625
With spiritual food he fed his servants well,
But free from flesh that made the Jews rebel;
And Moses' laws he held in more account,
For forty days of fasting in the mount.
  To speak the rest, who better are forgot,   630
Would tire a well-breathed witness of the Plot:
Yet, Corah, thou shalt from oblivion pass;
Erect thyself, thou monumental brass,
High as the serpent of thy metal made,
While nations stand secure beneath thy shade.   635
What tho' his birth were base, yet comets rise
From earthy vapors, ere they shine in skies.
Prodigious actions may as well be done
By weaver's issue, as by prince's son.

614-15. A reference to Bethel's pamphlet, *The Interest of Princes and States*.
617. *Rechabite:* cf. the Rechabite vow "to drink no wine all our days"
(Jeremiah 35:8). 618. *shrieval:* i.e., sheriff's. 619. *city feast:* Lavish hospitality was expected of the London sheriffs. 624. *burnt:* an allusion to the
great fire of London, 1665 (and to Bethel's frugality). 626. *spiritual food:*
Dryden wryly suggests that Bethel's stinginess to his servants is a Puritan
reinterpretation of the sacrament of the Eucharist, by which (in the
Prayer-Book phrase that Dryden echoes) we are fed with "spiritual food."
631. *a . . . Plot:* i.e., a witness as long-winded as many who testified against
the Catholics. 632. *Corah:* Titus Oates, the Plot's inventor. 633-4. Dryden
ironically compares Oates to the brass serpent by which Moses saved the
rebellious Israelites in the wilderness (Numbers 21:9).

This arch-attestor for the public good 640
By that one deed ennobles all his blood.
Who ever asked the witness's high race
Whose oath with martyrdom did Stephen grace?
Ours was a Levite, and as times went then,
His tribe were God Almighty's gentlemen. 645
Sunk were his eyes, his voice was harsh and loud,
Sure signs he neither choleric was nor proud:
His long chin proved his wit; his saintlike grace,
A church vermilion and a Moses' face.
His memory, miraculously great, 650
Could plots, exceeding man's belief, repeat;
Which therefore cannot be accounted lies,
For human wit could never such devise.
Some future truths are mingled in his book;
But where the witness failed, the prophet spoke: 655
Some things like visionary flights appear;
The spirit caught him up, the Lord knows where,
And gave him his rabbinical degree,
Unknown to foreign university.
His judgment yet his memory did excel, 660
Which pieced his wondrous evidence so well,
And suited to the temper of the times,
Then groaning under Jebusitic crimes.
Let Israel's foes suspect his heavenly call,
And rashly judge his writ apocryphal; 665
Our laws for such affronts have forfeits made:
He takes his life, who takes away his trade.
Were I myself in witness Corah's place,
The wretch who did me such a dire disgrace
Should whet my memory, tho' once forgot, 670
To make him an appendix of my Plot.
His zeal to Heaven made him his prince despise,
And load his person with indignities:
But zeal peculiar privilege affords,

---

644. *Levite:* cf. 519n. 649. *church vermilion:* florid well-fed complexion.
657. *spirit:* the Holy Spirit (from which many Puritans claimed to have
special communications). 665. *judge . . . apocryphal:* i.e., judge his deposi-
tions against the Catholics to be of doubtful authenticity. But, Dryden adds
(666-7), this doubt is an affront for which you might have to pay a forfeit, for you take a man's life when you deprive him of his trade (as informer, witness), and anybody who does doubt Oates will probably find
himself indicted next.

Indulging latitude to deeds and words;   675
And Corah might for Agag's murther call,
In terms as coarse as Samuel used to Saul.
What others in his evidence did join,
(The best that could be had for love or coin,)
In Corah's own predicament will fall;   680
For *witness* is a common name to all.
   Surrounded thus with friends of every sort,
Deluded Absalom forsakes the court:
Impatient of high hopes, urged with renown,
And fired with near possession of a crown.   685
Th' admiring crowd are dazzled with surprise
And on his goodly person feed their eyes:
His joy concealed, he sets himself to show,
On each side bowing popularly low;
His looks, his gestures, and his words he frames   690
And with familiar ease repeats their names.
Thus formed by nature, furnished out with arts,
He glides unfelt into their secret hearts:
Then, with a kind compassionating look,
And sighs, bespeaking pity ere he spoke,   695
Few words he said; but easy those and fit,
More slow than Hybla-drops, and far more sweet.
   "I mourn, my countrymen, your lost estate,
Tho' far unable to prevent your fate:
Behold a banished man, for your dear cause   700
Exposed a prey to arbitrary laws!
Yet O! that I alone could be undone,
Cut off from empire, and no more a son!
Now all your liberties a spoil are made;⎫
Egypt and Tyrus intercept your trade, ⎬   705
And Jebusites your sacred rites invade.⎭
My father, whom with reverence yet I name,
Charmed into ease, is careless of his fame:
And, bribed with petty sums of foreign gold,
Is grown in Bathsheba's embraces old: 710
Exalts his enemies, his friends destroys,
And all his power against himself employs.

---

676. *Agag:* Sir Edmund Godfrey, before whom Oates' deposition was taken
and who was murdered shortly after (according to Dryden's insinuation
here, at Oates' instigation). 677. Cf. 1 Samuel 15. 697. *Hybla-drops:* i.e.,
drops of honey, for which Hybla in Sicily was famous. 705. *Tyrus:*
Holland. 710. *Bathsheba:* the Duchess of Portsmouth, Charles's current
mistress.

He gives, and let him give, my right away;
But why should he his own and yours betray?
He, only he, can make the nation bleed,   715
And he alone from my revenge is freed.
Take then my tears (with that he wiped his eyes)
'Tis all the aid my present power supplies:
No court-informer can these arms accuse;
These arms may sons against their fathers use;   720
And 'tis my wish, the next successor's reign
May make no other Israelite complain."
    Youth, beauty, graceful action seldom fail:
But common interest always will prevail:
And pity never ceases to be shown   725
To him who makes the people's wrongs his own.
The crowd, that still believe their kings oppress,
With lifted hands their young Messiah bless:
Who now begins his progress to ordain
With chariots, horsemen, and a numerous train;   730
From east to west his glories he displays,
And, like the sun, the promised land surveys.
Fame runs before him as the morning star,
And shouts of joy salute him from afar:
Each house receives him as a guardian god,   735
And consecrates the place of his abode:
But hospitable treats did most commend
Wise Issachar, his wealthy western friend.
This moving court, that caught the people's eyes,
And seemed but pomp, did other ends disguise: 740
Achitophel had formed it, with intent
To sound the depths, and fathom, where it went,
The people's hearts; distinguish friends from foes,
And try their strength, before they came to blows.
Yet all was colored with a smooth pretense   745
Of specious love, and duty to their prince.
Religion, and redress of grievances,
Two names that always cheat and always please,
Are often urged; and good King David's life
Endangered by a brother and a wife.   750

---

729 ff. Monmouth made a journey through England to curry popular favor.
738. *Issachar:* Thomas Thynne of Wiltshire. 749-50. *and . . . wife:* Oates
tried to implicate both James and Queen Catherine in the plot against
Charles.

Thus in a pageant show a Plot is made,
And peace itself is war in masquerade.
O foolish Israel! never warned by ill!
Still the same bait, and circumvented still!
Did ever men forsake their present ease,   755
In midst of health imagine a disease;
Take pains contingent mischiefs to foresee,
Make heirs for monarchs, and for God decree?
What shall we think! Can people give away,
Both for themselves and sons, their native sway?   760
Then they are left defenseless to the sword
Of each unbounded, arbitrary lord:
And laws are vain, by which we right enjoy,
If kings unquestioned can those laws destroy.
Yet if the crowd be judge of fit and just,   765
And kings are only officers in trust,
Then this resuming covenant was declared
When kings were made, or is for ever barred:
If those who gave the scepter could not tie
By their own deed their own posterity,   770
How then could Adam bind his future race?
How could his forfeit on mankind take place?
Or how could heavenly justice damn us all,
Who ne'er consented to our father's fall?
Then kings are slaves to those whom they command,   775
And tenants to their people's pleasure stand.
Add, that the power for property allowed
Is mischievously seated in the crowd;
For who can be secure of private right,
If sovereign sway may be dissolved by might?   780
Nor is the people's judgment always true:
The most may err as grossly as the few;
And faultless kings run down, by common cry,
For vice, oppression, and for tyranny.
What standard is there in a fickle rout,   785
Which, flowing to the mark, runs faster out?
    Nor only crowds, but Sanhedrins may be
Infected with this public lunacy,
And share the madness of rebellious times,
To murther monarchs for imagined crimes.   790
If they may give and take whene'er they please,
Not kings alone, (the Godhead's images,)
But government itself at length must fall

To nature's state, where all have right to all.
Yet, grant our lords, the People, kings can make,   795
What prudent men a settled throne would shake?
For whatsoe'er their sufferings were before,
That change they covet makes them suffer more.
All other errors but disturb a state;
But innovation is the blow of fate.   800
If ancient fabrics nod, and threat to fall,
To patch the flaws, and buttress up the wall,
Thus far 'tis duty; but here fix the mark:
For all beyond it is to touch our Ark.
To change foundations, cast the frame anew,   805
Is work for rebels who base ends pursue,
At once divine and human laws control,
And mend the parts by ruin of the whole.
The tampering world is subject to this curse,
To physic their disease into a worse.   810
   Now what relief can righteous David bring?
How fatal 'tis to be too good a king!
Friends he has few, so high the madness grows;
Who dare be such, must be the people's foes:
Yet some there were, even in the worst of days;   815
Some let me name, and naming is to praise.
   In this short file Barzillai first appears;
Barzillai, crowned with honor and with years:
Long since, the rising rebels he withstood
In regions waste, beyond the Jordan's flood: 820
Unfortunately brave to buoy the State;
But sinking underneath his master's fate:
In exile with his godlike prince he mourned,
For him he suffered, and with him returned.
The court he practiced, not the courtier's art: 825
Large was his wealth, but larger was his heart:
Which well the noblest objects knew to choose,
The fighting warrior, and recording Muse.
His bed could once a fruitful issue boast;
Now more than half a father's name is lost.   830
His eldest hope, with every grace adorned,

---

804. *to . . . Ark:* to meddle with a sacred mystery (like the Hebrew *Ark*
of the covenant). 817. *Barzillai:* the Duke of Ormond, loyal supporter of
both Charles I and Charles II. 820. *beyond . . . flood:* in Ireland. 828.
Muse: i.e., the poet as recorder of great deeds. 829-30. Ormond had had
ten children, of whom six were now dead. 831. i.e., the Earl of Ossory,
who died at forty-six, after a distinguished career as a soldier.

By me (so Heaven will have it) always mourned,
And always honored, snatched in manhood's prime
B' unequal fates, and Providence's crime:
Yet not before the goal of honor won,   835
All parts fulfilled of subject and of son;
Swift was the race, but short the time to run.
O narrow circle, but of power divine,
Scanted in space, but perfect in thy line!
By sea, by land, thy matchless worth was known,   840
Arms thy delight, and war was all thy own:
Thy force, infused, the fainting Tyrians propped;
And haughty Pharaoh found his fortune stopped.
O ancient honor! O unconquered hand,
Whom foes unpunished never could withstand!   845
But Israel was unworthy of thy name;
Short is the date of all immoderate fame.
It looks as Heaven our ruin had designed,
And durst not trust thy fortune and thy mind.
Now, free from earth, thy disencumbered soul   850
Mounts up, and leaves behind the clouds and starry pole:
From thence thy kindred legions mayst thou bring,
To aid the guardian angel of thy king.
Here stop, my Muse, here cease thy painful flight;
No pinions can pursue immortal height: 855
Tell good Barzillai thou canst sing no more,
And tell thy soul she should have fled before.
Or fled she with his life, and left this verse
To hang on her departed patron's hearse?
Now take thy steepy flight from heaven, and see   860
If thou canst find on earth another *he*.
    Another *he* would be too hard to find;
See then whom thou canst see not far behind.
Zadoc the priest, whom, shunning power and place,
His lowly mind advanced to David's grace: 865
With him the Sagan of Jerusalem,
Of hospitable soul, and noble stem;
Him of the western dome, whose weighty sense

842-3. i.e., in the Anglo-Dutch wars against France 1677-8. 859. *hearse:* the
bier, on which verse tributes were often hung. 864. *Zadoc:* William San-
croft, Archbishop of Canterbury. 866. *Sagan:* Governor, i.e., the Bishop of
London (Henry Compton). 867. *stem:* family. Compton was an earl's
son. 868. *Him . . . dome:* the Dean of Westminster (John Dolben).

Flows in fit words and heavenly eloquence.
The prophets' sons, by such example led,   870
To learning and to loyalty were bred:
For colleges on bounteous kings depend,
And never rebel was to arts a friend.
To these succeed the pillars of the laws,
Who best could plead, and best can judge a cause.   875
Next them a train of loyal peers ascend:
Sharp-judging Adriel, the Muses' friend;
Himself a Muse:—in Sanhedrin's debate
True to his prince, but not a slave of state:
Whom David's love with honors did adorn,   880
That from his disobedient son were torn.
Jotham of piercing wit, and pregnant thought,
Endued by nature, and by learning taught
To move assemblies, who but only tried
The worse a while, then chose the better side;   885
Nor chose alone, but turned the balance too;
So much the weight of one brave man can do.
Hushai, the friend of David in distress,
In public storms, of manly steadfastness:
By foreign treaties he informed his youth,   890
And joined experience to his native truth.
His frugal care supplied the wanting throne;
Frugal for that, but bounteous of his own:
'Tis easy conduct when exchequers flow,
But hard the task to manage well the low;   895
For sovereign power is too depressed or high,
When kings are forced to sell, or crowds to buy.
    Indulge one labor more, my weary Muse,
For Amiel: who can Amiel's praise refuse?
Of ancient race by birth, but nobler yet   900
In his own worth, and without title great:
The Sanhedrin long time as chief he ruled,

---

870. *The . . . sons:* the boys of Westminster School. 877. *Adriel:* John
Sheffield, Earl of Mulgrave, *sharp-judging* because known for his critical
writings, *An Essay on Satire* and *An Essay on Poetry.* 880-1. In 1679,
Charles II had given Mulgrave two offices taken away from Monmouth.
882. *Jotham:* George Savile, Marquis of Halifax. 884-5. *who . . . while:*
from 1673-9 Halifax had been in the opposition party. 886-7. In the House
of Lords, Halifax's eloquence prevented passage of the Exclusion Bill. 888.
Hushai: Laurence Hyde, Viscount Hyde, made in 1679 First Lord of the
Treasury. 899. *Amiel:* Edward Seymour. 902. Seymour was speaker of
the House of Commons, 1673-9.

Their reason guided, and their passion cooled:
So dexterous was he in the crown's defense,
So formed to speak a loyal nation's sense,   905
That, as their band was Israel's tribes in small,
So fit was he to represent them all.
Now rasher charioteers the seat ascend,
Whose loose careers his steady skill commend:
They, like th' unequal ruler of the day,   910
Misguide the seasons, and mistake the way;
While he withdrawn at their mad labor smiles,
And safe enjoys the sabbath of his toils.

   These were the chief; a small but faithful band ⎫
Of worthies, in the breach who dared to stand ⎬ 915
And tempt th' united fury of the land. ⎭
With grief they viewed such powerful engines bent
To batter down the lawful government:
A numerous faction, with pretended frights,
In Sanhedrins to plume the regal rights;   920
The true successor from the court removed;
The Plot, by hireling witnesses, improved.
These ills they saw, and, as their duty bound,
They showed the king the danger of the wound;
That no concessions from the throne would please,   925
But lenitives fomented the disease;
That Absalom, ambitious of the crown,
Was made the lure to draw the people down;
That false Achitophel's pernicious hate
Had turned the Plot to ruin Church and State;   930
The council violent, the rabble worse:
That Shimei taught Jerusalem to curse.

   With all these loads of injuries oppressed,
And long revolving in his careful breast
Th' event of things; at last, his patience tired,   935
Thus from his royal throne, by Heaven inspired,
The godlike David spoke; with awful fear
His train their Maker in their master hear.

   "Thus long have I, by native mercy swayed,
My wrongs dissembled, my revenge delayed;   940
So willing to forgive th' offending age;
So much the father did the King assuage.

908-11. Referring to Phaeton's fatal attempt to drive the chariot of his
father the Sun. 920. *plume:* pluck away. 921. *The . . . successor:* James.
926. *lenitives fomented:* i.e., soothing medicines stimulated.

But now so far my clemency they slight,
Th' offenders question my forgiving right.
That one was made for many, they contend;   945
But 'tis to rule, for that's a monarch's end.
They call my tenderness of blood, my fear,
Tho' manly tempers can the longest bear.
Yet, since they will divert my native course,
'Tis time to shew I am not good by force.   950
Those heaped affronts that haughty subjects bring,
Are burthens for a camel, not a king.
Kings are the public pillars of the State,
Born to sustain and prop the nation's weight:
If my young Samson will pretend a call   955
To shake the column, let him share the fall:
But O that yet he would repent and live!
How easy 'tis for parents to forgive!
With how few tears a pardon might be won
From nature, pleading for a darling son!   960
Poor pitied youth, by my paternal care
Raised up to all the height his frame could bear:
Had God ordained his fate for empire born,
He would have given his soul another turn:
Gulled with a Patriot's name, whose modern sense   965
Is one that would by law supplant his prince;
The people's brave, the politician's tool;
Never was Patriot yet, but was a fool.
Whence comes it that religion and the laws
Should more be Absalom's than David's cause?   970
His old instructor, ere he lost his place,
Was never thought indued with so much grace.
Good heavens, how faction can a Patriot paint!
My rebel ever proves my people's saint.
Would *they* impose an heir upon the throne?   975
Let Sanhedrins be taught to give their own.
A king's at least a part of government,
And mine as requisite as their consent:
Without my leave a future king to choose,
Infers a right the present to depose.   980
True, they petition me t' approve their choice:

---

944. The Whigs had questioned Charles's right to extend pardons. 967.
brave: hero-bully. 971. *instructor*: Achitophel.

But Esau's hands suit ill with Jacob's voice.
My pious subjects for my safety pray;
Which to secure, they take my power away.
From plots and treasons Heaven preserve my years,   985
But save me most from my petitioners!
Unsatiate as the barren womb or grave;
God cannot grant so much as they can crave.
What then is left, but with a jealous eye
To guard the small remains of royalty?   990
The law shall still direct my peaceful sway,
And the same law teach rebels to obey:
Votes shall no more established power control,
Such votes as make a part exceed the whole:
No groundless clamors shall my friends remove   995
Nor crowds have power to punish ere they prove;
For gods and godlike kings their care express,
Still to defend their servants in distress.
O that my power to saving were confined:
Why am I forced, like Heaven, against my mind,   1000
To make examples of another kind?
Must I at length the sword of justice draw?
O curst effects of necessary law!
How ill my fear they by my mercy scan!
Beware the fury of a patient man.   1005
Law they require, let Law then shew her face;
They could not be content to look on Grace,
Her hinder parts, but with a daring eye
To tempt the terror of her front, and die.
By their own arts, 'tis righteously decreed,   1010
Those dire artificers of death shall bleed.
Against themselves their witnesses will swear,
Till viper-like their mother Plot they tear,
And suck for nutriment that bloody gore,
Which was their principle of life before.   1015

---

982. Alluding to the deception practiced by Jacob in securing Isaac's blessing (Genesis 29:22). 1004. i.e., how much they misestimate my power to terrify from my habit of being merciful. 1008. *hinder parts:* When Moses asks God to reveal his glory (Exodus 33:18 ff.), God replies that no man can see his face and live—only his "back parts." 1012-15. Many of the witnesses brought against the Catholics turned about-face later and testified against the Whigs.

Their Belial with their Belzebub will fight;
Thus on my foes, my foes shall do me right.
Nor doubt th' event; for factious crowds engage
In their first onset, all their brutal rage.
Then let 'em take an unresisted course;   1020
Retire, and traverse, and delude their force:
But, when they stand all breathless, urge the fight,
And rise upon 'em with redoubled might;
For lawful power is still superior found,
When long driven back, at length it stands the ground."   1025
   He said. Th' Almighty, nodding, gave consent;
And peals of thunder shook the firmament.
Henceforth a series of new time began,
The mighty years in long procession ran:
Once more the godlike David was restored,   1030
And willing nations knew their lawful lord.

❦

1018. *event:* outcome.

Jonathan Swift

An Argument against Abolishing Christianity
(1708)

𝒥 AM very sensible what a weakness and presumption it is, to reason against the general humour and disposition of the world. I remember it was with great justice, and a due regard to the freedom both of the publick and the press, forbidden upon several penalties to write, or discourse, or lay wagers against the Union even before [5 it was confirmed by Parliament; because that was looked upon as a design to oppose the current of the people, which besides the folly of it, is a manifest breach of the fundamental law, that makes this majority of opinions the voice of God. In like manner, and for the very same reasons, it may perhaps be neither safe nor prudent [10 to argue against the abolishing of Christianity, at a juncture when all parties seem so unanimously determined upon the point, as we cannot but allow from their actions, their discourses, and their writings. However, I know not how, whether from the affectation of singularity, or the perverseness of human nature, but so it unhappily falls [15 out, that I cannot be entirely of this opinion. Nay, though I were sure an order were issued out for my immediate prosecution by the Attorney-General, I should still confess, that in the present posture of our affairs at home or abroad, I do not yet see the absolute necessity of extirpating the Christian religion from among us. 20

This perhaps may appear too great a paradox even for our wise and paradoxical age to endure; therefore I shall handle it with all tenderness, and with the utmost deference to that great and profound majority which is of another sentiment.

---

5. *Union:* the union of Scotland and England, effected in 1707.

And yet the curious may please to observe, how much the   [25
genius of a nation is liable to alter in half an age: I have heard it
affirmed for certain by some very old people, that the contrary opinion
was even in their memories as much in vogue as the other is now;
and that a project for the abolishing of Christianity would then have
appeared as singular, and been thought as absurd, as it would   [30
be at this time to write or discourse in its defence.

Therefore I freely own, that all appearances are against me. The
system of the Gospel, after the fate of other systems, is generally anti-
quated and exploded; and the mass or body of the common people,
among whom it seems to have had its latest credit, are now   [35
grown as much ashamed of it as their betters; opinions, like fashions,
always descending from those of quality to the middle sort, and
thence to the vulgar, where at length they are dropped and vanish.

But here I would not be mistaken, and must therefore be so bold
as to borrow a distinction from the writers on the other side,   [40
when they make a difference betwixt nominal and real Trinitarians.
I hope no reader imagines me so weak to stand up in the defence of
real Christianity, such as used in primitive times (if we may believe
the authors of those ages) to have an influence upon men's belief and
actions: To offer at the restoring of that, would indeed be a   [45
wild project, it would be to dig up foundations; to destroy at one blow
all the wit, and half the learning of the kingdom; to break the entire
frame and constitution of things; to ruin trade, extinguish arts and
sciences, with the professors of them; in short, to turn our courts, exchanges, and shops into deserts; and would be full as absurd   [50
as the proposal of Horace, where he advises the Romans, all in a body,
to leave their city and seek a new seat in some remote part of the
world, by way of a cure for the corruption of their manners.

Therefore I think this caution was in itself altogether unnecessary,
(which I have inserted only to prevent all possibility of cavil-   [55
ling) since every candid reader will easily understand my discourse
to be intended only in defence of nominal Christianity, the other having been for some time wholly laid aside by general consent, as utterly
inconsistent with all our present schemes of wealth and power.

But why we should therefore cast off the name and title of   [60
Christians, although the general opinion and resolution be so violent
for it, I confess I cannot (with submission) apprehend the consequence
necessary. However, since the undertakers propose such wonderful
advantages to the nation by this project, and advance many plausible
objections against the system of Christianity, I shall briefly   [65

---

51. *Horace:* in Epode XVI. 63. *undertakers:* i.e., the "freethinkers," who
(according to Swift) are undertaking to abolish Christianity.

consider the strength of both, fairly allow them their greatest weight, and offer such answers as I think most reasonable. After which I will beg leave to shew what inconveniences may possibly happen by such an innovation, in the present posture of our affairs.

First, one great advantage proposed by the abolishing of   [70 Christianity is, that it would very much enlarge and establish liberty of conscience, that great bulwark of our nation, and of the Protestant religion, which is still too much limited by priest-craft, notwithstanding all the good intentions of the legislature, as we have lately found by a severe instance. For it is confidently reported, that two   [75 young gentlemen of real hopes, bright wit, and profound judgment, who, upon a thorough examination of causes and effects, and by the mere force of natural abilities, without the least tincture of learning, having made a discovery, that there was no God, and generously communicating their thoughts for the good of the publick, were   [80 some time ago, by an unparallell'd severity, and upon I know not what obsolete Law, broke for blasphemy. And as it hath been wisely observed, if persecution once begins, no man alive knows how far it may reach, or where it will end.

In answer to all which, with deference to wiser judgments,   [85 I think this rather shews the necessity of a nominal religion among us. Great wits love to be free with the highest objects; and if they cannot be allowed a God to revile or renounce, they will speak evil of dignities, abuse the Government, and reflect upon the Ministry, which I am sure few will deny to be of much more pernicious   [90 consequence, according to the saying of Tiberius, *Deorum offensa diis curae.* As to the particular fact related, I think it is not fair to argue from one instance, perhaps another cannot be produced: yet (to the comfort of all those who may be apprehensive of persecution) blasphemy we know is freely spoke a million of times in every   [95 coffee-house and tavern, or wherever else good company meet. It must be allowed indeed, that to break an English free-born officer only for blasphemy, was, to speak the gentlest of such an action, a very high strain of absolute power. Little can be said in excuse for the general; perhaps he was afraid it might give offence to the allies,   [100 among whom, for aught we know, it may be the custom of the country to believe a God. But if he argued, as some have done, upon a mistaken principle, that an officer who is guilty of speaking blasphemy, may some time or other proceed so far as to raise a mutiny, the consequence is by no means to be admitted: For, surely   [105

---

91. "Injuries done the gods are their own concern"—attributed to Tiberius in Tacitus's *Annales,* I lxxiii.

the commander of an English army is like to be but ill obeyed, whose soldiers fear and reverence him as little as they do a deity.

It is further objected against the Gospel system, that it obliges men to the belief of things too difficult for free-thinkers, and such who have shook off the prejudices that usually cling to a confined [110 education. To which I answer, that men should be cautious how they raise objections which reflect upon the wisdom of the nation. Is not every body freely allowed to believe whatever he pleases, and to publish his belief to the world whenever he thinks fit, especially if it serves to strengthen the party which is in the right? Would [115 any indifferent foreigner, who should read the trumpery lately written by Asgill, Tindall, Toland, Coward, and forty more, imagine the Gospel to be our rule of faith, and to be confirmed by Parliaments? Does any man either believe, or say he believes, or desire to have it thought that he says he believes one syllable of the matter? [120 and is any man worse received upon that score, or does he find his want of nominal faith a disadvantage to him in the pursuit of any civil or military employment? What if there be an old dormant statute or two against him, are they not now obsolete, to a degree, that Empson and Dudley themselves, if they were now alive, [125 would find it impossible to put them in execution?

It is likewise urged, that there are, by computation, in this kingdom, above ten thousand parsons, whose revenues, added to those of my Lords the Bishops, would suffice to maintain at least two hundred young gentlemen of wit and pleasure, and free-thinking ene- [130 mies to priest-craft, narrow principles, pedantry, and prejudices, who might be an ornament to the court and town: And then again, so great a number of able-bodied divines might be a recruit to our fleet and armies. This indeed appears to be a consideration of some weight: But then, on the other side, several things deserve to be con- [135 sidered likewise: as, first, whether it may not be thought necessary that in certain tracts of country, like what we call parishes, there should be one man at least, of abilities to read and write. Then it seems a wrong computation, that the revenues of the church through-out this island would be large enough to maintain two hun- [140 dred young gentlemen, or even half that number, after the present re-fined way of living, that is, to allow each of them such a rent, as in the

---

117. *Asgill . . . Coward:* writers of deistical tracts. In general, deism tended to deny the necessity and validity of the Christian Revelation. 125. *Empson, Dudley:* agents of Henry VII who extorted money from the people for his treasury by every kind of legal (and illegal) maneuver. 142. *rent:* income.

modern form of speech, would make them easy. But still there is in
this project a greater mischief behind; and we ought to beware of the
woman's folly, who killed the hen that every morning laid   [145
her a golden egg. For, pray what would become of the race of men
in the next age, if we had nothing to trust to besides the scrofulous
consumptive production furnished by our men of wit and pleasure,
when having squandered away their vigour, health, and estates, they
are forced, by some disagreeable marriage, to piece up their   [150
broken fortunes, and entail rottenness and politeness on their posterity? Now, here are ten thousand persons reduced, by the wise
regulations of Henry the Eighth, to the necessity of a low diet, and
moderate exercise, who are the only great restorers of our breed, without which the nation would in an age or two become one   [155
great hospital.

Another advantage proposed by the abolishing of Christianity, is
the clear gain of one day in seven, which is now entirely lost, and
consequently the kingdom one seventh less considerable in trade,
business, and pleasure; beside the loss to the publick of so   [160
many stately structures now in the hands of the clergy, which might be
converted into play-houses, exchanges, market-houses, common dormi-
tories, and other publick edifices.

I hope I shall be forgiven a hard word if I call this a perfect cavil.
I readily own there hath been an old custom, time out of   [165
mind, for people to assemble in the churches every Sunday, and that
shops are still frequently shut, in order, as it is conceived, to preserve
the memory of that ancient practice; but how this can prove a hin-
drance to business or pleasure, is hard to imagine. What if the men of
pleasure are forced, one day in the week, to game at home   [170
instead of the chocolate-house? Are not the taverns and coffee-houses
open? Can there be a more convenient season for taking a dose of
physick? Are fewer claps got upon Sundays than other days? Is not
that the chief day for traders to sum up the accounts of the week,
and for lawyers to prepare their briefs? But I would fain   [175
know how it can be pretended that the churches are misapplied.
Where are more appointments and rendezvouzes of gallantry? Where
more care to appear in the foremost box, with greater advantage of
dress? Where more meetings for business? Where more bargains
driven of all sorts? and where so many conveniencies or in-   [180
citements to sleep?

There is one advantage greater than any of the foregoing, proposed
by the abolishing of Christianity, that it will utterly extinguish parties

---

151. *rottenness:* diseases. 153. *the . . . Eighth:* referring to Henry VIII's
spoliation of church revenues.

among us, by removing those factious distinctions of High and Low
Church, of Whig and Tory, Presbyterian and Church of   [185
England, which are now so many mutual clogs upon public proceed-
ings, and are apt to prefer the gratifying themselves or depressing their
adversaries, before the most important interest of the state.

I confess, if it were certain that so great an advantage would redound to the nation by this expedient, I would submit, and be   [190
silent: But, will any man say, that if the words, whoring, drinking,
cheating, lying, stealing, were by Act of Parliament ejected out of the
English tongue and dictionaries, we should all awake next morning
chaste and temperate, honest and just, and lovers of truth? Is this a
fair consequence? Or if the physicians would forbid us to   [195
pronounce the words pox, gout, rheumatism, and stone, would that
expedient serve like so many talismans to destroy the diseases themselves? Are party and faction rooted in men's hearts no deeper than
phrases borrowed from religion, or founded upon no firmer principles?
And is our language so poor, that we cannot find other   [200
terms to express them? Are envy, pride, avarice and ambition such
ill nomenclators, that they cannot furnish appellations for their
owners? Will not heydukes and mamalukes, mandarins, and pat-
shaws, or any other words formed at pleasure, serve to distinguish
those who are in the ministry from others, who would be in   [205
it if they could? What, for instance, is easier than to vary the form
of speech, and instead of the word church, make it a question in
politicks, Whether the monument be in danger? Because religion was
nearest at hand to furnish a few convenient phrases, is our invention
so barren, we can find no other? Suppose, for argument sake,   [210
that the Tories favoured Margarita, the Whigs Mrs. Tofts, and the
Trimmers Valentini, would not Margaritians, Toftians, and Valen-
tinians be very tolerable marks of distinction? The Prasini and Veneti,
two most virulent factions in Italy, began (if I remember right) by a
distinction of colours in ribbons, which we might do with   [215
as good a Grace about the dignity of the blue and the green, and
serve as properly to divide the court, the Parliament, and the kingdom
between them, as any terms of art whatsoever, borrowed from religion.
And therefore I think there is little force in this objection against

205. *ministry:* i.e., ministry of state (not church). 211. *Margarita, Mrs.
Tofts* and *Valentini* were contemporary opera stars, each with an enthusiastic following. 212. *Trimmers* here means "compromisers"—from the
faction of that name in Charles II's reign who wished to restrain royal
prerogatives but opposed the Exclusion Bill: cf. Introduction, page 7.
213. The rivalry of the Prasini and Veneti (originating in chariot races
where their colors were green and blue) eventually broke out in civil war.

Christianity, or prospect of so great an advantage as is pro-   [220
posed in the abolishing of it.

'Tis again objected, as a very absurd ridiculous custom, that a set
of men should be suffered, much less employed and hired, to bawl one
day in seven against the lawfulness of those methods most in use
towards the pursuit of greatness, riches, and pleasure, which   [225
are the constant practice of all men alive on the other six. But this
objection is, I think, a little unworthy so refined an age as ours. Let
us argue this matter calmly; I appeal to the breast of any polite free-
thinker, whether, in the pursuit of gratifying a predominant passion,
he hath not always felt a wonderful incitement, by reflecting   [230
it was a thing forbidden: And therefore we see, in order to cultivate
this test, the wisdom of the nation hath taken special care, that the
ladies should be furnished with prohibited silks, and the men with
prohibited wine: And indeed it were to be wished, that some other
prohibitions were promoted, in order to improve the pleas-   [235
ures of the town; which, for want of such expedients, begin already,
as I am told, to flag and grow languid, giving way daily to cruel
inroads from the spleen.

'Tis likewise proposed, as a great advantage to the publick, that if
we once discard the system of the Gospel, all religion will of   [240
course be banished for ever, and consequently along with it, those
grievous prejudices of education, which, under the names of virtue,
conscience, honour, justice, and the like, are so apt to disturb the
peace of human minds, and the notions whereof are so hard to be
eradicated by right reason or free-thinking, sometimes during   [245
the whole course of our lives.

Here first I observe how difficult it is to get rid of a phrase which
the world is once grown fond of, tho' the occasion that first produced
it be entirely taken away. For some years past, if a man had but an
ill-favoured nose, the deep thinkers of the age would some   [250
way or other contrive to impute the cause to the prejudice of his
education. From this fountain were said to be derived all our foolish
notions of justice, piety, love of our country; all our opinions of God
or a future state, Heaven, Hell, and the like: And there might formerly perhaps have been some pretence for this charge.   [255
But so effectual care hath been since taken to remove those prejudices, by an entire change in the methods of education, that (with
honour I mention it to our polite innovators) the young gentlemen,
who are now on the scene, seem to have not the least tincture left
of those infusions, or string of those weeds; and by conse-   [260
quence the reason for abolishing nominal Christianity upon that pre-
text, is wholly ceased.

For the rest, it may perhaps admit a controversy, whether the banishing all notions of religion whatsoever, would be convenient for the vulgar. Not that I am in the least of opinion with   [265 those who hold religion to have been the invention of politicians, to keep the lower part of the world in awe by the fear of invisible powers; unless mankind were then very different from what it is now: For I look upon the mass or body of our people here in England, to be as free-thinkers, that is to say, as staunch unbelievers, as any   [270 of the highest rank. But I conceive some scattered notions about a superior power to be of singular use for the common people, as furnishing excellent materials to keep children quiet when they grow peevish, and providing topicks of amusement in a tedious winter night.

Lastly, 'tis proposed as a singular advantage, that the abol-   [275 ishing of Christianity will very much contribute to the uniting of Protestants, by enlarging the terms of communion so as to take in all sorts of dissenters, who are now shut out of the pale upon account of a few ceremonies, which all sides confess to be things indifferent: That this alone will effectually answer the great ends of a   [280 scheme for comprehension, by opening a large noble gate, at which all bodies may enter; whereas the chaffering with dissenters, and dodging about this or t'other ceremony, is but like opening a few wickets, and leaving them at jar, by which no more than one can get in at a time, and that not without stooping, and sideling, and   [285 squeezing his body.

To all this I answer, that there is one darling inclination of mankind, which usually affects to be a retainer to religion, though she be neither its parent, its godmother, nor its friend; I mean the spirit of opposition, that lived long before Christianity, and can   [290 easily subsist without it. Let us, for instance, examine wherein the opposition of sectaries among us consists; we shall find Christianity to have no share in it at all. Does the Gospel any where prescribe a starched squeezed countenance, a stiff formal gait, a singularity of manners and habit, or any affected forms and modes of speech   [295 different from the reasonable part of mankind? Yet, if Christianity did not lend its name to stand in the gap, and to employ or divert these humours, they must of necessity be spent in contraventions to the laws of the land, and disturbance of the publick peace. There is a portion of enthusiasm assigned to every nation, which if it   [300 hath not proper objects to work on, will burst out, and set all into a flame. If the quiet of a state can be bought by only flinging men a few ceremonies to devour, it is a purchase no wise man would refuse. Let the mastiffs amuse themselves about a sheep's skin stuffed

281. *comprehension:* inclusiveness. 284. *wickets:* gates. 293-6. Swift describes the bearing of some of the Puritan groups.

with hay, provided it will keep them from worrying the [305
flock. The institution of convents abroad, seems in one point a
strain of great wisdom, there being few irregularities in human
passions, which may not have recourse to vent themselves in some
of those orders, which are so many retreats for the speculative, the
melancholy, the proud, the silent, the politick, and the [310
morose, to spend themselves, and evaporate the noxious particles; for
each of whom we in this island are forced to provide a several sect
of religion, to keep them quiet; and whenever Christianity shall be
abolished, the legislature must find some other expedient to employ
and entertain them. For what imports it how large a gate [315
you open, if there will be always left a number who place a pride
and a merit in not coming in?

Having thus considered the most important objections against
Christianity, and the chief advantages proposed by the abolishing
thereof; I shall now with equal deference and submission to [320
wiser judgments, as before, proceed to mention a few inconveniences
that may happen, if the Gospel should be repealed; which perhaps
the projectors may not have sufficiently considered.

And first, I am very sensible how much the gentlemen of wit and
pleasure are apt to murmur, and be shocked at the sight [325
of so many daggled-tail parsons, that happen to fall in their way, and
offend their eyes; but at the same time these wise reformers do not
consider what an advantage and felicity it is, for great wits to be
always provided with objects of scorn and contempt, in order to
exercise and improve their talents, and divert their spleen [330
from falling on each other, or on themselves, especially when all this
may be done without the least imaginable danger to their persons.

And to urge another argument of a parallel nature: If Christianity
were once abolished, how could the free-thinkers, the strong rea-
soners, and the men of profound learning, be able to find [335
another subject so calculated in all points whereon to display their
abilities. What wonderful productions of wit should we be deprived
of, from those whose genius, by continual practice, hath been wholly
turned upon raillery and invectives against religion, and would
therefore never be able to shine or distinguish themselves [340
upon any other subject. We are daily complaining of the great
decline of wit among us, and would we take away the greatest, perhaps the only topick we have left? Who would ever have suspected
Asgill for a wit, or Toland for a philosopher, if the inexhaustible
stock of Christianity had not been at hand to provide them [345
with materials? What other subject through all art or nature could
have produced Tindall for a profound author, or furnished him with

317. *not . . . in:* i.e., not coming into the Church of England.

readers? It is the wise choice of the subject that alone adorns and distinguishes the writer. For had a hundred such pens as these been employed on the side of religion, they would have imme-   [350 diately sunk into silence and oblivion.

Nor do I think it wholly groundless, or my fears altogether imaginary, that the abolishing of Christianity may perhaps bring the church in danger, or at least put the senate to the trouble of another securing vote. I desire I may not be mistaken; I am far from   [355 presuming to affirm or think that the church is in danger at present, or as things now stand; but we know not how soon it may be so, when the Christian religion is repealed. As plausible as this project seems, there may a dangerous design lurk under it: Nothing can be more notorious, than that the atheists, deists, Socinians, anti-   [360 Trinitarians, and other subdivisions of free-thinkers, are persons of little zeal for the present ecclesiastical establishment: Their declared opinion is for repealing the sacramental test; they are very indifferent with regard to ceremonies; nor do they hold the *jus divinum* of episcopacy: Therefore this may be intended as one politick   [365 step towards altering the constitution of the church established, and setting up presbytery in the stead, which I leave to be further considered by those at the helm.

In the last place I think nothing can be more plain, than that by this expedient, we shall run into the evil we chiefly pretend   [370 to avoid; and that the abolishment of the Christian religion, will be the readiest course we can take to introduce popery. And I am the more inclined to this opinion, because we know it has been the constant practice of the Jesuits to send over emissaries, with instructions to personate themselves members of the several prevailing   [375 sects amongst us. So it is recorded, that they have at sundry times appeared in the guise of Presbyterians, Anabaptists, Independents, and Quakers, according as any of these were most in credit; so, since the fashion hath been taken up of exploding religion, the popish missionaries have not been wanting to mix with the free-   [380 thinkers; among whom Toland, the great oracle of the anti-Christians, is an Irish priest, the son of an Irish priest; and the most learned and ingenious author of a book called the *Rights of the Christian Church,* was in a proper juncture reconciled to the Romish faith, whose true son, as appears by a hundred passages in his   [385

---

354. *senate:* Parliament. 363. *sacramental test:* the act which excluded from political office (and many other privileges) all who would not take Communion according to the rites of the Church of England. 364. *jus divinum:* divine authority. 383. *author:* i.e., Tindal, one of the deistical writers mentioned earlier.

treatise, he still continues. Perhaps I could add some others to the number; but the fact is beyond dispute, and the reasoning they proceed by is right: For supposing Christianity to be extinguished, the people will never be at ease till they find out some other method of worship; which will as infallibly produce superstition, as [390 this will end in popery.

And therefore, if notwithstanding all I have said, it still be thought necessary to have a bill brought in for repealing Christianity, I would humbly offer an amendment, that instead of the word Christianity, may be put religion in general, which I conceive [395 will much better answer all the good ends proposed by the projectors of it. For, as long as we leave in being a God and his Providence, with all the necessary consequences which curious and inquisitive men will be apt to draw from such premises, we do not strike at the root of the evil, though we should ever so effectually annihilate [400 the present scheme of the Gospel; For of what use is freedom of thought, if it will not produce freedom of action, which is the sole end, how remote soever in appearance, of all objections against Christianity; and therefore, the free-thinkers consider it as a sort of edifice, wherein all the parts have such a mutual dependence [405 on each other, that if you happen to pull out one single nail, the whole fabrick must fall to the ground. This was happily exprest by him who had heard of a text brought for proof of the Trinity, which in an ancient manuscript was differently read; he thereupon immediately took the hint, and by a sudden deduction of a long [410 sorites, most logically concluded: Why, if it be as you say, I may safely whore and drink on, and defy the parson. From which, and many the like instances easy to be produced, I think nothing can be more manifest, than that the quarrel is not against any particular points of hard digestion in the Christian system, but against [415 religion in general, which, by laying restraints on human nature, is supposed the great enemy to the freedom of thought and action.

Upon the whole, if it shall still be thought for the benefit of church and state, that Christianity be abolished, I conceive however, it may be more convenient to defer the execution to a time of [420 peace, and not venture in this conjuncture to disoblige our Allies, who, as it falls out, are all Christians, and many of them, by the prejudices of their education, so bigoted, as to place a sort of pride in the appellation. If upon being rejected by them, we are to trust to an alliance with the Turk, we shall find our selves much de- [425 ceived: For, as he is too remote, and generally engaged in war with

---

397. *in being:* in existence. 411. *sorites:* chain of reasoning.

the Persian Emperor, so his people would be more scandalized at our infidelity, than our Christian neighbours. For they are not only strict observers of religious worship, but, what is worse believe a God; which is more than is required of us, even while we preserve   [430 the name of Christians.

To conclude: Whatever some may think of the great advantages to trade by this favourite scheme, I do very much apprehend, that in six months time after the act is passed for the extirpation of the Gospel, the Bank and East-India Stock may fall at least one   [435 per cent. And since that is fifty times more than ever the wisdom of our age thought fit to venture for the preservation of Christianity, there is no reason we should be at so great a loss, merely for the sake of destroying it.

❧

A Modest Proposal for Preventing the Children of Ireland from Being a Burden to Their Parents or Country

*I*T IS a melancholy object to those who walk through this great town or travel in the country, when they see the streets, the roads, and cabin-doors crowded with beggars of the female sex, followed by three, four, or six children, all in rags, and importuning every passenger for an alms. These mothers, instead of being able to work   [5 for their honest livelihood, are forced to employ all their time in strolling to beg sustenance for their helpless infants, who, as they grow up, either turn thieves for want of work, or leave their dear native country, to fight for the Pretender in Spain, or sell themselves to the Barbadoes.   10
I think it is agreed by all parties, that this prodigious number of children in the arms, or on the backs, or at the heels of their mothers, and frequently of their fathers, is in the present deplorable state of the kingdom a very great additional grievance; and therefore whoever could find out a fair, cheap, and easy method of making these   [15 children sound and useful members of the common-wealth, would deserve so well of the publick as to have his statue set up for a pre-server of the nation.

A MODEST PROPOSAL: 9. *Pretender:* The Catholic son of James II, exiled after the Revolution of 1688, which secured for England a Protestant crown.

But my intention is very far from being confined to provide only for the children of professed beggars; it is of a much greater   [20 extent, and shall take in the whole number of infants at a certain age, who are born of parents in effect as little able to support them, as those who demand our charity in the streets.

As to my own part, having turned my thoughts, for many years, upon this important subject, and maturely weighed the sev-   [25 eral schemes of other projectors, I have always found them grossly mistaken in their computation. It is true, a child just dropt from its dam may be supported by her milk for a solar year with little other nourishment, at most not above the value of two shillings, which the mother may certainly get, or the value in scraps, by her   [30 lawful occupation of begging; and it is exactly at one year old that I propose to provide for them in such a manner, as, instead of being a charge upon their parents, or the parish, or wanting food and raiment for the rest of their lives, they shall, on the contrary, con- tribute to the feeding and partly to the clothing of many   [35 thousands.

There is likewise another great advantage in my scheme, that it will prevent those voluntary abortions, and that horrid practice of women murdering their bastard children, alas! too frequent among us— sacrificing the poor innocent babes, I doubt, more to avoid   [40 the expense than the shame—which would move tears and pity in the most savage and inhuman breast.

The number of souls in this kingdom being usually reckoned one million and a half, of these I calculate there may be about two hundred thousand couple whose wives are breeders; from   [45 which number I substract thirty thousand couples, who are able to maintain their own children, although I apprehend there cannot be so many, under the present distresses of the kingdom; but this being granted, there will remain an hundred and seventy thousand breeders. I again substract fifty thousand, for those women who mis-   [50 carry, or whose children die by accident or disease within the year. There only remain an hundred and twenty thousand children of poor parents annually born: The question therefore is, How this number shall be reared, and provided for? which, as I have already said, under the present situation of affairs, is utterly impossible   [55 by all the methods hitherto proposed; for we can neither employ them in handicraft or agriculture; we neither build houses, (I mean in the country) nor cultivate land: They can very seldom pick up a livelihood by stealing till they arrive at six years old, except where they are of towardly parts, although, I confess, they learn the   [60 rudiments much earlier; during which time they can however be properly looked upon only as probationers; as I have been informed by a principal gentleman in the county of Cavan, who protested to me, that he never knew above one or two instances under the age of six, even in a part of the kingdom so renowned for the quick-   [65 est proficiency in that art.

I am assured by our merchants, that a boy or a girl before twelve years old, is no saleable commodity, and even when they come to this age, they will not yield above three pounds, or three pounds and half a crown at most, on the exchange; which cannot turn to   [70 account either to the parents or kingdom, the charge of nutriment and rags having been at least four times that value.

I shall now therefore humbly propose my own thoughts, which I hope will not be liable to the least objection.

ridiculous I have been assured by a very knowing American of my   [75 acquaintance in London, that a young healthy child well nursed is at a year old a most delicious nourishing and wholesome food, whether stewed, roasted, baked, or boiled; and I make no doubt that it will equally serve in a fricasee, or a ragout.

I do therefore humbly offer it to publick consideration, that   [80 of the hundred and twenty thousand children, already computed, twenty thousand may be reserved for breed, whereof only one fourth part to be males; which is more than we allow to sheep, black cattle, or swine, and my reason is, that these children are seldom the fruits of marriage, a circumstance not much regarded by our sav-   [85 ages; therefore, one male will be sufficient to serve four females. That the remaining hundred thousand may at a year old be offered in sale to the persons of quality and fortune, through the kingdom, always advising the mother to let them suck plentifully in the last month, so as to render them plump and fat for a good table. A child   [90 will make two dishes at an entertainment for friends, and when the family dines alone, the fore or hind quarter will make a reasonable dish, and seasoned with a little pepper or salt will be very good boiled on the fourth day, especially in winter.

I have reckoned upon a medium, that a child just born will   [95 weigh 12 pounds, and in a solar year, if tolerably nursed, encreaseth to 28 pounds.

I grant this food will be somewhat dear, and therefore very proper for landlords, who, as they have already devoured most of the parents seem to have the best title to the children.   100

Infant's flesh will be in season throughout the year, but more plentiful in March, and a little before and after; for we are told by a grave author, an eminent French physician, that fish being a pro-

---

79. *ragout:* stew.

lifick dyet, there are more children born in Roman Catholick coun- tries about nine months after Lent, than at any other season;   [105 therefore reckoning a year after Lent, the markets will be more glutted than usual, because the number of popish infants, is at least three to one in this kingdom, and therefore it will have one other collateral advantage, by lessening the number of papists among us.

I have already computed the charge of nursing a beggar's   [110 child (in which list I reckon all cottagers, labourers, and four fifths of the farmers) to be about two shillings per annum, rags included; and I believe no gentleman would repine to give ten shillings for the carcass of a good fat child, which, as I have said will make four dishes of excellent nutritive meat, when he hath only some   [115 particular friend, or his own family to dine with him. Thus the squire will learn to be a good landlord, and grow popular among his tenants; the mother will have eight shillings neat profit, and be fit for work till she produces another child.

Those who are more thrifty (as I must confess the times   [120 require) may flay the carcass; the skin of which, artificially dressed, will make admirable gloves for ladies, and summer boots for fine gentlemen.

As to our city of Dublin, shambles may be appointed for this pur- pose, in the most convenient parts of it, and butchers we may   [125 be assured will not be wanting; although I rather recommend buying the children alive, and dressing them hot from the knife, as we do roasting pigs.

A very worthy person, a true lover of his country, and whose vir- tues I highly esteem, was lately pleased, in discoursing on   [130 this matter, to offer a refinement upon my scheme. He said, that many gentlemen of this kingdom, having of late destroyed their deer, he conceived that the want of venison might be well supplied by the bodies of young lads and maidens, not exceeding fourteen years of age, nor under twelve; so great a number of both sexes in   [135 every country being now ready to starve, for want of work and service: And these to be disposed of by their parents if alive, or otherwise by their nearest relations. But with due deference to so excellent a friend, and so deserving a patriot, I cannot be altogether in his sentiments; for as to the males, my American acquaint-   [140 ance assured me from frequent experience, that their flesh was gen- erally tough and lean, like that of our schoolboys, by continual ex- ercise, and their taste disagreeable, and to fatten them would not answer the charge. Then as to the females, it would, I think with

---

121. *artificially:* skilfully. 124. *shambles:* slaughter-house.

humble submission, be a loss to the publick, because they   [145
soon would become breeders themselves: And besides it is not im-
probable that some scrupulous people might be apt to censure such
a practice (although indeed very unjustly) as a little bordering upon
cruelty, which, I confess, hath always been with me the strongest
objection against any project, how well soever intended.   150

But in order to justify my friend, he confessed, that this expedient
was put into his head by the famous Psalmanazar, a native of the
island Formosa, who came from thence to London, above twenty
years ago, and in conversation told my friend, that in his country
when any young person happened to be put to death, the   [155
executioner sold the carcass to persons of quality, as a prime dainty,
and that, in his time, the body of a plump girl of fifteen, who was
crucified for an attempt to poison the Emperor, was sold to his Imperial Majesty's prime minister of state, and other great mandarins
of the court, in joints from the gibbet, at four hundred   [160
crowns. Neither indeed can I deny, that if the same use were made
of several plump young girls in this town, who, without one single
groat to their fortunes, cannot stir abroad without a chair, and appear
at a play-house and assemblies in foreign fineries which they never
will pay for, the kingdom would not be the worse.   165

Some persons of a desponding spirit are in great concern about that
vast number of poor people, who are aged, diseased, or maimed, and
I have been desired to employ my thoughts what course may be
taken, to ease the nation of so grievous an encumbrance. But I am
not in the least pain upon that matter, because it is very well   [170
known, that they are every day dying, and rotting, by cold, and
famine, and filth, and vermin, as fast as can be reasonably expected.
And as to the younger labourers, they are now in almost as hopeful
a condition. They cannot get work, and consequently pine away for
want of nourishment, to a degree, that if at any time they   [175
are accidentally hired to common labour, they have not strength to
perform it, and thus the country and themselves are happily delivered
from the evils to come.

I have too long digressed, and therefore shall return to my subject.
I think the advantages by the proposal which I have made   [180
are obvious and many, as well as of the highest importance.

For *first,* as I have already observed, it would greatly lessen the
number of papists, with whom we are yearly over-run, being the
principal breeders of the nation, as well as our most dangerous
enemies, and who stay at home on purpose with a design to   [185

---

152. *Psalmanazar:* an eccentric Frenchman, who for a time passed himself
off as a Christianized native of Formosa and published (1704) a description
of Formosan life in which this incident is recorded.

deliver the kingdom to the Pretender, hoping to take their advantage by the absence of so many good Protestants, who have chosen rather to leave their country, than stay at home, and pay tithes against their conscience to an episcopal curate.

Secondly, the poorer tenants will have something valuable   [190 of their own which by law may be made liable to distress, and help to pay their landlord's rent, their corn and cattle being already seized, and money a thing unknown.

Thirdly, whereas the maintenance of an hundred thousand chil- dren, from two years old, and upwards, cannot be computed   [195 at less than ten shillings a piece per annum, the nation's stock will be thereby increased fifty thousand pounds per annum, besides the profit of a new dish, introduced to the tables of all gentlemen of fortune in the kingdom who have any refinement in taste, and the money will circulate among our selves, the goods being   [200 entirely of our own growth and manufacture.

Fourthly, the constant breeders, besides the gain of eight shillings sterling per annum, by the sale of their children, will be rid of the charge of maintaining them after the first year.

Fifthly, this food would likewise bring great custom to   [205 taverns, where the vintners will certainly be so prudent as to procure the best receipts for dressing it to perfection; and consequently have their houses frequented by all the fine gentlemen, who justly value themselves upon their knowledge in good eating; and a skilful cook, who understands how to oblige his guests, will contrive to   [210 make it as expensive as they please.

Sixthly, this would be a great inducement to marriage, which all wise nations have either encouraged by rewards, or enforced by laws and penalties. It would encrease the care and tenderness of mothers towards their children, when they were sure of a settlement   [215 for life to the poor babes, provided in some sort by the publick, to their annual profit instead of expence; we should soon see an honest emulation among the married women, which of them could bring the fattest child to the market. Men would become as fond of their wives during the time of their pregnancy, as they are now   [220 of their mares in foal, their cows in calf, or sows when they are ready to farrow, nor offer to beat or kick them (as is too frequent a practice) for fear of a miscarriage.

Many other advantages might be enumerated. For instance, the addition of some thousand carcasses in our exportation of   [225 barreled beef: the propagation of swine's flesh, and improvement in the art of making good bacon, so much wanted among us by the great destruction of pigs, too frequent at our tables, which are no way comparable in taste or magnificence to a well grown, fat yearling

child, which roasted whole will make a considerable figure   [230
at a Lord Mayor's feast, or any other publick entertainment. But this,
and many others, I omit, being studious of brevity.

Supposing that one thousand families in this city, would be constant customers for infant's flesh, besides others who might have it
at merry meetings, particularly at weddings and christenings,   [235
I compute that Dublin would take off annually about twenty thousand carcasses, and the rest of the kingdom (where probably they will
be sold somewhat cheaper) the remaining eighty thousand.

I can think of no one objection, that will possibly be raised against
this proposal, unless it should be urged, that the number of   [240
people will be thereby much lessened in the kingdom. This I freely
own, and 'twas indeed one principal design in offering it to the
world. I desire the reader will observe, that I calculate my remedy
for this one individual kingdom of Ireland, and for no other that
ever was, is, or, I think, ever can be upon earth. Therefore   [245
let no man talk to me of other expedients: of taxing our absentees at
five shillings a pound: of using neither clothes, nor household furniture, except what is of our own growth and manufacture: of utterly
rejecting the materials and instruments that promote foreign luxury:
of curing the expensiveness of pride, vanity, idleness, and   [250
gaming in our women: of introducing a vein of parsimony, prudence and temperance: of learning to love our country, wherein we
differ even from Laplanders, and the inhabitants of Topinamboo: of
quitting our animosities, and factions, nor act any longer like the
Jews, who were murdering one another at the very moment   [255
their city was taken: of being a little cautious not to sell our country
and consciences for nothing: of teaching landlords to have at least one
degree of mercy towards their tenants. Lastly, of putting a spirit of
honesty, industry, and skill into our shop-keepers, who, if a resolution could now be taken to buy only our native goods, would   [260
immediately unite to cheat and exact upon us in the price, the measure, and the goodness, nor could ever yet be brought to make one fair
proposal of just dealing, though often and earnestly invited to it.

Therefore I repeat, let no man talk to me of these and the like
expedients, till he hath at least some glimpse of hope, that   [265
there will ever be some hearty and sincere attempt to put them in
practice.

---

231. *Lord . . . feast:* Lord Mayors were expected to celebrate their tenure
of office with lavish hospitality. 246. *expedients:* The expedients which
follow had all been vainly advocated by Swift for years. *absentees:* Ab-
sentee landlords, especially impervious to the suffering caused by their
exactions because remote from it, were one of the chief causes of Ireland's
plight. 253. *Topinamboo:* a district in Brazil.

But as to my self, having been wearied out for many years with offering vain, idle, visionary thoughts, and at length utterly despairing of success, I fortunately fell upon this proposal, which as it is [270 wholly new, so it hath something solid and real, of no expense and little trouble, full in our own power, and whereby we can incur no danger in disobliging England. For this kind of commodity will not bear exportation, the flesh being of too tender a consistence to admit a long continuance in salt, although perhaps I could name a [275 country, which would be glad to eat up our whole nation without it.

After all, I am not so violently bent upon my own opinion, as to reject any offer, proposed by wise men, which shall be found equally innocent, cheap, easy, and effectual. But before something of that kind shall be advanced in contradiction to my scheme, and [280 offering a better, I desire the author or authors, will be pleased maturely to consider two points. *First,* as things now stand, how they will be able to find food and raiment for a hundred thousand useless mouths and backs. And *secondly,* there being a round million of creatures in human figure throughout this kingdom, whose [285 whole subsistence put into a common stock would leave them in debt two millions of pounds sterling—adding those who are beggars by profession, to the bulk of farmers, cottagers and labourers, with their wives and children, who are beggars in effect; I desire those politicians, who dislike my overture, and may perhaps be so [290 bold to attempt an answer, that they will first ask the parents of these mortals, whether they would not at this day think it a great happiness to have been sold for food at a year old, in the manner I prescribe, and thereby have avoided such a perpetual scene of misfortunes as they have since gone through, by the oppression of landlords, the [295 impossibility of paying rent without money or trade, the want of common sustenance, with neither house nor clothes to cover them from the inclemencies of the weather, and the most inevitable prospect of entailing the like, or greater miseries, upon their breed for ever.

I profess in the sincerity of my heart, that I have not the [300 least personal interest in endeavouring to promote this necessary work, having no other motive than the publick good of my country, by advancing our trade, providing for infants, relieving the poor, and giving some pleasure to the rich. I have no children by which I can propose to get a single penny; the youngest being nine years [305 old and my wife past child-bearing.

---

276. *a country:* England.

❧

Gulliver's Travels

(1726)

I. A VOYAGE TO LILLIPUT

CHAPTER ONE. *The Author giveth some account of himself and family; his first inducements to travel. He is shipwrecked, and swims for his life; gets safe on shore in the country of Lilliput; is made a prisoner, and carried up the country.*

. . . I lay down on the grass, which was very short and soft; where I slept sounder than ever I remember to have done in my life and, as I reckoned, above nine hours; for when I awaked, it was just daylight. I attempted to rise, but was not able to stir: for as I happened to lie on my back, I found my arms and legs were strongly   [5 fastened on each side to the ground; and my hair, which was long and thick, tied down in the same manner. I likewise felt several slender ligatures across my body, from my arm-pits to my thighs. I could only look upwards; the sun began to grow hot, and the light offended mine eyes. I heard a confused noise about me, but in   [10 the posture I lay, could see nothing except the sky. In a little time I felt something alive moving on my left leg, which advancing gently forward over my breast, came almost up to my chin; when bending mine eyes downwards as much as I could, I perceived it to be a human creature not six inches high, with a bow and arrow in his   [15 hands, and a quiver at his back. In the mean time, I felt at least forty more of the same kind (as I conjectured) following the first. I was in the utmost astonishment, and roared so loud, that they all ran back in a fright; and some of them, as I was afterwards told, were hurt with the falls they got by leaping from my sides   [20 upon the ground. However, they soon returned; and one of them, who ventured so far as to get a full sight of my face, lifting up his hands and eyes by way of admiration, cried out in a shrill but distinct voice, *"Hekinah degul"*: the others repeated the same words several times, but I then knew not what they meant. I lay all this   [25

1 ff. [On his first voyage Gulliver is shipwrecked; though exhausted by the effort, he manages to swim to a nearby shore.]

while, as the reader may believe, in great uneasiness: at length,
struggling to get loose, I had the fortune to break the strings, and
wrench out the pegs that fastened my left arm to the ground; for, by
lifting it up to my face, I discovered the methods they had taken to
bind me; and at the same time, with a violent pull, which   [30
gave me excessive pain, I a little loosened the strings that tied down
my hair on the left side, so that I was just able to turn my head about
two inches. But the creatures ran off a second time, before I could
seize them; whereupon there was a great shout in a very shrill accent,
and after it ceased, I heard one of them cry aloud, "*Tolgo*   [35
phonac"; when in an instant I felt above an hundred arrows discharged on my left hand, which pricked me like so many needles;
and besides, they shot another flight into the air, as we do bombs in
Europe; whereof many, I suppose, fell on my body (though I felt
them not) and some on my face, which I immediately covered   [40
with my left hand. When this shower of arrows was over, I fell a
groaning with grief and pain; and then striving again to get loose,
they discharged another volley larger than the first, and some of them
attempted with spears to stick me in the sides; but, by good luck, I
had on me a buff jerkin, which they could not pierce. I   [45
thought it the most prudent method to lie still; and my design was
to continue so till night, when, my left hand being already loose, I
could easily free myself: and as for the inhabitants, I had reason to
believe I might be a match for the greatest armies they could bring
against me, if they were all of the same size with him that   [50
I saw. But fortune disposed otherwise of me. When the people observed I was quiet, they discharged no more arrows; but, by the noise
increasing, I knew their numbers were greater; and about four yards
from me, over against my right ear, I heard a knocking for above
an hour, like people at work; when turning my head that way,   [55
as well as the pegs and strings would permit me, I saw a stage erected,
about a foot and a half from the ground, capable of holding four of
the inhabitants, with two or three ladders to mount it: from whence
one of them, who seemed to be a person of quality, made me a long
speech, whereof I understood not one syllable. But I should   [60
have mentioned, that before the principal person began his oration,
he cried out three times, "*Langro dehul san*" (these words and the
former were afterwards repeated and explained to me). Whereupon
immediately about fifty of the inhabitants came, and cut the strings
that fastened the left side of my head, which gave me the   [65
liberty of turning it to the right, and of observing the person and
gesture of him that was to speak. He appeared to be of a middle
age, and taller than any of the other three who attended him;

whereof one was a page that held up his train, and seemed to be
somewhat longer than my middle finger; the other two stood   [70
one on each side to support him. He acted every part of an orator;
and I could observe many periods of threatenings, and others of
promises, pity, and kindness. I answered in a few words, but in the
most submissive manner, lifting up my left hand and both mine eyes
to the sun, as calling him for a witness; and being almost   [75
famished with hunger, having not eaten a morsel for some hours
before I left the ship, I found the demands of nature so strong upon
me, that I could not forbear showing my impatience (perhaps against
the strict rules of decency) by putting my finger frequently on my
mouth, to signify that I wanted food. The *Hurgo* (for so   [80
they call a great lord, as I afterwards learnt) understood me very well.
He descended from the stage, and commanded that several ladders
should be applied to my sides, on which above an hundred of the
inhabitants mounted, and walked towards my mouth, laden with
baskets full of meat, which had been provided, and sent   [85
thither by the King's orders, upon the first intelligence he received of
me. I observed there was the flesh of several animals, but could not
distinguish them by the taste. There were shoulders, legs, and loins
shaped like those of mutton, and very well dressed, but smaller than
the wings of a lark. I ate them by two or three at a mouth-   [90
ful, and took three loaves at a time, about the bigness of musket bullets.
They supplied me as they could, showing a thousand marks of
wonder and astonishment at my bulk and appetite. I then made another sign that I wanted drink. They found by my eating that a small
quantity would not suffice me; and being a most ingenious   [95
people, they slung up with great dexterity one of their largest hogsheads; then rolled it towards my hand, and beat out the top; I drank
it off at a draught, which I might well do, for it did not hold half a
pint, and tasted like a small wine of Burgundy, but much more delicious. They brought me a second hogshead, which I drank   [100
in the same manner, and made signs for more, but they had none to
give me. When I had performed these wonders, they shouted for
joy, and danced upon my breast, repeating several times as they did
at first, *"Hekinah degul."* They made me a sign that I should throw
down the two hogsheads, but first warning the people be-   [105
low to stand out of the way, crying aloud, *"Borach mivola";* and
when they saw the vessels in the air, there was an universal shout of
"Hekinah degul." I confess I was often tempted, while they were
passing backwards and forwards on my body, to seize forty or fifty
of the first that came in my reach, and dash them against the   [110
ground. But the remembrance of what I had felt, which probably

might not be the worst they could do; and the promise of honour I made them, for so I interpreted my submissive behaviour, soon drove out those imaginations. Besides, I now considered myself as bound by the laws of hospitality to a people who had treated me with [115 so much expense and magnificence. However, in my thoughts I could not sufficiently wonder at the intrepidity of these diminutive mortals, who durst venture to mount and walk upon my body, while one of my hands was at liberty, without trembling at the very sight of so prodigious a creature as I must appear to them. After some time, [120 when they observed that I made no more demands for meat, there appeared before me a person of high rank from his Imperial Majesty. His Excellency, having mounted on the small of my right leg, advanced forwards up to my face, with about a dozen of his retinue. And producing his credentials under the Signet Royal, which [125 he applied close to mine eyes, spoke about ten minutes, without any signs of anger, but with a kind of determinate resolution; often pointing forwards, which, as I afterwards found, was towards the capital city, about half a mile distant, whither it was agreed by his Majesty in council that I must be conveyed. I answered in few words, [130 but to no purpose, and made a sign with my hand that was loose, putting it to the other (but over his Excellency's head, for fear of hurting him or his train) and then to my own head and body, to signify that I desired my liberty. It appeared that he understood me well enough, for he shook his head by way of disapprobation, and held [135 his hand in a posture to show that I must be carried as a prisoner. However, he made other signs to let me understand that I should have meat and drink enough, and very good treatment. Whereupon I once more thought of attempting to break my bonds; but again, when I felt the smart of their arrows upon my face and [140 hands, which were all in blisters, and many of the darts still sticking in them; and observing likewise that the number of my enemies increased; I gave tokens to let them know that they might do with me what they pleased. Upon this, the *Hurgo* and his train withdrew, with much civility and cheerful countenances. Soon after [145 I heard a general shout. . . .

These people are most excellent mathematicians, and arrived to a great perfection in mechanics by the countenance and encouragement of the Emperor, who is a renowned patron of learning. This prince hath several machines fixed on wheels, for the carriage of trees [150 and other great weights. He often buildeth his largest men of war, whereof some are nine foot long, in the woods where the timber grows, and has them carried on these engines three or four hundred yards to the sea. Five hundred carpenters and engineers were immediately

set at work to prepare the greatest engine they had. It was a   [155
frame of wood raised three inches from the ground, about seven foot
long and four wide, moving upon twenty-two wheels. The shout I
heard was upon the arrival of this engine, which, it seems, set out in
four hours after my landing. It was brought parallel to me as I lay.
But the principal difficulty was to raise and place me in this   [160
vehicle. Eighty poles, each of one foot high, were erected for this
purpose, and very strong cords of the bigness of packthread were
fastened by hooks to many bandages, which the workmen had girt
round my neck, my hands, my body, and my legs. Nine hundred of
the strongest men were employed to draw up these cords by   [165
many pulleys fastened on the poles; and thus, in less than three hours, I
was raised and slung into the engine, and there tied fast. All this I was
told; for while the whole operation was performing, I lay in a profound sleep, by the force of that soporiferous medicine infused into
my liquor. Fifteen hundred of the Emperor's largest horses,   [170
each about four inches and a half high, were employed to draw me
towards the metropolis, which, as I said, was half a mile distant. . . .

At the place where the carriage stopped, there stood an ancient
temple, esteemed to be the largest in the whole kingdom; which having been polluted some years before by an unnatural murder,   [175
was, according to the zeal of those people, looked on as profane,
and therefore had been applied to common use, and all the ornaments
and furniture carried away. In this edifice it was determined I should
lodge. The great gate fronting to the north was about four foot high,
and almost two foot wide, through which I could easily creep.   [180
On each side of the gate was a small window not above six inches
from the ground: into that on the left side, the King's smiths conveyed fourscore and eleven chains, like those that hang to a lady's watch
in Europe, and almost as large, which were locked to my left leg with six
and thirty padlocks. Over against this temple, on the other side   [185
of the great highway, at twenty foot distance, there was a turret
at least five foot high. Here the Emperor ascended with many principal lords of his court, to have an opportunity of viewing me, as
I was told, for I could not see them. It was reckoned that above an
hundred thousand inhabitants came out of the town upon   [190
the same errand; and in spite of my guards, I believe there could not
be fewer than ten thousand, at several times, who mounted upon my
body by the help of ladders. But a proclamation was soon issued to
forbid it, upon pain of death. When the workmen found it was impossible for me to break loose, they cut all the strings that   [195
bound me; whereupon I rose up with as melancholy a disposition as
ever I had in my life. . . .

CHAPTER TWO. *The Emperor of Lilliput, attended by several of the nobility, comes to see the Author in his confinement. The Emperor's person and habit described. Learned men appointed to teach the Author their language. He gains favour by his mild disposition. His pockets are searched, and his sword and pistols taken from him.*

*W*HEN I found myself on my feet, I looked about me, and must confess I never beheld a more entertaining prospect. The country round appeared like a continued garden, and the inclosed fields, which were generally forty foot square, resembled so many beds of flowers. These fields were intermingled with woods of half a stang, and   [5 the tallest trees, as I could judge, appeared to be seven foot high. I viewed the town on my left hand, which looked like the painted scene of a city in a theatre. . . .

The Emperor was already descended from the tower, and advancing on horseback towards me, which had like to have cost him   [10 dear; for the beast, though very well trained, yet wholly unused to such a sight, which appeared as if a mountain moved before him, reared up on his hinder feet: but that prince, who is an excellent horseman, kept his seat, till his attendants ran in, and held the bridle, while his master had time to dismount. When he alighted, he surveyed   [15 me round with great admiration, but kept beyond the length of my chains. He ordered his cooks and butlers, who were already prepared, to give me victuals and drink, which they pushed forward in a sort of vehicles upon wheels until I could reach them. I took these vehicles, and soon emptied them all; twenty of them were filled with   [20 meat, and ten with liquor; each of the former afforded me two or three good mouthfuls, and I emptied the liquor of ten vessels, which was contained in earthen vials, into one vehicle, drinking it off at a draught; and so I did with the rest. The Empress, and young Princes of the blood, of both sexes, attended by many ladies, sat at   [25 some distance in their chairs; but upon the accident that happened to the Emperor's horse, they alighted, and came near his person; which I am now going to describe. He is taller by almost the breadth of my nail than any of his court; which alone is enough to strike an awe into the beholders. His features are strong and masculine, with an   [30 Austrian lip and arched nose, his complexion olive, his countenance erect, his body and limbs well proportioned, all his motions graceful,

5. *half a stang:* about 8 feet.

and his deportment majestic. He was then past his prime, being twenty-eight years and three quarters old, of which he had reigned about seven, in great felicity, and generally victorious. For the [35 better convenience of beholding him, I lay on my side, so that my face was parallel to his, and he stood but three yards off: however, I have had him since many times in my hand, and therefore cannot be deceived in the description. His dress was very plain and simple, the fashion of it between the Asiatic and the European; but he [40 had on his head a light helmet of gold, adorned with jewels, and a plume on the crest. He held his sword drawn in his hand, to defend himself, if I should happen to break loose; it was almost three inches long, the hilt and scabbard were gold enriched with diamonds. His voice was shrill, but very clear and articulate, and I could [45 distinctly hear it when I stood up. The ladies and courtiers were all most magnificently clad, so that the spot they stood upon seemed to resemble a petticoat spread on the ground, embroidered with figures of gold and silver. His Imperial Majesty spoke often to me, and I returned answers, but neither of us could understand a syllable. [50 There were several of his priests and lawyers present (as I conjectured by their habits) who were commanded to address themselves to me, and I spoke to them in as many languages as I had the least smattering of, which were High and Low Dutch, Latin, French, Spanish, Italian, and Lingua Franca; but all to no purpose. After about two [55 hours the court retired, and I was left with a strong guard, to prevent the impertinence, and probably the malice of the rabble, who were very impatient to crowd about me as near as they durst; and some of them had the impudence to shoot their arrows at me as I sat on the ground by the door of my house; whereof one very narrowly [60 missed my left eye. But the colonel ordered six of the ringleaders to be seized, and thought no punishment so proper as to deliver them bound into my hands, which some of his soldiers accordingly did, pushing them forwards with the butt-ends of their pikes into my reach: I took them all in my right hand, put five of them into [65 my coat-pocket, and as to the sixth, I made a countenance as if I would eat him alive. The poor man squalled terribly, and the colonel and his officers were in much pain, especially when they saw me take out my penknife: but I soon put them out of fear; for, looking mildly, and immediately cutting the strings he was bound with, I set [70 him gently on the ground, and away he ran. I treated the rest in the same manner, taking them one by one out of my pocket; and I observed both the soldiers and people were highly obliged at this mark of my clemency, which was represented very much to my advantage at court. . . . 75

As the news of my arrival spread through the kingdom, it brought prodigious numbers of rich, idle, and curious people to see me; so that the villages were almost emptied, and great neglect of tillage and household affairs must have ensued, if his Imperial Majesty had not provided by several proclamations and orders of state against [80 this inconveniency. He directed that those who had already beheld me should return home, and not presume to come within fifty yards of my house, without license from court; whereby the secretaries of state got considerable fees.

In the mean time, the Emperor held frequent councils to [85 debate what course should be taken with me; and I was afterwards assured by a particular friend, a person of great quality, who was looked upon to be as much in the secret as any, that the court was under many difficulties concerning me. They apprehended my breaking loose, that my diet would be very expensive, and might [90 cause a famine. Sometimes they determined to starve me, or at least to shoot me in the face and hands with poisoned arrows, which would soon dispatch me: but again they considered, that the stench of so large a carcass might produce a plague in the metropolis, and probably spread through the whole kingdom. In the midst of these con- [95 sultations, several officers of the army went to the door of the great council-chamber; and two of them being admitted, gave an account of my behaviour to the six criminals above-mentioned; which made so favourable an impression in the breast of his Majesty and the whole board, in my behalf, that an Imperial Commission was issued [100 out, obliging all the villages nine hundred yards round the city, to deliver in every morning six beeves, forty sheep, and other victuals for my sustenance; together with a proportionable quantity of bread, and wine, and other liquors; for the due payment of which his Majesty gave assignments upon his treasury. For this prince lives [105 chiefly upon his own demesnes; seldom, except upon great occasions, raising any subsidies upon his subjects, who are bound to attend him in his wars at their own expense. An establishment was also made of six hundred persons to be my domestics, who had board-wages allowed for their maintenance, and tents built for them very [110 conveniently on each side of my door. It was likewise ordered, that three hundred tailors should make me a suit of clothes after the fashion of the country: that six of his Majesty's greatest scholars should be employed to instruct me in their language: and, lastly, that the Emperor's horses, and those of the nobility, and troops of [115 guards, should be exercised in my sight, to accustom themselves to me. All these orders were duly put in execution; and in about three weeks I made great progress in learning their language; during which

time the Emperor frequently honoured me with his visits, and was
pleased to assist my masters in teaching me. We began al-   [120
ready to converse together in some sort; and the first words I learnt
were to express my desire that he would please to give me my liberty,
which I every day repeated on my knees. His answer, as I could apprehend it, was, that this must be a work of time, not to be thought on
without the advice of his council; and that first I must *Lumos*   [125
kelmin pesso desmar lon emposo; that is, *swear a peace with him and
his kingdom.* However, that I should be used with all kindness; and
he advised me to acquire, by my patience and discreet behaviour, the
good opinion of himself and his subjects. He desired I would not
take it ill, if he gave orders to certain proper officers to search   [130
me; for probably I might carry about me several weapons, which must
needs be dangerous things, if they answered the bulk of so prodigious
a person. I said, his Majesty should be satisfied, for I was ready to
strip myself, and turn up my pockets before him. This I delivered,
part in words, and part in signs. He replied, that by the laws   [135
of the kingdom, I must be searched by two of his officers; that he
knew this could not be done without my consent and assistance; that
he had so good an opinion of my generosity and justice, as to trust
their persons in my hands: that whatever they took from me should
be returned when I left the country, or paid for at the rate   [140
which I would set upon them. I took up two officers in my hands,
put them first into my coat-pockets, and then into every other pocket
about me, except my two fobs, and another secret pocket which I
had no mind should be searched, wherein I had some little necessaries
that were of no consequence to any but myself. In one of my   [145
fobs there was a silver watch, and in the other a small quantity of gold
in a purse. These gentlemen, having pen, ink, and paper about them,
made an exact inventory of every thing they saw; and when they had
done, desired I would set them down, that they might deliver it to
the Emperor. This inventory I afterwards translated into   [150
English, and is word for word as follows.

Imprimis, In the right coat-pocket of the Great Man-Mountain (for
so I interpret the words *Quinbus Flestrin*) after the strictest search,
we found only one great piece of coarse cloth, large enough to be a
foot-cloth for your Majesty's chief room of state. In the left   [155
pocket we saw a huge silver chest, with a cover of the same metal,
which we, the searchers, were not able to lift. We desired it should be
opened; and one of us stepping into it, found himself up to the mid
leg in a sort of dust, some part whereof flying up to our faces, set us
both a sneezing for several times together. In his right waist-   [160

coat-pocket we found a prodigious bundle of white thin substances, folded one over another, about the bigness of three men, tied with a strong cable, and marked with black figures; which we humbly conceive to be writings, every letter almost half as large as the palm of our hands. In the left there was a sort of engine, from the [165 back of which were extended twenty long poles, resembling the palisados before your Majesty's court; wherewith we conjecture the Man-Mountain combs his head; for we did not always trouble him with questions, because we found it a great difficulty to make him understand us. In the large pocket on the right side of his [170 middle cover (so I translate the word *ramfu-lo,* by which they meant my breeches) we saw a hollow pillar of iron, about the length of a man, fastened to a strong piece of timber, larger than the pillar; and upon one side of the pillar were huge pieces of iron sticking out, cut into strange figures, which we know not what to make of. In [175 the left pocket, another engine of the same kind. In the smaller pocket on the right side, were several round flat pieces of white and red metal, of different bulk; some of the white, which seemed to be silver, were so large and heavy, that my comrade and I could hardly lift them. In the left pocket were two black pillars irregularly [180 shaped: we could not, without difficulty, reach the top of them as we stood at the bottom of his pocket. One of them was covered, and seemed all of a piece; but at the upper end of the other, there appeared a white round substance, about twice the bigness of our heads. Within each of these was enclosed a prodigious plate of steel; which, [185 by our orders, we obliged him to show us, because we apprehended they might be dangerous engines. He took them out of their cases, and told us, that in his own country his practice was to shave his beard with one of these, and to cut his meat with the other. There were two pockets which we could not enter: these he called [190 his fobs; they were two large slits cut into the top of his middle cover, but squeezed close by the pressure of his belly. Out of the right fob hung a great silver chain, with a wonderful kind of engine at the bottom. We directed him to draw out whatever was fastened to that chain; which appeared to be a globe, half silver, and half of [195 some transparent metal: for on the transparent side we saw certain strange figures circularly drawn, and thought we could touch them, till we found our fingers stopped with that lucid substance. He put this engine to our ears, which made an incessant noise like that of a watermill. And we conjecture it is either some unknown animal, [200 or the god that he worships; but we are more inclined to the latter opinion, because he assures us (if we understood him right, for he expressed himself very imperfectly) that he seldom did any thing

without consulting it. He called it his oracle, and said it pointed out
the time for every action of his life. From the left fob he   [205
took out a net almost large enough for a fisherman, but contrived to
open and shut like a purse, and served him for the same use: we
found therein several massy pieces of yellow metal, which, if they be
real gold, must be of immense value.

Having thus, in obedience to your Majesty's commands,   [210
diligently searched all his pockets, we observed a girdle about his waist
made of the hide of some prodigious animal; from which, on the left
side, hung a sword of the length of five men; and on the right, a bag
or pouch divided into two cells, each cell capable of holding three
of your Majesty's subjects. In one of these cells were several   [215
globes or balls of a most ponderous metal, about the bigness of our
heads, and required a strong hand to lift them: the other cell contained
a heap of certain black grains, but of no great bulk or weight, for we
could hold about fifty of them in the palms of our hands.

This is an exact inventory of what we found about the body   [220
of the Man-Mountain; who used us with great civility, and due respect
to your Majesty's commission. Signed and sealed on the fourth day
of the eighty-ninth moon of your Majesty's auspicious reign.

                        Clefren Frelock, Marsi Frelock.

When this inventory was read over to the Emperor, he di-   [225
rected me to deliver up the several particulars. He first called for my
scimitar, which I took out, scabbard and all. In the mean time he
ordered three thousand of his choicest troops, who then attended him,
to surround me at a distance, with their bows and arrows just ready
to discharge: but I did not observe it, for mine eyes were   [230
wholly fixed upon his Majesty. He then desired me to draw my scimitar, which, although it had got some rust by the sea-water, was in
most parts exceeding bright. I did so, and immediately all the troops
gave a shout between terror and surprise; for the sun shone clear,
and the reflection dazzled their eyes, as I waved the scimitar   [235
to and fro in my hand. His Majesty, who is a most magnanimous
prince, was less daunted than I could expect; he ordered me to return
it into the scabbard, and cast it on the ground as gently as I could,
about six foot from the end of my chain. The next thing he demanded
was one of the hollow iron pillars, by which he meant my   [240
pocket-pistols. I drew it out, and at his desire, as well as I could, expressed to him the use of it; and charging it only with powder, which
by the closeness of my pouch happened to escape wetting in the sea
(an inconvenience that all prudent mariners take special care to provide against) I first cautioned the Emperor not to be afraid;   [245

and then I let it off in the air. The astonishment here was much greater than at the sight of my scimitar. Hundreds fell down as if they had been struck dead; and even the Emperor, although he stood his ground, could not recover himself in some time. I delivered up both my pistols in the same manner as I had done my scimitar, [250 and then my pouch of powder and bullets; begging him that the former might be kept from fire, for it would kindle with the smallest spark, and blow up his imperial palace into the air. I likewise delivered up my watch, which the Emperor was very curious to see, and commanded two of his tallest yeomen of the guards to bear [255 it on a pole upon their shoulders, as draymen in England do a barrel of ale. He was amazed at the continual noise it made, and the motion of the minute-hand, which he could easily discern; for their sight is much more acute than ours. He asked the opinions of his learned men about him, which were various and remote, as the [260 reader may well imagine without my repeating; although indeed I could not very perfectly understand them. I then gave up my silver and copper money, my purse with nine large pieces of gold, and some smaller ones; my knife and razor, my comb and silver snuff-box, my handkerchief and journal-book. My scimitar, pistols, and [265 pouch, were conveyed in carriages to his Majesty's stores; but the rest of my goods were returned me. . . .

❧

CHAPTER THREE. *The Author diverts the Emperor and his nobility of both sexes, in a very uncommon manner. The diversions of the court of Lilliput described. The Author hath his liberty granted him upon certain conditions.*

*M*Y GENTLENESS and good behaviour had gained so far on the Emperor and his court, and indeed upon the army and people in general, that I began to conceive hopes of getting my liberty in a short time. I took all possible methods to cultivate this favourable disposition. The natives came by degrees to be less apprehensive [5 of any danger from me. I would sometimes lie down, and let five or six of them dance on my hand. And at last the boys and girls would venture to come and play at hide and seek in my hair. I had now made a good progress in understanding and speaking their language. The Emperor had a mind one day to entertain me with several [10 of the country shows, wherein they exceed all nations I have known, both for dexterity and magnificence. I was diverted with none so

much as that of the rope-dancers, performed upon a slender white
thread, extended about two foot, and twelve inches from the ground.
Upon which I shall desire liberty, with the reader's patience,   [15
to enlarge a little.

This diversion is only practised by those persons who are candidates
for great employments and high favour at court. They were trained
in this art from their youth, and are not always of the noble birth, or
liberal education. When a great office is vacant either by death   [20
or disgrace (which often happens), five or six of those candidates petition the Emperor to entertain his Majesty and the court with a dance
on the rope; and whoever jumps the highest without falling, succeeds
in the office. Very often the chief ministers themselves are commanded
to show their skill, and to convince the Emperor that they   [25
have not lost their faculty. Flimnap, the Treasurer, is allowed to cut
a caper on the straight rope, at least an inch higher than any other lord
in the whole empire. I have seen him do the summerset several times
together upon a trencher fixed on the rope, which is no thicker than
a common packthread in England. My friend Reldresal, prin-   [30
cipal Secretary for Private Affairs, is, in my opinion, if I am not partial, the second after the Treasurer; the rest of the great officers are
much upon a par.

These diversions are often attended with fatal accidents, whereof
great numbers are on record. I myself have seen two or three   [35
candidates break a limb. But the danger is much greater when the
ministers themselves are commanded to show their dexterity: for by
contending to excel themselves and their fellows, they strain so far,
that there is hardly one of them who hath not received a fall, and
some of them two or three. I was assured that a year or two   [40
before my arrival, Flimnap would have infallibly broke his neck, if one
of the King's cushions, that accidentally lay on the ground, had not
weakened the force of his fall.

There is likewise another diversion, which is only shown before the
Emperor and Empress, and first minister, upon particular oc-   [45
casions. The Emperor lays on a table three fine silken threads of six
inches long. One is blue, the other red, and the third green. These
threads are proposed as prizes for those persons whom the Emperor
hath a mind to distinguish by a peculiar mark of his favour. The
ceremony is performed in his Majesty's great chamber of state,   [50
where the candidates are to undergo a trial of dexterity very different

---

17. The following paragraphs are Swift's comment on the antics of
politicians. Specifically, Flimnap is probably Walpole; the "King's cushion,"
a royal mistress who helped restore Walpole to power; and the blue, red,
and green threads, the orders of the Garter, Bath, and Thistle.

from the former, and such as I have not observed the least resemblance of in any other country of the old or the new world. The Emperor holds a stick in his hands, both ends parallel to the horizon, while the candidates, advancing one by one, sometimes leap over the   [55 stick, sometimes creep under it backwards and forwards several times, according as the stick is advanced or depressed. Sometimes the Emperor holds one end of the stick, and his first minister the other; sometimes the minister has it entirely to himself. Whoever performs his part with most agility, and holds out the longest in *leaping*   [60 and *creeping,* is rewarded with the blue-coloured silk; the red is given to the next, and the green to the third, which they all wear girt twice round about the middle; and you see few great persons about this court who are not adorned with one of these girdles.

The horses of the army, and those of the royal stables, hav-   [65 ing been daily led before me, were no longer shy, but would come up to my very feet without starting. The riders would leap them over my hand as I held it on the ground, and one of the Emperor's huntsmen, upon a large courser, took my foot, shoe and all; which was indeed a prodigious leap. I had the good fortune to divert the   [70 Emperor one day, after a very extraordinary manner. I desired he would order several sticks of two foot high, and the thickness of an ordinary cane, to be brought me; whereupon his Majesty commanded the master of his woods to give directions accordingly; and the next morning six woodmen arrived with as many carriages, drawn   [75 by eight horses to each. I took nine of these sticks, and fixing them firmly in the ground in a quadrangular figure, two foot and a half square, I took four other sticks, and tied them parallel at each corner, about two foot from the ground; then I fastened my handkerchief to the nine sticks that stood erect, and extended it on all sides till   [80 it was as tight as the top of a drum; and the four parallel sticks rising about five inches higher than the handkerchief served as ledges on each side. When I had finished my work, I desired the Emperor to let a troop of his best horse, twenty-four in number, come and exercise upon this plain. His Majesty approved of the proposal, and I   [85 took them up one by one in my hands, ready mounted and armed, with the proper officers to exercise them. As soon as they got into order, they divided into two parties, performed mock skirmishes, discharged blunt arrows, drew their swords, fled and pursued, attacked and retired; and in short discovered the best military discipline   [90 I ever beheld. The parallel sticks secured them and their horses from falling over the stage; and the Emperor was so much delighted, that he ordered this entertainment to be repeated several days; and once was pleased to be lifted up and give the word of command; and, with great difficulty, persuaded even the Empress herself to let me   [95

hold her in her close chair, within two yards of the stage, from whence
she was able to take a full view of the whole performance. It was my
good fortune that no ill accident happened in these entertainments;
only once a fiery horse that belonged to one of the captains, pawing
with his foot struck a hole in my handkerchief, and his foot   [100
slipping, he overthrew his rider and himself; but I immediately relieved them both; for covering the hole with one hand, I set down the
troop with the other, in the same manner as I took them up. The
horse that fell was strained in the left shoulder, but the rider got no
hurt, and I repaired my handkerchief as well as I could: how-   [105
ever, I would not trust to the strength of it any more in such dangerous enterprises.

About two or three days before I was set at liberty, as I was entertaining the court with these kinds of feats, there arrived an express
to inform his Majesty that some of the subjects riding near   [110
the place where I was first taken up, had seen a great black substance lying on the ground, very oddly shaped, extending its edges
round as wide as his Majesty's bedchamber, and rising up in the middle as high as a man: that it was no living creature, as they at first
apprehended, for it lay on the grass without motion, and   [115
some of them had walked round it several times: that by mounting
upon each other's shoulders, they had got to the top, which was flat
and even; and stamping upon it they found it was hollow within: that
they humbly conceived it might be something belonging to the Man-
Mountain, and if his Majesty pleased, they would undertake   [120
to bring it with only five horses. I presently knew what they meant,
and was glad at heart to receive this intelligence. It seems, upon my
first reaching the shore after our shipwreck, I was in such confusion,
that before I came to the place where I went to sleep, my hat, which I
had fastened with a string to my head while I was rowing,   [125
and had stuck on all the time I was swimming, fell off after I came to
land; the string, as I conjecture, breaking by some accident which I
never observed, but thought my hat had been lost at sea. I entreated
his Imperial Majesty to give orders it might be brought to me as soon
as possible, describing to him the use and the nature of it: and   [130
the next day the waggoners arrived with it, but not in a very good condition; they had bored two holes in the brim, within an inch and
a half of the edge, and fastened two hooks in the holes; these hooks
were tied by a long cord to the harness, and thus my hat was dragged
along for above half an English mile: but the ground in that   [135
country being extremely smooth and level, it received less damage than
I expected. . . .

CHAPTER FOUR. *Mildendo, the metropolis of Lilliput, described, together with the Emperor's palace. A conversation between the Author and a principal Secretary, concerning the affairs of that empire: the Author's offers to serve the Emperor in his wars.*

. . . One morning, about a fortnight after I had obtained my liberty, Reldresal, principal Secretary (as they style him) of Private Affairs, came to my house attended only by one servant. He ordered his coach to wait at a distance, and desired I would give him an hour's audience; which I readily consented to, on account of his qual- [5 ity and personal merits, as well as the many good offices he had done me during my solicitations at court. I offered to lie down, that he might the more conveniently reach my ear; but he chose rather to let me hold him in my hand during our conversation. He began with compliments on my liberty; said he might pretend to some [10 merit in it; but, however, added, that if it had not been for the present situation of things at court, perhaps I might not have obtained it so soon. "For," said he, "as flourishing a condition as we may appear to be in to foreigners, we labour under two mighty evils; a violent faction at home, and the danger of an invasion by a most [15 potent enemy from abroad. As to the first, you are to understand, that for above seventy moons past, there have been two struggling parties in this empire, under the names of *Tramecksan* and *Slamecksan,* from the high and low heels on their shoes, by which they distinguish themselves.
20
"It is alleged indeed, that the high heels are most agreeable to our ancient constitution: but however this be, his Majesty hath determined to make use of only low heels in the administration of the government, and all offices in the gift of the Crown; as you cannot but observe; and particularly, that his Majesty's Imperial heels are lower at least [25 by a *drurr* than any of his court; (*drurr* is a measure about the fourteenth part of an inch). The animosities between these two parties run so high, that they will neither eat nor drink, nor talk with each other. We compute the *Tramecksan,* or High-Heels, to exceed us in number; but the power is wholly on our side. We apprehend [30

22-33. The *High-Heels* are the Tory and high-church party; the *Low-Heels* are the Whig and low-church party. George I favored the latter; his son (while Prince of Wales) favored both.

his Imperial Highness, the Heir to the Crown, to have some tendency towards the High-Heels; at least we can plainly discover one of his heels higher than the other, which gives him a hobble in his gait. Now, in the midst of these intestine disquiets, we are threatened with an invasion from the Island of Blefuscu, which is the other   [35 great empire of the universe, almost as large and powerful as this of his Majesty. For as to what we have heard you affirm, that there are other kingdoms and states in the world, inhabited by human creatures as large as yourself, our philosophers are in much doubt; and would rather conjecture that you dropped from the moon, or one of   [40 the stars; because it is certain, that an hundred mortals of your bulk would, in a short time, destroy all the fruits and cattle of his Majesty's dominions. Besides, our histories of six thousand moons make no mention of any other regions, than the two great empires of Lilliput and Blefuscu. Which two mighty powers have, as I was going   [45 to tell you, been engaged in a most obstinate war for six and thirty moons past. It began upon the following occasion. It is allowed on all hands, that the primitive way of breaking eggs before we eat them, was upon the larger end: but his present Majesty's grandfather, while he was a boy, going to eat an egg, and breaking it according to   [50 the ancient practice, happened to cut one of his fingers. Whereupon the Emperor his father published an edict, commanding all his subjects, upon great penalties, to break the smaller end of their eggs. The people so highly resented this law, that our histories tell us there have been six rebellions raised on that account; wherein one   [55 Emperor lost his life, and another his crown. These civil commotions were constantly fomented by the monarchs of Blefuscu; and when they were quelled, the exiles always fled for refuge to that empire. It is computed, that eleven thousand persons have, at several times, suffered death, rather than submit to break their eggs at the   [60 smaller end. Many hundred large volumes have been published upon this controversy: but the books of the Big-Endians have been long forbidden, and the whole party rendered incapable by law of holding employments. During the course of these troubles, the Emperors of Blefuscu did frequently expostulate by their ambassadors, ac-   [65 cusing us of making a schism in religion, by offending against a fundamental doctrine of our great prophet Lustrog, in the fifty-fourth chapter of the *Brundecral* (which is their Alcoran). This, however,

---

35. *Blefuscu:* France. 47. Swift refers in the passage that follows to the hostility of the English Roman Catholics (Big-Endians) and Protestants (Little-Endians), and to the recent wars between Catholic France and Protestant England.

is thought to be a mere strain upon the text: for the words are these; *That all true believers shall break their eggs at the convenient* [70 *end:* and which is the convenient end, seems, in my humble opinion, to be left to every man's conscience, or at least in the power of the chief magistrate to determine. Now the Big-Endian exiles have found so much credit in the Emperor of Blefuscu's court, and so much private assistance and encouragement from their party here at [75 home, that a bloody war hath been carried on between the two empires for six and thirty moons with various success; during which time we have lost forty capital ships, and a much greater number of smaller vessels, together with thirty thousand of our best seamen and soldiers; and the damage received by the enemy is reckoned to be some- [80 what greater than ours. However, they have now equipped a numer- ous fleet, and are just preparing to make a descent upon us; and his Imperial Majesty, placing great confidence in your valour and strength, hath commanded me to lay this account of his affairs before you." 85

I desired the Secretary to present my humble duty to the Emperor, and to let him know, that I thought it would not become me, who was a foreigner, to interfere with parties; but I was ready, with the hazard of my life, to defend his person and state against all invaders.

❧

CHAPTER FIVE. *The Author, by an extraordinary stratagem, prevents an invasion. A high title of honour is conferred upon him. Ambassadors arrive from the Emperor of Blefuscu, and sue for peace. The Empress's apartment on fire by an accident; the Author instrumental in saving the rest of the palace.*

THE Empire of Blefuscu is an island situated to the north-north-east side of Lilliput, from whence it is parted only by a channel of eight hundred yards wide. I had not yet seen it, and upon this notice of an intended invasion, I avoided appearing on that side of the coast, for fear of being discovered by some of the enemy's ships, who had [5 received no intelligence of me, all intercourse between the two empires having been strictly forbidden during the war, upon pain of death, and an embargo laid by our Emperor upon all vessels whatsoever. I communicated to his Majesty a project I had formed of seizing the enemy's whole fleet: which, as our scouts assured us, lay at [10 anchor in the harbour ready to sail with the first fair wind. I con- sulted the most experienced seamen, upon the depth of the channel, which they had often plumbed; who told me, that in the middle at high-water it was seventy *glumgluffs* deep, which is about six foot of European measure; and the rest of it fifty *glumgluffs* at [15 most. I walked to the north-east coast over against Blefuscu; where, lying down behind a hillock, I took out my small pocket perspective-glass, and viewed the enemy's fleet at anchor, consisting of about fifty men of war, and a great number of transports: I then came back to my house, and gave order (for which I had a warrant) for a [20 great quantity of the strongest cable and bars of iron. The cable was about as thick as packthread, and the bars of the length and size of a knitting-needle. I trebled the cable to make it stronger, and for the same reason I twisted three of the iron bars together, binding the extremities into a hook. Having thus fixed fifty hooks to as [25 many cables, I went back to the north-east coast, and putting off my coat, shoes, and stockings, walked into the sea in my leathern jerkin, about half an hour before high water. I waded with what haste I could, and swam in the middle about thirty yards till I felt ground; I arrived at the fleet in less than half an hour. The enemy [30 was so frighted when they saw me, that they leaped out of their ships, and swam to shore, where there could not be fewer than thirty thousand souls. I then took my tackling, and fastening a hook to the hole at the prow of each, I tied all the cords together at the end. While I was thus employed, the enemy discharged several thousand [35 arrows, many of which stuck in my hands and face; and besides the excessive smart, gave me much disturbance in my work. My greatest apprehension was for mine eyes, which I should have infallibly lost, if I had not suddenly thought of an expedient. I kept among other little necessaries a pair of spectacles in a private pocket, which, [40 as I observed before, had escaped the Emperor's searchers. These I took out and fastened as strongly as I could upon my nose, and thus armed went on boldly with my work in spite of the enemy's arrows, many of which stuck against the glasses of my spectacles, but without any other effect, further than a little to discompose them. I had [45 now fastened all the hooks, and taking the knot in my hand, began to pull; but not a ship would stir, for they were all too fast held by their anchors, so that the boldest part of my enterprise remained. I therefore let go the cord, and leaving the hooks fixed to the ships, I resolutely cut with my knife the cables that fastened the an- [50 chors, receiving about two hundred shots in my face and hands; then I took up the knotted end of the cables to which my hooks were tied, and with great ease drew fifty of the enemy's largest men-of-war after me.　　　　　　　　　　　　　　　　　　　　　　　54

The Blefuscudians, who had not the least imagination of what I intended, were at first confounded with astonishment. They had seen me cut the cables, and thought my design was only to let the ships run adrift, or fall foul on each other: but when they perceived the whole fleet moving in order, and saw me pulling at the end, they set up such a scream of grief and despair, that it is almost im-   [60 possible to describe or conceive. When I had got out of danger, I stopt awhile to pick out the arrows that stuck in my hands and face, and rubbed on some of the same ointment that was given me at my first arrival, as I have formerly mentioned. I then took off my spectacles, and waiting about an hour, till the tide was a little   [65 fallen, I waded through the middle with my cargo, and arrived safe at the royal port of Lilliput.

The Emperor and his whole court stood on the shore expecting the issue of this great adventure. They saw the ships move forward in a large half-moon, but could not discern me, who was up to my   [70 breast in water. When I advanced to the middle of the channel, they were yet in more pain, because I was under water to my neck. The Emperor concluded me to be drowned, and that the enemy's fleet was approaching in a hostile manner: but he was soon eased of his fears; for the channel growing shallower every step I made, I came   [75 in a short time within hearing, and holding up the end of the cable by which the fleet was fastened, I cried in a loud voice, *"Long live the most puissant Emperor of Lilliput!"* This great prince received me at my landing with all possible encomiums, and created me a *Nardac* upon the spot, which is the highest title of honour among them.   [80

His Majesty desired I would take some other opportunity of bringing all the rest of his enemy's ships into his ports. And so unmeasurable is the ambition of princes, that he seemed to think of nothing less than reducing the whole empire of Blefuscu into a province, and governing it by a Viceroy; of destroying the Big-Endian exiles,   [85 and compelling that people to break the smaller end of their eggs, by which he would remain the sole monarch of the whole world. But I endeavoured to divert him from this design, by many arguments drawn from the topics of policy as well as justice; and I plainly protested, that I would never be an instrument of bringing a   [90 free and brave people into slavery. And when the matter was debated in council, the wisest part of the ministry were of my opinion.

This open bold declaration of mine was so opposite to the schemes and politics of his Imperial Majesty, that he could never forgive me: he mentioned it in a very artful manner at council, where, I   [95 was told, that some of the wisest appeared, at least by their silence, to be of my opinion; but others, who were my secret enemies, could not forbear some expressions, which by a side-wind reflected on me.

And from this time began an intrigue between his Majesty and a junto of ministers maliciously bent against me, which broke out in less than two months. . . .   101

⧼

II. A VOYAGE TO BROBDINGNAG

CHAPTER ONE. *A great storm described. The long-boat sent to fetch water; the Author goes with it to discover the country. He is left on shore, is seized by one of the natives, and carried to a farmer's house. His reception there, with several accidents that happened there. A description of the inhabitants.*

. . . I saw our men already got into the boat, and rowing for life to the ship. I was going to hollo after them, although it had been to little purpose, when I observed a huge creature walking after them in the sea, as fast as he could: he waded not much deeper than his knees, and took prodigious strides: but our men had the   [5 start of him half a league, and the sea thereabouts being full of sharp-pointed rocks, the monster was not able to overtake the boat. This I was afterwards told, for I durst not stay to see the issue of that adventure; but ran as fast as I could the way I first went, and then climbed up a steep hill, which gave me some prospect of the country.   [10 I found it fully cultivated; but that which first surprised me was the length of the grass, which in those grounds that seemed to be kept for hay, was about twenty foot high.

I fell into a high road, for so I took it to be, although it served to the inhabitants only as a footpath through a field of barley.   [15 Here I walked on for some time, but could see little on either side, it being now near harvest, and the corn rising at least forty foot. I was an hour walking to the end of this field; which was fenced in with a hedge of at least one hundred and twenty foot high, and the trees so lofty that I could make no computation of their altitude. There   [20 was a stile to pass from this field into the next: it had four steps, and a stone to cross over when you came to the utmost. It was impossible

---

101. [As a result of this intrigue, Gulliver is indicted for high treason, flees to Blefuscu, supplies himself with a boat, and thence sails home.]

1 ff. [On his second voyage Gulliver goes ashore on a strange coast and is abandoned there by his companions through fright at what they have seen.]

for me to climb this stile, because every step was six foot high, and the upper stone above twenty. I was endeavouring to find some gap in the hedge, when I discovered one of the inhabitants in the   [25 next field advancing towards the stile, of the same size with him whom I saw in the sea pursuing our boat. He appeared as tall as an ordinary spire-steeple, and took about ten yards at every stride, as near as I could guess. I was struck with the utmost fear and astonishment, and ran to hide myself in the corn, from whence I saw him at   [30 the top of the stile, looking back into the next field on the right hand; and heard him call in a voice many degrees louder than a speaking-trumpet; but the noise was so high in the air, that at first I certainly thought it was thunder. Whereupon seven monsters like himself came towards him with reaping-hooks in their hands, each   [35 hook about the largeness of six scythes. These people were not so well clad as the first, whose servants or labourers they seemed to be. For, upon some words he spoke, they went to reap the corn in the field where I lay. I kept from them at as great a distance as I could, but was forced to move with extreme difficulty, for the stalks of   [40 the corn were sometimes not above a foot distant, so that I could hardly squeeze my body betwixt them. However, I made a shift to go forward till I came to a part of the field where the corn had been laid by the rain and wind: here it was impossible for me to advance a step; for the stalks were so interwoven that I could not creep   [45 through, and the beards of the fallen ears so strong and pointed that they pierced through my clothes into my flesh. At the same time I heard the reapers not above an hundred yards behind me. Being quite dispirited with toil, and wholly overcome with grief and despair, I lay down between two ridges, and heartily wished I might   [50 there end my days. I bemoaned my desolate widow, and fatherless children: I lamented my own folly and wilfulness in attempting a second voyage against the advice of all my friends and relations. In this terrible agitation of mind I could not forbear thinking of Lilliput, whose inhabitants looked upon me as the greatest prodigy that   [55 ever appeared in the world; where I was able to draw an Imperial Fleet in my hand, and perform those other actions which will be recorded for ever in the chronicles of that empire, while posterity shall hardly believe them, although attested by millions. I reflected what a mortification it must prove to me to appear as inconsiderable   [60 in this nation as one single Lilliputian would be among us. But this I conceived was to be the least of my misfortunes: for as human creatures are observed to be more savage and cruel in proportion to their bulk, what could I expect but to be a morsel in the mouth of

the first among these enormous barbarians who should happen   [65
to seize me? Undoubtedly philosophers are in the right when they
tell us, that nothing is great or little otherwise than by comparison.
It might have pleased fortune to let the Lilliputians find some nation,
where the people were as diminutive with respect to them, as they
were to me. And who knows but that even this prodigious   [70
race of mortals might be equally overmatched in some distant part
of the world, whereof we have yet no discovery?

Scared and confounded as I was, I could not forbear going on with
these reflections; when one of the reapers approaching within ten
yards of the ridge where I lay, made me apprehend that with   [75
the next step I should be squashed to death under his foot, or cut in
two with his reaping-hook. And therefore when he was again about
to move, I screamed as loud as fear could make me. Whereupon the
huge creature trod short, and looking round about under him for
some time, at last espied me as I lay on the ground. He   [80
considered a while with the caution of one who endeavours to lay
hold on a small dangerous animal in such a manner that it shall not be
able either to scratch or bite him, as I myself have sometimes done
with a weasel in England. At length he ventured to take me up behind by the middle between his forefinger and thumb, and   [85
brought me within three yards of his eyes, that he might behold my
shape more perfectly. I guessed his meaning, and my good fortune
gave me so much presence of mind, that I resolved not to struggle
in the least as he held me in the air about sixty foot from the ground,
although he grievously pinched my sides, for fear I should slip   [90
through his fingers. All I ventured was to raise mine eyes towards
the sun, and place my hands together in a supplicating posture, and
to speak some words in an humble melancholy tone, suitable to the
condition I then was in. For I apprehended every moment that he
would dash me against the ground, as we usually do any little   [95
hateful animal which we have in mind to destroy. But my good star
would have it, that he appeared pleased with my voice and gestures,
and began to look upon me as a curiosity; much wondering to hear
me pronounce articulate words, although he could not understand
them. In the mean time I was not able to forbear groaning   [100
and shedding tears, and turning my head towards my sides; letting
him know, as well as I could, how cruelly I was hurt by the pressure
of his thumb and finger. He seemed to apprehend my meaning; for,
lifting up the lappet of his coat, he put me gently into it, and immediately ran along with me to his master, who was a substantial   [105
farmer, and the same person I had first seen in the field.

The farmer having (as I supposed by their talk) received such an account of me as his servant could give him, took a piece of a small straw, about the size of a walking staff, and therewith lifted up the lappets of my coat; which it seems he thought to be some kind   [110 of covering that nature had given me. He blew my hairs aside to take a better view of my face. He called his hinds about him, and asked them (as I afterwards learned) whether they had ever seen in the fields any little creature that resembled me. He then placed me softly on the ground upon all four; but I got immediately   [115 up and walked slowly backwards and forwards, to let those people see I had no intent to run away. They all sat down in a circle about me, the better to observe my motions. I pulled off my hat, and made a low bow towards the farmer: I fell on my knees, and lifted up my hands and eyes, and spoke several words as loud as I could: I   [120 took a purse of gold out of my pocket, and humbly presented it to him. He received it on the palm of his hand, then applied it close to his eye, to see what it was, and afterwards turned it several times with the point of a pin (which he took out of his sleeve), but could make nothing of it. Whereupon I made a sign that he should place   [125 his hand on the ground: I then took the purse, and opening it, poured all the gold into his palm. There were six Spanish pieces of four pistoles each, beside twenty or thirty smaller coins. I saw him wet the tip of his little finger upon his tongue, and take up one of my largest pieces, and then another; but he seemed to be wholly   [130 ignorant what they were. He made me a sign to put them again into my purse, and the purse again into my pocket; which after offering to him several times, I thought it best to do.

The farmer by this time was convinced I must be a rational creature. He spoke often to me, but the sound of his voice pierced my   [135 ears like that of a water-mill; yet his words were articulate enough. I answered as loud as I could in several languages, and he often laid his ear within two yards of me, but all in vain, for we were wholly unintelligible to each other. He then sent his servants to their work, and taking his handkerchief out of his pocket, he doubled   [140 and spread it on his hand, which he placed flat on the ground with the palm upwards, making me a sign to step into it, as I could easily do, for it was not above a foot in thickness. I thought it my part to obey; and for fear of falling, laid myself at full length upon the hand-kerchief, with the remainder of which he lapped me up to   [145 the head for further security; and in this manner carried me home to his house. There he called his wife, and showed me to her; but she screamed and ran back as women in England do at the sight of a toad or a spider. However, when she had a while seen my be-haviour, and how well I observed the signs her husband   [150 made, she was soon reconciled, and by degrees grew extremely tender of me.

It was about twelve at noon, and a servant brought in dinner. It was only one substantial dish of meat (fit for the plain condition of an husbandman) in a dish of about four-and-twenty foot   [155 diameter. The company were the farmer and his wife, three children, and an old grandmother. When they were sat down, the farmer placed me at some distance from him on the table, which was thirty foot high from the floor. I was in a terrible fright, and kept as far as I could from the edge, for fear of falling. The wife minced a   [160 bit of meat, then crumbled some bread on a trencher, and placed it before me. I made her a low bow, took out my knife and fork, and fell to eat; which gave them exceeding delight. The mistress sent her maid for a small dram cup, which held about two gallons, and filled it with drink; I took up the vessel with much difficulty   [165 in both hands, and in a most respectful manner drank to her lady-ship's health, expressing the words as loud as I could in English; which made the company laugh so heartily, that I was almost deaf-ened with the noise. This liquor tasted like a small cyder, and was not unpleasant. Then the master made me a sign to come   [170 to his trencher side; but as I walked on the table, being in great sur-prise all the time, as the indulgent reader will easily conceive and excuse, I happened to stumble against a crust, and fell flat on my face, but received no hurt. I got up immediately, and observing the good people to be in much concern, I took my hat (which I held   [175 under my arm out of good manners) and waving it over my head, made three huzzas, to show I had got no mischief by my fall. But advancing forwards toward my master (as I shall henceforth call him) his youngest son who sat next him, an arch boy of about ten years old, took me up by the legs, and held me so high in   [180 the air, that I trembled every limb; but his father snatched me from him, and at the same time gave him such a box on the left ear, as would have felled an European troop of horse to the earth, ordering him to be taken from the table. But being afraid the boy might owe me a spite, and well remembering how mischievous all chil-   [185 dren among us naturally are to sparrows, rabbits, young kittens, and puppy dogs, I fell on my knees, and pointing to the boy, made my master to understand, as well as I could, that I desired his son might be pardoned. The father complied, and the lad took his seat again; whereupon I went to him and kissed his hand, which my   [190 master took, and made him stroke me gently with it.

In the midst of dinner, my mistress's favourite cat leapt into her lap. I heard a noise behind me like that of a dozen stocking-weavers at work; and turning my head, I found it proceeded from the purring of this animal, who seemed to be three times larger [195 than an ox, as I computed by the view of her head, and one of her paws, while her mistress was feeding and stroking her. The fierceness of this creature's countenance altogether discomposed me; although I stood at the farther end of the table, above fifty foot off; and although my mistress held her fast for fear she might [200 give a spring, and seize me in her talons. But it happened there was no danger; for the cat took not the least notice of me when my master placed me within three yards of her. And as I have been always told and found true by experience in my travels, that flying, or discovering fear before a fierce animal, is a certain way to make it pursue [205 or attack you; so I resolved in this dangerous juncture to show no manner of concern. I walked with intrepidity five or six times before the very head of the cat, and came within half a yard of her; whereupon she drew herself back, as if she were more afraid of me: I had less apprehension concerning the dogs, whereof three or four [210 came into the room, as it is usual in farmers' houses; one of which was a mastiff, equal in bulk to four elephants, and a greyhound, somewhat taller than the mastiff, but not so large.

When dinner was almost done, the nurse came in with a child of a year old in her arms, who immediately spied me, and began [215 a squall that you might have heard from London Bridge to Chelsea, after the usual oratory of infants, to get me for a plaything. The mother out of pure indulgence took me up, and put me towards the child, who presently seized me by the middle, and got my head in his mouth, where I roared so loud that the urchin was frighted, [220 and let me drop; and I should infallibly have broke my neck if the mother had not held her apron under me. The nurse to quiet her babe made use of a rattle, which was a kind of hollow vessel filled with great stones, and fastened by a cable to the child's waist: but all in vain, so that she was forced to apply the last remedy by [225 giving it suck. I must confess no object ever disgusted me so much as the sight of her monstrous breast, which I cannot tell what to compare with, so as to give the curious reader an idea of its bulk, shape and colour. It stood prominent six foot, and could not be less than sixteen in circumference. The nipple was about half [230 the bigness of my head, and the hue both of that and the dug so varified with spots, pimples and freckles, that nothing could appear more nauseous: for I had a near sight of her, she sitting down the more conveniently to give suck, and I standing on the table. This made me reflect upon the fair skins of our English ladies, [235 who appear so beautiful to us, only because they are of our own size, and their defects not to be seen but through a magnifying glass, where we find by experiment that the smoothest and whitest skins look rough and coarse, and ill coloured.

I remember when I was at Lilliput, the complexion of   [240 those diminutive people appeared to me the fairest in the world; and talking upon this subject with a person of learning there, who was an intimate friend of mine, he said that my face appeared much fairer and smoother when he looked on me from the ground, than it did upon a nearer view when he took him up in my hand and   [245 brought him close, which he confessed was at first a very shocking sight. He said he could discover great holes in my skin; that the stumps of my beard were ten times stronger than the bristles of a boar, and my complexion made up of several colours altogether disagreeable: although I must beg leave to say for myself, that   [250 I am as fair as most of my sex and country, and very little sunburnt by all my travels. On the other side, discoursing of the ladies in that Emperor's court, he used to tell me, one had freckles, another too wide a mouth, a third too large a nose; nothing of which I was able to distinguish. I confess this reflection was obvious enough;   [255 which however I could not forbear, lest the reader might think those vast creatures were actually deformed: for I must do them justice to say they are a comely race of people; and particularly the features of my master's countenance, although he were but a farmer, when I beheld him from the height of sixty foot, appeared very   [260 well proportioned.

When dinner was done, my master went out to his labourers; and as I could discover by his voice and gesture, gave his wife a strict charge to take care of me. I was very much tired and disposed to sleep, which my mistress perceiving, she put me on her own   [265 bed, and covered me with a clean white handkerchief, but larger and coarser than the mainsail of a man of war.

I slept about two hours, and dreamed I was at home with my wife and children, which aggravated my sorrows when I awaked and found myself alone in a vast room, between two and three   [270 hundred foot wide, and above two hundred high, lying in a bed twenty yards wide. My mistress was gone about her household affairs, and had locked me in. The bed was eight yards from the floor. Some natural necessities required me to get down; I durst not presume to call, and if I had, it would have been in vain   [275 with such a voice as mine at so great a distance from the room where I lay to the kitchen where the family kept. While I was under these circumstances, two rats crept up the curtains, and ran smelling back-

wards and forwards on the bed. One of them came up almost to my
face; whereupon I rose in a fright, and drew out my hanger   [280
to defend myself. These horrible animals had the boldness to attack
me on both sides, and one of them held his fore-feet at my collar;
but I had the good fortune to rip up his belly before he could do me
mischief. He fell down at my feet; and the other seeing the fate of
his comrade made his escape, but not without one good   [285
wound on the back, which I gave him as he fled, and made the blood
run trickling from him. After this exploit I walked gently to and
fro on the bed, to recover my breath and loss of spirits. These creatures were of the size of a large mastiff, but infinitely more nimble
and fierce; so that if I had taken off my belt before I went   [290
to sleep, I must have infallibly been torn to pieces and devoured. I
measured the tail of the dead rat, and found it to be two yards long,
wanting an inch; but it went against my stomach to drag the carcass
off the bed, where it lay still bleeding; I observed it had yet some
life, but with a strong slash cross the neck, I thoroughly dis-   [295
patched it. . . .

∾

CHAPTER TWO. *A description of the farmer's daughter. The Author
carried to a market-town, and then to the metropolis. The particulars of
his journey.*

My mistress had a daughter of nine years old, a child of
towardly parts for her age, very dexterous at her needle, and skilful
in dressing her baby. Her mother and she contrived to fit up the
baby's cradle for me against the night: the cradle was put into a small
drawer of a cabinet, and the drawer placed upon a hanging   [5
shelf for fear of the rats. This was my bed all the time I stayed with
those people, although made more convenient by degrees, as I began
to learn their language, and make my wants known. This young girl
was so handy, that after I had once or twice pulled off my clothes
before her, she was able to dress and undress me, although I   [10
never gave her that trouble when she would let me do either myself.
She made me seven shirts, and some other linen of as fine cloth as
could be got, which indeed was coarser than sackcloth; and these
she constantly washed for me with her own hands. She was likewise
my school-mistress to teach me the language: when I pointed   [15

to any thing, she told me the name of it in her own tongue, so that
in a few days I was able to call for whatever I had a mind to. She
was very good-natured, and not above forty foot high, being little for
her age. She gave me the name of *Grildrig*, which the family took
up, and afterwards the whole kingdom. The word imports   [20
what the Latins call *nanunculus*, the Italian *homunceletino*, and the
English *mannikin*. To her I chiefly owe my preservation in that
country: we never parted while I was there; I called her my *Glumdalclitch*, or little nurse: and I should be guilty of great ingratitude if
I omitted this honourable mention of her care and affection   [25
towards me, which I heartily wish it lay in my power to requite as
she deserves, instead of being the innocent but unhappy instrument
of her disgrace, as I have too much reason to fear.

It now began to be known and talked of in the neighbourhood,
that my master had found a strange animal in the field, about   [30
the bigness of a *splacknuck*, but exactly shaped in every part like a
human creature; which it likewise imitated in all its actions; seemed
to speak in a little language of its own, had already learned several
words of theirs, went erect upon two legs, was tame and gentle,
would come when it was called, do whatever it was bid, had   [35
the finest limbs in the world, and a complexion fairer than a nobleman's daughter of three years old. Another farmer who lived hard
by, and was a particular friend of my master, came on a visit on purpose to enquire into the truth of this story. I was immediately produced, and placed upon a table; where I walked as I was   [40
commanded, drew my hanger, put it up again, made my reverence
to my master's guest, asked him in his own language how he did,
and told him he was welcome, just as my little nurse had instructed
me. This man, who was old and dim-sighted, put on his spectacles to
behold me better, at which I could not forbear laughing very   [45
heartily; for his eyes appeared like the full moon shining into a
chamber at two windows. Our people, who discovered the cause of
my mirth, bore me company in laughing; at which the old fellow was
fool enough to be angry and out of countenance. He had the character of a great miser, and to my misfortune he well deserved   [50
it by the cursed advice he gave my master, to show me as a sight upon
a market-day in the next town, which was half an hour's riding,
about two and twenty miles from our house. I guessed there was
some mischief contriving, when I observed my master and his friend
whispering long together, sometimes pointing at me; and my   [55
fears made me fancy that I overheard and understood some of their
words. But the next morning Glumdalclitch my little nurse told me
the whole matter, which she had cunningly picked out from her

mother. The poor girl laid me on her bosom, and fell a weeping with shame and grief. She apprehended some mischief would hap-   [60 pen to me from rude vulgar folks, who might squeeze me to death, or break one of my limbs by taking me in their hands. She had also observed how modest I was in my nature, how nicely I regarded my honour, and what an indignity I should conceive it to be exposed for money as a public spectacle to the meanest of the people.   [65 She said, her papa and mamma had promised that Grildrig should be hers; but now she found they meant to serve her as they did last year, when they pretended to give her a lamb, and yet, as soon as it was fat, sold it to a butcher. For my own part, I may truly affirm that I was less concerned than my nurse. I had a strong hope   [70 which never left me, that I should one day recover my liberty; and as to the ignominy of being carried about for a monster, I considered myself to be a perfect stranger in the country, and that such a mis-fortune could never be charged upon me as a reproach, if ever I should return to England; since the King of Great Britain himself,   [75 in my condition, must have undergone the same distress.

My master, pursuant to the advice of his friend, carried me in a box the next market-day to the neighbouring town, and took along with him his little daughter my nurse upon a pillion behind him. The box was close on every side, with a little door for me to go in   [80 and out, and a few gimlet-holes to let in air. The girl had been so careful to put the quilt of her baby's bed into it, for me to lie down on. However, I was terribly shaken and discomposed in this journey, al-though it were but of half an hour. For the horse went about forty foot at every step, and trotted so high, that the agitation was   [85 equal to the rising and falling of a ship in a great storm, but much more frequent. Our journey was somewhat further than from London to St. Albans. My master alighted at an inn which he used to fre-quent; and after consulting a while with the innkeeper, and making some necessary preparations, he hired the *Grultrud,* or crier,   [90 to give notice through the town of a strange creature to be seen at the Sign of the Green Eagle, not so big as a *splacknuck* (an animal in that country very finely shaped, about six foot long) and in every part of the body resembling an human creature; could speak several words, and perform an hundred diverting tricks.   95

I was placed upon a table in the largest room of the inn, which might be near three hundred foot square. My little nurse stood on a low stool close to the table, to take care of me, and direct what I should do. My master, to avoid a crowd, would suffer only thirty people at a time to see me. I walked about on the table as the girl   [100 commanded; she asked me questions as far as she knew my understanding of the language reached, and I answered them as loud as I could. I turned about several times to the company, paid my humble respects, said they were welcome, and used some other speeches I had been taught. I took up a thimble filled with liquor, [105 which Glumdalclitch had given me for a cup, and drank their health. I drew out my hanger, and flourished with it after the manner of fencers in England. My nurse gave me part of a straw, which I exercised as a pike, having learned the art in my youth. I was that day shown to twelve sets of company, and as often forced to [110 go over again with the same fopperies, till I was half dead with weariness and vexation. For those who had seen me made such wonderful reports, that the people were ready to break down the doors to come in. My master for his own interest would not suffer any one to touch me except my nurse; and, to prevent danger, benches were set [115 round the table at such a distance as put me out of every body's reach. However, an unlucky school-boy aimed a hazel nut directly at my head, which very narrowly missed me; otherwise, it came with such violence, that it would have infallibly knocked out my brains, for it was almost as large as a small pumpion: but I had [120 the satisfaction to see the young rogue well beaten, and turned out of the room.

My master gave public notice that he would show me again the next market-day; and in the meantime he prepared a more convenient vehicle for me, which he had reason enough to do; for I was [125 so tired with my first journey, and with entertaining company for eight hours together, that I could hardly stand upon my legs or speak a word. It was at least three days before I recovered my strength; and that I might have no rest at home, all the neighbouring gentlemen from an hundred miles round, hearing of my [130 fame, came to see me at my master's own house. There could not be fewer than thirty persons with their wives and children (for the country is very populous); and my master demanded the rate of a full room whenever he showed me at home, although it were only to a single family. So that for some time I had but little ease [135 every day of the week (except Wednesday, which is their Sabbath) although I were not carried to the town.

My master finding how profitable I was like to be, resolved to carry me to the most considerable cities of the kingdom. Having therefore provided himself with all things necessary for a long journey, [140 and settled his affairs at home, he took leave of his wife; and upon the 17th of August, 1703, about two months after my arrival, we set

---

120. *pumpion:* pumpkin.

out for the metropolis, situated near the middle of that empire, and about three thousand miles distance from our house. My master made his daughter Glumdalclitch ride behind him. She carried me   [145 on her lap in a box tied about her waist. The girl had lined it on all sides with the softest cloth she could get, well quilted underneath; furnished it with her baby's bed, provided me with linen and other necessaries, and made everything as convenient as she could. We had no other company but a boy of the house, who rode after us with the luggage.
                                                                                    151
My master's design was to show me in all the towns by the way, and to step out of the road for fifty or an hundred miles, to any village or person of quality's house where he might expect custom. We made easy journeys of not above seven or eight score miles a day: [155 for Glumdalclitch, on purpose to spare me, complained she was tired with the trotting of the horse. She often took me out of my box at my own desire to give me air and show me the country, but always held me fast by leading-strings. We passed over five or six rivers many degrees broader and deeper than the Nile or the Ganges; and   [160 there was hardly a rivulet so small as the Thames at London Bridge. We were ten weeks in our journey, and I was shown in eighteen large towns, besides many large villages and private families.

On the 26th day of October, we arrived at the metropolis, called in their language *Lorbrulgrud,* or Pride of the Universe. My   [165 master took a lodging in the principal street of the city, not far from the royal palace; and put out bills in the usual form, containing an exact description of my person and parts. He hired a large room between three and four hundred foot wide. He provided a table sixty foot in diameter, upon which I was to act my part; and   [170 palisadoed it round three foot from the edge, and as many high, to prevent my falling over. I was shown ten times a day to the wonder and satisfaction of all people. I could now speak the language tolerably well, and perfectly understood every word that was spoken to me. Besides, I had learned their alphabet, and could make a   [175 shift to explain a sentence here and there; for Glumdalclitch had been my instructor while we were at home, and at leisure hours during our journey. She carried a little book in her pocket, not much larger than a Sanson's Atlas; it was a common treatise for the use of young girls, giving a short account of their religion: out of this   [180 she taught me my letters, and interpreted the words.

CHAPTER THREE. *The Author sent for to Court. The Queen buys him of his master the farmer, and presents him to the King. He disputes with his Majesty's great scholars. An apartment at Court provided for the Author. He is in high favour with the Queen. He stands up for the honour of his own country. His quarrels with the Queen's dwarf.*

. . . The Queen became so fond of my company, that she could not dine without me. I had a table placed upon the same at which her Majesty ate, just at her left elbow, and a chair to sit on. Glumdalclitch stood upon a stool on the floor, near my table, to assist and take care of me. I had an entire set of silver dishes and   [5 plates, and other necessaries, which, in proportion to those of the Queen, were not much bigger than what I have seen of the same kind in a London toy-shop, for the furniture of a babyhouse: these my little nurse kept in her pocket in a silver box, and gave me at meals as I wanted them, always cleaning them herself. No person   [10 dined with the Queen but the two Princesses Royal, the elder sixteen years old, and the younger at that time thirteen and a month. Her Majesty used to put a bit of meat upon one of my dishes, out of which I carved for myself; and her diversion was to see me eat in miniature. For the Queen (who had indeed but a weak stomach) took up   [15 at one mouthful as much as a dozen English farmers could eat at a meal, which to me was for some time a very nauseous sight. She would craunch the wing of a lark, bones and all, between her teeth, although it were nine times as large as that of a full-grown turkey; and put a bit of bread into her mouth, as big as two twelve-penny   [20 loaves. She drank out of a golden cup, above a hogshead at a draught. Her knives were twice as long as a scythe set straight upon the handle. The spoons, forks, and other instruments were all in the same proportion. I remember when Glumdalclitch carried me out of curiosity to see some of the tables at court, where ten or a   [25 dozen of these enormous knives and forks were lifted up together, I thought I had never till then beheld so terrible a sight.

It is the custom that every Wednesday (which, as I have before observed, was their Sabbath) the King and Queen, with the royal issue of both sexes, dine together in the apartment of his   [30 Majesty, to whom I was now become a favourite; and at these times my little chair and table were placed at his left hand, before one of the saltcellars. This prince took a pleasure in conversing with me; inquiring into the manners, religion, laws, government, and learning

of Europe; wherein I gave him the best account I was able. [35
His apprehension was so clear, and his judgment so exact, that he
made very wise reflections and observations upon all I said. But, I
confess, that after I had been a little too copious in talking of my own
beloved country; of our trade, and wars by sea and land, of our
schisms in religion, and parties in the state; the prejudices of [40
his education prevailed so far, that he could not forbear taking
me up in his right hand, and stroking me gently with the other, after
an hearty fit of laughing, asked me whether I were a Whig or a Tory.
Then turning to his first minister, who waited behind him with a
white staff, near as tall as the mainmast of the *Royal Sovereign,* [45
he observed how contemptible a thing was human grandeur, which
could be mimicked by such diminutive insects as I: "and yet,"
said he, "I dare engage, these creatures have their titles and distinctions of honour; they contrive little nests and burrows, that they call
houses and cities; they make a figure in dress and equipage; [50
they love, they fight, they dispute, they cheat, they betray." And thus
he continued on, while my colour came and went several times, with
indignation to hear our noble country, the mistress of arts and arms,
the scourge of France, the arbitress of Europe, the seat of virtue, piety,
honour and truth, the pride and envy of the world, so contemptuously
treated. 56

But as I was not in a condition to resent injuries, so, upon mature
thoughts, I began to doubt whether I were injured or no. For, after
having been accustomed several months to the sight and converse of
this people, and observed every object upon which I cast my [60
eyes to be of proportionable magnitude; the horror I had first conceived
from their bulk and aspect was so far worn off, that if I then beheld
a company of English lords and ladies in their finery and birth-day
clothes, acting their several parts in the most courtly manner of strut-
ting, and bowing and prating, to say the truth, I should have [65
been strongly tempted to laugh as much at them as this King and
his grandees did at me. Neither indeed could I forbear smiling
at myself, when the Queen used to place me upon her hand towards
a looking-glass, by which both our persons appeared before me in
full view together; and there could be nothing more ridiculous [70
than the comparison; so that I really began to imagine myself dwindled many degrees below my usual size. . . .

CHAPTER FIVE. *Several adventures that happened to the Author. The execution of a criminal. The Author shows his skill in navigation.*

I SHOULD have lived happy enough in that country, if my littleness had not exposed me to several ridiculous and troublesome accidents, some of which I shall venture to relate. Glumdalclitch often carried me into the gardens of the court in my smaller box, and would sometimes take me out of it and hold me in her hand, or set me [5 down to walk. I remember, before the dwarf left the Queen, he followed us one day into those gardens; and my nurse having set me down, he and I being close together, near some dwarf apple-trees, I must needs show my wit by a silly allusion between him and the trees, which happens to hold in their language as it doth in [10 ours. Whereupon, the malicious rogue watching his opportunity, when I was walking under one of them, shook it directly over my head, by which a dozen apples, each of them near as large as a Bristol barrel, came tumbling about my ears; one of them hit me on the back as I chanced to stoop, and knocked me down flat on my face, [15 but I received no other hurt; and the dwarf was pardoned at my desire, because I had given the provocation.

Another day Glumdalclitch left me on a smooth grass-plot to divert myself while she walked at some distance with her governess. In the meantime there suddenly fell such a violent shower of hail, [20 that I was immediately by the force of it struck to the ground: and when I was down, the hailstones gave me such cruel bangs all over the body, as if I had been pelted with tennis-balls; however I made a shift to creep on all four, and shelter myself by lying on the lee-side of a border of lemon thyme; but so bruised from head to foot that [25 I could not go abroad in ten days. Neither is this at all to be wondered at, because nature in that country observing the same proportion through all her operations, a hailstone is near eighteen hundred times as large as one in Europe; which I can assert upon experience, having been so curious to weigh and measure them.   30

But a more dangerous accident happened to me in the same garden, when my little nurse believing she had put me in a secure place, which I often entreated her to do, that I might enjoy my own thoughts; and having left my box at home to avoid the trouble of carrying it, went to another part of the garden with her governess and [35 some ladies of her acquaintance. While she was absent and out of hearing, a small white spaniel belonging to one of the chief gardeners, having got by accident into the garden, happened to range near the place where I lay. The dog following the scent, came directly up, and taking me in his mouth, ran straight to his master,   [40 wagging his tail, and set me gently on the ground. By good fortune he had been so well taught, that I was carried between his teeth without the least hurt, or even tearing my clothes. But the poor gardener, who knew me well, and had a great kindness for me, was in a terrible fright. He gently took me up in both his hands, and   [45 asked me how I did; but I was so amazed and out of breath, that I could not speak a word. In a few minutes I came to myself, and he carried me safe to my little nurse, who by this time had returned to the place where she left me, and was in cruel agonies when I did not appear, nor answer when she called; she severely repri-   [50 manded the gardener on account of his dog. But the thing was hushed up, and never known at court; for the girl was afraid of the Queen's anger; and truly as to myself, I thought it would not be for my reputation that such a story should go about.

This accident absolutely determined Glumdalclitch never to   [55 trust me abroad for the future out of her sight. I had been long afraid of this resolution, and therefore concealed from her some little unlucky adventures that happened in those times when I was left by myself. Once a kite hovering over the garden made a swoop at me, and if I had not resolutely drawn my hanger, and run under   [60 a thick espalier, he would have certainly carried me away in his talons. Another time walking to the top of a fresh mole-hill, I fell to my neck in the hole through which that animal had cast up the earth, and coined some lie, not worth remembering, to excuse myself for spoiling my clothes. I likewise broke my right shin   [65 against the shell of a snail, which I happened to stumble over, as I was walking alone, and thinking on poor England.

I cannot tell whether I were more pleased or mortified, to observe in those solitary walks that the smaller birds did not appear to be at all afraid of me; but would hop about within a yard dis-   [70 tance, looking for worms and other food, with as much indifference and security as if no creature at all were near them. I remembered a thrush had the confidence to snatch out of my hand with his bill a piece of cake that Glumdalclitch had just given me for my breakfast. When I attempted to catch any of these birds, they   [75 would boldly turn against me, endeavouring to pick my fingers, which I durst not venture within their reach; and then they would hop back unconcerned to hunt for worms or snails, as they did before. But one day I took a thick cudgel, and threw it with all my strength so luckily at a linnet that I knocked him down, and   [80 seizing him by the neck with both my hands, ran with him in triumph to my nurse. However, the bird, who had only been stunned, recovering himself, gave me so many boxes with his wings on both sides of my head and body, though I held him at arm's length, and was out of the reach of his claws, that I was twenty times [85 thinking to let him go. But I was soon relieved by one of our servants, who wrung off the bird's neck, and I had him next day for dinner, by the Queen's command. This linnet, as near as I can remember, seemed to be somewhat larger than an English swan.

The Maids of Honour often invited Glumdalclitch to their [90 apartments, and desired she would bring me along with her, on purpose to have the pleasure of seeing and touching me. They would often strip me naked from top to toe and lay me at full length in their bosoms; wherewith I was much disgusted; because, to say the truth, a very offensive smell came from their skins; which [95 I do not mention or intend to the disadvantage of those excellent ladies, for whom I have all manner of respect; but I conceive that my sense was more acute in proportion to my littleness; and that those illustrious persons were no more disagreeable to their lovers, or to each other, than people of the same quality are with [100 us in England. And, after all, I found their natural smell was much more supportable than when they used perfumes, under which I immediately swooned away. I cannot forget that an intimate friend of mine in Lilliput took the freedom in a warm day, when I had used a good deal of exercise, to complain of a strong smell [105 about me, although I am as little faulty that way as most of my sex: but I suppose his faculty of smelling was as nice with regard to me, as mine was to that of this people. Upon this point, I cannot forbear doing justice to the Queen my mistress, and Glumdalclitch my nurse, whose persons were as sweet as those of any lady in England.   110

That which gave me most uneasiness among these Maids of Honour, when my nurse carried me to visit them, was to see them use me without any manner of ceremony, like a creature who had no sort of consequence. For they would strip themselves to the skin, and put on their smocks in my presence, while I was placed [115 on their toilet directly before their naked bodies; which, I am sure, to me was very far from being a tempting sight, or from giving me any other emotions than those of horror and disgust. Their skins appeared so coarse and uneven, so variously coloured, when I saw them near, with a mole here and there as broad as a trencher, and [120 hairs hanging from it thicker than pack-threads, to say nothing fur-

---

116. *toilet:* dressing-table.

ther concerning the rest of their persons. Neither did they at all scruple, while I was by, to discharge what they had drunk, to the quantity of at least two hogsheads, in a vessel that held above three tuns. The handsomest among these Maids of Honour, a   [125 pleasant frolicsome girl of sixteen, would sometimes set me astride upon one of her nipples; with many other tricks, wherein the reader will excuse me for not being over particular. But I was so much displeased, that I entreated Glumdalclitch to contrive some excuse for not seeing that young lady any more.   130

One day a young gentleman, who was nephew to my nurse's governess, came and pressed them both to see an execution. It was of a man who had murdered one of that gentleman's intimate acquaintance. Glumdalclitch was prevailed on to be of the company, very much against her inclination, for she was naturally tender-   [135 hearted: and as for myself, although I abhorred such kind of spectacles, yet my curiosity tempted me to see something that I thought must be extraordinary. The malefactor was fixed in a chair upon a scaffold erected for the purpose, and his head cut off at a blow with a sword of about forty foot long. The veins and arteries   [140 spouted up such a prodigious quantity of blood, and so high in the air, that the great *jet d'eau* at Versailles was not equal for the time it lasted; and the head, when it fell on the scaffold floor, gave such a bounce, as made me start, although I were at least half an English mile distant.   145

The Queen, who often used to hear me talk of my sea-voyages, and took all occasions to divert me when I was melancholy, asked me whether I understood how to handle a sail or an oar, and whether a little exercise of rowing might not be convenient for my health. I answered that I understood both very well. For although   [150 my proper employment had been to be surgeon or doctor to the ship, yet often, upon a pinch, I was forced to work like a common mariner. But I could not see how this could be done in their country, where the smallest wherry was equal to a first-rate man of war among us, and such a boat as I could manage would never live in any of   [155 their rivers. Her Majesty said, if I would contrive a boat, her own joiner should make it, and she would provide a place for me to sail in. The fellow was an ingenious workman, and by my instructions in ten days finished a pleasure-boat with all its tackling, able conveniently to hold eight Europeans. When it was finished, the   [160 Queen was so delighted, that she ran with it in her lap to the King, who ordered it to be put in a cistern full of water, with me in it, by way of trial; where I could not manage my two sculls, or little oars, for want of room. But the Queen had before contrived another

project. She ordered the joiner to make a wooden trough of   [165
three hundred foot long, fifty broad, and eight deep, which being
well pitched to prevent leaking, was placed on the floor along the
wall, in an outer room of the palace. It had a cock near the bottom
to let out the water when it began to grow stale, and two servants
could easily fill it in half an hour. Here I often used to row   [170
for my own diversion, as well as that of the Queen and her ladies,
who thought themselves well entertained with my skill and agility.
Sometimes I would put up my sail, and then my business was only
to steer, while the ladies gave me a gale with their fans; and when
they were weary, some of the pages would blow my sail for-   [175
ward with their breath, while I showed my art by steering star-
board or larboard as I pleased. When I had done, Glumdalclitch
always carried my boat into her closet, and hung it on a nail to dry.

In this exercise I once met an accident which had like to have cost
me my life. For one of the pages having put my boat into   [180
the trough, the governess who attended Glumdalclitch very officiously
lifted me up to place me in the boat; but I happened to slip through
her fingers, and should have infallibly fallen down forty feet upon
the floor, if by the luckiest chance in the world, I had not been
stopped by a corking-pin that stuck in the good gentle-   [185
woman's stomacher; the head of the pin passed between my shirt
and the waistband of my breeches, and thus I was held by the middle
in the air until Glumdalclitch ran to my relief.

Another time, one of the servants, whose office it was to fill my
trough every third day with fresh water, was so careless to   [190
let a huge frog (not perceiving it) slip out of his pail. The frog lay
concealed till I was put into my boat, but then seeing a resting-place,
climbed up, and made it lean so much on one side, that I was forced
to balance it with all my weight on the other, to prevent overturning.
When the frog was got in, it hopped at once half the length   [195
of the boat, and then over my head, backwards and forwards, daub-
ing my face and clothes with its odious slime. The largeness of its
features made it appear the most deformed animal that can be conceived. However, I desired Glumdalclitch to let me deal with it
alone. I banged it a good while with one of my sculls, and   [200
at last forced it to leap out of the boat. . . .

I was every day furnishing the court with some ridiculous story;
and Glumdalclitch, although she loved me to excess, yet was   [295
arch enough to inform the Queen, whenever I committed any folly
that she thought would be diverting to her Majesty. The girl, who

---

185. *corking-pin:* a very large pin.

had been out of order, was carried by her governess to take the air about an hour's distance, or thirty miles from town. They alighted out of the coach near a small foot-path in a field, and Glum- [300 dalclitch setting down my travelling box, I went out of it to walk. There was a cow-dung in the patch, and I must needs try my activity by attempting to leap over it. I took a run, but unfortunately jumped short, and found myself just in the middle up to my knees. I waded through with some difficulty, and one of the footmen wiped [305 me as clean as he could with his handkerchief; for I was filthily be-mired, and my nurse confined me to my box till we returned home; where the Queen was soon informed of what had passed, and the footmen spread it about the court, so that all the mirth, for some days, was at my expense. 310

❧

CHAPTER SIX. *Several contrivances of the Author to please the King and Queen. He shows his skill in music. The King inquires into the state of Europe, which the Author relates to him. The King's observations thereon.*

. . . The King, who, as I before observed, was a prince of excellent understanding, would frequently order that I should be brought in my box, and set upon the table in his closet. He would then command me to bring one of my chairs out of the box, and sit down within three yards distance upon the top of the cabinet, which [5 brought me almost to a level with his face. In this manner I had several conversations with him. I one day took the freedom to tell his Majesty, that the contempt he discovered towards Europe, and the rest of the world, did not seem answerable to those excellent qualities of mind that he was master of. That reason did not [10 extend itself with the bulk of the body: on the contrary, we observed in our country that the tallest persons were usually least provided with it. That among other animals, bees and ants had the reputation of more industry, art and sagacity, than many of the larger kinds. And that, as inconsiderable as he took me to be, I hoped I might [15 live to do his Majesty some signal service. The King heard me with attention, and began to conceive a much better opinion of me than he had ever before. He desired I would give him as exact an account of the government of England as I possibly could; because, as fond as princes commonly are of their own customs (for so he con- [20 jectured of other monarchs, by my former discourses), he should be glad to hear of anything that might deserve imitation.

Imagine with thyself, courteous reader, how often I then wished for the tongue of Demosthenes or Cicero, that might have enabled me to celebrate the praise of my own dear native country [25 in a style equal to its merits and felicity.

I began my discourse by informing his Majesty that our dominions consisted of two islands, which composed three mighty kingdoms under one sovereign, beside our plantations in America. I dwelt long upon the fertility of our soil, and the temperature of our [30 climate. I then spoke at large upon the constitution of an English Parliament, partly made up of an illustrious body called the House of Peers, persons of the noblest blood, and of the most ancient and ample patrimonies. I described that extraordinary care always taken of their education in arts and arms, to qualify them for being [35 counsellors born to the king and kingdom; to have a share in the legislature, to be members of the highest Court of Judicature, from whence there could be no appeal; and to be champions always ready for the defence of their prince and country, by their valour, conduct, and fidelity. That these were the ornament and bulwark of the [40 kingdom, worthy followers of their most renowned ancestors, whose honour had been the reward of their virtue; from which their posterity were never once known to degenerate. To these were joined several holy persons, as part of that assembly, under the title of Bishops, whose peculiar business it is to take care of religion, and of those who [45 instruct the people therein. These were searched and sought out through the whole nation, by the prince and his wisest counsellors, among such of the priesthood as were most deservedly distinguished by the sanctity of their lives, and the depth of their erudition; who were indeed the spiritual fathers of the clergy and the people. [50

That the other part of the Parliament consisted of an assembly called the House of Commons, who were all principal gentlemen, *freely* picked and culled out by the people themselves, for their great abilities and love of their country, to represent the wisdom of the whole nation. And these two bodies make up the most [55 august assembly in Europe, to whom, in conjunction with the prince, the whole legislature is committed.

I then descended to the Courts of Justice, over which the Judges, those venerable sages and interpreters of the law, presided, for determining the disputed rights and properties of men, as well [60 as for the punishment of vice, and protection of innocence. I mentioned the prudent management of our treasury; the valour and achievements of our forces by sea and land. I computed the number of our people, by reckoning how many millions there might be of each religious sect, or political party among us. I did not [65 omit even our sports and pastimes, or any other particular which I thought might redound to the honour of my country. And I finished all with a brief historical account of affairs and events in England for about an hundred years past.

This conversation was not ended under five audiences, each [70 of several hours, and the King heard the whole with great attention, frequently taking notes of what I spoke, as well as memorandums of several questions he intended to ask me.

When I had put an end to these long discourses, his Majesty in a sixth audience consulting his notes, proposed many doubts, [75 queries, and objections, upon every article. He asked what methods were used to cultivate the minds and bodies of our young nobility, and in what kind of business they commonly spent the first and teachable part of their lives. What course was taken to supply that assembly when any noble family became extinct. What quali- [80 fications were necessary in those who were to be created new lords. Whether the humour of the prince, a sum of money to a court lady, or a prime minister, or a design of strengthening a party opposite to the public interest, ever happened to be motives in those advance- ments. What share of knowledge these lords had in the laws [85 of their country, and how they came by it, so as to enable them to decide the properties of their fellow-subjects in the last resort. Whether they were always so free from avarice, partialities, or want, that a bribe, or some other sinister view, could have no place among them. Whether those holy lords I spoke of were constantly promoted [90 to that rank upon account of their knowledge in religious matters, and the sanctity of their lives, had never been compliers with the times while they were common priests, or slavish prostitute chaplains to some nobleman, whose opinions they continued servilely to follow after they were admitted into that assembly. 95

He then desired to know what arts were practised in electing those whom I called commoners. Whether a stranger with a strong purse might not influence the vulgar voters to choose him before their own landlord, or the most considerable gentleman in the neighbourhood. How it came to pass, that people were so violently bent upon [100 getting into this assembly, which I allowed to be a great trouble and expense, often to the ruin of their families, without any salary or pension: because this appeared such an exalted strain of virtue and public spirit, that his Majesty seemed to doubt it might possibly not be always sincere: and he desired to know whether such [105 zealous gentlemen could have any views of refunding themselves for the charges and trouble they were at, by sacrificing the public good to the designs of a weak and vicious prince in conjunction with a corrupted ministry. He multiplied his questions, and sifted me thoroughly upon every part of this head, proposing numberless   [110 enquiries and objections, which I think it not prudent or convenient to repeat.

Upon what I said in relation to our Courts of Justice, his Majesty desired to be satisfied in several points: and this I was the better able to do, having been formerly almost ruined by a long suit in   [115 chancery, which was decreed for me with costs. He asked, what time was usually spent in determining between right and wrong, and what degree of expense. Whether advocates and orators had liberty to plead in causes manifestly known to be unjust, vexatious, or oppressive. Whether party in religion or politics were observed   [120 to be of any weight in the scale of justice. Whether those pleading orators were persons educated in the general knowledge of equity, or only in provincial, national, and other local customs. Whether they or their judges had any part in penning those laws which they assumed the liberty of interpreting and glossing upon at their   [125 pleasure. Whether they had ever at different times pleaded for and against the same cause, and cited precedents to prove contrary opinions. Whether they were a rich or a poor corporation. Whether they received any pecuniary reward for pleading or delivering their opinions. And particularly whether they were ever admitted as   [130 members in the lower senate.

He fell next upon the management of our treasury; and said he thought my memory had failed me, because I computed our taxes at about five or six millions a year, and when I came to mention the issues, he found they sometimes amounted to more than   [135 double; for the notes he had taken were very particular in this point; because he hoped, as he told me, that the knowledge of our conduct might be useful to him, and he could not be deceived in his calculations. But, if what I told him were true, he was still at a loss how a kingdom could run out of its estate like a private person.   [140 He asked me, who were our creditors? and where we should find money to pay them? He wondered to hear me talk of such chargeable and extensive wars; that certainly we must be a quarrelsome people, or live among very bad neighbours, and that our generals must needs be richer than our kings. He asked what business we   [145 had out of our own islands, unless upon the score of trade or treaty, or to defend the coasts with our fleet. Above all, he was amazed to hear me talk of a mercenary standing army in the midst of peace, and among a free people. He said, if we were governed by our own

consent in the persons of our representatives, he could not [150
imagine of whom we were afraid, or against whom we were to fight;
and would hear my opinion, whether a private man's house might not
better be defended by himself, his children, and family, than by half
a dozen rascals picked up at a venture in the streets, for small wages,
who might get an hundred times more by cutting their [155
throats.

He laughed at my odd kind of arithmetic (as he was pleased to call
it) in reckoning the numbers of our people by a computation drawn
from the several sects among us in religion and politics. He said
he knew no reason, why those who entertain opinions [160
prejudicial to the public, should be obliged to change, or should not
be obliged to conceal them. And as it was tyranny in any government
to require the first, so it was weakness not to enforce the second: for
a man may be allowed to keep poisons in his closet, but not to vend
them about for cordials. 165

He observed that among the diversions of our nobility and gentry
I had mentioned gaming. He desired to know at what age this entertainment was usually taken up, and when it was laid down; how
much of their time it employed; whether it ever went so high as
to affect their fortunes; whether mean vicious people, by [170
their dexterity in that art, might not arrive at great riches, and sometimes keep our very nobles in dependence, as well as habituate them
to vile companions, wholly take them from the improvement of their
minds; and force them, by the losses they have received, to learn and
practise that infamous dexterity upon others. 175

He was perfectly astonished with the historical account I gave him
of our affairs during the last century; protesting it was only an heap
of conspiracies, rebellions, murders, massacres, revolutions, banish-
ments, the very worst effects that avarice, faction, hypocrisy, perfidious-
ness, cruelty, rage, madness, hatred, envy, lust, malice, or [180
ambition could produce.

His Majesty in another audience was at the pains to recapitulate
the sum of all I had spoken; compared the questions he made with
the answers I had given; then taking me into his hands and stroking
me gently, delivered himself in these words, which I shall [185
never forget nor the manner he spoke them in. "My little friend
Grildrig, you have made a most admirable panegyric upon your
country. You have clearly proved that ignorance, idleness, and vice,
are the proper ingredients for qualifying a legislator. That laws are
best explained, interpreted, and applied by those whose inter- [190
ests and abilities lie in perverting, confounding, and eluding them. I
observe among you some lines of an institution, which in its original

might have been tolerable; but these half erased, and the rest wholly blurred and blotted by corruptions. It doth not appear from all you have said, how any one virtue is required towards the pro-   [195 curement of any one station among you; much less that men are ennobled on account of their virtue, that priests are advanced for their piety or learning, soldiers for their conduct or valour, judges for their integrity, senators for the love of their country, or counsellors for their wisdom. As for yourself" (continued the King) "who   [200 have spent the greatest part of your life in travelling, I am well disposed to hope you may hitherto have escaped many vices of your country. But by what I have gathered from your own relation, and the answers I have with much pains wringed and extorted from you, I cannot but conclude the bulk of your natives to be the most pernicious   [205 race of little odious vermin that nature ever suffered to crawl upon the surface of the earth."

❧

CHAPTER SEVEN. *The Author's love of his country. He makes a proposal of much advantage to the King; which is rejected. The King's great ignorance in politics. The learning of that country very imperfect and confined. Their laws, and military affairs, and parties in the State.*

*N*OTHING but an extreme of love of truth could have hindered me from concealing this part of my story. It was in vain to discover my resentments, which were always turned into ridicule: and I was forced to rest with patience while my noble and most beloved country was so injuriously treated. I am heartily sorry as any of my readers can   [5 possibly be, that such an occasion was given: but this prince happened to be so curious and inquisitive upon every particular, that it could not consist either with gratitude or good manners to refuse giving him what satisfaction I was able. Yet thus much I may be allowed to say in my own vindication; that I artfully eluded many   [10 of his questions; and gave to every point a more favourable turn by many degrees than the strictness of truth would allow. For I have always borne that laudable partiality to my own country, which Dionysius Halicarnassensis with so much justice recommends to an historian.

13-14. The historian Dionysius of Halicarnassus confesses in his *Archaeologia* a desire to illustrate the greatness of Rome. Swift satirically makes Gulliver misapply the precedent, since Dionysius, who was not a Roman, is an instance of admiration for greatness wherever found, not an instance of complacent patriotism.

I would hide the frailties and deformities of my political   [15
mother, and place her virtues and beauties in the most advantageous
light. This was my sincere endeavour in those many discourses I had
with that mighty monarch, although it unfortunately failed of success.

But great allowances should be given to a King who lives wholly
secluded from the rest of the world, and must therefore be al-   [20
together unacquainted with the manners and customs that most prevail in other nations: the want of which knowledge will ever produce
many *prejudices,* and a certain *narrowness of thinking;* from which
we and the politer countries of Europe are wholly exempted. And
it would be hard indeed, if so remote a prince's notions of   [25
virtue and vice were to be offered as a standard for all mankind.

To confirm what I have now said, and further, to show the miserable effects of a *confined education,* I shall here insert a passage which
will hardly obtain belief. In hopes to ingratiate myself farther into
his Majesty's favour, I told him of an invention discovered   [30
between three and four hundred years ago, to make a certain powder,
into an heap of which the smallest spark of fire falling, would kindle
the whole in a moment, although it were as big as a mountain, and
make it all fly up in the air together, with a noise and agitation greater
than thunder. That a proper quantity of this powder rammed   [35
into an hollow tube of brass or iron, according to its bigness, would
drive a ball of iron or lead with such violence and speed, as nothing
was able to sustain its force. That the largest balls thus discharged,
would not only destroy whole ranks of an army at once; but batter
the strongest walls to the ground; sink down ships with a   [40
thousand men in each, to the bottom of the sea; and, when linked
together by a chain, would cut through masts and rigging; divide
hundreds of bodies in the middle, and lay all waste before them. That
we often put this powder into large hollow balls of iron, and discharged them by an engine into some city we were besieging;   [45
which would rip up the pavements, tear the houses to pieces, burst
and throw splinters on every side, dashing out the brains of all who
came near. That I knew the ingredients very well, which were cheap,
and common; I understood the manner of compounding them, and
could direct his workmen how to make those tubes of a size   [50
proportionable to all other things in his Majesty's kingdom, and the
largest need not be above two hundred foot long; twenty or thirty of
which tubes, charged with the proper quantity of powder and balls,
would batter down the walls of the strongest town in his dominions
in a few hours; or destroy the whole metropolis, if ever it   [55
should pretend to dispute his absolute commands. This I humbly
offered to his Majesty, as a small tribute of acknowledgment in return

of so many marks that I had received of his royal favour and protection.

The King was struck with horror at the description I had [60 given of those terrible engines, and the proposal I had made. He was amazed how so impotent and grovelling an insect as I (these were his expressions) could entertain such inhuman ideas, and in so familiar a manner as to appear wholly unmoved at all the scenes of blood and desolation, which I had painted as the common effects of those [65 destructive machines; whereof he said some evil genius, enemy to mankind, must have been the first contriver. As for himself, he protested that although few things delighted him so much as new discoveries in art or in nature; yet he would rather lose half his kingdom than be privy to such a secret; which he commanded me, as I [70 valued my life, never to mention any more.

A strange effect of _narrow principles_ and _short views!_ that a prince possessed of every quality which procures veneration, love, and esteem; of strong parts, great wisdom, and profound learning; endued with admirable talents for government, and almost adored by his [75 subjects; should from a _nice unnecessary scruple,_ whereof in Europe we can have no conception, let slip an opportunity put into his hands, that would have made him absolute master of the lives, the liberties, and the fortunes of his people. Neither do I say this with the least intention to detract from the many virtues of that excellent [80 King, whose character I am sensible will on this account be very much lessened in the opinion of an English reader: but I take this defect among them to have risen from their ignorance; they not having hitherto reduced politics into a science, as the more acute wits of Europe have done. For I remember very well, in a discourse [85 one day with the King, when I happened to say there were several thousand books among us written upon the art of government; it gave him (directly contrary to my intention) a very mean opinion of our understandings. He professed both to abominate and despise all _mystery, refinement,_ and _intrigue,_ either in a prince or a minister. [90 He could not tell what I meant by _secrets of state,_ where an enemy or some rival nation were not in the case. He confined the knowledge of governing within very _narrow bounds;_ to common sense and reason, to justice and lenity, to the speedy determination of civil and criminal causes; with some other obvious topics which are not worth [95 considering. And he gave it for his opinion, that whoever could make two ears of corn or two blades of grass to grow upon a spot of ground where only one grew before, would deserve better of mankind, and do more essential service to his country than the whole race of politicians put together.   100

The learning of this people is very defective; consisting only in morality, history, poetry, and mathematics; wherein they must be allowed to excel. But the last of these is wholly applied to what may be useful in life, to the improvement of agriculture, and all mechanical arts; so that among us it would be little esteemed. And as to [105 ideas, entities, abstractions, and transcendentals, I could never drive the least conception into their heads. . . .

❧

CHAPTER EIGHT. *The King and Queen make a progress to the frontiers. The Author attends them. The manner in which he leaves the country very particularly related. He returns to England.*

. . . As I was on the road, observing the littleness of the houses, the trees, the cattle and the people, I began to think myself in Lilliput. I was afraid of trampling on every traveller I met, and often called aloud to have them stand out of my way, so that I had like to have gotten one or two broken heads for my impertinence.   5

When I came to my own house, for which I was forced to enquire, one of the servants opening the door, I bent down to go in (like a goose under a gate) for fear of striking my head. My wife ran out to embrace me, but I stooped lower than her knees, thinking she could otherwise never be able to reach my mouth. My daughter   [10 kneeled to ask my blessing, but I could not see her till she arose, having been so long used to stand with my head and eyes erect to above sixty foot; and then I went to take her up with one hand, by the waist. I looked down upon the servants and one or two friends who were in the house, as if they had been pigmies, and I a giant. I told   [15 my wife, she had been too thrifty; for I found she had starved herself and her daughter to nothing. In short, I behaved myself so unaccountably, that they were all of the Captain's opinion when he first saw me, and concluded I had lost my wits. . . .

❧

19. [The large wooden cage in which Gulliver is carried about in Brobdingnag is seized by a huge bird and dropped far out at sea. The cage floats, and being eventually sighted by a ship, he is rescued and returned to England.]

IV. A VOYAGE TO THE COUNTRY
OF THE HOUYHNHNMS

CHAPTER ONE. *The Author sets out as Captain of a ship. His men conspire against him, confine him a long time to his cabin, set him on shore in an unknown land. He travels up in the country. The Yahoos, a strange sort of animal, described. The Author meets two Houyhnhnms.*

. . . In this desolate condition I advanced forward, and soon got upon firm ground, where I sat down on a bank to rest myself, and consider what I had best to do. When I was a little refreshed, I went up into the country, resolving to deliver myself to the first savages I should meet, and purchase my life from them by some brace-   [5 lets, glass rings, and other toys, which sailors usually provide themselves with in those voyages, and whereof I had some about me. The land was divided by long rows of trees, not regularly planted, but naturally growing; there was great plenty of grass, and several fields of oats. I walked very circumspectly for fear of being sur-   [10 prised, or suddenly shot with an arrow from behind or on either side. I fell into a beaten road, where I saw many tracks of human feet, and some of cows, but most of horses. At last I beheld several animals in a field, and one or two of the same kind sitting in trees. Their shape was very singular and deformed, which a little discomposed   [15 me, so that I lay down behind a thicket to observe them better. Some of them coming forward near the place where I lay, gave me an opportunity of distinctly marking their form. Their heads and breasts were covered with a thick hair, some frizzled and others lank; they had beards like goats, and a long ridge of hair down their   [20 backs and the fore-parts of their legs and feet; but the rest of their bodies were bare, so that I might see their skins, which were of a brown buff colour. They had no tails, nor any hair at all on their buttocks, except about the anus; which, I presume, nature had placed there to defend them as they sat on the ground; for this pos-   [25 ture they used, as well as lying down, and often stood on their hind feet. They climbed high trees, as nimbly as a squirrel, for they had strong extended claws before and behind, terminating in sharp points,

---

1 ff. [On his final voyage, Gulliver's men mutiny and abandon him on a desert shore.]

hooked. They would often spring and bound and leap with prodigious
agility. The females were not so large as the males; they had   [30
long lank hair on their heads, and only a sort of down on the rest of
their bodies, except about the anus, and pudenda. Their dugs hung
between their fore-feet, and often reached almost to the ground as they
walked. The hair of both sexes was of several colours, brown, red,
black, and yellow. Upon the whole, I never beheld in all my   [35
travels so disagreeable an animal, or one against which I naturally
conceived so strong an antipathy. So that thinking I had seen enough,
full of contempt and aversion, I got up and pursued the beaten road,
hoping it might direct me to the cabin of some Indian. I had not got
far when I met one of these creatures full in my way, and com-   [40
ing up directly to me. The ugly monster, when he saw me, distorted
several ways every feature of his visage, and stared as at an object
he had never seen before; then approaching nearer, lifted up his fore-
paw, whether out of curiosity or mischief, I could not tell. But I drew
my hanger, and gave him a good blow with the flat side of it;   [45
for I durst not strike him with the edge, fearing the inhabitants might
be provoked against me, if they should come to know that I had killed
or maimed any of their cattle. When the beast felt the smart, he drew
back, and roared so loud that a herd of at least forty came flocking
about me from the next field, howling and making odious   [50
faces; but I ran to the body of a tree, and leaning my back against it,
kept them off by waving my hanger. Several of this cursed brood getting hold of the branches behind, leapt up into the tree, from whence
they began to discharge their excrements on my head; however, I
escaped pretty well, by sticking close to the stem of the tree,   [55
but was almost stifled with the filth, which fell about me on every side.

In the midst of this distress, I observed them all to run away on a
sudden as fast as they could; at which I ventured to leave the tree,
and pursue the road, wondering what it was that could put them into
this fright. But looking on my left hand, I saw a horse walk-   [60
ing softly in the field; which my persecutors having sooner discovered,
was the cause of their flight. The horse started a little when he came
near me, but soon recovering himself, looked full in my face with
manifest tokens of wonder; he viewed my hands and feet, walking
round me several times. I would have pursued my journey,   [65
but he placed himself directly in the way, yet looking with a very mild
aspect, never offering the least violence. We stood gazing at each
other for some time; at last I took the boldness to reach my hand
towards his neck, with a design to stroke it, using the common style
and whistle of jockeys when they are going to handle a strange   [70
horse. But this animal seeming to receive my civilities with disdain,

shook his head, and bent his brows, softly raising up his right fore-foot
to remove my hand. Then he neighed three or four times, but in so
different a cadence, that I almost began to think he was speaking to
himself in some language of his own.   75
    While he and I were thus employed, another horse came up; who
applying himself to the first in a very formal manner, they gently
struck each other's right hoof before, neighing several times by turns,
and varying the sound, which seemed to be almost articulate. They
went some paces off, as if it were to confer together, walking   [80
side by side, backward and forward, like persons deliberating upon
some affair of weight, but often turning their eyes towards me, as it
were to watch that I might not escape. I was amazed to see such
actions and behaviour in brute beasts, and concluded with myself, that
if the inhabitants of this country were endued with a propor-   [85
tionable degree of reason, they must needs be the wisest people upon
earth. This thought gave me so much comfort, that I resolved to go
forward until I could discover some house or village, or meet with
any of the natives, leaving the two horses to discourse together as they
pleased. But the first, who was a dapple gray, observing me to   [90
steal off, neighed after me in so expressive a tone, that I fancied myself
to understand what he meant; whereupon I turned back, and came
near him, to expect his farther commands, but concealing my fear
as much as I could, for I began to be in some pain, how this adventure might terminate; and the reader will easily believe I did   [95
not much like my present situation.
    The two horses came up close to me, looking with great earnestness
upon my face and hands. The gray steed rubbed my hat all round
with his right fore-hoof, and discomposed it so much that I was forced
to adjust it better, by taking it off, and settling it again;   [100
whereat both he and his companion (who was a brown bay) appeared
to be much surprised; the latter felt the lappet of my coat, and finding
it to hang loose about me, they both looked with new signs of wonder.
He stroked my right hand, seeming to admire the softness and colour;
but he squeezed it so hard between his hoof and his pastern,   [105
that I was forced to roar; after which they both touched me with all
possible tenderness. They were under great perplexity about my shoes
and stockings, which they felt very often, neighing to each other, and
using various gestures, not unlike those of a philosopher, when he
would attempt to solve some new and difficult phenomenon.   [110
    Upon the whole, the behaviour of these animals was so orderly and
rational, so acute and judicious, that I at last concluded they must
needs be magicians, who had thus metamorphosed themselves upon

some design, and seeing a stranger in the way, were resolved to divert themselves with him; or perhaps were really amazed at the   [115 sight of a man so very different in habit, feature, and complexion from those who might probably live in so remote a climate. Upon the strength of this reasoning, I ventured to address them in the following manner: "Gentlemen, if you be conjurers, as I have good cause to believe, you can understand any language; therefore I make   [120 bold to let your worships know that I am a poor distressed Englishman, driven by his misfortunes upon your coast, and I entreat one of you, to let me ride upon his back, as if he were a real horse, to some house or village, where I can be relieved. In return of which favour, I will make you a present of this knife and bracelet," (taking   [125 them out of my pocket). The two creatures stood silent while I spoke, seeming to listen with great attention; and when I had ended, they neighed frequently towards each other, as if they were engaged in serious conversation. I plainly observed, that their language expressed the passions very well, and the words might with little pains   [130 be resolved into an alphabet more easily than the Chinese.

I could frequently distinguish the word _Yahoo_, which was repeated by each of them several times; and although it were impossible for me to conjecture what it meant, yet while the two horses were busy in conversation, I endeavoured to practise this word upon my   [135 tongue; and as soon as they were silent, I boldly pronounced _Yahoo_ in a loud voice, imitating, at the same time, as near as I could, the neighing of a horse; at which they were both visibly surprised, and the gray repeated the same word twice, as if he meant to teach me the right accent, wherein I spoke after him as well as I could, and   [140 found myself perceivably to improve every time, although very far from any degree of perfection. Then the bay tried me with a second word, much harder to be pronounced; but reducing it to the English orthography, may be spelt thus, _Houyhnhnm_. I did not succeed in this so well as the former, but after two or three farther trials,   [145 I had better fortune; and they both appeared amazed at my capacity.

After some further discourse, which I then conjectured might relate to me, the two friends took their leaves, with the same compliment of striking each other's hoof; and the gray made me signs that I should walk before him; wherein I thought it prudent to comply,   [150 till I could find a better director. When I offered to slacken my pace, he would cry, _"Hhuun, Hhuun"_; I guessed his meaning, and gave him

---

144. _Houyhnhnm:_ pronounced "Whinnim"—in imitation of the whinny of horses.

to understand, as well as I could, that I was weary, and not able to walk faster; upon which he would stand a while to let me rest.

∾

CHAPTER TWO. *The Author conducted by a Houyhnhnm to his house. The house described. The Author's reception. The food of the Houyhnhnms. The Author in distress for want of meat, is at last relieved. His manner of feeding in that country.*

*H*AVING travelled about three miles, we came to a long kind of building, made of timber stuck in the ground, and wattled across; the roof was low, and covered with straw. I now began to be a little comforted, and took out some toys, which travellers usually carry for presents to the savage Indians of America and other parts, in   [5 hopes the people of the house would be thereby encouraged to receive me kindly. The horse made me a sign to go in first; it was a large room with a smooth clay floor, and a rack and manger extending the whole length on one side. There were three nags, and two mares, not eating, but some of them sitting down upon their hams,   [10 which I very much wondered at; but wondered more to see the rest employed in domestic business. The last seemed but ordinary cattle; however, this confirmed my first opinion, that a people who could so far civilize brute animals, must needs excel in wisdom all the nations of the world. The gray came in just after, and thereby pre-   [15 vented any ill treatment which the others might have given me. He neighed to them several times in a style of authority, and received answers.

Beyond this room there were three others, reaching the length of the house, to which you passed through three doors, opposite   [20 to each other, in the manner of a vista; we went through the second room towards the third; here the gray walked in first, beckoning me to attend: I waited in the second room, and got ready my presents for the master and mistress of the house: they were two knives, three bracelets of false pearl, a small looking-glass, and a bead neck-   [25 lace. The horse neighed three or four times, and I waited to hear some answers in a human voice, but I heard no other returns than in the same dialect, only one or two a little shriller than his. I began to think that this house must belong to some person of great note among them, because there appeared so much ceremony before   [30 I could gain admittance. But, that a man of quality should be served all by horses, was beyond my comprehension. I feared my brain was disturbed by my sufferings and misfortunes: I roused myself, and looked about me in the room where I was left alone; this was furnished as the first, only after a more elegant manner. I rubbed mine [35 eyes often, but the same objects still occurred. I pinched my arms and sides to awake myself, hoping I might be in a dream. I then absolutely concluded, that all these appearances could be nothing else but necromancy and magic. But I had no time to pursue these reflections; for the gray horse came to the door, and made me a sign to follow [40 him into the third room, where I saw a very comely mare, together with a colt and foal, sitting on their haunches, upon mats of straw, not unartfully made, and perfectly neat and clean.

The mare soon after my entrance, rose from her mat, and coming up close, after having nicely observed my hands and face, gave [45 me a most contemptuous look; then turning to the horse, I heard the word *Yahoo* often repeated betwixt them; the meaning of which word I could not then comprehend, although it were the first I had learned to pronounce; but I was soon better informed, to my everlasting mortification: for the horse beckoning me with his head, [50 and repeating the word *Hhuun, Hhuun,* as he did upon the road, which I understood was to attend him, led me out into a kind of court, where was another building at some distance from the house. Here we entered, and I saw three of those detestable creatures, whom I first met after my landing, feeding upon roots, and the flesh [55 of some animals, which I afterwards found to be that of asses and dogs, and now and then a cow dead by accident or disease. They were all tied by the neck with strong withes, fastened to a beam; they held their food between the claws of their fore-feet, and tore it with their teeth.
60

The master horse ordered a sorrel nag, one of his servants, to untie the largest of these animals, and take him into the yard. The beast and I were brought close together, and our countenances diligently compared, both by master and servant, who thereupon repeated several times the word *Yahoo*. My horror and astonishment are not to [65 be described, when I observed in this abominable animal a perfect human figure; the face of it indeed was flat and broad, the nose depressed, the lips large, and the mouth wide. But these differences are common to all savage nations, where the lineaments of the countenance are distorted by the natives suffering their infants to lie grovel- [70 ling on the earth, or by carrying them on their backs, nuzzling with their face against the mother's shoulders. The fore-feet of the Yahoo differed from my hands in nothing else but the length of the nails, the coarseness and brownness of the palms, and the hairiness on the backs. There was the same resemblance between our feet, with [75 the same differences, which I knew very well, though the horses did not, because of my shoes and stockings; the same in every part of our bodies, except as to hairiness and colour, which I have already described. [79

The great difficulty that seemed to stick with the two horses, was to see the rest of my body so very different from that of a Yahoo, for which I was obliged to my clothes, whereof they had no conception. The sorrel nag offered me a root, which he held (after their manner, as we shall describe in its proper place) between his hoof and pastern; I took it in my hand, and having smelt it, returned it to him [85 again as civilly as I could. He brought out of the Yahoo's kennel a piece of ass's flesh, but it smelt so offensively that I turned from it with loathing; he then threw it to the Yahoo, by whom it was greedily devoured. He afterwards showed me a wisp of hay, and a fetlock full of oats; but I shook my head, to signify that neither of these [90 were food for me. And indeed, I now apprehended that I must absolutely starve, if I did not get to some of my own species; for as to those filthy Yahoos, although there were few greater lovers of mankind, at that time, than myself, yet I confess I never saw any sensitive being so detestable on all accounts; and the more I came near [95 them, the more hateful they grew, while I stayed in that country. This the master horse observed in my behaviour, and therefore sent the Yahoo back to his kennel. He then put his fore-hoof to his mouth, at which I was much surprised, although he did it with ease, and with a motion that appeared perfectly natural, and made [100 other signs to know what I would eat; but I could not return him such an answer as he was able to apprehend; and if he had understood me, I did not see how it was possible to contrive any way for finding myself nourishment. While we were thus engaged, I observed a cow passing by; whereupon I pointed to her, and expressed a de- [105 sire to let me go and milk her. This had its effect; for he led me back into the house, and ordered a mare-servant to open a room, where a good store of milk lay in earthen and wooden vessels, after a very orderly and cleanly manner. She gave me a large bowl full, of which I drank very heartily, and found myself well refreshed. . . . [110

CHAPTER THREE. *The Author studious to learn the language, the Houyhnhnm his master assists in teaching him. The language described. Several Houyhnhnms of quality come out of curiosity to see the Author. He gives his master a short account of his voyage.*

*M*y PRINCIPAL endeavour was to learn the language, which my master (for so I shall henceforth call him), and his children, and every servant of his house, were desirous to teach me. For they looked upon it as a prodigy that a brute animal should discover such marks of a rational creature. I pointed to every thing and enquired   [5 the name of it, which I wrote down in my journal-book when I was alone, and corrected my bad accent by desiring those of the family to pronounce it often. In his employment, a sorrel nag, one of the under servants, was very ready to assist me. . . .   9

In about ten weeks' time I was able to understand most of his questions, and in three months could give him some tolerable answers. He was extremely curious to know from what part of the country I came, and how I was taught to imitate a rational creature; because the Yahoos (whom he saw I exactly resembled in my head, hands, and face, that were only visible), with some appearance of cunning,   [15 and the strongest disposition to mischief, were observed to be the most unteachable of all brutes. I answered that I came over the sea from a far place, with many others of my own kind, in a great hollow vessel made of the bodies of trees: that my companions forced me to land on this coast, and then left me to shift for myself. It was   [20 with some difficulty, and by the help of many signs, that I brought him to understand me. He replied, that I must needs be mistaken, or that I *said the thing which was not*. (For they have no word in their language to express lying or falsehood.) He knew it was impossible that there could be a country beyond the sea, or that a   [25 parcel of brutes could move a wooden vessel whither they pleased upon water. He was sure no Houyhnhnm alive could make such a vessel, or would trust Yahoos to manage it.

The word *Houyhnhnm*, in their tongue, signifies a *horse*, and in its etymology, *the perfection of nature*. I told my master, that   [30 I was at a loss for expression, but would improve as fast as I could; and hoped in a short time I should be able to tell him wonders: he was pleased to direct his own mare, his colt and foal, and the servants of the family to take all opportunities of instructing me; and every

day for two or three hours he was at the same pains himself.   [35
Several horses and mares of quality in the neighbourhood came often
to our house, upon the report spread of a wonderful Yahoo, that
could speak like a Houyhnhnm, and seemed in his words and actions to discover some glimmerings of reason. These delighted to
converse with me; they put many questions, and received such   [40
answers as I was able to return. By all which advantages I made so
great a progress that in five months from my arrival I understood
whatever was spoke, and could express myself tolerably well.

The Houyhnhnms who came to visit my master, out of a design
of seeing and talking with me, could hardly believe me to be   [45
a right Yahoo, because my body had a different covering from others
of my kind. They were astonished to observe me without the usual
hair or skin, except on my head, face, and hands; but I discovered
that secret to my master, upon an accident which happened about a
fortnight before.   50

I have already told the reader, that every night when the family
were gone to bed, it was my custom to strip and cover myself with my
clothes. It happened one morning early that my master sent for me
by the sorrel nag, who was his valet; when he came I was fast asleep,
my clothes fallen off on one side, and my shirt above my waist.   [55
I awaked at the noise he made, and observed him to deliver his message in some disorder; after which he went to my master, and in a
great fright gave him a very confused account of what he had seen.
This I presently discovered; for going as soon as I was dressed to pay
my attendance upon his Honour, he asked me the meaning of   [60
what his servant had reported, that I was not the same thing when I
slept as I appeared to be at other times; that his valet assured him,
some part of me was white, some yellow, at least not so white, and
some brown.   64

I had hitherto concealed the secret of my dress, in order to distinguish
myself as much as possible from that cursed race of Yahoos; but now
I found it in vain to do so any longer. Besides, I considered that my
clothes and shoes would soon wear out, which already were in a declining condition, and must be supplied by some contrivance from the
hides of Yahoos or other brutes; whereby the whole secret   [70
would be known. I therefore told my master that in the country
from whence I came, those of my kind always covered their bodies
with the hairs of certain animals prepared by art, as well for decency
as to avoid the inclemencies of air, both hot and cold; of which, as to
my own person, I would give him immediate conviction, if   [75
he pleased to command me; only desiring his excuse, if I did not
expose those parts that nature taught us to conceal. He said my dis-

course was all very strange, but especially the last part; for he could not understand why nature should teach us to conceal what nature had given. That neither himself nor family were ashamed of [80 any parts of their bodies; but however I might do as I pleased. Whereupon I first unbuttoned my coat and pulled it off. I did the same with my waistcoat; I drew off my shoes, stockings, and breeches. I let my shirt down to my waist, and drew up the bottom, fastening it like a girdle about my middle to hide my nakedness. 85

My master observed the whole performance with great signs of curiosity and admiration. He took up all my clothes in his pastern, one piece after another, and examined them diligently; he then stroked my body very gently and looked round me several times, after which he said it was plain I must be a perfect Yahoo; but that I [90 differed very much from the rest of my species, in the whiteness and smoothness of my skin, my want of hair in several parts of my body, the shape and shortness of my claws behind and before, and my affectation of walking continually on my two hinder feet. He desired to see no more, and gave me leave to put on my clothes again, [95 for I was shuddering with cold.

I expressed my uneasiness at his giving me so often the appellation of Yahoo, an odious animal for which I had so utter an hatred and contempt. I begged he would forbear applying that word to me, and take the same order in his family, and among his friends [100 whom he suffered to see me. I requested likewise that the secret of my having a false covering to my body might be known to none but himself, at least as long as my present clothing should last; for as to what the sorrel nag his valet had observed, his Honour might command him to conceal it. 105

All this my master very graciously consented to; and thus the secret was kept till my clothes began to wear out, which I was forced to supply by several contrivances that shall hereafter be mentioned. In the meantime he desired I would go on with my utmost diligence to learn their language, because he was more astonished at my [110 capacity for speech and reason than at the figure of my body, whether it were covered or no; adding that he waited with some impatience to hear the wonders which I promised to tell him.

From thenceforward he doubled the pains he had been at to instruct me; he brought me into all company, and made them [115 treat me with civility, because, as he told them privately, this would put me into good humour and make me more diverting.

Every day when I waited on him, beside the trouble he was at in teaching, he would ask me several questions concerning myself, which I answered as well as I could; and by these means he had al- [120 ready received some general ideas, although very imperfect. It would be tedious to relate the several steps by which I advanced to a more regular conversation: but the first account I gave of myself in any order and length, was to this purpose: 124

That I came from a very far country, as I already had attempted to tell him, with about fifty more of my own species; that we travelled upon the seas, in a great hollow vessel made of wood, and larger than his Honour's house. I described the ship to him in the best terms I could, and explained by the help of my handkerchief displayed, how it was driven forward by the wind. That upon a quarrel   [130 among us, I was set on shore on this coast, where I walked forward without knowing whither, till he delivered me from the persecution of those execrable Yahoos. He asked me who made the ship, and how it was possible that the Houyhnhnms of my country would leave it to the management of brutes? My answer was that I durst   [135 proceed no further in my relation, unless he would give me his word and honour that he would not be offended; and then I would tell him the wonders I had so often promised. He agreed; and I went on by assuring him that the ship was made by creatures like myself, who in all the countries I had travelled, as well as in my own, were   [140 the only governing, rational animals; and that upon my arrival hither I was much astonished to see the Houyhnhnms act like rational beings, as he or his friends could be in finding some marks of reason in a creature he was pleased to call a Yahoo; to which I owned my resemblance in every part, but could not account for their de-   [145 generate and brutal nature. I said farther that if good fortune ever restored me to my native country, to relate my travels hither, as I resolved to do, every body would believe that I *said the thing which was not;* that I invented the story out of my own head; and with all possible respect to himself, his family, and friends, and under   [150 his promise of not being offended, our countrymen would hardly think it probable, that a Houyhnhnm should be the presiding creature of a nation, and a Yahoo the brute.

CHAPTER FIVE. *The Author, at his master's command, informs him of the state of England. The causes of war among the princes of Europe. The Author begins to explain the English constitution.*

*T*HE reader may please to observe, that the following extract of many conversations I had with my master, contains a summary of the most material points which were discoursed at several times for

above two years; his Honour often desiring fuller satisfaction as I
farther improved in the Houyhnhnm tongue. I laid before   [5
him, as well as I could, the whole state of Europe; I discoursed of
trade and manufactures, of arts and sciences; and the answers I gave
to all the questions he made, as they arose upon several subjects,
were a fund of conversation not to be exhausted. But I shall here only
set down the substance of what passed between us concerning   [10
my own country, reducing it into order as well as I can, without any regard to time or other circumstances, while I strictly adhere to truth. My
only concern is that I shall hardly be able to do justice to my master's
arguments and expressions, which must needs suffer by my want of
capacity, as well as by a translation into our barbarous English.   [15

In obedience therefore to his Honour's commands, I related to
him the Revolution under the Prince of Orange; the long war with
France entered into by the said prince, and renewed by his successor
the present Queen; wherein the greatest powers of Christendom were
engaged, and which still continued: I computed at his request   [20
that about a million of Yahoos might have been killed in the whole
progress of it, and perhaps a hundred or more cities taken, and five
times as many ships burnt or sunk.

He asked me what were the usual causes or motives that made one
country go to war with another. I answered they were in-   [25
numerable, but I should only mention a few of the chief. Sometimes
the ambition of princes, who never think they have land or people
enough to govern; sometimes the corruption of ministers, who engage
their master in a war in order to stifle or divert the clamour of the
subjects against their evil administration. Difference in opin-   [30
ions hath cost many millions of lives: for instance, whether *flesh* be
bread, or *bread* be *flesh;* whether the juice of a certain *berry* be *blood*
or *wine;* whether *whistling* be a vice or a virtue; whether it be better
to *kiss a post,* or throw it into the fire; what is the best colour for a
coat, whether *black, white, red* or *gray;* and whether it should   [35
be *long* or *short, narrow* or *wide, dirty* or *clean;* with many more.
Neither are any wars so furious and bloody, or of so long continuance,
as those occasioned by difference in opinion, especially if it be in
things indifferent.   39

Sometimes the quarrel between two princes is to decide which
of them shall dispossess a third of his dominions, where neither of
them pretend to any right. Sometimes one prince quarrelleth with

---

36. Alluding to theological and ecclesiastical quarrels between Roman
Catholic, Church of England, and Dissenting communions about the character and function of the Eucharistic elements, the place of music in church
services, the use of the crucifix, and the proper kinds of vestments.

another, for fear the other should quarrel with him. Sometimes a war is entered upon, because the enemy is too *strong,* and sometimes because he is too *weak.* Sometimes our neighbours *want* the   [45 *things* which we *have,* or *have* the things which we *want;* and we both fight, till they take ours or give us theirs. It is a very justifiable cause of war to invade a country after the people have been wasted by famine, destroyed by pestilence, or embroiled by factions among themselves. It is justifiable to enter into war against our near-   [50 est ally, when one of his towns lies convenient for us, or a territory of land, that would render our dominions round and complete. If a prince sends forces into a nation where the people are poor and ignorant, he may lawfully put half of them to death, and make slaves of the rest, in order to civilize and reduce them from   [55 their barbarous way of living. It is a very kingly, honourable, and frequent practice, when one prince desires the assistance of another to secure him against an invasion, that the assistant, when he hath driven out the invader, should seize on the dominions himself, and kill, imprison or banish the prince he came to relieve. Alliance   [60 by blood or marriage is a frequent cause of war between princes; and the nearer the kindred is, the greater is their disposition to quarrel: *poor* nations are *hungry,* and *rich* nations are *proud;* and pride and hunger will ever be at variance. For these reasons, the trade of a soldier is held the most honourable of all others; because a   [65 soldier is a Yahoo hired to kill in cold blood as many of his own species, who have never offended him, as possibly he can.

There is likewise a kind of beggarly princes in Europe, not able to make war by themselves, who hire their troops to richer nations, for so much a day to each man; of which they keep three fourths   [70 to themselves, and it is the best part of their maintenance; such are those in Germany and other northern parts of Europe.

What you have told me, (said my master) upon the subject of war, does indeed discover most admirably the effects of that reason you pretend to: however, it is happy that the shame is greater than   [75 the danger; and that nature hath left you utterly uncapable of doing much mischief: for your mouths lying flat with your faces, you can hardly bite each other to any purpose, unless by consent. Then as to the claws upon your feet before and behind, they are so short and tender, that one of our Yahoos would drive a dozen of yours before   [80 him. And therefore in recounting the numbers of those who have been killed in battle, I cannot but think that you have *said the thing which is not.*

I could not forbear shaking my head and smiling a little at his ignorance. And being no stranger to the art of war, I gave   [85 him a description of cannons, culverins, muskets, carabines, pistols, powder, swords, bayonets, sieges, retreats, attacks, undermines, countermines, bombardments, sea fights; ships sunk with a thousand men, twenty thousand killed on each side; dying groans, limbs flying in the air: smoke, noise, confusion, trampling to death under   [90 horses' feet: flight, pursuit, victory; fields strewed with carcasses left for food to dogs, and wolves, and birds of prey; plundering, stripping, ravishing, burning, and destroying. And to set forth the valour of my own dear countrymen, I assured him that I had seen them blow up a hundred enemies at once in a siege, and as many in   [95 a ship, and beheld the dead bodies come down in pieces from the clouds, to the great diversion of the spectators.

I was going on to more particulars, when my master commanded me silence. He said whoever understood the nature of Yahoos might easily believe it possible for so vile an animal to be capable of   [100 every action I had named, if their strength and cunning equalled their malice. But as my discourse had increased his abhorrence of the whole species, so he found it gave him a disturbance in his mind, to which he was wholly a stranger before. He thought his ears being used to such abominable words, might by degrees admit them   [105 with less detestation. That although he hated the Yahoos of this country, yet he no more blamed them for their odious qualities, than he did a *gnnayh* (a bird of prey) for its cruelty or a sharp stone for cutting his hoof. But when a creature pretending to reason could be capable of such enormities, he dreaded lest the corruption   [110 of that faculty might be worse than brutality itself. He seemed therefore confident, that instead of reason, we were possessed of some quality fitted to increase our natural vices; as the reflection from a troubled stream returns the image of an ill-shapen body, not only larger, but more distorted.   115

He added, that he had heard too much upon the subject of war, both in this and some former discourses. There was another point which a little perplexed him at present. I had informed him, that some of our crew left their country on account of being ruined by *Law;* that I had already explained the meaning of the word; but he   [120 was at a loss how it should come to pass, that the law which was intended for every man's preservation, should be any man's ruin. Therefore he desired to be farther satisfied what I meant by *Law,* and the dispensers thereof, according to the present practice in my own country; because he thought nature and reason were sufficient   [125 guides for a reasonable animal, as we pretended to be, in showing us what we ought to do, and what to avoid.

I assured his Honour that law was a science wherein I had not

much conversed, further than by employing advocates, in vain, upon
some injustices that had been done me: however, I would   [130
give him all the satisfaction I was able.

I said there was a society of men among us, bred up from their
youth in the art of proving by words multiplied for the purpose, that
white is *black,* and *black* is *white,* according as they are paid. To
this society all the rest of the people are slaves.   135

For example, if my neighbour hath a mind to my cow, he hires a
lawyer to prove that he ought to have my cow from me. I must then
hire another to defend my right, it being against all rules of law that
any man should be allowed to speak for himself. Now in this case I
who am the right owner lie under two great disadvantages.   [140
First, my lawyer, being practised almost from his cradle in defending
falsehood, is quite out of his element when he would be advocate for
justice, which as an office unnatural, he always attempts with great
awkwardness, if not with ill-will. The second disadvantage is that
my lawyer must proceed with great caution, or else he will be   [145
reprimanded by the judges, and abhorred by his brethren, as one
that would lessen the practice of the law. And therefore I have but
two methods to preserve my cow. The first is to gain over my adversary's lawyer with a double fee, who will then betray his client by insinuating that he hath justice on his side. The second way is   [150
for my lawyer to make my cause appear as unjust as he can, by allowing the cow to belong to my adversary; and this, if it be skilfully done,
will certainly bespeak the favour of the bench.

Now, your Honour is to know that these judges are persons appointed to decide all controversies of property, as well as for   [155
the trial of criminals; and picked out from the most dexterous lawyers,
who are grown old or lazy; and having been biassed all their lives
against truth and equity, are under such a fatal necessity of favouring
fraud, perjury, and oppression, that I have known several of them
refuse a large bribe from the side where justice lay, rather   [160
than injure the faculty, by doing anything unbecoming their nature
or their office.

It is a maxim among these lawyers, that whatever hath been done
before may legally be done again: and therefore they take special care
to record all the decisions formerly made against common   [165
justice and the general reason of mankind. These, under the name
of *precedents,* they produce as authorities, to justify the most iniqui-
tous opinions; and the judges never fail of directing accordingly.

In pleading they studiously avoid entering into the merits of the
cause, but are loud, violent, and tedious in dwelling upon all   [170
circumstances which are not to the purpose. For instance, in the case

already mentioned, they never desire to know what claim or title my adversary hath to my cow; but whether the said cow were red or black, her horns long or short; whether the field I graze her in be round or square; whether she was milked at home or abroad; [175 what diseases she is subject to, and the like. After which they consult precedents, adjourn the cause from time to time, and in ten, twenty, or thirty years, come to an issue.

It is likewise to be observed, that this society hath a peculiar cant and jargon of their own, that no other mortal can understand, [180 and wherein all their laws are written, which they take special care to multiply; whereby they have wholly confounded the very essence of truth and falsehood, of right and wrong; so that it will take thirty years to decide whether the field left me by my ancestors for six generations belongs to me, or to a stranger three hundred [185 miles off.

In the trial of persons accused of crimes against the state the method is much more short and commendable: the judge first sends to sound the disposition of those in power, after which he can easily hang or save the criminal, strictly preserving all the forms of law.   190

Here my master, interposing, said it was a pity that creatures endowed with such prodigious abilities of mind as these lawyers, by the description I gave of them, must certainly be, were not rather encouraged to be instructors of others in wisdom and knowledge. In answer to which I assured his Honour that in all points [195 out of their own trade, they were usually the most ignorant and stupid generation among us, the most despicable in common conversation, avowed enemies to all knowledge and learning; and equally disposed to pervert the general reason of mankind in every other subject of discourse, as in that of their own profession.   200

&

CHAPTER SIX. *A continuation of the state of England under Queen Anne. The character of a first minister in the courts of Europe.*

*M*Y MASTER was yet wholly at a loss to understand what motives could incite this race of lawyers to perplex, disquiet, and weary themselves by engaging in a confederacy of injustice, merely for the sake of injuring their fellow-animals; neither could he comprehend what I meant in saying they did it for *hire*. Whereupon I was at [5 much pains to describe to him the use of _money_, the materials it was made of, and the value of the metals; that when a Yahoo had got a great store of this precious substance, he was able to purchase whatever he had a mind to; the finest clothing, the noblest houses, great tracts of land, the most costly meats and drinks; and have his   [10 choice of the most beautiful females. Therefore since money alone was able to perform all these feats, our Yahoos thought they could never have enough of it to spend or save, as they found themselves inclined from their natural bent either to profusion or avarice. That the rich man enjoyed the fruit of the poor man's labour, and   [15 the latter were a thousand to one in proportion to the former. That the bulk of our people were forced to live miserably, by labouring every day for small wages to make a few live plentifully. I enlarged myself much on these and many other particulars to the same purpose; but his Honour was still to seek; for he went upon a supposi-   [20 tion that all animals had a title to their share in the productions of the earth, and especially those who presided over the rest. Therefore he desired I would let him know what these costly meats were, and how any of us happened to want them. Whereupon I enumerated as many sorts as came into my head, with the various methods of   [25 dressing them, which could not be done without sending vessels to sea to every part of the world, as well for liquors to drink, as for sauces, and innumerable other conveniences. I assured him that this whole globe of earth must be at least three times gone round, before one of our better female Yahoos could get her breakfast or a   [30 cup to put it in. He said that must needs be a miserable country which cannot furnish food for its own inhabitants. But what he chiefly wondered at, was how such vast tracts of ground as I described should be wholly without _fresh water,_ and the people put to the necessity of sending over the sea for drink. I replied that Eng-   [35 land (the dear place of my nativity) was computed to produce three times the quantity of food, more than its inhabitants were able to consume, as well as liquors extracted from grain, or pressed out of the fruit of certain trees, which made excellent drink, and the same proportion in every other convenience of life. But, in order to   [40 feed the luxury and intemperance of the males, and the vanity of the females, we sent away the greatest part of our necessary things to other countries, from whence in return we brought the materials of diseases, folly, and vice, to spend among ourselves. Hence it follows of necessity that vast numbers of our people are compelled to   [45 seek their livelihood by begging, robbing, stealing, cheating, pimping, forswearing, flattering, suborning, forging, gaming, lying, fawning, hectoring, voting, scribbling, star-gazing, poisoning, whoring, canting, libelling, freethinking, and the like occupations: every one of which terms, I was at much pains to make him understand.   50

That wine was not imported among us from foreign countries, to supply the want of water or other drinks; but because it was a sort of liquid which made us merry by putting us out of our senses; diverted all melancholy thoughts, begat wild extravagant imaginations in the brain, raised our hopes, and banished our fears; suspended   [55 every office of reason for a time, and deprived us of the use of our limbs, till we fell into a profound sleep; although it must be confessed, that we always awaked sick and dispirited; and that the use of this liquor filled us with diseases, which made our lives uncomfortable and short.   60

But beside all this, the bulk of our people supported themselves by furnishing the necessities or conveniences of life to the rich, and to each other. For instance, when I am at home and dressed as I ought to be, I carry on my body the workmanship of an hundred trades-men; the building and furniture of my house employ as many   [65 more; and five times the number to adorn my wife.

I was going on to tell him of another sort of people, who get their livelihood by attending the sick, having upon some occasions informed his Honour that many of my crew had died of diseases. But here it was with the utmost difficulty that I brought him to appre-   [70 hend what I meant. He could easily conceive that a Houyhnhnm grew weak and heavy a few days before his death, or by some acci-dent might hurt a limb. But that nature, who worketh all things to perfection, should suffer any pains to breed in our bodies, he thought impossible, and desired to know the reason of so unaccountable   [75 an evil. I told him we fed on a thousand things which operated con-trary to each other; that we ate when we were not hungry, and drank without the provocation of thirst; that we sat whole nights drinking strong liquors without eating a bit; which disposed us to sloth, in-flamed our bodies, and precipitated or prevented digestion.   [80 That prostitute female Yahoos acquired a certain malady, which bred rottenness in the bones of those who fell into their embraces; that this and many other diseases were propagated from father to son, so that great numbers come into the world with complicated maladies upon them; that it would be endless to give him a catalogue   [85 of all diseases incident to human bodies; for they could not be fewer than five or six hundred, spread over every limb and joint; in short, every part, external and intestine, having diseases appropriated to them. To remedy which there was a sort of people bred up among us, in the profession or pretence of curing the sick. And be-   [90 cause I had some skill in the faculty, I would in gratitude to his Honour let him know the whole mystery and method by which they proceed.

Their fundamental is that all diseases arise from *repletion;* from whence they conclude that a great *evacuation* of the body is   [95 necessary, either through the natural passage or upwards at the mouth. Their next business is from herbs, minerals, gums, oils, shells, salts, juices, seaweed, excrements, barks of trees, serpents, toads, frogs, spiders, dead men's flesh and bones, birds, beasts and fishes, to form a composition for smell and taste the most abominable, nau-   [100 seous and detestable they can possibly contrive, which the stomach immediately rejects with loathing; and this they call a *vomit.* Or else from the same store-house, with some other poisonous additions, they command us to take in at the orifice *above* or *below* (just as the physician then happens to be disposed) a medicine equally   [105 annoying and disgustful to the bowels; which relaxing the belly, drives down all before it, and this they call a *purge* or a *clyster.* For nature (as the physicians allege) having intended the superior anterior orifice only for the *intromission* of solids and liquids, and the inferior posterior for ejection; these artists ingeniously considering   [110 that in all diseases nature is forced out of her seat; therefore to re-place her in it the body must be treated in a manner directly contrary, by interchanging the use of each orifice, forcing solids and liquids in at the anus, and making evacuations at the mouth.

But besides real diseases we are subject to many that are   [115 only imaginary, for which the physicians have invented imaginary cures; these have their several names, and so have the drugs that are proper for them, and with these our female Yahoos are always in-fested.

One great excellency in this tribe is their skill at prog-   [120 nostics, wherein they seldom fail; their predictions in real diseases, when they rise to any degree of malignity, generally portending death, which is always in their power, when recovery is not: and therefore, upon any unexpected signs of amendment, after they have pronounced their sentence, rather than be accused as false prophets, they   [125 know how to approve their sagacity to the world by a seasonable dose.

They are likewise of special use to husbands and wives who are grown weary of their mates; to eldest sons, to great ministers of state, and often to princes.

I had formerly upon occasion discoursed with my master   [130 upon the nature of *government* in general, and particularly of our own *excellent constitution,* deservedly the wonder and envy of the whole world. But having here accidentally mentioned a *minister of state,* he commanded me some time after to inform him what species of Yahoo I particularly meant by that appellation.   135

I told him that a First or Chief Minister of State, whom I intended to describe, was a creature wholly exempt from joy and grief, love and hatred, pity and anger; at least made use of no other passions but a violent desire of wealth, power, and titles; that he applies his words to all uses, except to the indication of his mind; that [140] he never tells a *truth* but with an intent that you should take it for a *lie;* nor a *lie* but with a design that you should take it for a *truth;* that those he speaks worst of behind their backs are in the surest way of preferment; and whenever he begins to praise you to others or to yourself, you are from that day forlorn. The worst mark you [145] can receive is a *promise,* especially when it is confirmed with an oath; after which every wise man retires, and gives over all hopes.

There are three methods by which a man may rise to be chief minister: the first is by knowing how with prudence to dispose of a wife, a daughter, or a sister: the second, by betraying or [150] undermining his predecessor: and the third is by a *furious zeal* in public assemblies against the corruptions of the court. But a wise prince would rather choose to employ those who practise the last of these methods; because such zealots prove always the most obsequious and subservient to the will and passions of their master. [155] That these ministers having all employments at their disposal, preserve themselves in power by bribing the majority of a senate or great council; and at last, by an expedient called an Act of Indemnity (whereof I described the nature to him) they secure themselves from after-reckonings, and retire from the public, laden with the [160] spoils of the nation.

The palace of a chief minister, is a seminary to breed up others in his own trade: the pages, lackeys, and porter, by imitating their master, become ministers of state in their several districts, and learn to excel in the three principal ingredients, of insolence, lying, [165] and bribery. Accordingly they have a subaltern court paid to them by persons of the best rank, and sometimes by the force of dexterity and impudence arrive through several gradations to be successors to their lord.

He is usually governed by a decayed wench or favourite [170] footman, who are the tunnels through which all graces are conveyed, and may properly be called, in the last resort, the governors of the kingdom.

One day my master, having heard me mention the *nobility* of my country, was pleased to make me a compliment which I [175] could not pretend to deserve: that he was sure I must have been born of some noble family, because I far exceeded in shape, colour, and cleanliness, all the Yahoos of his nation, although I seemed to fail in strength and agility, which must be imputed to my different way of living from those other brutes; and besides I was not only   [180 endowed with the faculty of speech, but likewise with some rudiments of reason, to a degree that with all his acquaintance I passed for a prodigy.

He made me observe, that among the Houyhnhnms, the white, the sorrel, and the iron-gray, were not so exactly shaped as the   [185 bay, the dapple-gray, and the black; nor born with equal talents of the mind, or a capacity to improve them; and therefore continued always in the condition of servants, without ever aspiring to match out of their own race, which in that country would be reckoned monstrous and unnatural.   190

I made his Honour my most humble acknowledgments for the good opinion he was pleased to conceive of me; but assured him at the same time that my birth was of the lower sort, having been born of plain honest parents, who were just able to give me a tolerable education; that nobility among us was altogether a different thing   [195 from the idea he had of it; that our young noblemen are bred from their childhood in idleness and luxury; that as soon as years will permit, they consume their vigour and contract odious diseases among lewd females; and when their fortunes are almost ruined, they marry some woman of mean birth, disagreeable person, and un-   [200 sound constitution, merely for the sake of money, whom they hate and despise. That the productions of such marriages are generally scrofulous, rickety, or deformed children; by which means the family seldom continues above three generations, unless the wife take care to provide a healthy father among her neighbours or domes-   [205 tics, in order to improve and continue the breed. That a weak diseased body, a meagre countenance, and sallow complexion, are the true marks of *noble blood;* and a healthy robust appearance is so disgraceful in a man of quality that the world concludes his real father to have been a groom or a coachman. The imperfections of   [210 his mind run parallel with those of his body, being a composition of spleen, dullness, ignorance, caprice, sensuality and pride.

Without the consent of this illustrious body no law can be enacted, repealed, or altered; and these have the decision of all our possessions without appeal.   215

CHAPTER SEVEN. *The Author's great love of his native country. His master's observations upon the constitution and administration of England, as described by the Author, with parallel cases and comparisons. His master's observations upon human nature.*

. . . I have related the substance of several conversations I had with my master, during the greatest part of the time I had the honour to be in his service, but have indeed for brevity sake omitted   [35 much more than is here set down.

When I had answered all his questions, and his curiosity seemed to be fully satisfied, he sent for me one morning early, and commanding me to sit down at some distance, (an honour which he had never before conferred upon me) he said he had been very seriously   [40 considering my whole story, as far as it related both to myself and my country: that he looked upon us as a sort of animals to whose share, by what accident he could not conjecture, some small pittance of Reason had fallen, whereof we made no other use than by its assistance to aggravate our *natural* corruptions, and to acquire new ones   [45 which nature had not given us. That we disarmed ourselves of the few abilities she had bestowed; had been very successful in multiplying our original wants, and seemed to spend our whole lives in vain endeavours to supply them by our own inventions. That as to myself, it was manifest I had neither the strength nor agility   [50 of a common Yahoo, that I walked infirmly on my hinder feet, had found out a contrivance to make my claws of no use or defence, and to remove the hair from my chin, which was intended as a shelter from the sun and the weather. Lastly, that I could neither run with speed, nor climb trees like my brethren (as he called them) the   [55 Yahoos in this country.

That our institutions of government and law were plainly owing to our gross defects in Reason, and by consequence, in Virtue; because Reason alone is sufficient to govern a *rational* creature; which was therefore a character we had no pretence to challenge,   [60 even from the account I had given of my own people; although he manifestly perceived that in order to favour them I had concealed many particulars, and often *said the thing which was not.*

He was the more confirmed in this opinion, because he observed that as I agreed in every feature of my body with other   [65 Yahoos, except where it was to my real disadvantage in point of strength, speed and activity, the shortness of my claws, and some other particulars where nature had no part; so from the representation

I had given him of our lives, our manners, and our actions, he found
as near a resemblance in the disposition of our minds. He   [70
said the Yahoos were known to hate one another more than they did
any different species of animals; and the reason usually assigned was
the odiousness of their own shapes, which all could see in the rest, but
not in themselves. He had therefore begun to think it not unwise
in us to *cover* our bodies, and by that invention conceal many   [75
of our deformities from each other, which would else be hardly supportable. But he now found he had been mistaken, and that the dis-
sensions of those brutes in his country were owing to the same cause
with ours, as I had described them. For if (said he) you throw
among five Yahoos as much food as would be sufficient for   [80
fifty, they will, instead of eating peaceably, fall together by the ears,
each single one impatient to *have all to itself;* and therefore a servant
was usually employed to stand by while they were feeding abroad,
and those kept at home were tied at a distance from each other.
That if a cow died of age or accident, before a Houyhnhnm   [85
could secure it for his own Yahoos, those in the neighbourhood would
come in herds to seize it, and then would ensue such a battle as I had
described, with terrible wounds made by their claws on both sides,
although they seldom were able to kill one another, for want of such
convenient instruments of death as we had invented. At other   [90
times, the like battles have been fought between the Yahoos of several neighbourhoods without any visible cause; those of one district
watching all opportunities to surprise the next before they are prepared. But if they find their project hath miscarried, they return
home, and, for want of enemies, engage in what I call a civil   [95
war among themselves.

That in some fields of his country there are certain *shining stones*
of several colours, whereof the Yahoos are violently fond; and when
part of these stones is fixed in the earth, as it sometimes happeneth,
they will dig with their claws for whole days to get them out,   [100
then carry them away, and hide them by heaps in their kennels; but
still looking round with great caution, for fear their comrades should
find out their treasure. My master said he could never discover the
reason of this unnatural appetite, or how these stones could be of
any use to a Yahoo; but now he believed it might proceed   [105
from the same principle of Avarice which I had ascribed to mankind.
That he had once, by way of experiment, privately removed a heap
of these stones from the place where one of his Yahoos had buried
it; whereupon the sordid animal missing his treasure, by his loud
lamenting brought the whole herd to the place, there miser-   [110
ably howled, then fell to biting and tearing the rest; began to pine
away, would neither eat nor sleep nor work, till he ordered a servant

privately to convey the stones into the same hole and hide them as before; which when his Yahoo had found, he presently recovered his spirits and good humour; but took good care to remove   [115 them to a better hiding-place, and hath ever since been a very serviceable brute.

My master farther assured me, which I also observed myself, that in the fields where these shining stones abound, the fiercest and most frequent battles are fought, occasioned by perpetual inroads   [120 of the neighbouring Yahoos.

He said it was common when two Yahoos discovered such a stone in a field, and were contending which of them should be the proprietor, a third would take the advantage, and carry it away from them both; which my master would needs contend to have   [125 some kind of resemblance with our Suits at Law; wherein I thought it for our credit not to undeceive him; since the decision he mentioned was much more equitable than many decrees among us; because the plaintiff and defendant there lost nothing beside the stone they contended for, whereas our Courts of Equity would   [130 never have dismissed the cause while either of them had any thing left.

My master continuing his discourse, said there was nothing that rendered the Yahoos more odious than their undistinguishing appetite to devour every thing that came in their way, whether herbs,   [135 roots, berries, the corrupted flesh of animals, or all mingled together; and it was peculiar in their temper that they were fonder of what they could get by rapine or stealth at a greater distance than much better food provided for them at home. If their prey held out, they would eat till they were ready to burst, after which nature   [140 had pointed out to them a certain root that gave them a general evacuation.

There was also another kind of root very juicy, but somewhat rare and difficult to be found, which the Yahoos sought for with much eagerness, and would suck it with great delight; it produced   [145 the same effects that wine hath upon us. It would make them sometimes hug, and sometimes tear one another; they would howl and grin, and chatter, and reel, and tumble, and then fall asleep in the dirt.

I did indeed observe that the Yahoos were the only animals   [150 in this country subject to any diseases; which, however, were much fewer than horses have among us, and contracted not by any ill-treatment they meet with, but by the nastiness and greediness of that sordid brute. Neither has their language any more than a general appellation for those maladies, which is borrowed from the   [155 name of the beast, and called *Hnea-Yahoo,* or the *Yahoo's evil,* and the cure prescribed is a mixture of their own dung and urine forcibly put down the Yahoo's throat. This I have since often known to have been taken with success, and do freely recommend it to my country-men, for the public good, as an admirable specific against all   [160 diseases produced by repletion.

As to learning, government, arts, manufactures, and the like, my master confessed he could find little or no resemblance between the Yahoos of that country and those in ours. For he only meant to observe what parity there was in our natures. He had heard   [165 indeed some curious Houyhnhnms observe that in most herds there was a sort of ruling Yahoo (as among us there is generally some leading or principal stag in a park), who was always more *deformed* in body and *mischievous in disposition* than any of the rest. That this leader had usually a favourite as like himself as he   [170 could get, whose employment was to *lick his master's feet and pos-teriors, and drive the female Yahoos to his kennel;* for which he was now and then rewarded with a piece of ass's flesh. This favourite is hated by the whole herd, and therefore to protect himself, keeps always near the person of his leader. He usually continues   [175 in office till a worse can be found; but the very moment he is dis-carded, his successor, at the head of all the Yahoos in that district, young and old, male and female, come in a body, and discharge their excrements upon him from head to foot. But how far this might be applicable to our courts and favourites, and ministers of state,   [180 my master said I could best determine.

I durst make no return to this malicious insinuation, which debased human understanding below the sagacity of a common hound, who has judgment enough to distinguish and follow the cry of the ablest dog in the pack, without being ever mistaken.   185

My master told me there were some qualities remarkable in the Yahoos, which he had not observed me to mention, or at least very slightly, in the accounts I had given him of human kind. He said those animals, like other brutes, had their females in common; but in this they differed, that the she Yahoo would admit the male   [190 while she was pregnant; and that the hes would quarrel and fight with the females as fiercely as with each other. Both which practices were such degrees of infamous brutality, that no other sensitive crea-ture ever arrived at.

Another thing he wondered at in the Yahoos was their   [195 strange disposition to nastiness and dirt, whereas there appears to be a natural love of cleanliness in all other animals. As to the two former accusations, I was glad to let them pass without any reply, because I had not a word to offer upon them in defence of my species, which otherwise I certainly had done from my own inclinations.   [200

But I could have easily vindicated human kind from the imputation of singularity upon the last article, if there had been any *swine* in that country (as unluckily for me there were not), which although it may be a *sweeter quadruped* than a *Yahoo,* cannot I humbly conceive in justice pretend to more cleanliness; and so his [205 Honour himself must have owned, if he had seen their filthy way of feeding, and their custom of wallowing and sleeping in the mud.

My master likewise mentioned another quality which his servants had discovered in several Yahoos, and to him was wholly unaccountable. He said, a fancy would sometimes take a Yahoo to re- [210 tire into a corner, to lie down and howl and groan, and spurn away all that came near him, although he were young and fat, wanted neither food nor water; nor did the servants imagine what could possibly ail him. And the only remedy they found was to set him to hard work, after which he would infallibly come to himself. [215 To this I was silent out of partiality to my own kind; yet here I could plainly discover the true seeds of *spleen,* which only seizeth on the lazy, the luxurious, and the rich; who, if they were forced to undergo the same regimen, I would undertake for the cure.

His Honour had further observed that a female Yahoo [220 would often stand behind a bank or a bush, to gaze on the young males passing by, and then appear, and hide, using many antic gestures and grimaces; at which time it was observed that she had a most offensive smell; and when any of the males advanced, would slowly retire, looking often back, and with a counterfeit show of [225 fear, run off into some convenient place where she knew the male would follow her.

At other times if a female stranger came among them, three or four of her own sex would get about her, and stare and chatter, and grin, and smell her all over; and then turn off with gestures that [230 seemed to express contempt and disdain.

Perhaps my master might refine a little in these speculations, which he had drawn from what he observed himself, or had been told him by others; however, I could not reflect without some amazement, and much sorrow, that the rudiments of lewdness, coquetry, cen- [235 sure, and scandal, should have place by instinct in womankind.

I expected every moment that my master would accuse the Yahoos of those unnatural appetites in both sexes, so common among us. But nature, it seems, hath not been so expert a school-mistress; and these politer pleasures are entirely the production of art and [240 reason, on our side of the globe.

CHAPTER EIGHT. *The Author relates several particulars of the Yahoos. The great virtues of the Houyhnhnms. The education and exercises of their youth. Their general assembly.*

As I ought to have understood human nature much better than I supposed it possible for my master to do, so it was easy to apply the character he gave of the Yahoos to myself and my countrymen; and I believed I could yet make farther discoveries from my own observation. I therefore often begged his favour to let me [5 go among the herds of Yahoos in the neighbourhood, to which he always very graciously consented, being perfectly convinced that the hatred I bore those brutes would never suffer me to be corrupted by them; and his Honour ordered one of his servants, a strong sorrel nag, very honest and good-natured, to be my guard, without [10 whose protection I durst not undertake such adventures. For I have already told the reader how much I was pestered by those odious animals upon my first arrival. I afterwards failed very narrowly three or four times of falling into their clutches, when I happened to stray at any distance without my hanger. And I have reason [15 to believe they had some imagination that I was their own species, which I often assisted myself, by stripping up my sleeves, and showing my naked arms and breast in their sight, when my protector was with me: at which times they would approach as near as they durst, and imitate my actions after the manner of monkeys, [20 but ever with great signs of hatred; as a tame jack-daw with cap and stockings is always persecuted by the wild ones, when he happens to be got among them.

They are prodigiously nimble from their infancy; however, I once caught a young male of three years old, and endeavoured by [25 all marks of tenderness to make it quiet; but the little imp fell a squalling and scratching and biting with such violence that I was forced to let it go; and it was high time, for a whole troop of old ones came about us at the noise; but finding the cub was safe (for away it ran), and my sorrel nag being by, they durst not ven- [30 ture near us. I observed the young animal's flesh to smell very rank, and the stink was somewhat between a weasel and a fox, but much more disagreeable. I forgot another circumstance (and perhaps I might have the reader's pardon if it were wholly omitted), that while I held the odious vermin in my hands, it voided its filthy ex- [35 crements of a yellow liquid substance, all over my clothes; but by good fortune there was a small brook hard by, where I washed myself as clean as I could; although I durst not come into my master's presence, until I were sufficiently aired.

By what I could discover, the Yahoos appear to be the [40 most unteachable of all animals, their capacities never reaching higher than to draw or carry burdens. Yet I am of opinion this defect ariseth chiefly from a perverse, restive disposition. For they are cunning, malicious, treacherous, and revengeful. They are strong and hardy, but of a cowardly spirit, and by consequence, insolent, abject, [45 and cruel. It is observed that the red-haired of both sexes are more libidinous and mischievous than the rest, whom yet they much exceed in strength and activity.

The Houyhnhnms keep the Yahoos for present use in huts not far from the house; but the rest are sent abroad to certain fields, [50 where they dig up roots, eat several kinds of herbs, and search about for carrion, or sometimes catch weasels and *luhimuhs* (a sort of wild rat), which they greedily devour. Nature hath taught them to dig deep holes with their nails on the side of a rising ground, wherein they lie by themselves; only the kennels of the females are larger, [55 sufficient to hold two or three cubs.

They swim from their infancy like frogs, and are able to continue long under water, where they often take fish, which the females carry home to their young. And upon this occasion, I hope the reader will pardon my relating an odd adventure. 60

Being one day abroad with my protector the sorrel nag, and the weather exceeding hot, I entreated him to let me bathe in a river that was near. He consented, and I immediately stripped myself stark naked, and went down softly into the stream. It happened that a young female Yahoo, standing behind a bank, saw the whole [65 proceeding, and inflamed by desire, as the nag and I conjectured, came running with all speed, and leaped into the water, within five yards of the place where I bathed. I was never in my life so terribly frighted; the nag was grazing at some distance, not suspecting any harm. She embraced me after a most fulsome manner; I [70 roared as loud as I could, and the nag came galloping towards me, whereupon she quitted her grasp, with the utmost reluctancy, and leaped upon the opposite bank, where she stood gazing and howling all the time I was putting on my clothes.

This was matter of diversion to my master and his family, [75 as well as of mortification to myself. For now I could no longer deny that I was a real Yahoo in every limb and feature, since the females had a natural propensity to me, as one of their own species. . . .

CHAPTER TEN. *The Author's economy, and happy life among the Houyhnhnms. His great improvement in virtue, by conversing with them. Their conversations. The Author has notice given him by his master that he must depart from the country. He falls into a swoon for grief, but submits. He contrives and finishes a canoe, by the help of a fellow-servant, and puts to sea at a venture.*

I HAD settled my little economy to my own heart's content. My master had ordered a room to be made for me after their manner, about six yards from the house; the sides and floors of which I plastered with clay, and covered with rush-mats of my own contriving: I had beaten hemp, which there grows wild, and made of it a   [5 sort of ticking; this I filled with the feathers of several birds I had taken with springes made of Yahoos' hairs, and were excellent food. I had worked two chairs with my knife, the sorrel nag helping me in the grosser and more laborious part. When my clothes were worn to rags, I made myself others with the skins of rabbits, and of   [10 a certain beautiful animal about the same size, called *muhnoh,* the skin of which is covered with a fine down. Of these I likewise made very tolerable stockings. I soled my shoes with wood which I cut from a tree and fitted to the upper leather, and when this was worn out, I supplied it with the skins of Yahoos dried in the sun. I often   [15 got honey out of hollow trees, which I mingled with water, or ate with my bread. No man could more verify the truth of these two maxims, *That nature is very easily satisfied;* and *That necessity is the mother of invention.* I enjoyed perfect health of body, and tranquillity of mind; I did not feel the treachery or inconstancy of a friend, nor the   [20 injuries of a secret or open enemy. I had no occasion of bribing, flattering, or pimping to procure the favour of any great man or of his opinion. I wanted no fence against fraud or oppression: here was neither physician to destroy my body, nor lawyer to ruin my fortune; no informer to watch my words and actions, or forge accusa-   [25 tions against me for hire; here were no gibers, censurers, backbiters, pickpockets, highwaymen, housebreakers, attorneys, bawds, buffoons, gamesters, politicians, wits, splenetics, tedious talkers, controvertists, ravishers, murderers, robbers, virtuosos; no leaders or followers of party and faction; no encouragers to vice, by seducement or ex-   [30 amples; no dungeon, axes, gibbets, whipping-posts, or pillories; no cheating shopkeepers or mechanics; no pride, vanity, or affectation; no fops, bullies, drunkards, strolling whores, or poxes; no ranting, lewd,

expensive wives; no stupid, proud pedants; no importunate, overbear-
ing, quarrelsome, noisy, roaring, empty, conceited, swearing [35
companions; no scoundrels raised from the dust for the sake of their
vices; or nobility thrown into it on account of their virtues; no lords,
fiddlers, judges, or dancing-masters.

I had the favour of being admitted to several Houyhnhnms, who
came to visit or dine with my master; where his Honour gra- [40
ciously suffered me to wait in the room, and listen to their discourse.
Both he and his company would often descend to ask me questions,
and receive my answers. I had also sometimes the honour of attending
my master in his visits to others. I never presumed to speak, except in
answer to a question; and then I did it with inward regret, be- [45
cause it was a loss of so much time for improving myself; but I was
infinitely delighted with the station of an humble auditor in such conversations, where nothing passed but what was useful, expressed in
the fewest and most significant words; where (as I have already said)
the greatest Decency was observed, without the least degree of [50
ceremony; where no person spoke without being pleased himself, and
pleasing his companions; where there was no interruption, tediousness,
heat, or difference of sentiments. They have a notion that when people
are met together, a short silence doth much improve conversation: this
I found to be true; for during those little intermissions of talk, [55
new ideas would arise in their minds, which very much enlivened the
discourse. Their subjects are generally on friendship and benevolence;
on order and economy; sometimes upon the visible operations of nature,
or ancient traditions; upon the bounds and limits of virtue; upon the
unerring rules of reason, or upon some determinations to be [60
taken at the next great assembly; and often upon the various excellencies
of poetry. I may add without vanity that my presence often gave them
sufficient matter for discourse, because it afforded my master an occasion
of letting his friends into the history of me and my country, upon which
they were all pleased to descant in a manner not very advanta- [65
geous to human kind; and for that reason I shall not repeat what they
said: only I may be allowed to observe that his Honour, to my great admiration, appeared to understand the nature of Yahoos much better
than myself. He went through all our vices and follies, and discovered
many which I had never mentioned to him, by only supposing [70
what qualities a Yahoo of their country, with a small proportion of
reason, might be capable of exerting; and concluded, with too much
probability, how vile as well as miserable such a creature must be.

I freely confess that all the little knowledge I have of any value was
acquired by the lectures I received from my master, and from [75
hearing the discourses of him and his friends; to which I should be

prouder to listen than to dictate to the greatest and wisest assembly in Europe. I admired the strength, comeliness, and speed of the inhabitants; and such a constellation of virtues in such amiable persons produced in me the highest veneration. At first, indeed, I did   [80 not feel that natural awe which the Yahoos and all other animals bear towards them; but it grew upon me by degrees, much sooner than I imagined, and was mingled with a respectful love and gratitude, that they would condescend to distinguish me from the rest of my species.

When I thought of my family, my friends, my countrymen,   [85 or human race in general, I considered them as they really were, Yahoos in shape and disposition, perhaps a little more civilized, and qualified with the gift of speech, but making no other use of reason than to improve and multiply those vices whereof their brethren in this country had only the share that nature allotted them.   [90 When I happened to behold the reflection of my own form in a lake or fountain, I turned away my face in horror and detestation of myself, and could better endure the sight of a common Yahoo than of my own person. By conversing with the Houyhnhnms, and looking upon them with delight, I fell to imitate their gait and gesture,   [95 which is now grown into an habit; and my friends often tell me in a blunt way, that *I trot like a horse:* which, however, I take for a great compliment. Neither shall I disown that in speaking I am apt to fall into the voice and manner of the Houyhnhnms, and hear myself ridiculed on that account without the least mortification.   100

In the midst of all this happiness, and when I looked upon myself to be fully settled for life, my master sent for me one morning a little earlier than his usual hour. I observed by his countenance that he was in some perplexity, and at a loss how to begin what he had to speak. After a short silence he told me he did not know how I   [105 would take what he was going to say: that in the last general assembly, when the affair of the Yahoos was entered upon, the representatives had taken offence at his keeping a Yahoo (meaning myself) in his family more like a Houyhnhnm than a brute animal. That he was known frequently to converse with me, as if he could receive   [110 some advantage or pleasure in my company; that such a practice was not agreeable to reason or nature, nor a thing ever heard of before among them. The assembly did therefore *exhort* him, either to employ me like the rest of my species, or command me to swim back to the place from whence I came. . . .   115

❧

CHAPTER ELEVEN. *The Author's dangerous voyage. He arrives at New Holland, hoping to settle there. Is wounded with an arrow by one of the natives. Is seized and carried by force into a Portuguese ship. The great civilities of the Captain, Pedro de Mendez. The Author arrives at England.*

. . . Our voyage passed without any considerable accident. In gratitude to the Captain I sometimes sat with him at his earnest re-   [1 quest, and strove to conceal my antipathy to human kind, although it often broke out; which he suffered to pass without observation. But the greatest part of the day I confined myself to my cabin, to avoid seeing any of the crew. The Captain had often entreated me to strip myself of my savage dress, and offered to lend me the best suit of   [5 clothes he had. This I would not be prevailed on to accept, abhorring to cover myself with any thing that had been on the back of a Yahoo. I only desired he would lend me two clean shirts, which having been washed since he wore them, I believed would not so much defile me. These I changed every second day, and washed them myself.   [10

We arrived at Lisbon, Nov. 5, 1715. At our landing the Captain forced me to cover myself with his cloak, to prevent the rabble from crowding about me. I was conveyed to his own house, and at my earnest request he led me up to the highest room backwards. I conjured him to conceal from all persons what I had told him of the Hou-   [15 yhnhnms; because the least hint of such a story would not only draw numbers of people to see me, but probably put me in danger of being imprisoned, or burnt by the Inquisition. The Captain persuaded me to accept a suit of clothes newly made; but I would not suffer the tailor to take my measure; however, Don Pedro being almost of my   [20 size, they fitted me well enough. He accoutred me with other necessaries all new, which I aired for twenty-four hours before I would use them.

[Gulliver is obliged by the Houyhnhnms to depart. Putting to sea in a large canoe, he reaches an island where he intends to make his home and from which he is rescued against his will by the crew of a Portuguese ship. They take him to their captain, Don Pedro de Mendez.]

The Captain had no wife, nor above three servants, none of which were suffered to attend at meals; and his whole deportment [25 was so obliging, added to very good *human* understanding, that I really began to tolerate his company. He gained so far upon me that I ventured to look out of the back window. By degrees I was brought into another room, from whence I peeped into the street, but drew my head back in a fright. In a week's time he seduced me down [30 to the door. I found my terror gradually lessened, but my hatred and contempt seemed to increase. I was at last bold enough to walk the street in his company, but kept my nose well stopped with rue, or sometimes with tobacco.

In ten days Don Pedro, to whom I had given some account [35 of my domestic affairs, put it upon me as a point of honour and conscience, that I ought to return to my native country, and live at home with my wife and children. He told me there was an English ship in the port just ready to sail, and he would furnish me with all things necessary. It would be tedious to repeat his arguments, and [40 my contradictions. He said it was altogether impossible to find such a solitary island as I had desired to live in; but I might command in my own house, and pass my time in a manner of recluse as I pleased.

I complied at last, finding I could not do better. I left Lisbon the twenty-fourth day of November, in an English merchantman, [45 but who was the master I never inquired. Don Pedro accompanied me to the ship, and lent me twenty pounds. He took kind leave of me, and embraced me at parting; which I bore as well as I could. During this last voyage I had no commerce with the master or any of his men; but pretending I was sick, kept close in my cabin. [50 On the fifth of December, 1715, we cast anchor in the Downs about nine in the morning, and at three in the afternoon I got safe to my house at Rotherhith.

My wife and family received me with great surprise and joy, because they concluded me certainly dead; but I must freely confess [55 the sight of them filled me only with hatred, disgust, and contempt; and the more by reflecting on the near alliance I had to them. For although since my unfortunate exile from the Houyhnhnm country, I had compelled myself to tolerate the sight of Yahoos, and to converse with Don Pedro de Mendez, yet my memory and imagina- [60 tion were perpetually filled with the virtues and ideas of those exalted Houyhnhnms. And when I began to consider that by copulating with one of the Yahoo species I had become a parent of more, it struck me with the utmost shame, confusion, and horror.

As soon as I entered the house, my wife took me in her [65

arms and kissed me; at which, having not been used to the touch of that odious animal for so many years, I fell in a swoon for almost an hour. At the time I am writing, it is five years since my last return to England: during the first year I could not endure my wife or children in my presence, the very smell of them was intol-   [70 erable; much less could I suffer them to eat in the same room. To this hour they dare not presume to touch my bread, or drink out of the same cup; neither was I ever able to let one of them take me by the hand. The first money I laid out was to buy two young stone-horses, which I keep in a good stable, and next to them the groom   [75 is my greatest favourite; for I feel my spirits revived by the smell he contracts in the stable. My horses understand me tolerably well; I converse with them at least four hours every day. They are strangers to bridle or saddle; they live in great amity with me, and friendship to each other   80

CHAPTER TWELVE. *The Author's veracity. His design in publishing this work. His censure of those travellers who swerve from the truth. The Author clears himself from any sinister ends in writing. An objection answered. The method of planting colonies. His native country commended. The right of the Crown to those countries described by the Author, is justified. The difficulty of conquering them. The Author takes his last leave of the reader; proposeth his manner of living for the future; gives good advice, and concludeth.*

. . . I began last week to permit my wife to sit at dinner with me, at the farthest end of a long table, and to answer (but with the utmost brevity) the few questions I ask her. Yet the smell of a Yahoo continuing very offensive, I always keep my nose well stopped with rue, lavender, or tobacco leaves. And although it be hard for a man   [5 late in life to remove old habits; I am not altogether out of hopes in some time to suffer a neighbour Yahoo in my company, with the apprehensions I am yet under of his teeth or his claws.

My reconcilement to the Yahoo-kind in general might not be so difficult, if they would be content with those vices and follies   [10 only which nature hath entitled them to. I am not in the least provoked at the sight of a lawyer, a pick-pocket, a colonel, a fool, a lord, a gamester, a politician, a whore-monger, a physician, an evidence, a

13. *evidence:* informer.

suborner, an attorney, a traitor, or the like: this is all according to the due course of things: but when I behold a lump of deformity [15 and diseases, both in body and mind, smitten with *pride,* it immediately breaks all the measures of my patience; neither shall I be ever able to comprehend how such an animal and such a vice could tally together.

.   .   .   .

John Gay

The Beggar's Opera
(1728)

DRAMATIS PERSONÆ — *London lowlife*

Men

PEACHUM
LOCKIT
MACHEATH — *triangle*
FILCH

JEMMY TWITCHER
CROOK-FINGERED JACK
WAT DREARY
ROBIN OF BAGSHOT
NIMMING NED
HARRY PADINGTON
MATT OF THE MINT
BEN BUDGE
BEGGAR
PLAYER

} *Macheath's gang*

Women

MRS. PEACHUM
POLLY PEACHUM
LUCY LOCKIT
DIANA TRAPES

MRS. COAXER
DOLLY TRULL
MRS. VIXEN
BETTY DOXY
JENNY DIVER
MRS. SLAMMEKIN
SUKY TAWDRY
MOLLY BRAZEN

} *Women of the town*

Constables, Drawers, Turnkey, etc.

INTRODUCTION

[BEGGAR, PLAYER.]

BEGGAR. If poverty be a title to poetry, I am sure nobody can dispute mine. I own myself of the company of beggars, and I make one at their weekly festivals at St. Giles's. I have a small yearly salary for

---

DRAM. PERS.: *Nimming:* To "nim" is to steal. INTROD.: 3. *St. Gile's:* London's Augustan equivalent of New York's Bowery.

my catches and am welcome to a dinner there whenever I please, which is more than most poets can say.   5

PLAYER. As we live by the muses, it is but gratitude in us to encourage poetical merit wherever we find it. The muses, contrary to all other ladies, pay no distinction to dress, and never partially mistake the pertness of embroidery for wit, nor the modesty of want for dullness. Be the author who he will, we push his play as far as it [10 will go. So (though you are in want) I wish you success heartily.

BEGGAR. This piece, I own, was originally writ for the celebrating the marriage of James Chanter and Moll Lay, two most excellent balladsingers. I have introduced the similes that are in your celebrated operas: the Swallow, the Moth, the Bee, the Ship, the Flower, [15 etc. Besides, I have a prison-scene, which the ladies always reckon charmingly pathetic. As to the parts, I have observed such a nice impartiality to our two ladies, that it is impossible for either of them to take offence. I hope I may be forgiven, that I have not made my opera throughout unnatural, like those in vogue; for I have [20 no recitative: excepting this, as I have consented to have neither prologue nor epilogue, it must be allowed an opera in all its forms. The piece indeed hath been heretofore frequently represented by ourselves in our great room at St. Giles's, so that I cannot too often acknowledge your charity in bringing it now on the stage.   25

PLAYER. But I see 'tis time for us to withdraw; the actors are preparing to begin. Play away the overture.   [*Exeunt.*

Act I

SCENE I. PEACHUM'S *house.*

[PEACHUM *sitting at a table with a large book of accounts before him.*]

AIR I—*An old woman clothed in gray, etc.*

Through all the employments of life,
  Each neighbor abuses his brother;
Whore and rogue they call husband and wife:
  All professions be-rogue one another.
The priest calls the lawyer a cheat,   5

---

4. *catches:* songs. 6. *As . . . muses:* i.e., by acting in the works of men who write. 18. *two ladies:* referring to a notorious quarrel between two operatic stars, Cuzzoni and Faustina: cf. also Polly's and Lucy's quarrel in II xiii.

> The lawyer be-knaves the divine;
> And the statesman, because he's so great,
> Thinks his trade as honest as mine.

A lawyer is an honest employment; so is mine. Like me, too, he acts
in a double capacity, both against rogues and for 'em; for 'tis　　[10
but fitting that we should protect and encourage cheats, since we
live by 'em.

SCENE II

[PEACHUM, FILCH.]

FILCH. Sir, Black Moll hath sent word her trial comes on in the afternoon, and she hopes you will order matters so as to bring her off.

PEACHUM. Why, she may plead her belly at worst; to my knowledge she hath taken care of that security. But as the wench is very
active and industrious, you may satisfy her that I'll soften the　　[5
evidence.

FILCH. Tom Gagg, sir, is found guilty.

PEACHUM. A lazy dog! When I took him the time before, I told
him what he would come to if he did not mend his hand. This is
death without reprieve. I may venture to book him. (*Writes.*)　　[10
For Tom Gagg, forty pounds. Let Betty Sly know that I'll save her
from transportation, for I can get more by her staying in England.

FILCH. Betty hath brought more goods into our lock to-year, than
any five of the gang; and in truth, 'tis a pity to lose so good a customer.

PEACHUM. If none of the gang take her off, she may, in the　　[15
common course of business, live a twelve-month longer. I love to let
women 'scape. A good sportsman always lets the hen partridges fly,
because the breed of the game depends upon them. Besides, here the
law allows us no reward; there is nothing to be got by the death of
women—except our wives.　　　20

FILCH. Without dispute, she is a fine woman! 'Twas to her I was
obliged for my education, and (to say a bold word) she hath trained
up more young fellows to the business than the gaming-table.

PEACHUM. Truly, Filch, thy observation is right. We and the surgeons are more beholden to women than all the professions　　[25
besides.

ACT I, SCENE II: 3. *her belly:* i.e., her pregnancy. 13. *lock:* i.e., "fence"
(depot for stolen goods). 14. *customer:* two meanings besides the usual one
are relevant, especially the second: (1) one who collects a tax on the
public: cf. I iii 22; (2) a prostitute: cf. III vi 23.

FILCH.

AIR II—*The bonny gray-eyed morn, etc.*

'Tis woman that seduces all mankind,
　　By her we first were taught the wheedling arts;
Her very eyes can cheat; when most she's kind,
　　She tricks us of our money with our hearts.   30
For her, like wolves by night we roam for prey,
　　And practise every fraud to bribe her charms;
For suits of love, like law, are won by pay,
　　And beauty must be fee'd into our arms.

PEACHUM. But make haste to Newgate, boy, and let my   [35
friends know what I intend; for I love to make them easy one way
or other.

FILCH. When a gentleman is long kept in suspense, penitence may
break his spirit ever after. Besides, certainty gives a man a good air
upon his trial, and makes him risk another without fear or   [40
scruple. But I'll away, for 'tis a pleasure to be the messenger of comfort to friends in affliction.   [*Exit.*

SCENE III

[PEACHUM.]

PEACHUM. But 'tis now high time to look about me for a decent
execution against next sessions. I hate a lazy rogue, by whom one can
get nothing till he is hanged. A register of the gang: (*Reading.*)
"Crook-fingered Jack. A year and a half in the service." Let me see
how much the stock owes to his industry; one, two, three, four,   [5
five gold watches, and seven silver ones.—A mighty clean-handed fellow!—Sixteen snuff-boxes, five of them of true gold. Six dozen of
handkerchiefs, four silver-hilted swords, half a dozen of shirts, three
tie-periwigs, and a piece of broadcloth.—Considering these are only the
fruits of his leisure hours, I don't know a prettier fellow, for   [10
no man alive hath a more engaging presence of mind upon the road.
"Wat Dreary, alias Brown Will"—an irregular dog, who hath an
underhand way of disposing of his goods. I'll try him only for a sessions or two longer upon his good behavior. "Harry Padington"—a

---

35. *Newgate:* Newgate prison.
　　SCENE III: 2. *sessions:* of the criminal court. 11. *upon the road:* in a highway robbery.

poor petty-larceny rascal, without the least genius; that fellow, [15
though he were to live these six months, will never come to the gallows with any credit. "Slippery Sam"—he goes off the next sessions,
for the villain hath the impudence to have views of following his
trade as a tailor, which he calls an honest employment. "Matt of the
Mint"—listed not above a month ago, a promising sturdy fel- [20
low, and diligent in his way: somewhat too bold and hasty, and may
raise good contributions on the public, if he does not cut himself short
by murder. "Tom Tipple"—a guzzling, soaking sot, who is always
too drunk to stand himself, or to make others stand. A cart is absolutely necessary for him. "Robin of Bagshot, alias Gorgon, [25
alias Bluff Bob, alias Carbuncle, alias Bob Booty!—"

SCENE IV

[PEACHUM, MRS. PEACHUM.]

MRS. PEACHUM. What of Bob Booty, husband? I hope nothing bad
hath betided him. You know, my dear, he's a favorite customer of
mine. 'Twas he made me a present of this ring.

PEACHUM. I have set his name down in the black list, that's all, my
dear; he spends his life among women, and as soon as his [5
money is gone, one or other of the ladies will hang him for the reward,
and there's forty pound lost to us forever.

MRS. PEACHUM. You know, my dear, I never meddle in matters of
death; I always leave those affairs to you. Women indeed are bitter
bad judges in these cases, for they are so partial to the brave [10
that they think every man handsome who is going to the camp or
the gallows.

AIR III—*Cold and raw, etc.*

If any wench Venus's girdle wear,
    Though she be never so ugly,
Lilies and roses will quickly appear,   15
    And her face look wondrous smugly.
Beneath the left ear so fit but a cord,
    (A rope so charming a zone is!)
The youth in his cart hath the air of a lord,
    And we cry, There dies an Adonis!   20

---

24. *cart:* hangman's cart. 25-6. references to Walpole. 25. *Bagshot:* Bagshot Heath, a place notorious for robberies.
SCENE IV: 11. *The camp:* military service.

But really, husband, you should not be too hard-hearted, for you never had a finer, braver set of men than at present. We have not had a murder among them all, these seven months. And truly, my dear, that is a great blessing.

PEACHUM. What a dickens is the woman always a-whim- [25 p'ring about murder for? No gentleman is ever looked upon the worse for killing a man in his own defence; and if business cannot be carried on without it, what would you have a gentleman do?

MRS. PEACHUM. If I am in the wrong, my dear, you must excuse me, for nobody can help the frailty of an over-scrupulous con- [30 science.

PEACHUM. Murder is as fashionable a crime as a man can be guilty of. How many fine gentlemen have we in Newgate every year, purely upon that article! If they have wherewithal to persuade the jury to bring it in manslaughter, what are they the worse for it? So [35 my dear, have done upon this subject. Was Captain Macheath here this morning, for the bank-notes he left with you last week?

MRS. PEACHUM. Yes, my dear; and though the bank has stopped payment, he was so cheerful and so agreeable! Sure there is not a finer gentleman upon the road than the captain! If he comes from [40 Bagshot at any reasonable hour he hath promised to make one this evening with Polly and me, and Bob Booty, at a party of quadrille. Pray, my dear, is the captain rich?

PEACHUM. The captain keeps too good company ever to grow rich. Marybone and the chocolate-houses are his undoing. The man [45 that proposes to get money by play should have the education of a fine gentleman, and be trained up to it from his youth.

MRS. PEACHUM. Really, I am sorry upon Polly's account the captain hath not more discretion. What business hath he to keep company with lords and gentlemen? he should leave them to prey upon [50 one another.

PEACHUM. Upon Polly's account! What a plague does the woman mean?—Upon Polly's account!

MRS. PEACHUM. Captain Macheath is very fond of the girl.

PEACHUM. And what then?   55

MRS. PEACHUM. If I have any skill in the ways of women, I am sure Polly thinks him a very pretty man.

PEACHUM. And what then? You would not be so mad to have the wench marry him! Gamesters and highwaymen are generally very good to their whores, but they are very devils to their wives. [60

MRS. PEACHUM. But if Polly should be in love, how should we help

---

45. *Marybone:* a gambling resort.

her, or how can she help herself? Poor girl, I am in the utmost concern about her.

AIR IV—*Why is your faithful slave disdained? etc.*

> If love the virgin's heart invade,
> How, like a moth, the simple maid   65
>   Still plays about the flame!
> If soon she be not made a wife,
> Her honour's singed, and then, for life,
> She's—what I dare not name.

PEACHUM. Look ye, wife. A handsome wench in our way of   [70
business is as profitable as at the bar of a Temple coffee-house, who
looks upon it as her livelihood to grant every liberty but one. You see
I would indulge the girl as far as prudently we can,—in anything but
marriage! After that, my dear, how shall we be safe? Are we not
then in her husband's power? For a husband hath the abso-   [75
lute power over all a wife's secrets but her own. If the girl had the
discretion of a court lady, who can have a dozen young fellows at her
ear without complying with one, I should not matter it; but Polly is
tinder, and a spark will at once set her on a flame. Married! If the
wench does not know her own profit, sure she knows her own   [80
pleasure better than to make herself a property! My daughter to me
should be, like a court lady to a minister of state, a key to the whole
gang. Married! if the affair is not already done, I'll terrify her from
it, by the example of our neighbors.

MRS. PEACHUM. Mayhap, my dear, you may injure the girl.   [85
She loves to imitate the fine ladies, and she may only allow the captain
liberties in the view of interest.

PEACHUM. But 'tis your duty, my dear, to warn the girl against her
ruin, and to instruct her how to make the most of her beauty. I'll go
to her this moment, and sift her. In the meantime, wife, rip   [90
out the coronets and marks of these dozen of cambric handkerchiefs,
for I can dispose of them this afternoon to a chap in the city.   [*Exit.*

SCENE V

[MRS. PEACHUM.]

MRS. PEACHUM. Never was a man more out of the way in an argu-

---

71. *Temple:* the section of London where the Inns of Court (Inner and
Middle Temple) are located. 81. *property:* cf. I v 6. 92. *chap:* chapman,
i.e., customer.

ment than my husband! Why must our Polly, forsooth, differ from
her sex, and love only her husband? And why must Polly's marriage,
contrary to all observation, make her the less followed by other men?
All men are thieves in love, and like a woman the better for   [5
being another's property.

AIR v—*Of all the simple things we do, etc.*

A maid is like the golden ore,
    Which hath guineas intrinsical in't;
Whose worth is never known, before
    It is tried and impressed in the mint.   10
A wife's like a guinea in gold,
    Stamped with the name of her spouse;
Now here, now there; is bought, or is sold;
    And is current in every house.

SCENE VI

[MRS. PEACHUM, FILCH.]

MRS. PEACHUM. Come hither, Filch. I am as fond of this child as
though my mind misgave me he were my own. He hath as fine a hand
at picking a pocket as a woman, and is as nimble-fingered as a juggler.
If an unlucky session does not cut the rope of thy life, I pronounce,
boy, thou wilt be a great man in history. Where was your   [5
post last night, my boy?

FILCH. I plied at the opera, madam; and considering 'twas neither
dark nor rainy, so that there was no great hurry in getting chairs and
coaches, made a tolerable hand on't. These seven handkerchiefs,
madam.   10

MRS. PEACHUM. Colored ones, I see. They are of sure sale from our
warehouse at Redriff among the seamen.

FILCH. And this snuff-box.

MRS. PEACHUM. Set in gold! A pretty encouragement this to a young
beginner.   15

FILCH. I had a fair tug at a charming gold watch. Pox take the
tailors for making the fobs so deep and narrow. It stuck by the way,
and I was forced to make my escape under a coach. Really, madam,
I fear, I shall be cut off in the flower of my youth, so that every now
and then (since I was pumped) I have thoughts of taking up   [20
and going to sea.

12. *Redriff:* London's dock section. 20. *pumped:* punished (as young offenders often were) by being held under the public pump.

MRS. PEACHUM. You should go to Hockley-in-the-Hole and to Mary-bone, child, to learn valor. These are the schools that have bred so many brave men. I thought, boy, by this time, thou hadst lost fear as well as shame.—Poor lad! how little does he know as yet of   [25 the Old Bailey! For the first fact I'll insure thee from being hanged; and going to sea, Filch, will come time enough upon a sentence of transportation. But now, since you have nothing better to do, even go to your book, and learn your catechism; for really a man makes but an ill figure in the ordinary's paper, who cannot give a satis-   [30 factory answer to his questions. But, hark you, my lad. Don't tell me a lie; for you know I hate a liar. Do you know of anything that hath passed between Captain Macheath and our Polly?

FILCH. I beg you, madam, don't ask me; for I must either tell a lie to you or to Miss Polly—for I promised her I would not tell.   [35

MRS. PEACHUM. But when the honor of our family is concerned—

FILCH. I shall lead a sad life with Miss Polly if ever she come to know that I told you. Besides, I would not willingly forfeit my own honor by betraying anybody.

MRS. PEACHUM. Yonder comes my husband and Polly. Come,   [40 Filch, you shall go with me into my own room, and tell me the whole story. I'll give thee a glass of a most delicious cordial that I keep for my own drinking.   [*Exeunt.*

SCENE VII

[PEACHUM, POLLY.]

POLLY. I know as well as any of the fine ladies how to make the most of myself and of my man too. A woman knows how to be mercenary, though she hath never been in a court or at an assembly. We have it in our natures, papa. If I allow Captain Macheath some trifling liberties, I have this watch and other visible marks of his   [5 favor to show for it. A girl who cannot grant some things, and refuse what is most material, will make but a poor hand of her beauty, and soon be thrown upon the common.

AIR VI—*What shall I do to show how much I love her, etc.*

Virgins are like the fair flower in its lustre,
   Which in the garden enamels the ground;   10
Near it the bees in play flutter and cluster,

---

23. *to . . . valor:* because Hockley-in-the-Hole was the scene of bloody sports like bear-baiting. 26. *Old Bailey:* London's criminal court. 30. *ordinary's paper:* the prison chaplain's report of confessions.

And gaudy butterflies frolic around.
But, when once plucked, 'tis no longer alluring;
    To Covent-garden 'tis sent (as yet sweet),
There fades, and shrinks, and grows past all enduring,   15
    Rots, stinks, and dies, and is trod under feet.

PEACHUM. You know, Polly, I am not against your toying and trifling
with a customer in the way of business, or to get out a secret or so.
But if I find out that you have played the fool and are married, you
jade you, I'll cut your throat, hussy! Now you know my mind.   [20

SCENE VIII

[PEACHUM, POLLY, MRS. PEACHUM. MRS. PEACHUM
in a very great passion.]

AIR VII—*Oh London is a fine town.*

Our Polly is a sad slut! nor heeds what we have taught her.
I wonder any man alive will ever rear a daughter!
For she must have both hoods and gowns, and hoops to swell her pride,
With scarfs and stays, and gloves and lace; and she will have men
    beside;
And when she's dressed with care and cost, all-tempting fine and
    gay,   5
As men should serve a cowcumber, she flings herself away.

You baggage, you hussy! you inconsiderate jade! Had you been
hanged, it would not have vexed me, for that might have been your
misfortune; but to do such a mad thing by choice! The wench is
married, husband.   10
    PEACHUM. Married! The captain is a bold man, and will risk any-
thing for money; to be sure, he believes her a fortune!—Do you think
your mother and I should have lived comfortably so long together, if
ever we had been married? Baggage!
    MRS. PEACHUM. I knew she was always a proud slut; and now   [15
the wench hath played the fool and married because, forsooth, she
would do like the gentry. Can you support the expense of a husband,
hussy, in gaming, drinking, and whoring? Have you money enough
to carry on the daily quarrels of man and wife about who shall squan-
der most? There are not many husbands and wives who can   [20
bear the charges of plaguing one another in a handsome way. If you
must be married, could you introduce nobody into our family but a

---

SCENE VII: 14. *Covent-garden:* London's flower market.
SCENE VIII: 6. *cowcumber:* cucumber.

highwayman? Why, thou foolish jade, thou wilt be as ill used, and as much neglected, as if thou hadst married a lord!

PEACHUM. Let not your anger, my dear, break through the   [25
rules of decency, for the captain looks upon himself in the military capacity, as a gentleman by his profession. Besides what he hath already, I know he is in a fair way of getting, or of dying; and both these ways, let me tell you, are most excellent chances for a wife.— Tell me, hussy, are you ruined or no?   30

MRS. PEACHUM. With Polly's fortune, she might very well have gone off to a person of distinction. Yes, that you might, you pouting slut!

PEACHUM. What, is the wench dumb? Speak, or I'll make you plead by squeezing out an answer from you. Are you really bound wife to him, or are you only upon liking?   35

[*Pinches her.*

POLLY (*screaming*). Oh!

MRS. PEACHUM. How the mother is to be pitied who hath handsome daughters! Locks, bolts, bars, and lectures of morality are nothing to them; they break through them all. They have as much pleasure in cheating a father and mother as in cheating at cards.   40

PEACHUM. Why, Polly, I shall soon know if you are married, by Macheath's keeping from our house.

POLLY.

AIR VIII—*Grim king of the ghosts, etc.*

Can love be controlled by advice?
    Will Cupid our mothers obey?
Though my heart were as frozen as ice,   45
    At his flame 'twould have melted away.

When he kissed me, so closely he pressed,
    'Twas so sweet that I must have complied,
So I thought it both safest and best
    To marry, for fear you should chide.   50

MRS. PEACHUM. Then all the hopes of our family are gone for ever and ever!

PEACHUM. And Macheath may hang his father- and mother-in-law, in hope to get into their daughter's fortune!

POLLY. I did not marry him (as 'tis the fashion) coolly and   [55
deliberately for honor or money—but I love him.

MRS. PEACHUM. Love him! Worse and worse! I thought the girl had been better bred. O husband, husband! her folly makes me mad! my head swims! I'm distracted! I can't support myself—Oh!

[*Faints.*

PEACHUM. See, wench, to what a condition you have reduced   [60
your poor mother! a glass of cordial, this instant. How the poor
woman takes it to heart! (*Polly goes out and returns with it.*) Ah,
hussy, now this is the only comfort your mother has left!

POLLY. Give her another glass, sir; my mama drinks double the
quantity whenever she is out of order.—This, you see, fetches   [65
her.

MRS. PEACHUM. The girl shows such a readiness, and so much concern, that I could almost find in my heart to forgive her.

AIR IX—*O Jenny, O Jenny, where hast thou been.*

O Polly, you might have toyed and kissed;
By keeping men off, you keep them on.   70

POLLY.

But he so teased me,
And he so pleased me,
What I did, you must have done—

MRS. PEACHUM. Not with a highwayman.—You sorry slut!

PEACHUM. A word with you, wife. 'Tis no new thing for a   [75
wench to take man without consent of parents. You know 'tis the
frailty of woman, my dear.

MRS. PEACHUM. Yes, indeed, the sex is frail. But the first time a
woman is frail, she should be somewhat nice, methinks, for then or
never is the time to make her fortune. After that, she hath   [80
nothing to do but to guard herself from being found out, and she may
do what she pleases.

PEACHUM. Make yourself a little easy; I have a thought shall soon
set all matters again to rights. Why so melancholy, Polly? Since what
is done cannot be undone, we must all endeavor to make the   [85
best of it.

MRS. PEACHUM. Well, Polly, as far as one woman can forgive another, I forgive thee.—Your father is too fond of you, hussy.

POLLY. Then all my sorrows are at an end.

MRS. PEACHUM. A mighty likely speech in troth, for a wench   [90
who is just married.

POLLY.

AIR X—*Thomas, I cannot, etc.*

I, like a ship in storms, was tossed,
Yet afraid to put into land;
For seized in the port, the vessel's lost,
Whose treasure is contraband.   95
The waves are laid,

My duty's paid,
Oh, joy beyond expression!
Thus, safe ashore,
I ask no more,   100
My all is in my possession.

PEACHUM. I hear customers in t'other room. Go, talk with 'em, Polly; but come to us again as soon as they are gone.—But, hark ye, child, if 'tis the gentleman who was here yesterday about the repeating watch, say, you believe we can't get intelligence of it till to- [105 morrow—for I lent it to Suky Straddle, to make a figure with to-night at a tavern in Drury Lane. If t'other gentleman calls for the silver-hilted sword, you know beetle-browed Jemmy hath it on, and he doth not come from Tunbridge till Tuesday night; so that it cannot be had till then.   110

[*Exit* POLLY.

SCENE IX

[PEACHUM, MRS. PEACHUM.]

PEACHUM. Dear wife, be a little pacified. Don't let your passion run away with your senses. Polly, I grant you, hath done a rash thing.

MRS. PEACHUM. If she had had only an intrigue with the fellow, why, the very best families have excused and huddled up a frailty of [5 that sort. 'Tis marriage, husband, that makes it a blemish.

PEACHUM. But money, wife, is the true fuller's earth for reputations; there is not a spot or a stain but what it can take out. A rich rogue nowadays is fit company for any gentleman, and the world, my dear, hath not such a contempt for roguery as you imagine. I tell [10 you, wife, I can make this match turn to our advantage.

MRS. PEACHUM. I am very sensible, husband, that Captain Macheath is worth money, but I am in doubt whether he hath not two or three wives already, and then if he should die in a session or two, Polly's dower would come into dispute.   15

PEACHUM. That, indeed, is a point which ought to be considered.

AIR XI—*A soldier and a sailor.*

A fox may steal your hens, sir,
A whore your health and pence, sir,
Your daughter rob your chest, sir,
Your wife may steal your rest, sir,   20

---

100. *Tunbridge:* a town north of London.

> A thief your goods and plate.
> But this is all but picking;
> With rest, pence, chest, and chicken;
> It ever was decreed, sir,
> If lawyer's hand is fee'd, sir,   25
> He steals your whole estate.

The lawyers are bitter enemies to those in our way. They don't care
that anybody should get a clandestine livelihood but themselves.

SCENE X

[MRS. PEACHUM, PEACHUM, POLLY.]

POLLY. 'Twas only Nimming Ned. He brought in a damask win-
dow-curtain, a hoop petticoat, a pair of silver candlesticks, a periwig,
and one silk stocking, from the fire that happened last night.

PEACHUM. There is not a fellow that is cleverer in his way and
saves more goods out of the fire, than Ned. But now, Polly, to   [5
your affair; for matters must not be left as they are. You are married
then, it seems?

POLLY. Yes, sir.

PEACHUM. And how do you propose to live, child?

POLLY. Like other women, sir,—upon the industry of my   [10
husband.

MRS. PEACHUM. What, is the wench turned fool? A highwayman's
wife, like a soldier's, hath as little of his pay as of his company.

PEACHUM. And had not you the common views of a gentlewoman
in your marriage, Polly?   15

POLLY. I don't know what you mean, sir.

PEACHUM. Of a jointure, and of being a widow.

POLLY. But I love him, sir; how then could I have thoughts of parting with him?   19

PEACHUM. Parting with him! Why, that is the whole scheme and
intention of all marriage articles. The comfortable estate of widowhood is the only hope that keeps up a wife's spirits. Where is the
woman who would scruple to be a wife, if she had it in her power to
be a widow whenever she pleased? If you have any views of this sort,
Polly, I shall think the match not so very unreasonable.   25

POLLY. How I dread to hear your advice! Yet I must beg you to
explain yourself.

PEACHUM. Secure what he hath got, have him peached the next
sessions, and then at once you are made a rich widow.

SCENE X: 17. *jointure:* a property settled on a woman by her husband
for her support after his death. 28. *peached:* informed against, indicted.

POLLY. What, murder the man I love! The blood runs cold   [30
at my heart with the very thought of it.

PEACHUM. Fie, Polly! What hath murder to do in the affair? Since
the thing sooner or later must happen, I dare say the captain himself
would like that we should get the reward for his death sooner than a
stranger. Why, Polly, the captain knows that as 'tis his em-   [35
ployment to rob, so 'tis ours to take robbers; every man in his business.
So that there is no malice in the case.

MRS. PEACHUM. Ay, husband, now you have nicked the matter. To
have him peached is the only thing could ever make me forgive
her.   40

POLLY.

> AIR XII—*Now ponder well, ye parents dear.*
>
> Oh, ponder well! be not severe;
>   So save a wretched wife!
> For on the rope that hangs my dear
>   Depends poor Polly's life.

MRS. PEACHUM. But your duty to your parents, hussy, obliges   [45
you to hang him. What would many a wife give for such an opportunity!

POLLY. What is a jointure, what is widowhood to me? I know my
heart. I cannot survive him.

> AIR XIII—*Le printemps rappelle aux armes.*
>
> The turtle thus with plaintive crying,   50
>   Her lover dying,
> The turtle thus with plaintive crying,
>   Laments her dove.
> Down she drops, quite spent with sighing;
>   Paired in death, as paired in love.   55

Thus, sir, it will happen to your poor Polly.

MRS. PEACHUM. What, is the fool in love in earnest then? I hate
thee for being particular. Why, wench, thou art a shame to thy very
sex.

POLLY. But hear me, mother,—if you ever loved—   60

MRS. PEACHUM. Those cursed play-books she reads have been her
ruin. One word more, hussy, and I shall knock your brains out, if
you have any.

---

36. *every . . . business:* Cf. *1 Henry IV,* I ii 116: "'Tis no sin for a man
to labor in his vocation."

PEACHUM. Keep out of the way, Polly, for fear of mischief, and
consider what is proposed to you.   65
MRS. PEACHUM. Away, hussy! Hang your husband, and be dutiful.

SCENE XI

[MRS. PEACHUM, PEACHUM, POLLY *listening.*]

MRS. PEACHUM. The thing, husband, must and shall be done. For
the sake of intelligence, we must take other measures and have him
peached the next session without her consent. If she will not know
her duty, we know ours.

PEACHUM. But really, my dear, it grieves one's heart to take   [5
off a great man. When I consider his personal bravery, his fine stratagem, how much we have already got by him, and how much more
we may get, methinks I can't find in my heart to have a hand in his
death. I wish you could have made Polly undertake it.

MRS. PEACHUM. But in a case of necessity—our own lives   [10
are in danger.

PEACHUM. Then, indeed, we must comply with the customs of the
world, and make gratitude give way to interest. He shall be taken
off.

MRS. PEACHUM. I'll undertake to manage Polly.   15
PEACHUM. And I'll prepare matters for the Old Bailey.   [*Exeunt.*

SCENE XII

[POLLY.]

POLLY. Now I'm a wretch, indeed—methinks I see him already in
the cart, sweeter and more lovely than the nosegay in his hand!—I
hear the crowd extolling his resolution and intrepidity!—What volleys
of sighs are sent from the windows of Holborn, that so comely a
youth should be brought to disgrace!—I see him at the tree!   [5
The whole circle are in tears!—even butchers weep!—Jack Ketch himself hesitates to perform his duty, and would be glad to lose his fee,
by a reprieve. What then will become of Polly? As yet I may inform
him of their design, and aid him in his escape. It shall be so!—But
then he flies, absents himself, and I bar myself from his dear,   [10

SCENE XI: 6-7. *stratagem:* strategy (in robberies).
SCENE XII: 4. *Holborn:* a squalid London district lying on the route between Newgate prison and the gallows at Tyburn. 5. *tree:* gallows. 6.
Jack Ketch: a seventeenth-century hangman whose name came to be applied to all hangmen.

dear conversation! That too will distract me. If he keep out of the way, my papa and mama may in time relent, and we may be happy. If he stays, he is hanged, and then he is lost forever! He intended to lie concealed in my room till the dusk of evening. If they are abroad, I'll this instant let him out, lest some accident should prevent   [15 him.   [*Exit, and returns.*

SCENE XIII

[POLLY, MACHEATH.]

MACHEATH.   AIR XIV—*Pretty Parrot, say.*

        Pretty Polly, say,
        When I was away,
    Did your fancy never stray
        To some newer lover?

POLLY.

        Without disguise,   5
        Heaving sighs,
        Doating eyes,
    My constant heart discover.
        Fondly let me loll!

MACHEATH.

        O pretty, pretty Poll.   10

POLLY. And are *you* as fond as ever, my dear?

MACHEATH. Suspect my honor, my courage—suspect anything but my love. May my pistols miss fire, and my mare slip her shoulder while I am pursued, if I ever forsake thee!

POLLY. Nay, my dear, I have no reason to doubt you, for I   [15 find in the romance you lent me, none of the great heroes were ever false in love.

MACHEATH.

        AIR XV—*Pray, fair one, be kind*

        My heart was so free,
        It roved like the bee,
    Till Polly my passion requited;   20
        I sipped each flower,
        I changed every hour,
    But here every flower is united.

POLLY. Were you sentenced to transportation, sure, my dear, you could not leave me behind you,—could you?   25

MACHEATH. Is there any power, any force that could tear me from thee? You might sooner tear a pension out of the hands of a courtier, a fee from a lawyer, a pretty woman from a looking glass, or any woman from quadrille. But to tear me from thee is impossible!

AIR XVI—*Over the hills and far away.*

Were I laid on Greenland's coast, 30
And in my arms embraced my lass;
Warm amidst eternal frost,
Too soon the half year's night would pass.

POLLY.

Were I sold on Indian soil,
Soon as the burning day was closed, 35
I could mock the sultry toil,
When on my charmer's breast reposed.
MACHEATH. And I would love you all the day,
POLLY. Every night would kiss and play,
MACHEATH. If with me you'd fondly stray 40
POLLY. Over the hills and far away.

POLLY. Yes, I would go with thee. But oh!—how shall I speak it? I must be torn from thee. We must part.

MACHEATH. How! Part!

POLLY. We must, we must. My papa and mama are set [45 against thy life. They now, even now, are in search after thee. They are preparing evidence against thee. Thy life depends upon a moment.

AIR. XVII—*'Gin thou wert mine awn thing.*

Oh, what pain it is to part!
Can I leave thee, can I leave thee? 50
Oh, what pain it is to part!
Can thy Polly ever leave thee?
But lest death my love should thwart
And bring thee to the fatal cart,
Thus I tear thee from my bleeding heart! 55
Fly hence, and let me leave thee.

One kiss and then,—one kiss. Begone,—farewell.

MACHEATH. My hand, my heart, my dear, is so riveted to thine, that I cannot unloose my hold.

POLLY. But my papa may intercept thee, and then I should [60 lose the very glimmering of hope. A few weeks, perhaps, may reconcile us all. Shall thy Polly hear from thee?

MACHEATH. Must I then go?

POLLY. And will not absence change your love?

MACHEATH. If you doubt it, let me stay—and be hanged.   65

POLLY. Oh, I fear! how I tremble!—Go—but when safety will give you leave, you will be sure to see me again; for till then Polly is wretched.

> [*Parting, and looking back at each other with fondness;
> he at one door, she at the other.*]

MACHEATH.

AIR XVIII—*Oh the broom, etc.*

The miser thus a shilling sees,
   Which he's obliged to pay,   70
With sighs resigns it by degrees,
   And fears 'tis gone for aye.

POLLY.

The boy, thus, when his sparrow's flown,
   The bird in silence eyes;
But soon as out of sight 'tis gone,   75
   Whines, whimpers, sobs, and cries.

Act II

SCENE I. *A tavern near Newgate.*

[JEMMY TWITCHER, CROOK-FINGERED JACK, WAT DREARY, ROBIN OF BAG-
SHOT, NIMMING NED, HARRY PADINGTON, MATT OF THE MINT, BEN
BUDGE, *and the rest of the gang, at the table, with wine, brandy,
and tobacco.*]

BEN. But prithee, Matt, what is become of thy brother Tom? I have not seen him since my return from transportation.

MATT. Poor brother Tom had an accident this time twelve-month, and so clever a made fellow he was, that I could not save him from those flaying rascals the surgeons; and now, poor man, he is   [5
among the anatomies at Surgeons' Hall.

BEN. So, it seems, his time was come.

JEM. But the present time is ours, and nobody alive hath more. Why are the laws levelled at us? Are we more dishonest than the rest of mankind? What we win, gentlemen, is our own by the   [10
law of arms and the right of conquest.

ACT II, SCENE I: 6. *anatomies:* skeletons.

JACK. Where shall we find such another set of practical philosophers, who to a man are above the fear of death?

WAT. Sound men, and true!

ROBIN. Of tried courage, and indefatigable industry!   15

NED. Who is there here that would not die for his friend?

HARRY. Who is there here that would betray him for his interest?

MATT. Show me a gang of courtiers that can say as much.

BEN. We are for a just partition of the world, for every man hath a right to enjoy life.   20

MATT. We retrench the superfluities of mankind. The world is avaricious, and I hate avarice. A covetous fellow, like a jackdaw, steals what he was never made to enjoy, for the sake of hiding it. These are the robbers of mankind, for money was made for the free-hearted and generous; and where is the injury of taking   [25 from another, what he hath not the heart to make use of?

JEM. Our several stations for the day are fixed. Good luck attend us! Fill the glasses.

MATT.

AIR XIX—*Fill ev'ry glass, etc.*

Fill every glass, for wine inspires us,
    And fires us,   30
With courage, love, and joy.
Women and wine should life employ.
Is there aught else on earth desirous?

CHORUS.

    Fill every glass, etc.

SCENE II

[*To them enter* MACHEATH.]

MACHEATH. Gentlemen, well met. My heart hath been with you this hour, but an unexpected affair hath detained me. No ceremony, I beg you.

MATT. We were just breaking up to go upon duty. Am I to have the honor of taking the air with you, sir, this evening upon   [5 the heath? I drink a dram now and then with the stage-coachmen in the way of friendship and intelligence, and I know that about this time there will be passengers upon the Western Road who are worth speaking with.

MACHEATH. I was to have been of that party—but—   10

MATT. But what, sir?

MACHEATH. Is there any man who suspects my courage?—

MATT. We have all been witnesses of it.—

MACHEATH. My honor and truth to the gang?

MATT. I'll be answerable for it.   15

MACHEATH. In the division of our booty, have I ever shown the least marks of avarice or injustice?

MATT. By these questions something seems to have ruffled you. Are any of us suspected?

MACHEATH. I have a fixed confidence, gentlemen, in you all,   [20 as men of honor, and as such I value and respect you. Peachum is a man that is useful to us.

MATT. Is he about to play us any foul play? I'll shoot him through the head.

MACHEATH. I beg you, gentlemen, act with conduct and dis-   [25 cretion. A pistol is your last resort.

MATT. He knows nothing of this meeting.

MACHEATH. Business cannot go on without him. He is a man who knows the world, and is a necessary agent to us. We have had a slight difference, and till it is accommodated I shall be obliged   [30 to keep out of his way. Any private dispute of mine shall be of no ill consequence to my friends. You must continue to act under his direction, for the moment we break loose from him, our gang is ruined.

MATT. As a bawd to a whore, I grant you, he is to us of great   [35 convenience.

MACHEATH. Make him believe I have quitted the gang, which I can never do but with life. At our private quarters I will continue to meet you. A week or so will probably reconcile us.

MATT. Your instructions shall be observed. 'Tis now high   [40 time for us to repair to our several duties; so till the evening at our quarters in Moor-fields we bid you farewell.

MACHEATH. I shall wish myself with you. Success attend you.

[Sits down melancholy at the table.

MATT.

AIR XX—*March in Rinaldo, with drums and trumpets*

Let us take the road.
        Hark! I hear the sound of coaches!   45
        The hour of attack approaches,
To your arms, brave boys, and load.

        See the ball I hold!
Let the chymists toil like asses,

AIR TITLE: *Rinaldo:* one of Handel's operas.

Our fire their fire surpasses,   50
And turns all our lead to gold.

[*The gang, ranged in the front of the stage, load their pistols, and
stick them under their girdles, then go off singing the first part
in chorus.*]

SCENE III

[MACHEATH, DRAWER.]

MACHEATH. What a fool is a fond wench! Polly is most confound-
edly bit—I love the sex. And a man who loves money might be as
well contented with one guinea, as I with one woman. The town
perhaps hath been as much obliged to me, for recruiting it with free-
hearted ladies, as to any recruiting officer in the army. If it   [5
were not for us, and the other gentlemen of the sword, Drury Lane
would be uninhabited.

AIR XXI—*Would you have a young virgin, etc.*

If the heart of a man is depressed with cares,
The mist is dispelled when a woman appears;
Like the notes of a fiddle, she sweetly, sweetly   10
Raises the spirits, and charms our ears.
Roses and lilies her cheeks disclose,
But her ripe lips are more sweet than those.
Press her,
Caress her   15
With blisses,
Her kisses
Dissolve us in pleasure and soft repose.

I must have women. There is nothing unbends the mind like them.
Money is not so strong a cordial for the time. Drawer!—   20

[*Enter* DRAWER.]

Is the porter gone for all the ladies, according to my directions?
DRAWER. I expect him back every minute. But you know, sir, you
sent him as far as Hockley-in-the-Hole for three of the ladies, for one
in Vinegar Yard, and for the rest of them somewhere about Lewk-
ner's Lane. Sure some of them are below, for I hear the bar   [25
bell. As they come I will show them up. Coming! coming!   [*Exit.*

---

51. *gold:* punning on alchemical transmutation of metals by "projection."
SCENE III: 6. *Drury Lane:* a resort of prostitutes. 23-5 Places frequented
by the city's riff-raff.

SCENE IV

[MACHEATH, MRS. COAXER, DOLLY TRULL, MRS. VIXEN, BETTY DOXY, JENNY DIVER, MRS. SLAMMEKIN, SUKY TAWDRY, *and* MOLLY BRAZEN.]

MACHEATH. Dear Mrs. Coaxer, you are welcome. You look charmingly to-day. I hope you don't want the repairs of quality, and lay on paint.—Dolly Trull! kiss me, you slut; are you as amorous as ever, hussy? You are always so taken up with stealing hearts, that you don't allow yourself time to steal anything else. Ah Dolly,　　[5 thou wilt ever be a coquette.—Mrs. Vixen, I'm yours! I always loved a woman of wit and spirit; they make charming mistresses, but plaguy wives.—Betty Doxy! come hither, hussy. Do you drink as hard as ever? You had better stick to good, wholesome beer; for in troth, Betty, strong waters will, in time, ruin your constitution. You　　[10 should leave those to your betters.—What! and my pretty Jenny Diver too! As prim and demure as ever! There is not any prude, though ever so high bred, hath a more sanctified look, with a more mischievous heart. Ah! thou art a dear artful hypocrite!—Mrs. Slammekin! as careless and genteel as ever! all you fine ladies, who　　[15 know your own beauty, affect an undress.—But see, here's Suky Tawdry come to contradict what I was saying. Everything she gets one way, she lays out upon her back. Why, Suky, you must keep at least a dozen tally-men.—Molly Brazen! (*She kisses him.*) That's well done. I love a free-hearted wench. Thou hast a most agree-　　[20 able assurance, girl, and art as willing as a turtle.—But hark! I hear music. The harper is at the door. "If music be the food of love, play on." Ere you seat yourselves, ladies, what think you of a dance? Come in.

[*Enter* HARPER.]

Play the French tune that Mrs. Slammekin was so fond of.　　25

[*A dance à la ronde in the French manner; near the end of it this song and chorus.*]

AIR XXII—*Cotillion*

Youth's the season made for joys,
Love is then our duty;
She alone who that employs,

SCENE IV: 19. *tally-men:* merchants who sold on credit. 21. *turtle:* turtledove. 22. *Twelfth Night,* I i 1.

> Well deserves her beauty.
>   Let's be gay,   30
>   While we may,
> Beauty's a flower despised in decay.

CHORUS.

>   Youth's the season, etc.

> Let us drink and sport to-day,
>   Ours is not to-morrow.   35
> Love with youth flies swift away,
>   Age is nought but sorrow.
>   Dance and sing,
>   Time's on the wing,
> Life never knows the return of spring.   40

CHORUS.

>   Let us drink, etc.

MACHEATH. Now pray, ladies, take your places. Here, fellow. (*Pays the* HARPER.) Bid the drawer bring us more wine.   [*Exit* HARPER. If any of the ladies choose gin, I hope they will be so free to call for it.

JENNY. You look as if you meant me. Wine is strong   [45 enough for me. Indeed, sir, I never drink strong waters but when I have the colic.

MACHEATH. Just the excuse of the fine ladies! Why, a lady of quality is never without the colic. I hope, Mrs. Coaxer, you have had good success of late in your visits among the mercers.   50

MRS. COAXER. We have so many interlopers. Yet, with industry, one may still have a little picking. I carried a silver-flowered lute-string and a piece of black padesoy to Mr. Peachum's lock but last week.

MRS. VIXEN. There's Molly Brazen hath the ogle of a rattlesnake. She riveted a linen-draper's eye so fast upon her, that he was   [55 nicked of three pieces of cambric before he could look off.

MOLLY BRAZEN. Oh, dear madam! But sure nothing can come up to your handling of laces! And then you have such a sweet deluding tongue! To cheat a man is nothing; but the woman must have fine parts indeed who cheats a woman!   60

MRS. VIXEN. Lace, madam, lies in a small compass, and is of easy conveyance. But you are apt, madam, to think too well of your friends.

MRS. COAXER. If any woman hath more art than another, to be sure, 'tis Jenny Diver. Though her fellow be never so agreeable,   [65

---

50. *mercers:* textile merchants. 52-3. *a . . . padesoy:* expensive fabrics. 54. *ogle:* gaze.

she can pick his pocket as coolly as if money were her only pleasure. Now, that is a command of the passions uncommon in a woman!

JENNY. I never go to the tavern with a man but in the view of business. I have other hours, and other sort of men for my pleasure. But had I your address, madam—   70

MACHEATH. Have done with your compliments, ladies, and drink about. You are not so fond of me, Jenny, as you use to be.

JENNY. 'Tis not convenient, sir, to show my kindness among so many rivals. 'Tis your own choice, and not the warmth of my inclination, that will determine you.   75

> AIR XXIII—*All in a misty morning, etc.*
>
> Before the barn-door crowing,
>   The cock by hens attended,
> His eyes around him throwing,
>   Stands for a while suspended.
> Then one he singles from the crew,   80
>   And cheers the happy hen;
> With "How do you do," and "How do you do,"
>   And "How do you do" again.

MACHEATH. Ah Jenny! thou art a dear slut.

TRULL. Pray, madam, were you ever in keeping?   85

TAWDRY. I hope, madam, I han't been so long upon the town but I have met with some good fortune as well as my neighbors.

TRULL. Pardon me, madam, I meant no harm by the question; 'twas only in the way of conversation.

TAWDRY. Indeed, madam, if I had not been a fool, I might   [90 have lived very handsomely with my last friend. But upon his missing five guineas, he turned me off. Now, I never suspected he had counted them.

SLAMMEKIN. Who do you look upon, madam, as your best sort of keepers?   95

TRULL. That, madam, is thereafter as they be.

SLAMMEKIN. I, madam, was once kept by a Jew; and bating their religion, to women they are a good sort of people.

TAWDRY. Now for my part, I own I like an old fellow; for we always make them pay for what they can't do.   100

VIXEN. A spruce prentice, let me tell you, ladies, is no ill thing; they bleed freely. I have sent at least two or three dozen of them in my time to the plantations.

102-3. *bleed . . . plantations:* i.e., prentices pay high (with their masters' money) and so are deported.

JENNY. But to be sure, sir, with so much good fortune as you have
had upon the road, you must be grown immensely rich.   105

MACHEATH. The road, indeed, hath done me justice, but the gaming-
table hath been my ruin.

JENNY.

AIR XXIV—*When once I lay with another man's wife, etc.*

The gamesters and lawyers are jugglers alike,
  If they meddle, your all is in danger:
Like gypsies, if once they can finger a souse,   110
  Your pockets they pick, and they pilfer your house,
And give your estate to a stranger.

A man of courage should never put anything to the risque, but his life.
These are the tools of a man of honor. Cards and dice are only fit for
cowardly cheats, who prey upon their friends.   115
          [*She takes up his pistol.* TAWDRY *takes up the other.*
TAWDRY. This, sir, is fitter for your hand. Besides your loss of
money, 'tis a loss to the ladies. Gaming takes you off from women.
How fond could I be of you!—but before company, 'tis ill-bred.

MACHEATH. Wanton hussies!

JENNY. I must and will have a kiss, to give my wine a zest.   [120
[*They take him about the neck, and make signs to Peachum and Constables, who rush in upon him.*]

SCENE V

[*To them* PEACHUM *and* CONSTABLES.]

PEACHUM. I seize you, sir, as my prisoner.

MACHEATH. Was this well done, Jenny? Women are decoy ducks:
who can trust them? Beasts, jades, jilts, harpies, furies, whores!

PEACHUM. Your case, Mr. Macheath, is not particular. The greatest
heroes have been ruined by women. But, to do them justice,   [5
I must own they are a pretty sort of creatures, if we could trust them.
You must now, sir, take your leave of the ladies, and if they have
a mind to make you a visit, they will be sure to find you at home.
This gentleman, ladies, lodges in Newgate. Constables, wait upon
the captain to his lodgings.   10

MACHEATH.

AIR XXV—*When first I laid siege to my Chloris, etc.*

At the tree I shall suffer with pleasure,
At the tree I shall suffer with pleasure;

---

110. *souse: sou.*

SCENE V: 2. *Was . . . done: Cf. Antony and Cleopatra, V ii 328.*

Let me go where I will,
In all kinds of ill,
I shall find no such furies as these are.   15

PEACHUM. Ladies, I'll take care the reckoning shall be discharged.
[*Exit* MACHEATH, *guarded, with* PEACHUM
and CONSTABLES.]

SCENE VI

[*The* WOMEN *remain.*]

VIXEN. Look ye, Mrs. Jenny; though Mr. Peachum may have made
a private bargain with you and Suky Tawdry for betraying the captain, as we were all assisting, we ought all to share alike.

COAXER. I think Mr. Peachum, after so long an acquaintance, might
have trusted me as well as Jenny Diver.   5

SLAMMEKIN. I am sure at least three men of his hanging, and in
a year's time too, (if he did me justice) should be set down to my
account.

TRULL. Mrs. Slammekin, that is not fair. For you know one of them
was taken in bed with me.   10

JENNY. As far as a bowl of punch or a treat, I believe Mrs. Suky will
join with me. As for anything else, ladies, you cannot in conscience
expect it.

SLAMMEKIN. Dear madam—

TRULL. I would not for the world—

SLAMMEKIN. 'Tis impossible for me—   15

TRULL. As I hope to be saved, madam—

SLAMMEKIN. Nay, then I must stay here all night.—

TRULL. Since you command me.   [*Exeunt with great ceremony.*

SCENE VII. *Newgate.*

[LOCKIT, TURNKEYS, MACHEATH, CONSTABLES.]

LOCKIT. Noble captain, you are welcome. You have not been a
lodger of mine this year and half. You know the custom, sir. Garnish,
captain, garnish! Hand me down those fetters there.

MACHEATH. Those, Mr. Lockit, seem to be the heaviest of the whole
set! With your leave, I should like the further pair better.   5

LOCKIT. Look ye, captain, we know what is fittest for our prisoners.

SCENE VI: 14-19. Each lady (with a curtsy parodying that of ladies of
fashion) insists that the other precede her through the door.
SCENE VII: 3. *Garnish:* i.e., fee me. The treatment accorded prisoners
depended on the amount they paid the prison keeper.

When a gentleman uses me with civility, I always do the best I can to please him.—Hand them down, I say.—We have them of all prices, from one guinea to ten, and 'tis fitting every gentleman should please himself.   10

MACHEATH. I understand you, sir. (*Gives money.*) The fees here are so many, and so exorbitant, that few fortunes can bear the expense of getting off handsomely, or of dying like a gentleman.

LOCKIT. Those, I see, will fit the captain better. Take down the further pair. Do but examine them, sir,—never was better work.   [15 How genteelly they are made! They will fit as easy as a glove, and the nicest man in England might not be ashamed to wear them. (*He puts on the chains.*) If I had the best gentleman in the land in my custody, I could not equip him more handsomely. And so, sir—I now leave you to your private meditations.   20

SCENE VIII

[MACHEATH.]

AIR XXVI—*Courtiers, courtiers, think it no harm, etc.*

> Man may escape from rope and gun;
> Nay, some have outlived the doctor's pill;
> Who takes a woman must be undone,
>   That basilisk is sure to kill.

> The fly that sips treacle is lost in the sweets,   5
> So he that tastes woman, woman, woman,
>   He that tastes woman, ruin meets.

To what a woeful plight have I brought myself! Here must I (all day long, till I am hanged) be confined to hear the reproaches of a wench who lays her ruin at my door. I am in the custody of her fa-   [10 ther, and to be sure if he knows of the matter, I shall have a fine time on't betwixt this and my execution. But I promised the wench marriage. What signifies a promise to a woman? Does not a man in marriage itself promise a hundred things that he never means to perform? Do all we can, women will believe us; for they look   [15 upon a promise as an excuse for following their own inclinations.— But here comes Lucy, and I cannot get from her. Would I were deaf!

SCENE IX

[MACHEATH, LUCY.]

LUCY. You base man, you, how can you look me in the face after what hath passed between us?—See here, perfidious wretch, how I am forced to bear about the load of infamy you have laid upon me—O Macheath! thou hast robbed me of my quiet—to see thee tortured would give me pleasure.

5

AIR XXVII—*A lovely lass to a friar came, etc.*

> Thus when a good housewife sees a rat
> In a trap in the morning taken,
> With pleasure her heart goes pit-a-pat
> In revenge for her loss of bacon.
> Then she throws him   10
> To the dog or cat,
> To be worried, crushed, and shaken.

MACHEATH. Have you no bowels, no tenderness, my dear Lucy, to see a husband in these circumstances?

LUCY. A husband!

15

MACHEATH. In every respect but the form, and that, my dear, may be said over us at any time. Friends should not insist upon ceremonies. From a man of honor, his word is as good as his bond.

LUCY. 'Tis the pleasure of all you fine men to insult the women you have ruined.

20

AIR XXVIII—*'Twas when the sea was roaring, etc.*

> How cruel are the traitors
> Who lie and swear in jest,
> To cheat unguarded creatures
> Of virtue, fame, and rest!
>
> Whoever steals a shilling   25
> Through shame the guilt conceals;
> In love, the perjured villain
> With boasts the theft reveals.

MACHEATH. The very first opportunity my dear, (have but patience) you shall be my wife in whatever manner you please.

30

LUCY. Insinuating monster! And so you think I know nothing of the affair of Miss Polly Peachum. I could tear thy eyes out!

MACHEATH. Sure, Lucy, you can't be such a fool as to be jealous of Polly!

LUCY. Are you not married to her, you brute, you?

35

MACHEATH. Married! Very good. The wench gives it out only to vex thee, and to ruin me in thy good opinion. 'Tis true I go to the

SCENE IX: 4. See *1 Henry IV*, V iv 77. "O Harry, thou hast robbed me of my youth!"

house; I chat with the girl, I kiss her, I say a thousand things to her (as all gentlemen do) that mean nothing, to divert myself; and now the silly jade hath set it about that I am married to her, to let   [40 me know what she would be at. Indeed, my dear Lucy, these violent passions may be of ill consequence to a woman in your condition.

LUCY. Come, come, captain, for all your assurance, you know that Miss Polly hath put it out of your power to do me the justice you promised me.   45

MACHEATH. A jealous woman believes everything her passion suggests. To convince you of my sincerity, if we can find the ordinary, I shall have no scruples of making you my wife—and I know the consequence of having two at a time.   49

LUCY. That you are only to be hanged, and so get rid of them both.

MACHEATH. I am ready, my dear Lucy, to give you satisfaction—if you think there is any in marriage. What can a man of honor say more?

LUCY. So then it seems—you are not married to Miss Polly.

MACHEATH. You know, Lucy, the girl is prodigiously con-   [55 ceited. No man can say a civil thing to her, but (like other fine ladies) her vanity makes her think he's her own for ever and ever.

AIR XXIX—*The sun had loosed his weary teams, etc.*

> The first time at the looking-glass
>   The mother sets her daughter,
> The image strikes the smiling lass   60
>   With self-love ever after.
> Each time she looks, she, fonder grown,
>   Thinks every charm grows stronger.
> But alas, vain maid, all eyes but your own
>   Can see you are not younger.   65

When women consider their own beauties, they are all alike unreasonable in their demands; for they expect their lovers should like them as long as they like themselves.

LUCY. Yonder is my father. Perhaps this way we may light upon the ordinary, who shall try if you will be as good as your word;   [70 for I long to be made an honest woman.   · [*Exeunt.*

SCENE X. [*Lockit's room in Newgate*]

[PEACHUM, LOCKIT *with an account-book.*]

LOCKIT. In this last affair, brother Peachum, we are agreed. You have consented to go halves in Macheath.

---

70. *ordinary:* chaplain.

PEACHUM. We shall never fall out about an execution. But as to that article, pray how stands our last year's account?

LOCKIT. If you will run your eye over it, you'll find 'tis fair   [5
and clearly stated.

PEACHUM. This long arrear of the government is very hard upon us! Can it be expected that we should hang our acquaintance for nothing, when our betters will hardly save theirs without being paid for it? Unless the people in employment pay better, I promise them   [10
for the future, I shall let other rogues live besides their own.

LOCKIT. Perhaps, brother, they are afraid these matters may be carried too far. We are treated, too, by them with contempt, as if our profession were not reputable.

PEACHUM. In one respect, indeed, our employment may be   [15
reckoned dishonest, because, like great statesmen, we encourage those who betray their friends.

LOCKIT. Such language, brother, anywhere else might turn to your prejudice. Learn to be more guarded, I beg you.

AIR XXX—*How happy are we, etc.*

When you censure the age,   20
Be cautious and sage,
Lest the courtiers offended should be.
If you mention vice or bribe,
'Tis so pat to all the tribe
Each cries—That was levelled at me.   25

PEACHUM. Here's poor Ned Clincher's name, I see. Sure, brother Lockit, there was a little unfair proceeding in Ned's case; for he told me in the condemned hold, that for value received, you had promised him a session or two longer without molestation.

LOCKIT. Mr. Peachum, this is the first time my honor was   [30
ever called in question.

PEACHUM. Business is at an end, if once we act dishonorably.

LOCKIT. Who accuses me?

PEACHUM. You are warm, brother.

LOCKIT. He that attacks my honor, attacks my livelihood.   [35
And this usage, sir, is not to be borne.

PEACHUM. Since you provoke me to speak, I must tell you too, that Mrs. Coaxer charges you with defrauding her of her information-money, for the apprehending of curl-pated Hugh. Indeed, indeed, brother, we must punctually pay our spies, or we shall have   [40
no information.

SCENE X: *7. arrear:* i.e., failure to pay up the rewards promised for the capture and conviction of criminals. *10. employment:* official position.

LOCKIT. Is this language to me, sirrah? Who have saved you from the gallows, sirrah!   [*Collaring each other.*

PEACHUM. If I am hanged, it shall be for ridding the world of an arrant rascal.   45

LOCKIT. This hand shall do the office of the halter you deserve, and throttle you, you dog!   [*They break apart.*

PEACHUM. —Brother, brother,—we are both losers in the dispute— for you know we have it in our power to hang each other. You should not be so passionate.   50

LOCKIT. Nor you so provoking.

PEACHUM. 'Tis our mutual interest, 'tis for the interest of the world, we should agree. If I said anything, brother, to the prejudice of your character, I ask pardon.

LOCKIT. Brother Peachum, I can forgive as well as resent.   [55 —Give me your hand. Suspicion does not become a friend.

PEACHUM. I only meant to give you occasion to justify yourself. But I must now step home, for I expect the gentleman about this snuff-box that Filch nimmed two nights ago in the park. I appointed   [59 him at this hour.   [*Exit.*

SCENE XI

[LOCKIT, LUCY.]

LOCKIT. Whence come you, hussy?

LUCY. My tears might answer that question.

LOCKIT. You have then been whimpering and fondling, like a span- iel, over the fellow that hath abused you.

LUCY. One can't help love; one can't cure it. 'Tis not in my   [5 power to obey you, and hate him.

LOCKIT. Learn to bear your husband's death like a reasonable woman. 'Tis not the fashion, nowadays, so much as to affect sorrow upon these occasions. No woman would ever marry if she had not the chance of mortality for a release. Act like a woman of   [10 spirit, hussy, and thank your father for what he is doing.

LUCY.

AIR XXXI—*Of a noble race was Shenkin.*

Is then his fate decreed, sir?
    Such a man can I think of quitting?
When first we met, so moves me yet,
    Oh, see how my heart is splitting!   15

LOCKIT. Look ye, Lucy—there is no saving him—so, I think, you must even do like other widows,—buy yourself weeds, and be cheer- ful.

AIR XXXII

You'll think, ere many days ensue,
    This sentence not severe;   20
I hang your husband, child, 'tis true,
    But with him hang your care.
        Twang dang dillo dee.

Like a good wife, go moan over your dying husband; that, child, is
your duty.—Consider, girl, you can't have the man and the   [25
money too—so make yourself as easy as you can by getting all you can
from him.   [*Exeunt.*

SCENE XII. *Another part of the prison.*

[LUCY, MACHEATH.]

LUCY. Though the ordinary was out of the way to-day, I hope, my
dear, you will, upon the first opportunity, quiet my scruples.—Oh, sir!
—my father's hard heart is not to be softened, and I am in the utmost
despair.

MACHEATH. But if I could raise a small sum—would not   [5
twenty guineas, think you, move him?—Of all the arguments in the
way of business, the perquisite is the most prevailing.—Your father's
perquisites for the escape of prisoners must amount to a considerable
sum in the year. Money well timed and properly applied will do
anything.   10

AIR XXXIII—*London ladies.*

If you at an office solicit your due,
    And would not have matters neglected;
You must quicken the clerk with the perquisite too,
    To do what his duty directed.
Or would you the frowns of a lady prevent,   15
    She too has this palpable failing,
The perquisite softens her into consent;
    That reason with all is prevailing.

LUCY. What love or money can do shall be done, for all my comfort
depends upon your safety.   20

SCENE XIII

[LUCY, MACHEATH, POLLY.]

POLLY. Where is my dear husband?—Was a rope ever intended for
this neck?—Oh, let me throw my arms about it, and throttle thee with

love!—Why dost thou turn away from me?—'Tis thy Polly—'tis thy wife.

MACHEATH. Was there ever such an unfortunate rascal as I [5 am!

LUCY. Was there ever such another villain!

POLLY. O Macheath! was it for this we parted? Taken! imprisoned! tried! hanged!—cruel reflection! I'll stay with thee till death—no force shall tear thy dear wife from thee now.—What means my [10 love?—not one kind word!—not one kind look! Think what thy Polly suffers to see thee in this condition.

AIR XXXIV—All in the downs, etc.

Thus when the swallow, seeking prey,
 Within the sash is closely pent,
His consort, with bemoaning lay,   15
 Without, sits pining for the event.
Her chattering lovers all around her skim;
She heeds them not (poor bird)—her soul's with him.

MACHEATH. I must disown her.—(*Aside.*) The wench is distracted.

LUCY. Am I then bilked of my virtue? Can I have no rep- [20 aration? Sure, men were born to lie, and women to believe them. O villain! villain!

POLLY. Am I not thy wife? Thy neglect of me, thy aversion to me, too severely proves it.—Look on me. Tell me; am I not thy wife?

LUCY. Perfidious wretch!   25

POLLY. Barbarous husband!

LUCY. Hadst thou been hanged five months ago, I had been happy.

POLLY. And I too. If you had been kind to me till death, it would not have vexed me—and that's no very unreasonable request (though from a wife) to a man who hath not above seven or eight days [30 to live.

LUCY. Art thou then married to another? Hast thou two wives, monster?

MACHEATH. If women's tongues can cease for an answer—hear me.

LUCY. I won't! Flesh and blood can't bear my usage.   35

POLLY. Shall I not claim my own? Justice bids me speak.

MACHEATH.

AIR XXXV—Have you heard of a frolicsome ditty, etc.

How happy I could be with either,
 Were t'other dear charmer away!
But while you thus tease me together,

> To neither a word will I say;   40
>   But tol de rol, etc.

POLLY. Sure, my dear, there ought to be some preference shown to
a wife! At least she may claim the appearance of it.—He must be
distracted with his misfortunes, or he could not use me thus!

LUCY. O villain, villain! thou hast deceived me—I could   [45
even inform against thee with pleasure. Not a prude wishes more
heartily to have facts against her intimate acquaintance, than I now
wish to have facts against thee. I would have her satisfaction, and
they should all out.

AIR XXXVI—Irish Trot.

POLLY. I'm bubbled.
LUCY.   —I'm bubbled!
POLLY. Oh how I am troubled!   50
LUCY. Bamboozled, and bit!
POLLY.   —My distresses are doubled.
LUCY.

> When you come to the tree, should the hangman refuse,
>   These fingers, with pleasure, could fasten the noose.

POLLY. I'm bubbled, etc.
                                                            55
MACHEATH. Be pacified, my dear Lucy!—This is all a fetch of Polly's
to make me desperate with you in case I get off. If I am hanged, she
would fain have the credit of being thought my widow.—Really, Polly,
this is no time for a dispute of this sort; for whenever you are talking
of marriage, I am thinking of hanging.   60

POLLY. And hast thou the heart to persist in disowning me?

MACHEATH. And hast thou the heart to persist in persuading me that
I am married? Why, Polly, dost thou seek to aggravate my misfortunes?   64

LUCY. *Really*, Miss Peachum, you but expose yourself. Besides, 'tis
barbarous in you to worry a gentleman in his circumstances.

POLLY.

AIR XXXVII

> Cease your funning,
>   Force or cunning
> Never shall my heart trepan.
>   All these sallies   70
>   Are but malice
> To seduce my constant man.

SCENE XIII: 50. *bubbled:* cheated. 69. *trepan:* deceive.

'Tis most certain,
By their flirting,
Women oft have envy shown;   75
Pleased to ruin
Other's wooing;
Never happy in their own!

LUCY. Decency, madam, methinks, might teach you to behave yourself with some reserve with the husband while his wife is   [80
present.

MACHEATH. But, seriously, Polly, this is carrying the joke a little too
far.

LUCY. If you are determined, madam, to raise a disturbance in the
prison, I shall be obliged to send for the turnkey to show you   [85
the door. I am sorry, madam, you force me to be so ill-bred.

POLLY. Give me leave to tell you, madam; these forward airs don't
become you in the least, madam. And my duty, madam, obliges me
to stay with my husband, madam.

LUCY.

AIR XXXVIII—*Good-morrow, gossip Joan.*

Why, how now, Madam Flirt?   90
If you thus must chatter;
And are for flinging dirt,
Let's try who best can spatter!
Madam Flirt!

POLLY.

Why, how now, saucy jade;   95
Sure the wench is tipsy!
How can you see me made   [*To him.*
The scoff of such a gipsy?
Saucy jade!   [*To her.*

SCENE XIV

[LUCY, MACHEATH, POLLY, PEACHUM.]

PEACHUM. Where's my wench? Ah hussy! hussy!—Come you home,
you slut; and when your fellow is hanged, hang yourself, to make your
family some amends.

POLLY. Dear, dear father, do not tear me from him! I must speak;
I have more to say to him. (*To* MACHEATH.) Oh! twist thy   [5
fetters about me, that he may not haul me from thee!

PEACHUM. Sure, all women are alike! If ever they commit the folly, they are sure to commit another by exposing themselves.—**Away**—not a word more—you are my prisoner now, hussy!

POLLY (*Holding* MACHEATH, PEACHUM *pulling her*).

AIR XXXIX—*Irish howl.*

No power on earth can e'er divide   10
The knot that sacred love hath tied.
When parents draw against our mind,
The true-love's knot they faster bind.
  Oh, oh ray, oh amborah—Oh, oh, etc.

[*Exeunt* POLLY *and* PEACHUM.

SCENE XV

[LUCY, MACHEATH.]

MACHEATH. I am naturally compassionate, wife, so that I could not use the wench as she deserved, which made you at first suspect there was something in what she said.

LUCY. Indeed, my dear, I was strangely puzzled.

MACHEATH. If that had been the case, her father would never   [5
have brought me into this circumstance. No, Lucy,—I had rather die than be false to thee.

LUCY. How happy am I if you say this from your heart! For I love thee so, that I could sooner bear to see thee hanged than in the arms of another.   10

MACHEATH. But couldst thou bear to see me hanged?

LUCY. O Macheath, I can never live to see that day.

MACHEATH. You see, Lucy; in the account of love you are in my debt, and you must now be convinced that I rather choose to die than to be another's. Make me, if possible, love thee more, and let   [15
me owe my life to thee. If you refuse to assist me, Peachum and your father will immediately put me beyond all means of escape.

LUCY. My father, I know, hath been drinking hard with the prisoners, and I fancy he is now taking his nap in his own room. If I can procure the keys, shall I go off with thee, my dear?   20

MACHEATH. If we are together, 'twill be impossible to lie concealed. As soon as the search begins to be a little cool, I will send to thee—till then, my heart is thy prisoner.

LUCY. Come then, my dear husband—owe thy life to me—and though you love me not—be grateful. But that Polly runs in   [25
my head strangely.

MACHEATH. A moment of time may make us unhappy forever.

LUCY.

AIR XL—*The lass of Patie's mill, etc.*

I like the fox shall grieve,
　　Whose mate hath left her side,
Whom hounds, from morn till eve,   30
　　Chase o'er the country wide,
Where can my lover hide?
　　Where cheat the wary pack?
If love be not his guide,
　　He never will come back!   35

Act III

SCENE I. *Newgate.*

[LOCKIT, LUCY.]

LOCKIT. To be sure, wench, you must have been aiding and abetting to help him to this escape.

LUCY. Sir, here hath been Peachum and his daughter Polly, and to be sure they know the ways of Newgate as well as if they had been born and bred in the place all their lives. Why must all your   [5 suspicion light upon me?

LOCKIT. Lucy, Lucy, I will have none of these shuffling answers.

LUCY. Well then—if I know anything of him, I wish I may be burnt!

LOCKIT. Keep your temper, Lucy, or I shall pronounce you guilty.

LUCY. Keep yours, sir. I do wish I may be burnt, I do. And   [10 what can I say more to convince you.

LOCKIT. Did he tip handsomely? How much did he come down with? Come, hussy, don't cheat your father, and I shall not be angry with you. Perhaps you have made a better bargain with him than I could have done. How much, my good girl?   15

LUCY. You know, sir, I am fond of him, and would have given money to have kept him with me.

LOCKIT. Ah, Lucy! thy education might have put thee more upon thy guard; for a girl in the bar of an ale-house is always besieged.

LUCY. Dear sir, mention not my education—for 'twas to that   [20 I owe my ruin.

AIR XLI—*If love's a sweet passion, etc.*

When young, at the bar you first taught me to score,
And bid me be free of my lips, and no more.

I was kissed by the parson, the squire, and the sot;
When the guest was departed, the kiss was forgot.   25
But his kiss was so sweet, and so closely he prest,
That I languished and pined till I granted the rest.

If you can forgive me, sir, I will make a fair confession, for to be sure he hath been a most barbarous villain to me.

LOCKIT. And so you have let him escape, hussy, have you?   30

LUCY. When a woman loves, a kind look, a tender word can persuade her to anything,—and I could ask no other bribe.

LOCKIT. Thou wilt always be a vulgar slut, Lucy. If you would not be looked upon as a fool, you should never do anything but upon the foot of interest. Those that act otherwise are their own   [35 bubbles.

LUCY. But love, sir, is a misfortune that may happen to the most discreet woman, and in love we are all fools alike. Not withstanding all he swore, I am now fully convinced that Polly Peachum is actually his wife. Did I let him escape (fool that I was) to go to   [40 her? Polly will wheedle herself into his money, and then Peachum will hang him, and cheat us both.

LOCKIT. So I am to be ruined, because, forsooth, you must be in love! —a very pretty excuse!   44

LUCY. I could murder that impudent happy strumpet! I gave him his life, and that creature enjoys the sweets of it. Ungrateful Macheath!

AIR XLII—*South-sea Ballad.*

My love is all madness and folly,
          Alone I lie,
              Toss, tumble, and cry;
What a happy creature is Polly!   50
Was e'er such a wretch as I!
With rage I redden like scarlet,
That my dear, inconstant varlet,
          Stark blind to my charms,
          Is lost in the arms   } *bis*   55
Of that jilt, that inveigling harlot! |
This, this my resentment alarms.

LOCKIT. And so, after all this mischief, I must stay here to be entertained with your catewauling, mistress Puss! Out of my   [60 sight, wanton strumpet! You shall fast and fortify yourself into reason,

ACT III, SCENE I: 36. *bubbles:* dupes.

with now and then a little handsome discipline to bring you to your
senses. Go!   [*Exit* LUCY.

SCENE II

[LOCKIT.]

—Peachum then intends to outwit me in this affair, but I'll be even
with him. The dog is leaky in his liquor; so I'll ply him that way,
get the secret from him, and turn this affair to my own advantage.
Lions, wolves, and vultures don't live together in herds, droves, or
flocks. Of all animals of prey, man is the only sociable one.   [5
Every one of us preys upon his neighbor, and yet we herd together.
Peachum is my companion, my friend. According to the custom of
the world, indeed, he may quote thousands of precedents for cheating
me. And shall not I make use of the privilege of friendship to make
him a return?   10

AIR XLIII—*Packington's Pound.*

Thus gamesters united in friendship are found,
Though they know that their industry all is a cheat;
They flock to their prey at the dice-box's sound,
And join to promote one another's deceit.
But if by mishap   15
They fail of a chap,
To keep in their hands, they each other entrap.
Like pikes, lank with hunger, who miss of their ends,
They bite their companions, and prey on their friends.

Now, Peachum, you and I, like honest tradesmen, are to have   [20
a fair trial which of us two can over-reach the other. (*Calls.*) Lucy!

[*Enter* LUCY.]

Are there any of Peachum's people now in the house?

LUCY. Filch, sir, is drinking a quartern of strong waters in the next
room with Black Moll.   24
LOCKIT. Bid him come to me.   [*Exit* LUCY.

SCENE III

[LOCKIT, FILCH.]

LOCKIT. Why, boy, thou lookest as if thou wert half starved—like a
shotten herring.

SCENE III: 2. *a . . . herring:* a herring that having cast its roe is scrawny.
Cf. 1 *Henry IV*, II iv 143.

FILCH. One had need have the constitution of a horse to go through the business. Since the favorite child-getter was disabled by mishap, I have picked up a little money by helping the ladies to a preg-   [5 nancy against their being called down to sentence. But if a man cannot get an honest livelihood any easier way, I am sure 'tis what I can't undertake for another session.

LOCKIT. Truly, if that great man should tip off, 'twould be an irrep- arable loss. The vigor and prowess of a knight-errant never   [10 saved half of the ladies in distress that he hath done.—But, boy, canst thou tell me where thy master is to be found?

FILCH. At his lock, sir, at the Crooked Billet.

LOCKIT. Very well. I have nothing more with you. (*Exit* FILCH.) I'll go to him there, for I have many important affairs to   [15 settle with him; and in the way of those transactions, I'll artfully get into his secret, so that Macheath shall not remain a day longer out o' my clutches.

SCENE IV. *A gaming-house.*

[MACHEATH *in a fine tarnished coat,* BEN BUDGE, MATT OF THE MINT.]

MACHEATH. I am sorry, gentlemen, the road was so barren of money. When my friends are in difficulties, I am always glad that my   [20 fortune can be serviceable to them. (*Gives them money.*) You see, gentlemen, I am not a mere court friend, who professes everything and will do nothing.

AIR XLIV—*Lillibullero.*

The modes of the court so common are grown,
 That a true friend can hardly be met;   25
Friendship for interest is but a loan,
 Which they let out for what they can get.
   'Tis true, you find
   Some friends so kind,
Who will give you good counsel themselves to defend. 30
   In sorrowful ditty,
   They promise, they pity,
But shift you, for money, from friend to friend.

But we, gentlemen, have still honor enough to break through the corruptions of the world. And while I can serve you, you may   [35 command me.

BEN. It grieves my heart that so generous a man should be involved in such difficulties as oblige him to live with such ill company, and herd with gamesters.

MATT. See the partiality of mankind! One man may steal a   [40
horse, better than another look over a hedge. Of all mechanics, of all
servile handicrafts-men, a gamester is the vilest. But yet, as many of
the quality are of the profession, he is admitted amongst the politest
company. I wonder we are not more respected.

MACHEATH. There will be deep play tonight at Marybone and   [45
consequently money may be picked up upon the road. Meet me there,
and I'll give you the hint who is worth setting.

MATT. The fellow with a brown coat with a narrow gold binding,
I am told, is never without money.

MACHEATH. What do you mean, Matt? Sure you will not   [50
think of meddling with him! He's a good honest kind of a fellow,
and one of us.

BEN. To be sure, sir, we will put ourselves under your direction.

MACHEATH. Have an eye upon the money-lenders. A rouleau or
two would prove a pretty sort of an expedition. I hate extortion.   [55

MATT. These rouleaus are very pretty things. I hate your bank bills.
There is such a hazard in putting them off.

MACHEATH. There is a certain man of distinction who in his time
hath nicked me out of a great deal of the ready. He is in my cash,
Ben. I'll point him out to you this evening, and you shall draw   [60
upon him for the debt.—The company are met; I hear the dice-box
in the other room. So, gentlemen, your servant! You'll meet me at
Marybone.   [*Exeunt.*

SCENE V. PEACHUM's *lock. A table with wine, brandy,
pipes and tobacco.*

[PEACHUM, LOCKIT.]

LOCKIT. The Coronation account, brother Peachum, is of so intricate
a nature, that I believe it will never be settled.

PEACHUM. It consists, indeed, of a great variety of articles. It was
worth to our people, in fees of different kinds, above ten installments.
This is part of the account, brother, that lies open before us.   [5

LOCKIT. A lady's tail of rich brocade—that, I see, is disposed of—

PEACHUM. To Mrs. Diana Trapes, the tallywoman, and she will
make a good hand on't in shoes and slippers, to trick out young
ladies upon their going into keeping.

LOCKIT. But I don't see any article of the jewels.   10

SCENE IV: 47. *setting:* robbing. 54. *rouleau:* roll of (gold) coins.

SCENE V: 1. *Coronation account:* i.e., the pickings from the crowd at the
coronation of George II in 1727. 6. *tail:* train.

PEACHUM. Those are so well known that they must be sent abroad. You'll find them entered under the article of exportation. As for the snuff-boxes, watches, swords, etc., I thought it best to enter them under their several heads.

LOCKIT. Seven and twenty women's pockets complete, with   [15
the several things therein contained—all sealed, numbered, and entered.

PEACHUM. But, brother, it is impossible for us now to enter upon this affair.—We should have the whole day before us.—Besides, the account of the last half-year's plate is in a book by itself, which   [20
lies at the other office.

LOCKIT. Bring us then more liquor.—Today shall be for pleasure—tomorrow for business.—Ah, brother, those daughters of ours are two slippery hussies. Keep a watchful eye upon Polly, and Macheath in a day or two shall be our own again.   25

LOCKIT.

AIR XLV.—*Down in the North Country, etc.*

What gudgeons are we men!
    Every woman's easy prey;
Though we have felt the hook, again
    We bite and they betray.
The bird that hath been trapped,   30
    When he hears his calling mate,
To her he flies, again he's clapped
    Within the wiry grate.

PEACHUM. But what signifies catching the bird if your daughter Lucy will set open the door of the cage?   35

LOCKIT. If men were answerable for the follies and frailities of their wives and daughters, no friends could keep a good correspondence together for two days.—This is unkind of you, brother; for among good friends, what they say or do goes for nothing.

[*Enter* A SERVANT.]

SERVANT. Sir, here's Mrs. Diana Trapes wants to speak with   [40
you.

PEACHUM. Shall we admit her, brother Lockit?

LOCKIT. By all means—she's a good customer, and a fine-spoken woman—and a woman who drinks and talks so freely will enliven the conversation.   45

PEACHUM. Desire her to walk in.   [*Exit* SERVANT.

26. *gudgeon:* a variety of fish easily caught; hence, "dupe."

SCENE VI

[PEACHUM, LOCKIT, MRS. TRAPES.]

PEACHUM. Dear Mrs. Dye, your servant—one may know by your kiss, that your gin is excellent.

TRAPES. I was always very curious in my liquors.

LOCKIT. There is no perfumed breath like it. I have been long acquainted with the flavor of those lips—han't I, Mrs. Dye?   [5

TRAPES. Fill it up.—I take as large draughts of liquor as I did of love.—I hate a flincher in either.

AIR XLVI—*A shepherd kept sheep, etc.*

In the days of my youth I could bill like a dove, fa, la, la, etc.
Like a sparrow at all times was ready for love, fa, la, la, etc.
The life of all mortals in kissing should pass,   10
Lip to lip while we're young—then lip to the glass, fa, la, etc.

But now, Mr. Peachum, to our business.—If you have blacks of any kind, brought in of late; mantoes—velvet scarfs—petticoats—let it be what it will, I am your chap—for all my ladies are very fond of mourning.   15

PEACHUM. Why, look ye, Mrs. Dye—you deal so hard with us, that we can afford to give the gentlemen who venture their lives for the goods, little or nothing.

TRAPES. The hard times oblige me to go very near in my dealing. To be sure, of late years I have been a great sufferer by the   [20 parliament.—Three thousand pounds would hardly make me amends. —The act for destroying the Mint was a severe cut upon our business —till then, if a customer stepped out of the way—we knew where to have her. No doubt you know Mrs. Coaxer—there's a wench now (till to-day) with a good suit of clothes of mine upon her back,   [25 and I could never set eyes upon her for three months together. Since the act, too, against imprisonment for small sums, my loss there too hath been very considerable; and it must be so, when a lady can borrow a handsome petticoat, or a clean gown, and I not have the least hank upon her! And, o' my conscience, nowadays most ladies take a   [30 delight in cheating, when they can do it with safety!

PEACHUM. Madam, you had a handsome gold watch of us t'other day for seven guineas. Considering we must have our profit—to a

---

SCENE VI: 3. *curious:* particular. 13. *mantoes:* manteaus. 22. *Mint:* Southwark Mint, a rendezvous of criminals. 29. *hank:* control.

gentleman upon the road, a gold watch will be scarce worth the
taking.   35

TRAPES. Consider, Mr. Peachum, that watch was remarkable and
not of very safe sale. If you have any black velvet scarfs—they are
handsome winter wear, and take with most gentlemen who deal with
my customers. 'Tis I that put the ladies upon a good foot. 'Tis not
youth or beauty that fixes their price. The gentlemen always   [40
pay according to their dress, from half a crown to two guineas; and
yet those hussies make nothing of bilking me. Then, too, allowing
for accidents.—I have eleven fine customers now down under the
surgeon's hands; what with fees and other expenses, there are great
goings-out, and no comings-in, and not a farthing to pay for   [45
at least a month's clothing. We run great risks—great risks indeed.

PEACHUM. As I remember, you said something just now of a Mrs.
Coaxer.

TRAPES. Yes, sir. To be sure, I stripped her of a suit of my own
clothes about two hours ago, and have left her as she should be,   [50
in her shift, with a lover of hers, at my house. She called him upstairs
as he was going to Marybone in a hackney coach. And I hope, for
her sake and mine, she will persuade the captain to redeem her, for
the captain is very generous to the ladies.

LOCKIT. What captain?   55

TRAPES. He thought I did not know him—an intimate acquaintance
of yours, Mr. Peachum—only Captain Macheath—as fine as a lord.

PEACHUM. To-morrow, dear Mrs. Dye, you shall set your own price
upon any of the goods you like. We have at least half a dozen velvet
scarfs, and all at your service. Will you give me leave to make   [60
you a present of this suit of nightclothes for your own wearing?—
But are you sure it is Captain Macheath?

TRAPES. Though he thinks I have forgot him, nobody knows him
better. I have taken a great deal of the captain's money in my time
at second-hand, for he always loved to have his ladies well-   [65
dressed.

PEACHUM. Mr. Lockit and I have a little business with the captain—
you understand me—and we will satisfy you for Mrs. Coaxer's debt.

LOCKIT. Depend upon it—we will deal like men of honor.

TRAPES. I don't enquire after your affairs—so whatever hap-   [70
pens, I wash my hands on't. It hath always been my maxim, that
one friend should assist another.—But if you please, I'll take one of
the scarfs home with me. 'Tis always good to have something in
hand.

43-4. i.e., for pregnancies or venereal diseases.

SCENE VII. *Newgate.*

[LUCY.]

LUCY. Jealousy, rage, love, and fear are at once tearing me to pieces. How I am weatherbeaten and shattered with distresses!

AIR XLVII—*One evening, having lost my way, etc.*

I'm like a skiff on the ocean tossed,
Now high, now low, with each billow borne;
With her rudder broke, and her anchor lost,   5
    Deserted and all forlorn.
While thus I lie rolling and tossing all night,
That Polly lies sporting on seas of delight!
    Revenge, revenge, revenge,
Shall appease my restless sprite.   10

—I have the ratsbane ready. I run no risk; for I can lay her death upon the gin, and so many die of that naturally that I shall never be called in question. But say I were to be hanged—I never could be hanged for anything that would give me greater comfort than the poisoning that slut.   15

[*Enter* FILCH.]

FILCH. Madam, here's our Miss Polly come to wait upon you.
LUCY. Show her in.

SCENE VIII

[LUCY, POLLY.]

LUCY. Dear madam, your servant. I hope you will pardon my passion when I was so happy to see you last. I was so overrun with the spleen, that I was perfectly out of myself. And really when one hath the spleen, everything is to be excused by a friend.

AIR XLVIII—*Now Roger, I'll tell thee, because thou'rt my son, etc.*

When a wife's in her pout,   5
(As she's sometimes, no doubt);
The good husband, as meek as a lamb,
    Her vapors to still,
    First grants her her will,
And the quieting draught is a dram.   10
Poor man! And the quieting draught is a dram.

—I wish all our quarrels might have so comfortable a reconciliation.

POLLY. I have no excuse for my own behavior, madam, but my misfortunes. And really, madam, I suffer too upon your account.

LUCY. But, Miss Polly—in the way of friendship, will you   [15
give me leave to propose a glass of cordial to you?

POLLY. Strong waters are apt to give me the headache; I hope, madam, you will excuse me.

LUCY. Not the greatest lady in the land could have better in her closet, for her own private drinking. You seem mighty low   [20
in spirits, my dear.

POLLY. I am sorry, madam, my health will not allow me to accept of your offer. I should not have left you in the rude manner I did when we met last, madam, had not my papa hauled me away so unexpectedly. I was indeed somewhat provoked, and perhaps   [25
might use some expressions that were disrespectful. But really, madam, the captain treated me with so much contempt and cruelty, that I deserved your pity, rather than your resentment.

LUCY. But since his escape, no doubt, all matters are made up again. —Ah Polly! Polly! 'tis I am the unhappy wife, and he loves   [30
you as if you were only his mistress.

POLLY. Sure, madam, you cannot think me so happy as to be the object of your jealousy! A man is always afraid of a woman who loves him too well—so that I must expect to be neglected and avoided.

LUCY. Then our cases, my dear Polly, are exactly alike. Both   [35
of us, indeed, have been too fond.

AIR XLIX—*O Bessy Bell.*

> POLLY. A curse attends that woman's love,
>   Who always would be pleasing.
> LUCY. The pertness of the billing dove,
>   Like tickling, is but teasing.   40
> POLLY. What then in love can woman do?
> LUCY. If we grow fond they shun us.
> POLLY. And when we fly them, they pursue.
> LUCY. But leave us when they've won us.

LUCY. Love is so very whimsical in both sexes, that it is   [45
impossible to be lasting. But my heart is particular, and contradicts my own observation.

POLLY. But really, mistress Lucy, by his last behavior, I think I ought to envy you. When I was forced from him, he did not shew the least

---

SCENE VIII: 20. *private:* It was a pose of fashionable women that they touched nothing stronger than wine: cf. III x 4 ff.

tenderness. But perhaps he hath a heart not capable of it.   50

AIR L—*Would fate to me Belinda give.*

> Among the men, coquets we find,
> Who court by turns all womankind;
> And we grant all their hearts desired,
> When they are flattered and admired.

The coquets of both sexes are self-lovers, and that is a love no   [55
other whatever can dispossess. I fear, my dear Lucy, our husband is
one of those.

LUCY. Away with these melancholy reflections!—indeed, my dear
Polly, we are both of us a cup too low. (*Going.*) Let me prevail upon
you to accept of my offer.   60

AIR LI—*Come, sweet lass, etc.*

> Come, sweet lass,
> Let's banish sorrow
> 'Till to-morrow;
> Come, sweet lass,
> Let's take a chirping glass.   65
>   Wine can clear
>   The vapors of despair;
>   And make us light as air;
>   Then drink, and banish care.

I can't bear, child, to see you in such low spirits. And I must   [70
persuade you to what I know will do you good. (*Aside.*) I shall now
soon be even with the hypocritical strumpet.   [*Exit* LUCY.

SCENE IX

[POLLY.]

POLLY. All this wheedling of Lucy cannot be for nothing—at this
time too, when I know she hates me!—The dissembling of a woman
is always the forerunner of mischief.—By pouring strong waters down
my throat, she thinks to pump some secret out of me. I'll be upon
my guard and won't taste a drop of her liquor, I'm resolved.   5

SCENE X

[LUCY, *with strong waters;* POLLY.]

LUCY. Come, Miss Polly.

POLLY. Indeed, child, you have given yourself trouble to no purpose.
—You must, my dear, excuse me.

LUCY. Really, Miss Polly, you are so squeamishly affected about taking a cup of strong waters as a lady before company. I vow,   [5
Polly, I shall take it monstrously ill if you refuse me.—Brandy and men (though women love them never so well) are always taken by us with some reluctance—unless 'tis in private.

POLLY. I protest, madam, it goes against me. What do I see! Macheath again in custody!—Now every glimmering of happiness   [10 is lost. [*Drops the glass of liquor on the ground.*]

LUCY (*aside*). Since things are thus, I am glad the wench hath escaped: for by this event, 'tis plain, she was not happy enough to deserve to be poisoned.

SCENE XI

[LOCKIT, MACHEATH, PEACHUM, LUCY, POLLY.]

LOCKIT. Set your heart to rest, captain.—You have neither the chance of love, or money for another escape; for you are ordered to be called down upon your trial immediately.

PEACHUM. Away, hussies!—This is not a time for a man to be hampered with his wives. You see, the gentleman is in chains   [5 already.

LUCY. O husband, husband, my heart longed to see thee; but to see thee thus distracts me!

POLLY. Will not my dear husband look upon his Polly? Why hadst thou not flown to me for protection? With me thou hadst   [10 been safe.

AIR LII—*The last time I went o'er the moor.*

POLLY. Hither, dear husband, turn your eyes.
LUCY. Bestow one glance to cheer me.
POLLY. Think, with that look, thy Polly dies.
LUCY. Oh shun me not—but hear me.   15
POLLY. 'Tis Polly sues.
LUCY.   —'Tis Lucy speaks.
POLLY. Is thus true love requited?
LUCY. My heart is bursting.
POLLY.   —Mine too breaks.
LUCY. Must I?
POLLY.   —Must I be slighted?

MACHEATH. What would you have me say, ladies?—You see,   [20 this affair will soon be at an end without my disobliging either of you.

PEACHUM. But the settling this point, captain, might prevent a lawsuit between your two widows.

MACHEATH.

AIR LIII—Tom Tinker's my true love.

Which way shall I turn me? How can I decide?
Wives, the day of our death, are as fond as a bride.   25
One wife is too much for most husbands to hear,
But two at a time there's no mortal can bear.
This way, and that way, and which way I will,
What would comfort the one, t'other wife would take ill.

POLLY (*aside*). But if his own misfortunes have made him   [30
insensible to mine—a father sure will be more compassionate.—(*To*
PEACHUM.) Dear, dear sir, sink the material evidence, and bring him
off at his trial! Polly upon her knees begs it of you.

AIR LIV—I am a poor shepherd undone.

When my hero in court appears,
    And stands arraigned for his life;   35
Then think of poor Polly's tears;
    For ah! poor Polly's his wife.
Like the sailor he holds up his hand,
    Distressed on the dashing wave.
To die a dry death at land,   40
    Is as bad as a watery grave.
        And alas, poor Polly;
        Alack, and well-a-day!
        Before I was in love,
        Oh, every month was May!   45

LUCY (*to* LOCKIT). If Peachum's heart is hardened, sure you, sir,
will have more compassion on a daughter. I know the evidence is in
your power. How can you be a tyrant to me?   [*Kneeling.*

AIR LV—Ianthe the lovely, etc.

When he holds up his hand arraigned for his life,
Oh, think of your daughter, and think I'm his wife!   50
What are cannons, or bombs, or clashing of swords?
For death is more certain by witnesses' words.
Then nail up their lips; that dread thunder allay;
And each month of my life will hereafter be May.

LOCKIT. Macheath's time is come, Lucy. We know our own   [55
affairs; therefore let us have no more whimpering or whining.

AIR LVI—*A cobbler there was, etc.*

Ourselves, like the great, to secure a retreat,
When matters require it, must give up our gang.
    And good reason why,
    Or instead of the fry,
    Even Peachum and I,
Like poor petty rascals, might hang, hang;
Like poor petty rascals might hang.

PEACHUM. Set your heart at rest, Polly. Your husband is to die
to-day! therefore, if you are not already provided, 'tis high   [65
time to look about for another.—There's comfort for you, you slut.

LOCKIT. We are ready, sir, to conduct you to the Old Bailey.

MACHEATH.

AIR LVII—*Bonny Dundee.*

The charge is prepared; the lawyers are met,
The judges all ranged (a terrible show!).
I go, undismayed—for death is a debt,   70
A debt on demand. So, take what I owe.
Then farewell, my love—dear charmers, adieu.
Contented I die—'tis the better for you.
Here ends all dispute the rest of our lives,
    For this way at once I please all my wives.   75

Now, gentlemen, I am ready to attend you.

                [*Exeunt* MACHEATH, LOCKIT *and* PEACHUM.

SCENE XII

[LUCY, POLLY, FILCH.]

POLLY. Follow them, Filch, to the court; and when the trial is over,
bring me a particular account of his behavior, and of everything that
happened.—You'll find me here with Miss Lucy. [*Exit* FILCH.] But
why is all this music?

LUCY. The prisoners whose trials are put off till next sessions   [5
are diverting themselves.

POLLY. Sure there is nothing so charming as music! I'm fond of it
to distraction! But alas! now, all mirth seems an insult upon my

---

SCENE XI: 60. *fry:* small fish. 70. *Death* and *debt* were originally pronounced alike: cf. 1 Henry IV, V i 127 ff.

affliction.—Let us retire, my dear Lucy, and indulge our sor-   [9
rows.—The noisy crew, you see, are coming upon us.   [*Exeunt.*
[*A dance of prisoners in chains, etc.*]

SCENE XIII. *The condemned hold.*

[MACHEATH *in a melancholy posture.*]

AIR LVIII—*Happy groves.*

O cruel, cruel, cruel case!
Must I suffer this disgrace?

AIR LVIX—*Of all the girls that are so smart.*

Of all the friends in time of grief,
  When threatening death looks grimmer,
Not one so sure can bring relief,   5
  As this best friend, a brimmer.   [*Drinks.*

AIR LX—*Britons, strike home.*

Since I must swing,—I scorn, I scorn to wince or whine.
          [*Rises.*

AIR LXI—*Chevy Chase.*

But now again my spirits sink;
I'll raise them high with wine.
          [*Drinks a glass of wine.*

AIR LXII—*To old Sir Simon the king.*

But valor the stronger grows,   10
The stronger liquor we're drinking.
And how can we feel our woes,
When we've left the trouble of thinking?
          [*Drinks.*

AIR LXIII—*Joy to great Cæsar.*

If thus—a man can die.
Much bolder with brandy.   15
          [*Pours out a bumper of brandy.*

AIR LXIV—*There was an old woman.*

So I drink off this bumper.—And now I can stand the test.
And my comrades shall see that I die as brave as the best.
          [*Drinks.*

AIR LXV—*Did you ever hear of a gallant sailor.*

> But can I leave my pretty hussies,
>   Without one tear, or tender sigh?

AIR LXVI—*Why are mine eyes still flowing.*

> Their eyes, their lips, their busses,   20
>   Recall my love.—Ah, must I die?

AIR LXVII—*Green sleeves.*

Since laws were made for every degree,
To curb vice in others, as well as me,
I wonder we han't better company,
        Upon Tyburn tree!   25
But gold from law can take out the sting;
And if rich men like us were to swing,
'Twould thin the land, such numbers to string
        Upon Tyburn tree!

[Enter a JAILOR.]

JAILOR. Some friends of yours, captain, desire to be ad-   [30
mitted.—I leave you together.   [*Exit.*

SCENE XIV

[MACHEATH, BEN BUDGE, MATT OF THE MINT.]

MACHEATH. For my having broke prison, you see, gentlemen, I am
ordered immediate execution. The sheriff's officers, I believe, are now
at the door. That Jemmy Twitcher should peach me, I own, surprised
me! 'Tis a plain proof that the world is all alike, and that even our
gang can no more trust one another than other people. There-   [5
fore, I beg you, gentlemen, look well to yourselves, for in all probability you may live some months longer.

MATT. We arc heartily sorry, captain, for your misfortune.—But 'tis
what we must all come to.

MACHEATH. Peachum and Lockit, you know, are infamous   [10
scoundrels. Their lives are as much in your power, as yours are in
theirs. Remember your dying friend!—'Tis my last request. Bring
those villains to the gallows before you, and I am satisfied.

MATT. We'll do't.

[Re-enter JAILOR.]

SCENE XIII: 20. *busses:* kisses.

JAILOR. Miss Polly and Miss Lucy entreat a word with you.　　15
MACHEATH. Gentlemen, adieu.　　[*Exeunt* BEN, MATT, *and* JAILOR.

SCENE XV

[LUCY, MACHEATH, POLLY.]

MACHEATH. My dear Lucy—my dear Polly! Whatsoever hath passed between us is now at an end. If you are fond of marrying again, the best advice I can give you is to ship yourselves off for the West Indies, where you'll have a fair chance of getting a husband apiece—or by good luck, two or three, as you like best.　　5

POLLY. How can I support this sight!

LUCY (*aside*). There is nothing moves one so much as a great man in distress.

AIR LXVIII—*All you that must take a leap, etc.*

LUCY. Would I might be hanged!
POLLY.　　　　　　　　　—And I would so too!
LUCY. To be hanged with you.
POLLY.　　　　　　　—My dear, with you.　　10
MACHEATH. Oh, leave me to thought! I fear! I doubt!
I tremble! I droop!—See, my courage is out.
　　　　　　　　　　　　　　　[*Turns up the empty bottle.*

POLLY. No token of love?
MACHEATH.　　　　　　—See, my courage is out.
　　　　　　　　　　　　　　　[*Turns up the empty pot.*

LUCY. No token of love?
POLLY.　　　　　　Adieu.
LUCY.　　　　　　　Farewell!
MACHEATH. But hark! I hear the toll of the bell!　　15
CHORUS. Tol de rol lol, etc.

[*Enter* JAILOR.]

JAILOR. Four women more, captain, with a child apiece! See, here they come.

[*Enter* WOMEN *and* CHILDREN.]

MACHEATH. What—four wives more!—This is too much.—Here, tell the Sheriff's officers I am ready.　　20
　　　　　　　　　　　　　　　[*Exit* MACHEATH *guarded.*

SCENE XVI

[To them enter PLAYER *and* BEGGAR.]

PLAYER. But, honest friend, I hope you don't intend that Macheath shall be really executed.

BEGGAR. Most certainly, sir. To make the piece perfect, I was for doing strict poetical justice. Macheath is to be hanged; and for the other personages of the drama, the audience must have sup-   [5 posed they were all either hanged or transported.

PLAYER. Why then, friend, this is a downright deep tragedy. The catastrophe is manifestly wrong, for an opera must end happily.

BEGGAR. Your objection, sir, is very just, and is easily removed; for you must allow that in this kind of drama, 'tis no matter how   [10 absurdly things are brought about. So—you rabble there! run and cry a reprieve!—let the prisoner be brought back to his wives in triumph.

PLAYER. All this we must do, to comply with the taste of the town.

BEGGAR. Through the whole piece you may observe such a similitude of manners in high and low life, that it is difficult to deter-   [15 mine whether (in the fashionable vices) the fine gentlemen imitate the gentlemen of the road, or the gentlemen of the road the fine gentlemen. Had the play remained as I at first intended, it would have carried a most excellent moral. 'Twould have shown that the lower sort of people have their vices in a degree as well as the rich,   [20 and that they are punished for them.

SCENE XVII

[To them MACHEATH, *with rabble, etc.]*

MACHEATH. So it seems I am not left to my choice, but must have a wife at last.—Look ye, my dears, we will have no controversy now. Let us give this day to mirth, and I am sure she who thinks herself my wife will testify her joy by a dance.

ALL. Come, a dance—a dance!   5

MACHEATH. Ladies, I hope you will give me leave to present a partner to each of you. And (if I may without offence) for this time, I take Polly for mine. *[To* POLLY.] And for life, you slut, for we were really married. As for the rest—but at present keep your own secret.

A Dance

AIR LXIX—*Lumps of pudding, etc.*

Thus I stand like the Turk, with his doxies around;　　10
From all sides their glances his passion confound:
For black, brown, and fair, his inconstancy burns,
And the different beauties subdue him by turns.
Each calls forth her charms, to provoke his desires;
Though willing to all, with but one he retires.　　15
But think of this maxim, and put off your sorrow,
The wretch of to-day may be happy to-morrow.

CHORUS. But think of this maxim, etc.

Alexander Pope

An Essay on Criticism

I

'T is hard to say, if greater want of skill
Appear in writing or in judging ill;
But, of the two, less dangerous is th' offence.
To tire our patience, than mislead our sense.
Some few in that, but numbers err in this,   5
Ten censure wrong for one who writes amiss;
A fool might once himself alone expose,
Now one in verse makes many more in prose.
    'Tis with our judgments as our watches, none
Go just alike, yet each believes his own.   10
In Poets as true genius is but rare,
True taste as seldom is the Critic's share;
Both must alike from Heaven derive their light,
These born to judge, as well as those to write.
Let such teach others who themselves excel,   15
And censure freely who have written well.
Authors are partial to their wit, 'tis true,
But are not Critics to their judgment too?
    Yet if we look more closely, we shall find
Most have the seeds of judgment in their mind: 20
Nature affords at least a glimmering light;
The lines, tho' touched but faintly, are drawn right.

---

17. *wit:* Pope uses this word in several senses; here, to mean an author's
writings (and perhaps also the creative power which produces them).

But as the slightest sketch, if justly traced,
Is by ill-colouring but the more disgraced,
So by false learning is good sense defaced: 25
Some are bewildered in the maze of schools,
And some made coxcombs Nature meant but fools.
In search of wit these lose their common sense,
And then turn Critics in their own defence:
Each burns alike, who can, or cannot write,   30
Or with a Rival's, or an Eunuch's spite.
All fools have still an itching to deride,
And fain would be upon the laughing side.
If Mævius scribble in Apollo's spite,
There are who judge still worse than he can write.   35
   Some have at first for Wits, then Poets past,
Turned Critics next, and proved plain fools at last.
Some neither can for Wits nor Critics pass,
As heavy mules are neither horse nor ass.
Those half-learn'd witlings, numerous in our isle,   40
As half-formed insects on the banks of Nile;
Unfinished things, one knows not what to call,
Their generation's so equivocal:
To tell 'em, would a hundred tongues require,
Or one vain Wit's, that might a hundred tire.   45
   But you who seek to give and merit fame,
And justly bear a Critic's noble name,
Be sure yourself and your own reach to know,
How far your genius, taste, and learning go;
Launch not beyond your depth, but be discreet,   50
And mark that point where sense and dulness meet.
   Nature to all things fixed the limits fit,
And wisely curbed proud man's pretending wit.
As on the land while here the ocean gains,
In other parts it leaves wide sandy plains;   55
Thus in the soul while memory prevails,
The solid power of understanding fails;
Where beams of warm imagination play,
The memory's soft figures melt away.

---

23. *traced:* drawn. 26. *schools:* i.e., of criticism. 27. *coxcombs:* pretenders
to wit and learning. 28. *wit:* striking literary effect. 34. *Maevius:* traditional name for a poetaster. *Apollo:* patron of poetry. 36. *Wits:* Men who
are (or fancy themselves) imaginatively and artistically gifted. 41. Egyptian insects were believed to be spontaneously generated in Nile mud by the
sun's heat. 44. *tell:* count. 53. *pretending wit:* aspiring intellect.

One science only will one genius fit;   60
So vast is art, so narrow human wit:
Not only bounded to peculiar arts,
But oft in those confined to single parts.
Like kings we lose the conquests gained before,
By vain ambition still to make them more;   65
Each might his several province well command,
Would all but stoop to what they understand.
    First follow Nature, and your judgment frame
By her just standard, which is still the same:
Unerring NATURE, still divinely bright,   70
One clear, unchanged, and universal light,
Life, force, and beauty, must to all impart,
At once the source, and end, and test of Art.
Art from that fund each just supply provides,
Works without show, and without pomp presides: 75
In some fair body thus th' informing soul
With spirits feeds, with vigour fills the whole,
Each motion guides, and every nerve sustains;
Itself unseen, but in th' effects, remains.
Some, to whom Heaven in wit has been profuse,   80
Want as much more, to turn it to its use;
For wit and judgment often are at strife,
Tho' meant each other's aid, like man and wife.
'Tis more to guide, than spur the Muse's steed;
Restrain his fury, than provoke his speed;   85
The wingèd courser, like a generous horse,
Shows most true mettle when you check his course.
    Those RULES of old discovered, not devised,
Are Nature still, but Nature methodized;
Nature, like liberty, is but restrained   90
By the same laws which first herself ordained.
    Hear how learn'd Greece her useful rules indites,
When to repress, and when indulge our flights:
High on Parnassus' top her sons she showed,
And pointed out those arduous paths they trod;   95
Held from afar, aloft, th' immortal prize,
And urged the rest by equal steps to rise.

---

60. *One science:* one art, or one type of knowledge. 62. *peculiar:* particular.
68. *Nature:* See the Introduction. 80. *wit:* imaginative power. 84. *more:*
more important. *Muse's steed:* Pegasus. 86. *Generous:* high-bred.

Just precepts thus from great examples given,
She drew from them what they derived from Heaven.
The generous Critic fanned the Poet's fire,   100
And taught the world with reason to admire.
Then Criticism the Muses' handmaid proved,
To dress her charms, and make her more beloved:
But following Wits from that intention strayed,
Who could not win the mistress, wooed the maid;   105
Against the Poets their own arms they turned,
Sure to hate most the men from whom they learned.
So modern 'Pothecaries, taught the art
By Doctor's bills to play the Doctor's part,
Bold in the practice of mistaken rules,   110
Prescribe, apply, and call their masters fools.
Some on the leaves of ancient authors prey,
Nor time nor moths e'er spoiled so much as they.
Some drily plain, without invention's aid,
Write dull receipts how poems may be made.   115
These leave the sense, their learning to display,
And those explain the meaning quite away.
    You then whose judgment the right course would steer,
Know well each ANCIENT's proper character;
His fable, subject, scope in every page;   120
Religion, Country, genius of his Age:
Without all these at once before your eyes,
Cavil you may, but never criticize.
Be Homer's works your study and delight,
Read them by day, and meditate by night;   125
Thence form your judgment, thence your maxims bring,
And trace the Muses upward to their spring.
Still with itself compared, his text peruse;
And let your comment be the Mantuan Muse.
    When first young Maro in his boundless mind   130
A work t' outlast immortal Rome designed,
Perhaps he seemed above the critic's law,

---

109. *bills:* prescriptions. 110. *mistaken:* misinterpreted. 119. *proper:* distinctive. 120. *fable:* plot. *scope:* aim. 124. *Homer* is instanced because he is the father of epic, the literary genre prized above all others by the Augustans. 127. *spring:* with punning reference to the Pierian spring, home of the Muses. 129. i.e., let your commentary on Homer's epics be Virgil's epic. On *Mantuan,* cf. 707-8n. 130. *Maro:* Virgil.

And but from Nature's fountains scorned to draw:
But when t' examine every part he came,
Nature and Homer were, he found, the same.   135
Convinced, amazed, he checks the bold design;⎫
And rules as strict his laboured work confine, ⎬
As if the Stagirite o'erlooked each line.   ⎭
Learn hence for ancient rules a just esteem;
To copy nature is to copy them.   140
  Some beauties yet no Precepts can declare,
For there's a happiness as well as care.
Music resembles Poetry, in each   ⎫
Are nameless graces which no methods teach,   ⎬
And which a master-hand alone can reach.   ⎭   145
If, where the rules not far enough extend,
(Since rules were made but to promote their end)
Some lucky Licence answer to the full
Th' intent proposed, that Licence is a rule.
Thus, Pegasus, a nearer way to take,   150
May boldly deviate from the common track.
Great wits sometimes may gloriously offend,
And rise to faults true Critics dare not mend;
From vulgar bounds with brave disorder part,
And snatch a grace beyond the reach of art,   155
Which without passing thro' the judgment, gains
The heart, and all its end at once attains.
In prospects thus, some objects please our eyes,⎫
Which out of nature's common order rise,   ⎬
The shapeless rock, or hanging precipice.   ⎭   160
But tho' the Ancients thus their rules invade,
(As Kings dispense with laws themselves have made)
Moderns, beware! or if you must offend
Against the precept, ne'er transgress its End;
Let it be seldom, and compelled by need;   165
And have, at least, their precedent to plead.
The Critic else proceeds without remorse,
Seizes your fame, and puts his laws in force.
  I know there are, to whose presumptuous thoughts
Those freer beauties, even in them, seem faults.   170

---

138. *the Stagirite:* Aristotle (so called from his birthplace, Stagyra), whose observations on epic were particularly influential at this time. 141. *declare:* elucidate. 142. *happiness:* felicity in expression. 154. *brave:* fine. 170. *faults:* a perfect rhyme with *thoughts* in Pope's day.

Some figures monstrous and mis-shaped appear,
Considered singly, or beheld too near,
Which, but proportioned to their light, or place,
Due distance reconciles to form and grace.
A prudent chief not always must display   175
His powers in equal ranks, and fair array,
But with th' occasion and the place comply,
Conceal his force, nay seem sometimes to fly.
Those oft are stratagems which errors seem,
Nor is it Homer nods, but we that dream.   180
  Still green with bays each ancient Altar stands,
Above the reach of sacrilegious hands;
Secure from Flames, from Envy's fiercer rage,
Destructive War, and all-involving Age.
See, from each clime the learn'd their incense bring!   185
Hear, in all tongues consenting Pæans ring!
In praise so just let every voice be joined,
And fill the general chorus of mankind.
Hail, Bards triumphant! born in happier days;
Immortal heirs of universal praise!   190
Whose honours with increase of ages grow,
As streams roll down, enlarging as they flow;
Nations unborn your mighty names shall sound,
And worlds applaud that must not yet be found!
Oh may some spark of your celestial fire,   195
The last, the meanest of your sons inspire,
(That on weak wings, from far, pursues your flights;
Glows while he reads, but trembles as he writes)
To teach vain Wits a science little known,
T' admire superior sense, and doubt their own!   200

II

  Of all the Causes which conspire to blind
Man's erring judgment, and misguide the mind,
What the weak head with strongest bias rules,
Is _Pride,_ the never-failing vice of fools.
Whatever nature has in worth denied,   205
She gives in large recruits of needful pride;

---

184. *involving:* enfolding. 186. *consenting:* harmonious (as in musical 'con-
cent'). 187. *joined:* a perfect rhyme with *kind* in Pope's day. 206. *recruits:*
reinforcements.

For as in bodies, thus in souls, we find
What wants in blood and spirits, swelled with wind:
Pride, where wit fails, steps in to our defence,
And fills up all the mighty Void of sense.   210
If once right reason drives that cloud away,
Truth breaks upon us with resistless day.
Trust not yourself; but your defects to know,
Make use of every friend—and every foe.
A *little learning* is a dangerous thing;   215
Drink deep, or taste not the Pierian spring.
There shallow draughts intoxicate the brain,
And drinking largely sobers us again.
Fired at first sight with what the Muse imparts,
In fearless youth we tempt the heights of Arts,   220
While from the bounded level of our mind
Short views we take, nor see the lengths behind;
But more advanced, behold with strange surprise
New distant scenes of endless science rise!
So pleased at first the towering Alps we try,   225
Mount o'er the vales, and seem to tread the sky,
Th' eternal snows appear already past,
And the first clouds and mountains seem the last;
But, those attained, we tremble to survey
The growing labours of the lengthened way,   230
Th' increasing prospect tires our wandering eyes,
Hills peep o'er hills, and Alps on Alps arise!
A perfect Judge will read each work of wit
With the same spirit that its author writ:
Survey the WHOLE, nor seek slight faults to find   235
Where nature moves, and rapture warms the mind;
Nor lose, for that malignant dull delight,
The generous pleasure to be charmed with Wit.
But in such lays as neither ebb, nor flow,
Correctly cold, and regularly low,   240
That shunning faults, one quiet tenour keep,
We cannot blame indeed —— but we may sleep.
In wit, as nature, what affects our hearts
Is not th' exactness of peculiar parts;

---

208. *wants:* is lacking. 216. Pierian: cf. 127n. 220. *tempt:* attempt. 222. *behind:* lying still further ahead. 224. *science:* knowledge. 233. *wit:* literature. 240. i.e., correct but cold: obedient to the rules, but uninspired. 244. *peculiar:* cf. 62n.

'Tis not a lip, or eye, we beauty call,   245
But the joint force and full result of all.
Thus when we view some well-proportioned dome,
(The world's just wonder, and even thine, O Rome!)
No single parts unequally surprize,
All comes united to th' admiring eyes;   250
No monstrous height, or breadth, or length appear;
The Whole at once is bold, and regular.

Whoever thinks a faultless piece to see,
Thinks what ne'er was, nor is, nor e'er shall be.
In every work regard the writer's End,   255
Since none can compass more than they intend;
And if the means be just, the conduct true,
Applause, in spite of trivial faults, is due;
As men of breeding, sometimes men of wit,
T' avoid great errors, must the less commit: 260
Neglect the rules each verbal Critic lays,
For not to know some trifles, is a praise.
Most Critics, fond of some subservient art,
Still make the Whole depend upon a Part:
They talk of principles, but notions prize,   265
And all to one loved Folly sacrifice.

Once on a time, La Mancha's Knight, they say,
A certain bard encountering on the way,
Discoursed in terms as just, with looks as sage,
As e'er could Dennis of the Grecian stage;   270
Concluding all were desperate sots and fools,
Who durst depart from Aristotle's rules.
Our Author, happy in a judge so nice,
Produced his Play, and begged the Knight's advice;
Made him observe the subject, and the plot,   275
The manners, passions, unities; what not?
All which, exact to rule, were brought about,
Were but a Combat in the lists left out.
"What! leave the Combat out?" exclaims the Knight;
Yes, or we must renounce the Stagirite.   280

---

248. *dome*: building (but perhaps here with special reference to domed buildings like the Pantheon and St. Peter's.) 257. *conduct*: arrangement of the parts. 261. *verbal critic*: a critic concerned only with niceties of language, esp. grammar. 265. *notions*: prejudices, whims. 267. *La Mancha's knight*: Cervantes' *Don Quixote* (with reference to an episode in the sequel of the novel added by an unknown author). 270. *Dennis*: cf. 585-7n.

"Not so by Heaven" (he answers in a rage),
"Knights, squires, and steeds, must enter on the stage."
So vast a throng the stage can ne'er contain.
"Then build a new, or act it in a plain."
  Thus Critics, of less judgment than caprice,   285
Curious not knowing, not exact but nice,
Form short Ideas; and offend in arts
(As most in manners) by a love to parts.
  Some to *Conceit* alone their taste confine,
And glittering thoughts struck out at every line;   290
Pleased with a work where nothing's just or fit;
One glaring Chaos and wild heap of wit.
Poets like painters, thus, unskilled to trace
The naked nature and the living grace,
With gold and jewels cover every part,   295
And hide with ornaments their want of art.
True Wit is Nature to advantage dressed,
What oft was thought, but ne'er so well expressed;
Something, whose truth convinced at sight we find,
That gives us back the image of our mind.   300
As shades more sweetly recommend the light,
So modest plainness sets off sprightly wit.
For works may have more wit than does 'em good,
As bodies perish thro' excess of blood.
  Others for *Language* all their care express,   305
And value books, as women men, for Dress:
Their praise is still,—the Style is excellent:
The Sense, they humbly take upon content.
Words are like leaves; and where they most abound,
Much fruit of sense beneath is rarely found: 310
False Eloquence, like the prismatic glass,
Its gaudy colours spreads on every place;
The face of Nature we no more survey,
All glares alike, without distinction gay:
But true expression, like th' unchanging Sun,   315
Clears and improves whate'er it shines upon,
It gilds all objects, but it alters none.
Expression is the dress of thought, and still

286. *curious:* difficult to satisfy, 'fussy.' *nice:* fastidious. 289. *conceit:* extraordinary or far-fetched thoughts, comparisons, fancies. 304. e.g., in an apoplexy. 308. *content:* trust (with a pun).

Appears more decent, as more suitable;
A vile conceit in pompous words expressed,   320
Is like a clown in regal purple dressed:
For different styles with different subjects sort,
As several garbs with country, town, and court.
Some by old words to fame have made pretence,
Ancients in phrase, mere moderns in their sense;   325
Such laboured nothings, in so strange a style,
Amaze th' unlearn'd, and make the learnèd smile.
Unlucky, as Fungoso in the play,
These sparks with awkward vanity display
What the fine gentleman wore yesterday;   330
And but so mimic ancient wits at best,
As apes our grandsires, in their doublets drest.
In words, as fashions, the same rule will hold;
Alike fantastic, if too new, or old:
Be not the first by whom the new are tried,   335
Nor yet the last to lay the old aside.
   But most by *Numbers* judge a Poet's song;
And smooth or rough, with them is right or wrong:
In the bright Muse, though thousand charms conspire,
Her voice is all these tuneful fools admire;   340
Who haunt Parnassus but to please their ear,
Not mend their minds; as some to Church repair,
Not for the doctrine, but the music there.
These equal syllables alone require,
Tho' oft the ear the open vowels tire;   345
While expletives their feeble aid do join;
And ten low words oft creep in one dull line:
While they ring round the same unvaried chimes,
With sure returns of still expected rhymes;
Where-e'er you find "the cooling western breeze,"   350
In the next line, it "whispers through the trees:"
If crystal streams "with pleasing murmurs creep,"
The reader's threatened (not in vain) with "sleep:"

---

319. *decent:* attractive. 321. *clown:* rustic. 328. *play:* Jonson's *Every Man Out of His Humor.* 337. *Numbers:* versification (especially the sound). 345. Pope illustrates the effect he criticizes in *Tho' oft, the ear,* and *the open.* 346. *do join:* again an illustration of the fault in question. 347. Likewise an illustration. But Pope's warning is not so much against monosyllabic lines as against *dull* ones in which *low words creep.* 349. *expected rhymes:* illustrated in 348-53, along with *cliché* phrasings in 350-3.

Then, at the last and only couplet fraught
With some unmeaning thing they call a thought,   355
A needless Alexandrine ends the song
That, like a wounded snake, drags its slow length along.
Leave such to tune their own dull rhymes, and know
What's roundly smooth or languishingly slow;
And praise the easy vigour of a line,   360
Where Denham's strength, and Waller's sweetness join.
True ease in writing comes from art, not chance,
As those move easiest who have learned to dance.
'Tis not enough no harshness gives offence,
The sound must seem an Echo to the sense: 365
Soft is the strain when Zephyr gently blows,
And the smooth stream in smoother numbers flows;
But when loud surges lash the sounding shore,
The hoarse, rough verse should like the torrent roar:
When Ajax strives some rock's vast weight to throw,   370
The line too labours, and the words move slow;
Not so, when swift Camilla scours the plain,
Flies o'er the unbending corn, and skims along the main.
Hear how Timotheus' varied lays surprize,
And bid alternate passions fall and rise!   375
While, at each change, the son of Libyan Jove
Now burns with glory, and then melts with love,
Now his fierce eyes with sparkling fury glow,
Now sighs steal out, and tears begin to flow:
Persians and Greeks like turns of nature found,   380
And the world's victor stood subdued by Sound!
The power of Music all our hearts allow,
And what Timotheus was, is DRYDEN now.
  Avoid Extremes; and shun the fault of such,
Who still are pleased too little or too much.   385
At every trifle scorn to take offence—

---

356. *Alexandrine:* a line of twelve syllables and six stresses (illustrated in
357). 361. *strength, sweetness:* characteristics regularly attributed by the
Augustans to the versification of these two seventeenth-century poets. 365.
Pope variously illustrates the mating of sound with sense in 366-73. 370.
Alluding to Homer's *Iliad,* vii 268 ff. or xii 380 ff. 372. *Camilla:* a warrior
maiden whose movement is described in Virgil's *Aeneid,* vii 808 ff.—a
passage Pope here echoes. 374. *Timotheus:* musician to Alexander the
Great: cf. Dryden's *Alexander's Feast* for the effects here ascribed to his
music. 376. *son . . . Jove:* Alexander the Great. 380. *turns of nature:* emotions.

That always shows great pride, or little sense;
Those heads, as stomachs, are not sure the best,
Which nauseate all, and nothing can digest.
Yet let not each gay turn thy rapture move;   390
For fools admire, but men of sense approve:
As things seem large which we thro' mists descry,
Dulness is ever apt to magnify.

Some foreign writers, some our own despise;
The Ancients only, or the Moderns prize.   395
Thus Wit, like Faith, by each man is applied
To one small sect, and all are damned beside.
Meanly they seek the blessing to confine,
And force that sun but on a part to shine,
Which not alone the southern wit sublimes,   400
But ripens spirits in cold northern climes;
Which from the first has shone on ages past,
Enlights the present, and shall warm the last;
Tho' each may feel increases and decays,
And see now clearer and now darker days.   405
Regard not then if Wit be old or new,
But blame the false, and value still the true.

Some ne'er advance a Judgment of their own,
But catch the spreading notion of the Town;
They reason and conclude by precedent,   410
And own stale nonsense which they ne'er invent.
Some judge of author's names, not works, and then
Nor praise nor blame the writings, but the men.
Of all this servile herd the worst is he
That in proud dulness joins with Quality: 415
A constant Critic at the great man's board,
To fetch and carry nonsense for my Lord.
What woful stuff this madrigal would be,
In some starved hackney sonneteer, or me?
But let a Lord once own the happy lines,   420
How the wit brightens! how the style refines!
Before his sacred name flies every fault,
And each exalted stanza teems with thought!

The Vulgar thus through Imitation err;
As oft the Learn'd by being singular;   425
So much they scorn the crowd, that if the throng

---

391. *admire:* stand agape. *approve:* test. 400. Alluding to ancient literature as the product of a warm Mediterranean sun. 415. *Quality:* the aristocracy.

By chance go right, they purposely go wrong;
So Schismatics the plain believers quit,
And are but damned for having too much wit.
Some praise at morning what they blame at night; 430
But always think the last opinion right.
A Muse by these is like a mistress used,
This hour she's idolized, the next abused;
While their weak heads like towns unfortified,
'Twixt sense and nonsense daily change their side. 435
Ask them the cause; they're wiser still, they say;
And still to-morrow's wiser than to-day.
We think our fathers fools, so wise we grow,
Our wiser sons, no doubt, will think us so.
Once School-divines this zealous isle o'er-spread; 440
Who knew most Sentences, was deepest read;
Faith, Gospel, all, seemed made to be disputed,
And none had sense enough to be confuted:
Scotists and Thomists, now, in peace remain,
Amidst their kindred cobwebs in Duck-lane. 445
If Faith itself has different dresses worn,
What wonder modes in Wit should take their turn?
Oft, leaving what is natural and fit,
The current folly proves the ready wit;
And authors think their reputation safe, 450
Which lives as long as fools are pleased to laugh.
  Some valuing those of their own side or mind,
Still make themselves the measure of mankind:
Fondly we think we honour merit then,
When we but praise ourselves in other men. 455
Parties in Wit attend on those of State,
And public faction doubles private hate.
Pride, Malice, Folly, against Dryden rose,
In various shapes of Parsons, Critics, Beaus;
But sense survived, when merry jests were past; 460
For rising merit will buoy up at last.

---

436. *still:* always. 440. *School-divines:* scholastic theologians. *zealous:* with reference to religious zeal. 441. *Sentences:* i.e., theological maxims and precepts like those in Peter Lombard's *Sententiae.* 444. *Scotists, Thomists:* disciples respectively of Duns Scotus and St. Thomas Aquinas. 445. *Duck-lane:* London street where second-hand books were sold. 454. *fondly:* foolishly. 456. In Pope's time, approval of an author's work often depended on approval of his politics (as Whig or Tory).

Might he return, and bless once more our eyes,
New Blackmores and new Milbourns must arise:
Nay should great Homer lift his awful head,
Zoilus again would start up from the dead.   465
Envy will merit, as its shade, pursue;
But like a shadow, proves the substance true;
For envied Wit, like Sol eclipsed, makes known
Th' opposing body's grossness, not its own,
When first that sun too powerful beams displays,   470
It draws up vapours which obscure its rays;
But even those clouds at last adorn its way,
Reflect new glories, and augment the day.

Be thou the first true merit to befriend;
His praise is lost, who stays till all commend.   475
Short is the date, alas, of modern rhymes,
And 't is but just to let them live betimes.
No longer now that golden age appears,
When Patriarch-wits survived a thousand years:
Now length of Fame (our second life) is lost,   480
And bare threescore is all even that can boast;
Our sons their fathers' failing language see;
And such as Chaucer is, shall Dryden be.
So when the faithful pencil has designed
Some bright Idea of the master's mind,   485
Where a new world leaps out at his command,
And ready Nature waits upon his hand;
When the ripe colours soften and unite,
And sweetly melt into just shade and light;
When mellowing years their full perfection give,   490
And each bold figure just begins to live,
The treacherous colours the fair art betray,
And all the bright creation fades away!

Unhappy Wit, like most mistaken things,
Atones not for that envy which it brings.   495
In youth alone its empty praise we boast,
But soon the short-lived vanity is lost:
Like some fair flower the early spring supplies,

---

463. Sir Richard *Blackmore* and Luke *Milbourn* were among those who
attacked Dryden and his work. 465. *Zoilus:* ancient grammarian, whose
severe strictures upon Homer have made his name synonymous with
pedantic criticism. 478. Pope mistakenly anticipates here a further change
in the language, such as would render Dryden's English as difficult as
Chaucer's.

That gaily blooms, but even in blooming dies.
What is this Wit, which must our cares employ?   500
The owner's wife, that other men enjoy;
Then most our trouble still when most admired,
And still the more we give, the more required;
Whose fame with pains we guard, but lose with ease,
Sure some to vex, but never all to please;   505
'Tis what the vicious fear, the virtuous shun,
By fools 'tis hated, and by knaves undone!
   If Wit so much from Ignorance undergo,
Ah let not Learning too commence its foe!
Of old, those met rewards who could excel,   510
And such were praised who but endeavoured well:
Tho' triumphs were to generals only due,
Crowns were reserved to grace the soldiers too.
Now, they who reach Parnassus' lofty crown,
Employ their pains to spurn some others down;   515
And while self-love each jealous writer rules,
Contending wits become the sport of fools:
But still the worst with most regret commend,
For each ill Author is as bad a Friend.
To what base ends, and by what abject ways,   520
Are mortals urged thro' sacred lust of praise!
Ah ne'er so dire a thirst of glory boast,
Nor in the Critic let the Man be lost.
Good-nature and good-sense must ever join;
To err is human, to forgive, divine.   525
   But if in noble minds some dregs remain
Not yet purged off, of spleen and sour disdain;
Discharge that rage on more provoking crimes,
Nor fear a dearth in these flagitious times.
No pardon vile Obscenity should find,   530
Tho' wit and art conspire to move your mind;
But Dulness with Obscenity must prove
As shameful sure as Impotence in love.
In the fat age of pleasure, wealth, and ease,
Sprung the rank weed, and thrived with large increase: 535
When love was all an easy Monarch's care;
Seldom at council, never in a war:
Jilts ruled the state, and statesmen farces writ;

---

509. *commence:* begin to be. 521. *sacred:* the term also means 'accursed,'
from Virgil's phrase *'auri sacra fames'* (Aeneid iii 57). 534. *age . . . ease:*
the reign of Charles II.

Nay Wits had pensions, and young Lords had wit:
The Fair sat panting at a Courtier's play,   540
And not a Mask went unimproved away:
The modest fan was lifted up no more,
And Virgins smiled at what they blushed before.
The following licence of a Foreign reign
Did all the dregs of bold Socinus drain;   545
Then unbelieving priests reformed the nation,
And taught more pleasant methods of salvation;
Where Heaven's free subjects might their rights dispute,
Lest God himself should seem too absolute:
Pulpits their sacred satire learned to spare,   550
And Vice admired to find a flatterer there!
Encouraged thus, Wit's Titans braved the skies,
And the press groaned with licensed blasphemies.
These monsters, Critics! with your darts engage,
Here point your thunder, and exhaust your rage!   555
Yet shun their fault, who, scandalously nice,
Will needs mistake an author into vice;
All seems infected that th' infected spy,
As all looks yellow to the jaundiced eye.

III

  Learn then what MORALS Critics ought to show,   560
For 'tis but half a Judge's task, to know.
'Tis not enough, taste, judgment, learning, join;
In all you speak, let truth and candour shine:
That not alone what to your sense is due
All may allow; but seek your friendship too.   565
  Be silent always when you doubt your sense;
And speak, tho' sure, with seeming diffidence:
Some positive, persisting fops we know,
Who, if once wrong, will needs be always so;
But you, with pleasure own your errors past,   570
And make each day a crítique on the last.
  'Tis not enough, your counsel still be true;

---

540. *The Fair:* i.e., women. 541. *Mask:* Restoration women of fashion wore masks when attending the theater. *unimproved:* uninstructed in obscenity. 544. *foreign reign:* that of William III, a Hollander. 545. *Socinus:* founder of Unitarian doctrine. 552. *braved:* defied (with reference to the Titans mounting into heaven to make war on Zeus. 553. *licensed:* alluding to the Licensing Act (which expired in 1695) and to the licentiousness of the books.

Blunt truths more mischief than nice falsehoods do;
Men must be taught as if you taught them not,
And things unknown proposed as things forgot. 575
Without Good Breeding, truth is disapproved;
That only makes superior sense beloved.
  Be niggards of advice on no pretence;
For the worst avarice is that of sense.
With mean complacence ne'er betray your trust, 580
Nor be so civil as to prove unjust.
Fear not the anger of the wise to raise;
Those best can bear reproof, who merit praise.
  'Twere well might critics still this freedom take,
But Appius reddens at each word you speak, 585
And stares, tremendous, with a threatening eye,
Like some fierce Tyrant in old tapestry.
Fear most to tax an Honourable fool,
Whose right it is, uncensured, to be dull;
Such, without wit, are Poets when they please, 590
As without learning they can take Degrees.
Leave dangerous truths to unsuccessful Satires,
And flattery to fulsome Dedicators,
Whom, when they praise, the world believes no more,
Than when they promise to give scribbling o'er. 595
'Tis best sometimes your censure to restrain,
And charitably let the dull be vain:
Your silence there is better than your spite,
For who can rail so long as they can write?
Still humming on, their drowsy course they keep, 600
And lashed so long, like tops, are lashed asleep.
False steps but help them to renew the race,
As, after stumbling, Jades will mend their pace.
What crowds of these, impenitently bold,
In sounds and jingling syllables grown old, 605
Still run on Poets, in a raging vein,
Even to the dregs and squeezings of the brain,

585-7. Pope alludes to John Dennis, a literary critic of some talent and much self-esteem, whose tragedy *Appius and Virginia* had failed miserably in 1709, and who was very fond of the word *tremendous* (586). 580. *complacence:* zeal to please. 588. *tax:* criticize. *Honorable:* noble. 591. Noblemen were formerly admitted to an unearned M.A. at English universities. 601. *asleep:* A top is said to 'sleep' when it turns so fast and smoothly that its motion is imperceptible. 606. *run on:* continue as.

Strain out the last dull droppings of their sense,
And rhyme with all the rage of Impotence.
   Such shameless Bards we have; and yet 'tis true,   610
There are as mad abandoned Critics too.
The bookful blockhead, ignorantly read,
With loads of learnèd lumber in his head,
With his own tongue still edifies his ears,
And always listening to himself appears.   615
All books he reads, and all he reads assails,
From Dryden's Fables down to Durfey's Tales.
With him, most authors steal their works, or buy;
Garth did not write his own Dispensary.
Name a new Play, and he's the Poet's friend,   620
Nay, showed his faults—but when would Poets mend?
No place so sacred from such fops is barred,
Nor is Paul's church more safe than Paul's churchyard:
Nay, fly to altars; there they'll talk you dead:
For Fools rush in where Angels fear to tread.   625
Distrustful sense with modest caution speaks, ⎫
It still looks home, and short excursions makes; ⎬
But rattling nonsense in full volleys breaks, ⎭
And never shocked, and never turned aside,
Bursts out, resistless, with a thundering tide.   630
   But where's the man, who counsel can bestow,
Still pleased to teach, and yet not proud to know
Unbiassed, or by favour, or by spite;
Not dully prepossessed, nor blindly right;
Tho' learn'd, well-bred; and tho' well-bred, sincere,   635
Modestly bold, and humanly severe:
Who to a friend his faults can freely show,
And gladly praise the merit of a foe?
Blest with a taste exact, yet unconfined;
A knowledge both of books and human kind: 640
Generous converse; a soul exempt from pride;
And love to praise, with reason on his side?
   Such once were Critics; such the happy few,
Athens and Rome in better ages knew.

---

617. *Fables:* a collection (mainly) of stories in verse. *Durfey:* Thomas
Durfey, dramatist, song-writer, and literary hack, whose name was synonymous with bad writing. 619. *Dispensary:* the title of a poem by Pope's
friend, Sir Samuel Garth. 623. *Paul's church:* In the Restoration, St. Paul's
cathedral was used as a general social and business *rendez-vous.* 629.
shocked: stopped.

The mighty Stagirite first left the shore,   645
Spread all his sails, and durst the deeps explore:
He steered securely, and discovered far,
Led by the light of the Mæonian Star.
Poets, a race long unconfined, and free,
Still fond and proud of savage liberty,   650
Received his laws; and stood convinced 'twas fit,
Who conquered Nature, should preside o'er Wit.
  Horace still charms with graceful negligence,
And without method talks us into sense,
Will, like a friend, familiarly convey   655
The truest notions in the easiest way.
He, who supreme in judgment, as in wit,
Might boldly censure, as he boldly writ,
Yet judged with coolness, tho' he sung with fire;
His Precepts teach but what his works inspire.   660
Our Critics take a contrary extreme,
They judge with fury, but they write with fle'me:
Nor suffers Horace more in wrong Translations
By Wits, than Critics in as wrong Quotations.
  See Dionysius Homer's thoughts refine,   665
And call new beauties forth from every line!
  Fancy and art in gay Petronius please,
The scholar's learning, with the courtier's ease.
  In grave Quintilian's copious work, we find
The justest rules, and clearest method joined: 670
Thus useful arms in magazines we place,
All ranged in order, and disposed with grace,
But less to please the eye, than arm the hand,
Still fit for use, and ready at command.
  Thee, bold Longinus! all the Nine inspire,   675
And bless their Critic with a Poet's fire.

---

645 ff. Pope now begins a catalogue of critics. 646 ff. Alluding to Aristotle's *Poetics* (and, in 652, to his scientific works). 648. *Maeonian star:* Homer. 654 ff. Alluding especially to Horace's *Ars Poetica,* which is in the form of a verse letter. 662. *fle'me:* phlegm, i.e., coldness, heaviness. 666. *Dionysius:* Dionysius of Halicarnassus (1st cent., B.C.), Greek rhetorician and critic. 667. *Petronius:* Roman author (1st cent., A.D.), whose *Satyricon* contains a small amount of criticism. 669. *Quintilian:* Roman author (1st cent., A.D.) of a famous treatise of rhetoric, *De Institutione Oratoria.* 675. *Longinus:* attributed author of the treatise *On Elevated Style* (often called *On the Sublime*), the influence of which increased the opposition of the English Augustans to a literature of 'rules.'

An ardent Judge, who zealous in his trust,
With warmth gives sentence, yet is always just;
Whose own example strengthens all his laws;
And is himself that great Sublime he draws.   680

    Thus long succeeding Critics justly reigned,
Licence repressed, and useful laws ordained.
Learning and Rome alike in empire grew;
And Arts still followed where her Eagles flew;
From the same foes, at last, both felt their doom,   685
And the same age saw Learning fall, and Rome.
With Tyranny, then Superstition joined,
As that the body, this enslaved the mind;
Much was believed, but little understood,
And to be dull was construed to be good;   690
A second deluge Learning thus o'er-run,
And the Monks finished what the Goths begun.

    At length Erasmus, that great injured name,
(The glory of the Priesthood, and the shame!)
Stemmed the wild torrent of a barbarous age,   695
And drove those holy Vandals off the stage.

    But see! each Muse, in Leo's golden days,
Starts from her trance, and trims her withered bays,
Rome's ancient Genius, o'er its ruins spread,
Shakes off the dust, and rears his reverend head   700
Then Sculpture and her sister-arts revive;
Stones leaped to form, and rocks began to live;
With sweeter notes each rising Temple rung;
A Raphael painted, and a Vida sung.
Immortal Vida: on whose honoured brow   705
The Poet's bays and Critic's ivy grow:
Cremona now shall ever boast thy name,
As next in place to Mantua, next in fame!

    But soon by impious arms from Latium chased,
Their ancient bounds the banished Muses passed;   710
Thence Arts o'er all the northern world advance,

---

693. *Erasmus:* leader of the new humanistic and anti-scholastic learning of
the Renaissance: *glory of the priesthood* because a priest, its *shame* because
he (1) exposed its weaknesses, (2) was persecuted by it. 698. *Leo:*
Pope Leo X (1513-21) a great patron of the arts. 704. *Vida:* Renaissance
Latin poet (1488-1566), author of a verse treatise on poetics which Pope
occasionally echoes in this poem. 707-8. *Cremona, Mantua:* Vida's and
Virgil's birthplaces. 709. Rome was sacked by the French in 1527.

But Critic-learning flourished most in France:
The Rules, a nation born to serve obeys;
And Boileau still in right of Horace sways.
But we, brave Britons, foreign laws despised,   715
And kept unconquered, and uncivilized;
Fierce for the liberties of wit, and bold,
We still defied the Romans, as of old.
Yet some there were, among the sounder few
Of those who less presumed, and better knew,   720
Who durst assert the juster ancient cause,
And here restored Wit's fundamental laws.
Such was the Muse, whose rules and practice tell,
"Nature's chief Master-piece is writing well."
Such was Roscommon, not more learn'd than good,   725
With manners generous as his noble blood;
To him the wit of Greece and Rome was known,
And every author's merit, but his own.
Such late was Walsh—the Muse's judge and friend,
Who justly knew to blame or to commend;   730
To failings mild, but zealous for desert;
The clearest head, and the sincerest heart.
This humble praise, lamented shade! receive,
This praise at least a grateful Muse may give:
The Muse, whose early voice you taught to sing,   735
Prescribed her heights, and pruned her tender wing,
(Her guide now lost) no more attempts to rise,
But in low numbers short excursions tries:
Content, if hence th' unlearn'd their wants may view,
The learn'd reflect on what before they knew: 740
Careless of censure, nor too fond of fame;
Still pleased to praise, yet not afraid to blame,
Averse alike to flatter, or offend;
Not free from faults, nor yet too vain to mend.

~❧~

714. *Boileau:* Referring especially to his *L'Art poétique* (1673). 723. *the Muse:* John Sheffield (1648-1721), from whose *Essay on Poetry* Pope takes the next line. 725. *Roscommon:* Wentworth Dillon, fourth Earl of Roscommon (1633?-85), author of a verse *Essay on Translated Verse.* 729. *Walsh:* William Walsh (1633-1708), whose critical judgment was highly valued by both Pope and Dryden.

The Rape of the Lock

(1714)

CANTO I

*W*HAT dire offence from amorous causes springs, *Uses run-on*
What mighty contests rise from trivial things, *for epic effect*
I sing—This verse to CARYL, Muse! is due:
This, even Belinda may vouchsafe to view:
Slight is the subject, but not so the praise, (5)
If She inspire, and He approve my lays.

invocation
  Say what strange motive, Goddess! could compel
A well-bred Lord t' assault a gentle Belle?
O say what stranger cause, yet unexplored,
Could make a gentle Belle reject a Lord? 10
In tasks so bold, can little men engage,
And in soft bosoms dwells such mighty Rage?

  Sol thro' white curtains shot a timorous ray,
And oped those eyes that must eclipse the day:
Now lap-dogs give themselves the rousing shake, 15
And sleepless lovers, just at twelve, awake:
Thrice rung the bell, the slipper knocked the ground,
And the pressed watch returned a silver sound.
Belinda still her downy pillow prest
epithean Her guardian SYLPH prolonged the balmy rest: 20
'Twas He had summoned to her silent bed
dream of The morning-dream that hovered o'er her head;
A Youth more glittering than a Birth-night Beau,
dream good (That even in slumber caused her cheek to glow)
Seemed to her ear his winning lips to lay, 25
And thus in whispers said, or seemed to say.

  "Fairest of mortals, thou distinguished care
Of thousand bright Inhabitants of Air!

---

  1 ff. A parody of the epic invocation: cf. *Par. Lost,* I 1 ff. 14. *those eyes:*
Belinda's. 17. Belinda summons her maid. 18. *pressed watch:* A watch for
night use, which, when pressed, sounded the hour and quarter hour just
past. 19. Belinda has fallen asleep again. 23. *Birth-night:* i.e., dressed in
finery for a royal birthday.

If e'er one vision touched thy infant thought,
Of all the Nurse and all the Priest have taught: 30
Of airy Elves by moonlight shadows seen,
The silver token, and the circled green,
Or virgins visited by Angel-powers,
With golden crowns and wreaths of heavenly flowers;
Hear and believe! thy own importance know,   35
Nor bound thy narrow views to things below.
Some secret truths, from learnèd pride concealed,
To Maids alone and Children are revealed:
What tho' no credit doubting Wits may give?
The Fair and Innocent shall still believe.   40
Know, then, unnumbered Spirits round thee fly,
The light Militia of the lower sky:
These, tho' unseen, are ever on the wing,
Hang o'er the Box, and hover round the Ring.
Think what an equipage thou hast in Air,   45
And view with scorn two Pages and a Chair.
As now your own, our beings were of old,
And once enclosed in Woman's beauteous mould;
Thence, by a soft transition, we repair
From earthly Vehicles to these of air.   50
Think not, when Woman's transient breath is fled
That all her vanities at once are dead;
Succeeding vanities she still regards,
And tho' she plays no more, o'erlooks the cards.
Her joy in gilded Chariots, when alive,   55
And love of Ombre, after death survive.
For when the Fair in all their pride expire,
To their first Elements their Souls retire:
The Sprites of fiery Termagants in Flame
Mount up, and take a Salamander's name.   60
Soft yielding minds to Water glide away,
And sip, with Nymphs, their elemental Tea.
The graver Prude sinks downward to a Gnome,
In search of mischief still on Earth to roam.

---

32. *silver token:* the sixpence that fairies leave in the shoe of maids they
approve. 44. *Box:* theatre-box. *Ring:* a circular drive in London's Hyde
Park where fashionable ladies aired themselves in their coaches. 46. *Chair:*
sedan chair. 50. *Vehicles:* i.e., bodies (with punning reference to *equipage*
and *Chair*). 55. *Chariots:* contemporary name for carriage (used here for
its epic associations). 56. *Ombre:* Cf. III 27 ff. 59. *Termagants:* scolds.

The light Coquettes in Sylphs aloft repair,   65
And sport and flutter in the fields of Air.
  "Know further yet; whoever fair and chaste
Rejects mankind, is by some Sylph embraced:
For Spirits, freed from mortal laws, with ease
Assume what sexes and what shapes they please.   70
What guards the purity of melting Maids,
In courtly balls, and midnight masquerades,
Safe from the treacherous friend, the daring spark,
The glance by day, the whisper in the dark,
When kind occasion prompts their warm desires,   75
When music softens, and when dancing fires?
'Tis but their Sylph, the wise Celestials know,
Tho' Honour is the word with Men below.
  "Some nymphs there are, too conscious of their face
For life predestined to the Gnomes' embrace.   80
These swell their prospects and exalt their pride,
When offers are disdained, and love denied:
Then gay Ideas crowd the vacant brain,
While Peers, and Dukes, and all their sweeping train,
And Garters, Stars, and Coronets appear,   85
And in soft sounds, Your Grace salutes their ear.
'Tis these that early taint the female soul,
Instruct the eyes of young Coquettes to roll,
Teach Infant-cheeks a bidden blush to know,
And little hearts to flutter at a Beau.   90
  "Oft, when the world imagine women stray,
The Sylphs thro' mystic mazes guide their way,
Thro' all the giddy circle they pursue,
And old impertinence expel by new.
What tender maid but must a victim fall   95
To one man's treat, but for another's ball?
When Florio speaks, what virgin could withstand,
If gentle Damon did not squeeze her hand?
With varying vanities, from every part,
They shift the moving Toyshop of their heart;   100
Where wigs with wigs, with sword-knots sword-knots strive,
Beaux banish beaux, and coaches coaches drive.
This erring mortals Levity may call;
Oh blind to truth! the Sylphs contrive it all.

---

73. *spark:* beau. 89. *a . . . blush:* i.e., by rouge. 94. *impertinence:* folly, trifling. 101. *sword-knots:* ribbons on sword-hilts.

"Of these am I, who thy protection claim,   105
A watchful sprite, and Ariel is my name.
Late, as I ranged the crystal wilds of air,
In the clear mirror of thy ruling Star
I saw, alas! some dread event impend,
Ere to the main this morning sun descend,   110
But heaven reveals not what, or how, or where:
Warned by the Sylph, oh pious maid, beware!
This to disclose is all thy guardian can:
Beware of all, but most beware of Man!"

He said; when Shock, who thought she slept too long,
Leaped up, and waked his mistress with his tongue.
'Twas then, Belinda, if report say true,
Thy eyes first opened on a Billet-doux;
Wounds, Charms, and Ardors were no sooner read,
But all the Vision vanished from thy head.   120

And now, unveiled, the Toilet stands displayed,
Each silver Vase in mystic order laid.
First, robed in white, the Nymph intent adores,   *arming*
With head uncovered, the Cosmetic powers.
A heavenly image in the glass appears,   125
To that she bends, to that her eyes she rears;
Th' inferior Priestess, at her altar's side,
Trembling begins the sacred rites of Pride.
Unnumbered treasures ope at once, and here
The various offerings of the world appear;   130
From each she nicely culls with curious toil,
And decks the Goddess with the glittering spoil.
This casket India's glowing gems unlocks,
And all Arabia breathes from yonder box.
The Tortoise here and Elephant unite,   135
Transformed to combs, the speckled, and the white.
Here files of pins extend their shining rows,
Puffs, Powders, Patches, Bibles, Billet-doux
Now awful Beauty puts on all its arms;) *hero preparing for battle*
The fair each moment rises in her charms,   140
Repairs her smiles, awakens every grace,

---

105 ff. A parody of epic warnings. 119. *Wounds . . . Ardors:* i.e., the affected phraseology of the *billet-doux.* 125. Belinda is presented as the principal, and her maid as the inferior, priestess: the goddess is Belinda's *image in
the glass.* In the scheme of epic parodies, this scene represents the arming
of the champion (cf. 139). 132. *spoil:* again, a term with epic associations.
138. *Patches:* beauty-patches.

And calls forth all the wonders of her face;
Sees by degrees a purer blush arise,
And keener lightnings quicken in her eyes.
The busy Sylphs surround their darling care,   145
These set the head, and those divide the hair,
Some fold the sleeve, whilst others plait the gown;
And Betty's praised for labours not her own.

❧

CANTO II

*N*OT with more glories, in th' etherial plain,
The Sun first rises o'er the purpled main,
Than, issuing forth, the rival of his beams   — *comparison*
Launched on the bosom of the silver Thames.
Fair Nymphs, and well-drest Youths around her shone,   5
But every eye was fixed on her alone.
On her white breast a sparkling Cross she wore,
Which Jews might kiss, and Infidels adore.
Her lively looks a sprightly mind disclose,
Quick as her eyes, and as unfixed as those: 10
Favours to none, to all she smiles extends;
Oft she rejects, but never once offends.
Bright as the sun, her eyes the gazers strike,
And, like the sun, they shine on all alike.
Yet graceful ease, and sweetness void of pride,   15
Might hide her faults, if Belles had faults to hide:
If to her share some female errors fall,
Look on her face, and you'll forget 'em all.
   This Nymph, to the destruction of mankind,
Nourished two Locks, which graceful hung behind   20
In equal curls, and well conspired to deck
With shining ringlets the smooth ivory neck.
Love in these labyrinths his slaves detains,
And mighty hearts are held in slender chains.
With hairy springes we the birds betray,   25
Slight lines of hair surprise the finny prey,
Fair tresses man's imperial race ensnare,
And beauty draws us with a single hair.

148. *Betty:* the maid.

   CANTO II: 14. So God "maketh his sun to rise on the evil and on the good" (Matthew 5:45).

Th' adventurous Baron the bright locks admired;
He saw, he wished, and to the prize aspired.   30
Resolved to win, he meditates the way,
By force to ravish, or by fraud betray;
For when success a Lover's toil attends,
Few ask, if fraud or force attained his ends.

For this, ere Phœbus rose, he had implored   35
Propitious heaven, and every power adored,
But chiefly Love—to Love an Altar built,
Of twelve vast French Romances, neatly gilt.
There lay three garters, half a pair of gloves;
And all the trophies of his former loves;   40
With tender Billet-doux he lights the pyre,
And breathes three amorous sighs to raise the fire.
Then prostrate falls, and begs with ardent eyes
Soon to obtain, and long possess the prize:
The powers gave ear, and granted half his prayer,   45
The rest, the winds dispersed in empty air.

But now secure the painted vessel glides,
The sun-beams trembling on the floating tides:
While melting music steals upon the sky,
And softened sounds along the waters die;   50
Smooth flow the waves, the Zephyrs gently play,
Belinda smiled, and all the world was gay.
All but the Sylph—with careful thoughts opprest,
Th' impending woe sat heavy on his breast.
He summons strait his Denizens of air;   55
The lucid squadrons round the sails repair:
Soft o'er the shrouds aërial whispers breathe,
That seemed but Zephyrs to the train beneath.
Some to the sun their insect-wings unfold,
Waft on the breeze, or sink in clouds of gold;   60
Transparent forms, too fine for mortal sight,
Their fluid bodies half dissolved in light.
Loose to the wind their airy garments flew,
Thin glittering textures of the filmy dew,
Dipt in the richest tincture of the skies,   65
Where light disports in ever-mingling dyes,
While every beam new transient colours flings,
Colours that change whene'er they wave their wings.
Amid the circle, on the gilded mast,

---

35 ff. Parody of an epic sacrifice and prayer.

Superior by the head, was Ariel placed;   70
His purple pinions opening to the sun,
He raised his azure wand, and thus begun.
    "Ye Sylphs and Sylphids, to your chief give ear!
Fays, Fairies, Genii, Elves, and Dæmons, hear!
Ye know the spheres and various tasks assigned   75
By laws eternal to th' aërial kind.
Some in the fields of purest Æther play,
And bask and whiten in the blaze of day.
Some guide the course of wandering orbs on high,
Or roll the planets thro' the boundless sky.   80
Some less refined, beneath the moon's pale light
Pursue the stars that shoot athwart the night,
Or suck the mists in grosser air below,
Or dip their pinions in the painted bow,
Or brew fierce tempests on the wintry main,   85
Or o'er the glebe distil the kindly rain.
Others on earth o'er human race preside,
Watch all their ways, and all their actions guide:
Of these the chief the care of Nations own,
And guard with Arms divine the British Throne.   90
    "Our humbler province is to tend the Fair,
Not a less pleasing, tho' less glorious care;
To save the powder from too rude a gale,
Nor let th' imprisoned essences exhale;
To draw fresh colours from the vernal flowers;   95
To steal from rainbows ere they drop in showers
A brighter wash; to curl their waving hairs,
Assist their blushes, and inspire their airs;
Nay oft, in dreams, invention we bestow,
To change a Flounce, or add a Furbelow.   100
    "This day, black Omens threat the brightest Fair
That e'er deserved a watchful spirit's care;
Some dire disaster, or by force, or slight;
But what, or where, the fates have wrapt in night:
Whether the nymph shall break Diana's law,   105
Or some frail China jar receive a flaw;

---

70. *Superior . . . head:* i.e., taller than his followers (as the epic hero always is). 73-4. Parody of the elaborate addresses to the several ranks of angels in Milton's Hell and Heaven. 89. i.e., the chief sprites (among those who look after human beings) guard important political personages. 97. *wash:* lotion. 103. *slight:* cunning. 105. *Diana's law:* chastity.

Or stain her honour or her new brocade;
Forget her prayers, or miss a masquerade;
Or lose her heart, or necklace, at a ball;
Or whether Heaven has doomed that Shock must fall.   110
Haste, then, ye spirits! to your charge repair:
The fluttering fan be Zephyretta's care;
The drops to thee, Brillante, we consign;
And, Momentilla, let the watch be thine;
Do thou, Crispissa, tend her favorite Lock;   115
Ariel himself shall be the guard of Shock.
  "To fifty chosen Sylphs, of special note,
We trust th' important charge, the Petticoat:
Oft have we known that seven-fold fence to fail,
Tho' stiff with hoops, and armed with ribs of whale;   120
Form a strong line about the silver bound,
And guard the wide circumference around.
  "Whatever spirit, careless of his charge,
His post neglects, or leaves the Fair at large,
Shall feel sharp vengeance soon o'ertake his sins,   125
Be stopped in vials, or transfixed with pins;
Or plunged in lakes of bitter washes lie,
Or wedged whole ages in a bodkin's eye:
Gums and Pomatums shall his flight restrain,
While clogged he beats his silken wings in vain;   130
Or Alum styptics with contracting power
Shrink his thin essence like a riveled flower:
Or, as Ixion fixed, the wretch shall feel
The giddy motion of the whirling Mill,
In fumes of burning Chocolate shall glow,   135
And tremble at the sea that froths below!"
  He spoke; the spirits from the sails descend;
Some, orb in orb, around the nymph extend;
Some thrid the mazy ringlets of her hair;
Some hang upon the pendants of her ear: 140
With beating hearts the dire event they wait,
Anxious, and trembling for the birth of Fate.

112-15. The sylphs' names (roughly equivalent to "Fluttering," "Sparkling,"
"Timing," and "Curling") imply their functions. 113. *drops:* diamond ear-
rings. 128. *bodkin's:* needle's. 129. *Pomatums:* pomades. 132. *riveled:*
shriveled. 134. *Mill:* beater (used to agitate the hot chocolate). 138. *orb in
orb:* like the angels in *Par. Lost*, V 596. 139. *thrid:* thread. 140. *pendants:*
Cf. 113, *drops.*

CANTO III

Close by those meads, for ever crowned with flowers,
Where Thames with pride surveys his rising towers,
There stands a structure of majestic frame,
Which from the neighbouring Hampton takes its name.
Here Britain's statesmen oft the fall foredoom   5
Of foreign Tyrants and of Nymphs at home;
Here thou, great Anna! whom three realms obey,
Dost sometimes counsel take—and sometimes Tea.
Hither the heroes and the nymphs resort,
To taste awhile the pleasures of a Court;   10
In various talk th' instructive hours they past,
Who gave the ball, or paid the visit last;
One speaks the glory of the British Queen,
And one describes a charming Indian screen;
A third interprets motions, looks, and eyes;   15
At every word a reputation dies.
Snuff, or the fan, supply each pause of chat,
With singing, laughing, ogling, _and all that._
   Mean while, declining from the noon of day,
The sun obliquely shoots his burning ray;   20
The hungry Judges soon the sentence sign,
And wretches hang that jury-men may dine;
The merchant from th' Exchange returns in peace,
And the long labours of the Toilet cease.
Belinda now, whom thirst of fame invites,   25
Burns to encounter two adventurous Knights,
At Ombre singly to decide their doom;
And swells her breast with conquests yet to come.
Straight the three bands prepare in arms to join,
Each band the number of the sacred Nine.   30
Soon as she spreads her hand, th' aërial guard
Descend, and sit on each important card:

CANTO III: i.e., Hampton Court, one of the royal residences. 25 ff. The game as a whole parodies the single combats between knights in epic poetry; 37 ff. parodies an epic review of troops, and 47 ff., an epic joining of battle. 29. _bands:_ i.e., hands of cards. 30. _Nine:_ the Muses.

First Ariel perched upon a Matadore,
Then each, according to the rank they bore;
For Sylphs, yet mindful of their ancient race,
Are, as when women, wondrous fond of place.   35
  Behold, four Kings in majesty revered,
With hoary whiskers and a forky beard;
And four fair Queens whose hands sustain a flower,
Th' expressive emblem of their softer power;
Four Knaves in garbs succinct, a trusty band,   40
Caps on their heads, and halberts in their hand;
And particoloured troops, a shining train,
Draw forth to combat on the velvet plain.
  The skilful Nymph reviews her force with care: 45
Let Spades be trumps! she said, and trumps they were.
  Now move to war her sable Matadores,
In show like leaders of the swarthy Moors.
Spadillio first, unconquerable Lord!
Led off two captive trumps, and swept the board.   50
As many more Manillio forced to yield,
And marched a victor from the verdant field.
Him Basto followed, but his fate more hard
Gained but one trump and one Plebian card.
With his broad sabre next, a chief in years,   55
The hoary Majesty of Spades appears,
Puts forth one manly leg, to sight revealed,
The rest, his many-coloured robe concealed.
The rebel Knave, who dares his prince engage,
Proves the just victim of his royal rage.   60
Even mighty Pam, that Kings and Queens o'erthrew
And mowed down armies in the fights of Lu,
Sad chance of war! now destitute of aid,
Falls undistinguished by the victor spade!
  Thus far both armies to Belinda yield;   65
Now to the Baron fate inclines the field.

---

41. *succinct:* tucked up. 44. *velvet plain:* velvet surface of the card table.
46. Cf. Genesis 1:3: "And God said, 'Let there be light,' and there was light."
47. *Matadores:* In Ombre, the three highest trumps: ace of spades (Spadillio), lowest card of the trump suit (Manillio), ace of clubs (Basto). Since
in Belinda's game, spades are trumps, her Matadores are *all* sable. 49 ff.
Belinda now takes four successive tricks (of the nine possible in Ombre).
61. *mighty Pam:* Knave of Clubs, top trump in the game of Loo.

His warlike Amazon her host invades,
Th' imperial consort of the crown of Spades.
The Club's black Tyrant first her victim died,
Spite of his haughty mien, and barbarous pride: 70
What boots the regal circle on his head,
His giant limbs, in state unwieldy spread;
That long behind he trails his pompous robe,
And of all monarchs only grasps the globe?

   The Baron now his Diamonds pours apace;   75
Th' embroidered King who shows but half his face,
And his refulgent Queen, with powers combined,
Of broken troops an easy conquest find.
Clubs, Diamonds, Hearts, in wild disorder seen,
With throngs promiscuous strow the level green.   80
Thus when dispersed a routed army runs,
Of Asia's troops, and Afric's sable sons,
With like confusion different nations fly,
Of various habit, and of various dye,
The pierced battalions dis-united fall,   85
In heaps on heaps; one fate o'erwhelms them all.

   The Knave of Diamonds tries his wily arts,
And wins (oh shameful chance!) the Queen of Hearts.
At this, the blood the virgin's cheek forsook,
A livid paleness spreads o'er all her look;   90
She sees, and trembles at th' approaching ill,
Just in the jaws of ruin, and Codille.
And now (as oft in some distempered State)
On one nice Trick depends the general fate.
An Ace of Hearts steps forth: The King unseen   95
Lurked in her hand, and mourned his captive Queen:
He springs to Vengeance with an eager pace,
And falls like thunder on the prostrate Ace.
The nymph exulting fills with shouts the sky;
The walls, the woods, and long canals reply.   100

   Oh thoughtless mortals! ever blind to fate,
Too soon dejected, and too soon elate.
Sudden, these honours shall be snatched away,

---

67 ff. The baron also takes four tricks. 81 ff. Parody of the epic simile.
92. *Codille:* the equivalent of being "set" in bridge (but used here with
overtones appropriate to the serious amatory game in which Belinda and
the baron are engaged). 98. In the red suits in Ombre, the king is high.
99 ff. Mock-epic "pride," to be followed by a fall.

And cursed for ever this victorious day.

For lo! the board with cups and spoons is crowned,   105
The berries crackle, and the mill turns round; *feast*
On shining Altars of Japan they raise
The silver lamp; the fiery spirits blaze:
From silver spouts the grateful liquors glide,
While China's earth receives the smoking tide: 110
At once they gratify their scent and taste,
And frequent cups prolong the rich repast.
Straight hover round the Fair her airy band;
Some, as she sipped, the fuming liquor fanned,
Some o'er her lap their careful plumes displayed,   115
Trembling, and conscious of the rich brocade.
Coffee (which makes the politician wise,
And see thro' all things with his half-shut eyes)
Sent up in vapours to the Baron's brain
New Stratagems, the radiant Lock to gain.   120
Ah cease, rash youth! desist ere 'tis too late,
Fear the just Gods, and think of Scylla's Fate!
Changed to a bird, and sent to flit in air,
She dearly pays for Nisus' injured hair!

But when to mischief mortals bend their will,   125
How soon they find fit instruments of ill!
Just then, Clarissa drew with tempting grace
A two-edged weapon from her shining case:
So Ladies in Romance assist their Knight,
Present the spear, and arm him for the fight.   130
He takes the gift with reverence, and extends
The little engine on his fingers' ends;
This just behind Belinda's neck he spread,
As o'er the fragrant steams she bends her head.
Swift to the Lock a thousand Sprites repair,   135
A thousand wings, by turns, blow back the hair;

---

105 ff. Parody of an epic feast. 106. *berries:* i.e., coffee. 107. *Altars of Japan:*
japanned, i.e., lacquered, tables. 110. The pun on *China's earth* brings together the actual china cups and the epic habit of pouring out on the
ground a libation to the gods. 122-4. Nisus's daughter Scylla plucked from
his head a purple hair on which his kingdom's prosperity was known to
depend, in order to give it to an enemy of Nisus with whom she was in
love. The enemy repudiated her for this act of impiety and both he and
she were changed into birds.

And thrice they twitched the diamond in her ear;
Thrice she looked back, and thrice the foe drew near.
Just in that instant, anxious Ariel sought
The close recesses of the Virgin's thought;   140
As on the nosegay in her breast reclined,
He watched th' Ideas rising in her mind,
Sudden he viewed, in spite of all her art,
An earthly Lover lurking at her heart.
Amazed, confused, he found his power expired,   145
Resigned to fate, and with a sigh retired.

    The Peer now spreads the glittering Forfex wide,
T' inclose the Lock; now joins it, to divide.
Even then, before the fatal engine closed,
A wretched Sylph too fondly interposed;   150
Fate urged the shears, and cut the Sylph in twain,
(But airy substance soon unites again)
The meeting points the sacred hair dissever
From the fair head, for ever, and for ever!

    Then flashed the living lightning from her eyes,   155
And screams of horror rend th' affrighted skies.
Not louder shrieks to pitying heaven are cast,
When husbands, or when lap-dogs breathe their last;
Or when rich China vessels fallen from high,
In glittering dust and painted fragments lie!   160

    "Let wreaths of triumph now my temples twine
(The victor cried) the glorious Prize is mine!
While fish in streams, or birds delight in air,
Or in a coach and six the British Fair,
As long as Atalantis shall be read,   165
Or the small pillow grace a Lady's bed,
While visits shall be paid on solemn days,
When numerous wax-lights in bright order blaze,
While nymphs take treats, or assignations give,
So long my honour, name, and praise shall live!"   170

    What Time would spare, from Steel receives its date,
And monuments, like men, submit to fate!
Steel could the labour of the Gods destroy,
And strike to dust th' imperial towers of Troy;
Steel could the works of mortal pride confound,   175
And hew triumphal arches to the ground.

---

142. *Ideas:* images. 145. Cf. I 67. 165. *Atalantis:* a slanderous "novel" of the day.

What wonder then, fair nymph! thy hairs should feel,
The conquering force of unresisted steel?

CANTO IV

*B*UT anxious cares the pensive nymph oppressed,
And secret passions laboured in her breast.
Not youthful kings in battle seized alive,
Not scornful virgins who their charms survive,
Not ardent lovers robbed of all their bliss,   5
Not ancient ladies when refused a kiss,
Not tyrants fierce that unrepenting die,
Not Cynthia when her manteau's pinned awry,
E'er felt such rage, resentment, and despair,
As thou, sad Virgin! for thy ravished Hair.   10
For, that sad moment, when the Sylphs withdrew
And Ariel weeping from Belinda flew,
Umbriel, a dusky, melancholy sprite,
As ever sullied the fair face of light,
Down to the central earth, his proper scene,   15
Repaired to search the gloomy Cave of Spleen.
Swift on his sooty pinions flits the Gnome,
And in a vapour reached the dismal dome.
No cheerful breeze this sullen region knows,
The dreaded East is all the wind that blows.   20
Here in a grotto, sheltered close from air,
And screened in shades from day's detested glare,
She sighs for ever on her pensive bed,
Pain at her side, and Megrim at her head.
Two handmaids wait the throne: alike in place,   25
But differing far in figure and in face.

CANTO IV: 15 ff. A parody of the epic visit to the underworld. 16. *Spleen:*
a vague term used in Pope's time for a variety of ailments, but in the poem
usually for those that would today be called neurotic. 17 ff. It is important
to remember throughout the rest of the poem that the gnomes are the
sprites of women who were prudes—i.e., affectedly virtuous. 18. *vapour:*
used in both its senses of "mist" and "peevishness." 20. *East:* This wind was
supposed to cause the spleen. 24. i.e., Spleen's two attendants are placed
where the pains of spleen were oftenest found—in the side and in the head.
Megrim is "migraine," a severe headache.

Here stood Ill-nature like an ancient maid,
Her wrinkled form in black and white arrayed;
With store of prayers, for mornings, nights, and noons,
Her hand is filled; her bosom with lampoons.   30
    There Affectation, with a sickly mien,
Shows in her cheek the roses of eighteen,
Practised to lisp, and hang the head aside,
Faints into airs, and languishes with pride;
On the rich quilt sinks with becoming woe,   35
Wrapt in a gown, for sickness, and for show.
The fair ones feel such maladies as these,
When each new night-dress gives a new disease.
    A constant Vapour o'er the palace flies;
Strange phantoms rising as the mists arise;   40
Dreadful, as hermit's dreams in haunted shades,
Or bright, as visions of expiring maids.
Now glaring fiends, and snakes on rolling spires,
Pale spectres, gaping tombs, and purple fires:
Now lakes of liquid gold, Elysian scenes,   45
And crystal domes, and angels in machines.
    Unnumbered throngs on every side are seen,
Of bodies changed to various forms by Spleen.
Here living Tea-pots stand, one arm held out,
One bent; the handle this, and that the spout: 50
A Pipkin there, like Homer's Tripod walks;
Here sighs a Jar, and there a Goose-pie talks;
Men prove with child, as powerful fancy works,
And maids, turned bottles, call aloud for corks.
    Safe passed the Gnome thro' this fantastic band,   55
A branch of healing Spleenwort in his hand.
Then thus addressed the power: "Hail, wayward Queen!
Who rule the sex to fifty from fifteen:
Parent of vapours and of female wit,
Who give th' hysteric, or poetic fit,   60
On various tempers act by various ways,
Make some take physic, others scribble plays;
Who cause the proud their visits to delay,
And send the godly in a pet to pray.
A nymph there is, that all thy power disdains,   65
And thousands more in equal mirth maintains.
But oh! if e'er thy Gnome could spoil a grace,

---

49 ff. Delusions to which the splenetic were believed subject.

Or raise a pimple on a beauteous face,
Like Citron-waters matrons' cheeks inflame,
Or change complexions at a losing game;   70
If e'er with airy horns I planted heads,
Or rumpled petticoats, or tumbled beds,
Or caused suspicion when no soul was rude,
Or discomposed the head-dress of a Prude,
Or e'er to costive lap-dog gave disease,   75
Which not the tears of brightest eyes could ease:
Hear me, and touch Belinda with chagrin,
That single act gives half the world the spleen."
　　The Goddess with a discontented air
Seems to reject him, tho' she grants his prayer.   80
A wondrous Bag with both her hands she binds,
Like that where once Ulysses held the winds;
There she collects the force of female lungs,
Sighs, sobs, and passions, and the war of tongues.
A Vial next she fills with fainting fears,   85
Soft sorrows, melting griefs, and flowing tears.
The Gnome rejoicing bears her gifts away,
Spreads his black wings, and slowly mounts to day.
　　Sunk in Thalestris' arms the nymph he found,
Her eyes dejected and her hair unbound.   90
Full o'er their heads the swelling bag he rent,
And all the Furies issued at the vent.
Belinda burns with more than mortal ire,
And fierce Thalestris fans the rising fire.
"O wretched maid!" she spread her hands, and cried,   95
(While Hampton's echoes, "Wretched maid!" replied)
"Was it for this you took such constant care
The bodkin, comb, and essence to prepare?
For this your locks in paper durance bound,
For this with torturing irons wreathed around?   100
For this with fillets strained your tender head,
And bravely bore the double loads of lead?
Gods! shall the ravisher display your hair,
While the Fops envy, and the Ladies stare!
Honour forbid! at whose unrivalled shrine   105

69. *Citron-waters:* brandy flavored with citron-peel. 70. Cf. III 89. 71. *heads:*
i.e., of those believed to be cuckolds. 82. *where . . . winds:* cf. *Odyssey*
x 19 ff. 98. *bodkin:* The term is used here (and in v 95) to mean a hairpin.
99. *durance:* i.e., curlers. 101. *fillets:* headbands.

Ease, pleasure, virtue, all, our sex resign.
Methinks already I your tears survey,
Already hear the horrid things they say,
Already see you a degraded toast, *honored for beauty, but degra...*
And all your honour in a whisper lost!   110
How shall I, then, your helpless fame defend?
'Twill then be infamy to seem your friend!
And shall this prize, th' inestimable prize,
Exposed thro' crystal to the gazing eyes,
And heightened by the diamond's circling rays,   115
On that rapacious hand for ever blaze?
Sooner shall grass in Hyde-park Circus grow,
And wits take lodgings in the sound of Bow;
Sooner let earth, air, sea, to Chaos fall,
Men, monkeys, lap-dogs, parrots, perish all!"   120
    She said: then raging to Sir Plume repairs,
And bids her Beau demand the precious hairs:
(Sir Plume of amber snuff-box justly vain,   *shallow*
And the nice conduct of a clouded cane)   *ineffectual*
With earnest eyes, and round unthinking face,   125
He first the snuff-box opened, then the case,
And thus broke out—"My Lord, why, what the devil?
Z—ds! damn the lock! 'fore Gad you must be civil!
Plague on 't! 'tis past a jest—nay prithee, pox!
Give her the hair"—he spoke, and rapped his box.   130
    "It grieves me much" (replied the Peer again)
"Who speaks so well should ever speak in vain.
But by this Lock, this sacred Lock, I swear,
(Which never more shall join its parted hair;
Which never more its honours shall renew,   135
Clipped from the lovely head where late it grew)
That while my nostrils draw the vital air,
This hand, which won it, shall for ever wear."
He spoke, and speaking, in proud triumph spread
The long-contended honours of her head.   140
    But Umbriel, hateful Gnome! forbears not so;
He breaks the Vial whence the sorrows flow.
Then see! the nymph in beauteous grief appears,

114-15. i.e., the lock will be made up in a ring. 117. *Hyde-park Circus:* the
"Ring" of I 44. 118. *in . . . Bow:* within earshot of the bells of St. Mary-le-
Bow—i.e., in the unfashionable mercantile section. 124. *clouded:* mottled.
140. *honours:* beauties, i.e., hairs.

Her eyes half-languishing, half-drowned in tears;
On her heaved bosom hung her drooping head, 145
Which, with a sigh, she raised; and thus she said.
  "For ever cursed be this detested day,
Which snatched my best, my favourite curl away!
Happy! ah ten times happy had I been,
If Hampton-Court these eyes had never seen! 150
Yet am not I the first mistaken maid,
By love of Courts to numerous ills betrayed.
Oh had I rather un-admired remained
In some lone isle; or distant Northern land;
Where the gilt Chariot never marks the way, 155
Where none learn Ombre, none e'er taste Bohea!
There kept my charms concealed from mortal eye,
Like roses, that in deserts bloom and die.
What moved my mind with youthful Lords to roam?
Oh had I stayed, and said my prayers at home! 160
'Twas this, the morning omens seemed to tell,
Thrice from my trembling hand the patch-box fell;
The tottering China shook without a wind,
Nay, Poll sat mute, and Shock was most unkind!
A Sylph too warned me of the threats of fate, 165
In mystic visions, now believed too late!
See the poor remnants of these slighted hairs!
My hands shall rend what even thy rapine spares:
These in two sable ringlets taught to break,
Once gave new beauties to the snowy neck; 170
The sister-lock now sits uncouth, alone,
And in its fellow's fate foresees its own;
Uncurled it hangs, the fatal shears demands,
And tempts once more thy sacrilegious hands.
Oh hadst thou, cruel! been content to seize 175
Hairs less in sight, or any hairs but these!"

❧

CANTO V

SHE said: the pitying audience melt in tears.
But Fate and Jove had stopped the Baron's ears.

---

156. *Bohea:* a kind of tea. 161 ff. Parody of epic omens.

In vain Thalestris with reproach assails,
For who can move when fair Belinda fails?
Not half so fixed the Trojan could remain,   5
While Anna begged and Dido raged in vain.
Then grave Clarissa graceful waved her fan;
Silence ensued, and thus the nymph began.
    "Say why are Beauties praised and honoured most,
The wise man's passion, and the vain man's toast?   10
Why decked with all that land and sea afford,
Why Angels called, and Angel-like adored?
Why round our coaches crowd the white-gloved Beaux,
Why bows the side-box from its inmost rows;
How vain are all these glories, all our pains,   15
Unless good sense preserve what beauty gains:
That men may say, when we the front-box grace:
'Behold the first in virtue as in face!'
Oh! if to dance all night, and dress all day,
Charmed the small-pox, or chased old-age away;   20
Who would not scorn what housewife's cares produce,
Or who would learn one earthly thing of use?
To patch, nay ogle, might become a Saint,
Nor could it sure be such a sin to paint.
But since, alas! frail beauty must decay,   25
Curled or uncurled, since Locks will turn to grey;
Since painted, or not painted, all shall fade,
And she who scorns a man, must die a maid;
What then remains but well our power to use,
And keep good-humour still whate'er we lose?   30
And trust me, dear! good-humour can prevail,
When airs, and flights, and screams, and scolding fail.
Beauties in vain their pretty eyes may roll;
Charms strike the sight, but merit wins the soul."
    So spoke the Dame, but no applause ensued;   35
Belinda frowned, Thalestris called her Prude.
"To arms, to arms!" the fierce Virago cries,
And swift as lightning to the combat flies.
All side in parties, and begin th' attack;
Fans clap, silks rustle, and tough whalebones crack;   40

CANTO V: 5-6. Alluding to Dido's pleas (seconded by her sister Anna) that
Aeneas remain with her. 9 ff. The lines echo one of the most famous of
heroic speeches—Glaucus's address to Sarpedon in *Iliad*, XII. 37. *Virago*:
manlike woman. 39 ff. Parody of an epic mêlée.

Heroes' and Heroines' shouts confusedly rise,
And bass, and treble voices strike the skies.
No common weapons in their hands are found,
Like Gods they fight, nor dread a mortal wound.

    So when bold Homer makes the Gods engage,   45
And heavenly breasts with human passions rage;
'Gainst Pallas, Mars; Latona, Hermes arms;
And all Olympus rings with loud alarms:
Jove's thunder roars, heaven trembles all around,
Blue Neptune storms, the bellowing deeps resound: 50
Earth shakes her nodding towers, the ground gives way,
And the pale ghosts start at the flash of day!

    Triumphant Umbriel on a sconce's height
Clapped his glad wings, and sate to view the fight:
Propped on their bodkin spears, the Sprites survey   55
The growing combat, or assist the fray.

    While thro' the press enraged Thalestris flies,
And scatters death around from both her eyes,
A Beau and Witling perished in the throng,
One died in metaphor, and one in song.   60
"O cruel nymph! a living death I bear,"
Cried Dapperwit, and sunk beside his chair.
A mournful glance Sir Fopling upwards cast,
"Those eyes are made so killing"—was his last.
Thus on Mæander's flowery margin lies   65
Th' expiring Swan, and as he sings he dies.

    When bold Sir Plume had drawn Clarissa down,
Chloë stepped in, and killed him with a frown;
She smiled to see the doughty hero slain,
But, at her smile, the Beau revived again.   70

    Now Jove suspends his golden scales in air,
Weighs the Men's wits against the Lady's hair;
The doubtful beam long nods from side to side;
At length the wits mount up, the hairs subside.

    See, fierce Belinda on the Baron flies,   75
With more than usual lightning in her eyes:
Nor feared the Chief th' unequal fight to try,
Who sought no more than on his foe to die.
But this bold Lord with manly strength endued,
She with one finger and a thumb subdued: 80

---

53. *sconce:* wall-bracket (for candles). 57 ff. Beneath the epic references in
this "battle" lurks the old sense of "dying" as sexual consummation.

Just where the breath of life his nostrils drew,
A charge of Snuff the wily virgin threw;
The Gnomes direct, to every atom just,
The pungent grains of titillating dust.
Sudden, with starting tears each eye o'erflows,   85
And the high dome re-echoes to his nose.
   "Now meet thy fate," incensed Belinda cried,
And drew a deadly bodkin from her side.
(The same, his ancient personage to deck,
Her great great grandsire wore about his neck,   90
In three seal-rings; which after, melted down,
Formed a vast buckle for his widow's gown:
Her infant grandame's whistle next it grew,
The bells she jingled, and the whistle blew;
Then in a bodkin graced her mother's hairs,   95
Which long she wore, and now Belinda wears.)
   "Boast not my fall" (he cried) "insulting foe!
Thou by some other shalt be laid as low,
Nor think, to die dejects my lofty mind:
All that I dread is leaving you behind!   100
Rather than so, ah let me still survive,
And burn in Cupid's flames—but burn alive."
   "Restore the Lock!" she cries; and all around
"Restore the Lock!" the vaulted roofs rebound.
Not fierce Othello in so loud a strain   105
Roared for the handkerchief that caused his pain.
But see how oft ambitious aims are crossed,
And chiefs contend 'till all the prize is lost!
The Lock, obtained with guilt, and kept with pain,
In every place is sought, but sought in vain: 110
With such a prize no mortal must be blest,
So heaven decrees! with heaven who can contest?
   Some thought it mounted to the Lunar sphere,
Since all things lost on earth are treasured there.
There Heroes' wits are kept in ponderous vases,   115
And beaux', in snuff-boxes and tweezer-cases.
There broken vows and death-bed alms are found,
And lovers' hearts with ends of riband bound,
The courtier's promises, and sick man's prayers,
The smiles of harlots, and the tears of heirs,   120
Cages for gnats, and chains to yoke a flea,
Dried butterflies, and tomes of casuistry.

89 ff. Parody of epic descriptions of the origin of a piece of armour.

But trust the Muse—she saw it upward rise,
Tho' marked by none but quick, poetic eyes:
(So Rome's great founder to the heavens withdrew,   125
To Proculus alone confessed in view)
A sudden Star, it shot thro' liquid air,
And drew behind a radiant trail of hair.
Not Berenice's Locks first rose so bright,
The heavens bespangling with dishevelled light.   130
The Sylphs behold it kindling as it flies,
And pleased pursue its progress thro' the skies.

   This the Beau monde shall from the Mall survey,
And hail with music its propitious ray.
This the blest Lover shall for Venus take,   135
And send up vows from Rosamonda's lake.
This Partridge soon shall view in cloudless skies,
When next he looks thro' Galileo's eyes;
And hence th' egregious wizard shall foredoom
The fate of Louis, and the fall of Rome.   140

   Then cease, bright Nymph! to mourn thy ravished hair,
Which adds new glory to the shining sphere!
Not all the tresses that fair head can boast,
Shall draw such envy as the Lock you lost.
For, after all the murders of your eye,   145
When after millions slain, yourself shall die:
When those fair suns shall set, as set they must,
And all those tresses shall be laid in dust,
This Lock, the Muse shall consecrate to fame,
And 'midst the stars inscribe Belinda's name.   150

[handwritten margin notes: "Partridge Almanac / Swift predicted death"; "one of seriousness / beauty must die"; "Tribute to offset satire"]

❧

125-6. Romulus's translation to heaven was confirmed by one of the Roman senators, Proculus. 129. The hair of Berenice (queen of Ptolemy III), dedicated as a votive offering to ensure her husband's safe return from battle, was said to have been translated to the skies and become the constellation *Coma Berenices.* 133. *the Mall:* a fashionable promenade in St. James's Park, often the scene of impromptu music. 136. *Rosamonda's Lake:* a pond in St. James's Park identified with unhappy love. Cf. *Of the Characters of Women,* 92 n. 137. *Partridge:* a star-gazing quack, whose almanacs pretended to foretell the future. 140. *Louis:* Louis XIV of France.

[handwritten at bottom: "Uses a lot from 'Paradise Lost' / Grandeur reveals triviality of human acts"]

An Essay on Man

To

H. ST. JOHN LORD BOLINGBROKE

(1733-4)

Argument of Epistle I

OF THE NATURE AND STATE OF MAN, WITH RESPECT TO THE UNIVERSE

Of Man in the abstract. I. That we can judge only with regard to our own system, being ignorant of the relations of systems and things, v. 17, &c. II. That Man is not to be deemed imperfect, but a Being suited to his place and rank in the creation, agreeable to the general Order of things, and conformable to Ends and Relations to him unknown, v. 35, &c. III. That it is partly upon his ignorance of future events, and partly upon the hope of a future state, that all his happiness in the present depends, v. 77, &c. IV. The pride of aiming at more knowledge, and pretending to more Perfection, the cause of Man's error and misery. The impiety of putting himself in the place of God, and judging of the fitness or unfitness, perfection or imperfection, justice or injustice of his dispensations, v. 113, &c. V. The absurdity of conceiting himself the final cause of the creation, or expecting that perfection in the moral world, which is not in the natural, v. 131, &c. VI. The unreasonableness of his complaints against Providence, while on the one hand he demands the Perfections of the Angels, and on the other the bodily qualifications of the Brutes; though, to possess any of the sensitive faculties in a higher degree, would render him miserable, v. 173, &c. VII. That throughout the whole visible world, an universal order and gradation in the sensual and mental faculties is observed, which causes a subordination of creature to creature, and of all creatures to Man. The gradations of sense, instinct, thought, reflection, reason; that Reason alone countervails all the other faculties, v. 207. VIII. How much further this order and subordination of living creatures may extend, above and below us; were any part of which broken, not that part only, but the whole connected creation must be destroyed, v. 233. IX. The extravagance, madness, and pride of such a desire, v. 259. X. The consequence of all,

the absolute submission due to Providence, both as to our present and
future state, v. 281, &c. to the end.

EPISTLE I *Sat.*

Awake, my St. John! leave all meaner things
To low ambition, and the pride of Kings.   — *attitude of Pope*
Let us (since Life can little more supply   *man not important*
Than just to look about us and to die)
Expatiate free o'er all this scene of Man;   5
A mighty maze! but not without a plan;
A Wild, where weeds and flowers promiscuous shoot;
Or Garden, tempting with forbidden fruit.   → *Pope and Bolingbroke*
Together let us beat this ample field,
Try what the open, what the covert yield;   10
The latent tracts, the giddy heights, explore
Of all who blindly creep, or sightless soar;
Eye Nature's walks, shoot Folly as it flies,
And catch the Manners living as they rise;
Laugh where we must, be candid where we can;   *like milton*   15
But vindicate the ways of God to Man.

   I. Say first, of God above, or Man below,
What can we reason, but from what we know?
Of Man, what see we but his station here,
From which to reason, or to which refer?   20
Thro' worlds unnumbered tho' the God be known,
'Tis ours to trace him only in our own.
He, who thro' vast immensity can pierce,
See worlds on worlds compose one universe,
Observe how system into system runs,   25
What other planets circle other suns,
What varied Being peoples every star,
May tell why Heaven has made us as we are.

---

  1. *St. John:* Henry St. John, Viscount Bolingbroke, Pope's philosophically
minded friend who had promised to set down his own speculations in prose
while Pope was setting down his in verse; Bolingbroke had so far failed to
keep the bargain, and hence is told to *awake*. 7-8. Here and in 216 Pope
indicates the relation of his *theme* to Milton's in *Par. Lost:* the Garden of
Eden has now become the world we all live in; good and evil are everywhere mixed; but there remain the old problems of how evil originated and
how it may be avoided. 9-14. Through the informality of the garden and
hunting images Pope indicates the relation of his *tone* to Milton's: he is not
writing an epic, but an "essay."

But of this frame the bearings, and the ties,
The strong connexions, nice dependencies,   30
Gradations just, has thy pervading soul
Looked thro'? or can a part contain the whole?
  Is the great chain, that draws all to agree,
And drawn supports, upheld by God, or thee?
  II. Presumptuous Man! the reason wouldst thou find,   35
Why formed so weak, so little, and so blind?
First, if thou canst, the harder reason guess,
Why formed no weaker, blinder, and no less?
Ask of thy mother earth, why oaks are made
Taller or stronger than the weeds they shade?   40
Or ask of yonder argent fields above,
Why Jove's satellites are less than Jove?
  Of Systems possible, if 'tis confest
That Wisdom infinite must form the best,
Where all must full or not coherent be,   45
And all that rises, rise in due degree;
Then, in the scale of reasoning life, 'tis plain,
There must be, somewhere, such a rank as Man:
And all the question (wrangle e'er so long)
Is only this, if God has placed him wrong?   50
  Respecting Man, whatever wrong we call,
May, must be right, as relative to all.
In human works, tho' laboured on with pain,
A thousand movements scarce one purpose gain;
In God's, one single can its end produce;   55
Yet serves to second too some other use.
So Man, who here seems principal alone,
Perhaps acts second to some sphere unknown,
Touches some wheel, or verges to some goal;
'Tis but a part we see, and not a whole.   60

---

33. *the . . . chain:* the chain or ladder of beings from uncreated nothing up
to the Creator. 42. *Jove:* the planet Jupiter (but possibly with added reference to the hierarchy of the Olympian gods). 43-6. These were common as-
sumptions about the cosmos from classical times on: that God would choose
to create the best world possible; that the best world is necessarily the one
that permits existence to the greatest number of kinds of being—i.e., is *full* of
ranks of being; and that all these ranks must mount by even steps (*degree*).
48-50. It was a traditional complaint against God's providence and goodness
that, in comparison with the other creatures, man had been slighted. 51 ff.
Pope argues that what men now take to be defects would be seen to be
good in the universe as a whole—if only men could see the whole.

When the proud steed shall know why Man restrains
His fiery course, or drives him o'er the plains:
When the dull Ox, why now he breaks the clod,
Is now a victim, and now Ægypt's God:
Then shall Man's pride and dulness comprehend   65
His actions', passions', being's, use and end;
Why doing, suffering, checked, impelled; and why
This hour a slave, the next a deity.
    Then say not Man's imperfect, Heaven in fault;
Say rather, Man's as perfect as he ought: 70
His knowledge measured to his state and place;
His time a moment, and a point his space.
If to be perfect in a certain sphere,
What matter, soon or late, or here or there?
The blest to day is as completely so,   75
As who began a thousand years ago.
    III. Heaven from all creatures hides the book of Fate,
All but the page prescribed, their present state:
From brutes what men, from men what spirits know:
Or who could suffer Being here below?   80
The lamb thy riot dooms to bleed to-day,
Had he thy Reason, would he skip and play?
Pleased to the last, he crops the flowery food,
And licks the hand just raised to shed his blood.
Oh blindness to the future! kindly given,   85
That each may fill the circle marked by Heaven:
Who sees with equal eye, as God of all,
A hero perish, or a sparrow fall,
Atoms or systems into ruin hurled,
And now a bubble burst, and now a world.   90
    Hope humbly then; with trembling pinions soar;
Wait the great teacher Death; and God adore.
What future bliss, he gives not thee to know,
But gives that Hope to be thy blessing now.

---

61 ff. An analogy between the animals' unawareness of man's intelligible
purposes and man's unawareness of his Creator's presumably intelligible purposes. 73. I.e., if man is to become a perfect being (rather than a limited
one) in a future existence. 75-6. I.e., beatitude is beatitude: one does not
have more of it by beginning earlier. 77 ff. Further analogies to suggest that
man's limitations—for instance, his lack of foreknowledge—are actually
blessings. 88. Matthew 10:29-31: "Are not two sparrows sold for a farthing?
and one of them shall not fall on the ground without your Father. . . .
Fear ye not therefore, ye are of more value than many sparrows."

Hope springs eternal in the human breast: *aft quoted* 95
Man never Is, but always To be blest:
The soul, uneasy and confined from home,
Rests and expatiates in a life to come.

  Lo, the poor Indian! whose untutored mind *very popular*
Sees God in clouds, or hears him in the wind: *attitude towards* 100
His soul, proud Science never taught to stray *the indian*
Far as the solar walk, or milky way;
Yet simple Nature to his hope has given,
Behind the cloud-topt hill, an humbler heaven;
Some safer world in depth of woods embraced,   105
Some happier island in the watry waste,
Where slaves once more their native land behold,
No fiends torment, no Christians thirst for gold.
To Be, contents his natural desire,
He asks no Angel's wing, no Seraph's fire;   110
But thinks, admitted to that equal sky,
His faithful dog shall bear him company.

  IV. Go, wiser thou! and, in thy scale of sense,
Weigh thy Opinion against Providence;
Call imperfection what thou fancy'st such,   115
Say, here he gives too little, there too much:
Destroy all Creatures for thy sport or gust,
Yet cry, If Man's unhappy, God's unjust;
If Man alone engross not Heaven's high care,
Alone made perfect here, immortal there: 120
Snatch from his hand the balance and the rod,
Re-judge his justice, be the GOD of GOD.
In Pride, in reasoning Pride, our error lies;
All quit their sphere, and rush into the skies.
Pride still is aiming at the blest abodes,   125
Men would be Angels, Angels would be Gods.
Aspiring to be Gods, if Angels fell,
Aspiring to be Angels, Men rebel:
And who but wishes to invert the laws
Of ORDER, sins against th' Eternal Cause.   130

  V. Ask for what end the heavenly bodies shine,
Earth for whose use? Pride answers, " 'Tis for mine:

---

99 ff. Cf. IV. 177-8. 116. *he:* God. 126-8. A further notice of the relation of
Pope's theme to Milton's. 131-40. The attitude of the anthropocentrist, who
believes God made the universe for man.

For me kind Nature wakes her genial Power,
Suckles each herb, and spreads out every flower;
Annual for me, the grape, the rose renew   135
The juice nectareous, and the balmy dew;
For me, the mine a thousand treasures brings;
For me, health gushes from a thousand springs;
Seas roll to waft me, suns to light me rise;
My foot-stool earth, my canopy the skies."   140
    But errs not Nature from this gracious end,
From burning suns when livid deaths descend,
When earthquakes swallow, or when tempests sweep
Towns to one grave, whole nations to the deep?
"No, ('tis replied) the first Almighty Cause   145
Acts not by partial, but by general laws;
Th' exceptions few; some change since all began:
And what created perfect?"—Why then Man?
If the great end be human Happiness,
Then Nature deviates; and can Man do less?   150
As much that end a constant course requires
Of showers and sun-shine, as of Man's desires;
As much eternal springs and cloudless skies,
As Men for ever temperate, calm, and wise.
If plagues or earthquakes break not Heaven's design,   155
Why then a Borgia, or a Catiline?
Who knows but he, whose hand the lightning forms,
Who heaves old Ocean, and who wings the storms;
Pours fierce Ambition in a Cæsar's mind,
Or turns young Ammon loose to scourge mankind?   160
From pride, from pride, our very reasoning springs;
Account for moral, as for natural things:
Why charge we Heaven in those, in these acquit?
In both, to reason right is to submit.

[handwritten margin notes: "natural forces of evil" (near line 148); "moral failures of man" (near line 155)]

---

141 ff. Certain facts in the natural world show that the whole is not planned for man alone. So do certain facts in the moral world—e.g., man's capacity (having freedom to choose and passions to mislead him) for evil. 147. *some . . . began:* alluding possibly to Newton's idea that the cosmos was deteriorating, possibly to the traditional idea that the world was altered for the worse since the Fall. 148. *And . . . perfect?* i.e., no created thing can be perfect, since perfection belongs only to God the Creator. 156 *Catiline:* a debauched Roman who sought to wipe out the Senate, plunder the treasury, and burn the city (63 b.c.). 160. *Ammon:* Alexander the Great (who was deified as son—*Young Ammon*—to Jupiter Ammon).

Better for Us, perhaps, it might appear,   165
Were there all harmony, all virtue here;
That never air or ocean felt the wind;
That never passion discomposed the mind.
But ALL subsists by elemental strife;
And Passions are the elements of Life.   170
The general ORDER, since the whole began,
Is kept in Nature, and is kept in Man.
    VI. What would this Man? Now upward will he soar,
And little less than Angel, would be more;
Now looking downwards, just as grieved appears   175
To want the strength of bulls, the fur of bears.
Made for his use all creatures if he call,
Say what their use, had he the powers of all?
Nature to these, without profusion, kind,
The proper organs, proper powers assigned;   180
Each seeming want compénsated of course,
Here with degrees of swiftness, there of force;
All in exact proportion to the state;
Nothing to add, and nothing to abate.
Each beast, each insect, happy in its own: 185
Is Heaven unkind to Man, and Man alone?
Shall he alone, whom rational we call,
Be pleased with nothing, if not blessed with all?
    The bliss of Man (could Pride that blessing find)
Is not to act or think beyond mankind;   190
No powers of body or of soul to share,
But what his nature and his state can bear.
Why has not Man a microscopic eye?
For this plain reason, Man is not a Fly.
Say what the use, were finer optics given,   195
T' inspect a mite, not comprehend the heaven?
Or touch, if tremblingly alive all o'er,
To smart and agonize at every pore?
Or quick effluvia darting thro' the brain,
Die of a rose in aromatic pain?   200
If nature thundered in his opening ears,
And stunned him with the music of the spheres,

173-76. A traditional complaint of the Epicurean philosophers against providence. 195. *optics:* eyes (with reference also to optic glasses like the micro-
scope, which was still a novelty). 199. *effluvia:* stream of (odorous) particles. 202. *the . . . spheres:* the harmony supposed to result from each
sphere's musical note as it turned.

How would he wish that Heaven had left him still
The whispering Zephyr, and the purling rill?
Who finds not Providence all good and wise,   205
Alike in what it gives, and what it denies?
  VII. Far as Creation's ample range extends,
The scale of sensual, mental powers ascends:
Mark how it mounts, to Man's imperial race,
From the green myriads in the peopled grass: 210
What modes of sight betwixt each wide extreme,
The mole's dim curtain, and the lynx's beam:
Of smell, the headlong lioness between,
And hound sagacious on the tainted green:
Of hearing, from the life that fills the Flood,   215
To that which warbles thro' the vernal wood:
The spider's touch, how exquisitely fine!
Feels at each thread, and lives along the line:
In the nice bee, what sense so subtly true
From poisonous herbs extracts the healing dew?   220
How Instinct varies in the groveling swine,
Compared, half-reasoning elephant, with thine!
'Twixt that, and Reason, what a nice barriér,
For ever separate, yet for ever near!
Remembrance and Reflection how allied;   225
What thin partitions Sense from Thought divide:
And Middle natures, how they long to join,
Yet never pass th' insuperable line!
Without this just gradation, could they be
Subjected, these to those, or all to thee?   230
The powers of all subdued by thee alone,
Is not thy Reason all these powers in one?   *man only diarmed with reason*
  VIII. See, thro' this air, this ocean, and this earth,
All matter quick, and bursting into birth.
Above, how high, progressive life may go!   235
Around, how wide! how deep extend below!
Vast chain of Being! which from God began,
Natures ethereal, human, angel, man,

---

212. *lynx:* traditionally believed the keenest-sighted of all animals. 214
sagacious: quick of scent. 223. *that:* i.e., instinct (regarded as the highest
faculty in animals, as reason is in man). 225. Animals were accredited with
simple memory; men, with the ability to look before and after, draw conclusions, make plans. 226. *Sense, Thought:* sensateness; rationality. 227.
Middle natures: those whose characteristics bridge two classes—like bats.

Beast, bird, fish, insect, what no eye can see,
No glass can reach; from Infinite to thee,   240
From thee to Nothing.—On superior powers
Were we to press, inferior might on ours:
Or in the full creation leave a void,
Where, one step broken, the great scale's destroyed:
From Nature's chain whatever link you strike,   245
Tenth or ten thousandth, breaks the chain alike.
  And, if each system in gradation roll
Alike essential to th' amazing Whole,
The least confusion but in one, not all
That system only, but the Whole must fall.   250
Let Earth unbalanced from her orbit fly,
Planets and Suns run lawless thro' the sky;
Let ruling angels from their spheres be hurled,
Being on Being wrecked, and world on world;
Heaven's whole foundations to their centre nod,   255
And Nature tremble to the throne of God.
All this dread ORDER break—for whom? for thee?
Vile worm!—Oh Madness! Pride! Impiety!
  IX. What if the foot, ordained the dust to tread,
Or hand, to toil, aspired to be the head?   260
What if the head, the eye, or ear repined
To serve mere engines to the ruling Mind?
Just as absurd for any part to claim
To be another, in this general frame:
Just as absurd, to mourn the tasks or pains,   265
The great directing MIND of ALL ordains.
  All are but parts of one stupendous whole,
Whose body Nature is, and God the soul;
That, changed thro' all, and yet in all the same,
Great in the earth, as in th' ethereal frame,   270
Warms in the sun, refreshes in the breeze,
Glows in the stars, and blossoms in the trees;
Lives thro' all life, extends thro' all extent,
Spreads undivided, operates unspent;
Breathes in our soul, informs our mortal part,   275
As full, as perfect, in a hair as heart:
As full, as perfect, in vile Man that mourns,
As the rapt Seraph that adores and burns:

---

259 ff. Pope echoes St. Paul's analogy of the body and the members (1 Corinthians, 12).

To him no high, no low, no great, no small;
He fills, he bounds, connects, and equals all. 280
  X. Cease then, nor ORDER Imperfection name:
Our proper bliss depends on what we blame.
Know thy own point: This kind, this due degree
Of blindness, weakness, Heaven bestows on thee.
Submit.—In this, or any other sphere, 285
Secure to be as blest as thou canst bear:
Safe in the hand of one disposing Power,
Or in the natal, or the mortal hour.
All Nature is but Art, unknown to thee;
All Chance, Direction, which thou canst not see; 290
All Discord, Harmony, not understood;
All Partial Evil, universal Good:
And, spite of Pride, in erring Reason's spite,
One truth is clear, WHATEVER IS, IS RIGHT.

❧

Argument of Epistle II

OF THE NATURE AND STATE OF MAN WITH RESPECT TO HIMSELF, AS AN INDIVIDUAL

    I. The business of Man not to pry into God, but to study himself. His Middle Nature; his Powers and Frailties, v. 1 to 18. The Limits of his Capacity, v. 19, &c. II. The two Principles of Man, Self-love and Reason, both necessary, v. 53, &c. Self-love the stronger, and why, v. 67, &c. Their end the same, v. 81, &c. III. The Passions, and their use, v. 93 to 130. The predominant Passion, and its force, v. 131 to 160. Its Necessity, in directing Men to different purposes, v. 165, &c. Its providential Use, in fixing our Principle, and ascertaining our Virtue, v. 177. IV. Virtue and Vice joined in our mixed Nature; the limits near, yet the things separate and evident: What is the Office of Reason, v. 203 to 216. V. How odious Vice in itself, and how we deceive ourselves into it, v. 217. VI. That, however, the Ends of Providence and general Good are answered in our Passions and Imperfections, v. 231, &c. How usefully these are distributed to all Orders of Men, v. 241. How useful they are to Society, v. 251. And to the Individuals, v. 261. In every state, and every age of life, v. 271, &c.

---

280. *equals all:* makes all equal. Creatures may be of different ranks, but all are equally "filled" (and cared for: cf. I 87) by God.

EPISTLE II

I. Know then thyself, presume not God to scan;
The proper study of Mankind is Man.
Placed on this isthmus of a middle state,
A Being darkly wise, and rudely great:
With too much knowledge for the Sceptic side,   5
With too much weakness for the Stoic's pride,
He hangs between; in doubt to act, or rest;
In doubt to deem himself a God, or Beast;
In doubt his Mind or Body to prefer;
Born but to die, and reasoning but to err;   10
Alike in ignorance, his reason such,
Whether he thinks too little, or too much:
Chaos of Thought and Passion, all confused;
Still by himself abused, or disabused;
Created half to rise, and half to fall;   15
Great lord of all things, yet a prey to all;
Sole judge of Truth, in endless Error hurled:
The glory, jest, and riddle of the world!

Go, wondrous creature! mount where Science guides,
Go, measure earth, weigh air, and state the tides;   20
Instruct the planets in what orbs to run,
Correct old Time, and regulate the Sun;
Go, soar with Plato to th' empyreal sphere,
To the first good, first perfect, and first fair;
Or tread the mazy round his followers trod,   25
And quitting sense call imitating God;
As Eastern priests in giddy circles run,
And turn their heads to imitate the Sun.
Go, teach Eternal Wisdom how to rule—
Then drop into thyself, and be a fool!   30

---

1. *scan:* pry into and carp at. 6. The *Stoic's pride* is the notion that passions can be extirpated and man become an entirely intellectual creature. 19 ff. Pope argues that despite the self-intoxication with intellect to which man is subject (instanced in neo-Platonism and scientism) his real task is the ethical culture of his nature as it is—partly rational, partly passional. 23. *empyreal sphere:* home of the Platonic absolutes, or "Forms," named in l. 24. 26. *quitting sense:* i.e., leaving the body behind (in trance-like ascents of the soul to the "first fair," etc.)

   Superior beings, when of late they saw
A mortal Man unfold all Nature's law,
Admired such wisdom in an earthly shape,
And shewed a NEWTON as we shew an Ape.

of what use to discovery to men

   Could he, whose rules the rapid Comet bind,   35
Describe or fix one movement of his Mind?
Who saw its fires here rise, and there descend,
Explain his own beginning, or his end?
Alas what wonder! Man's superior part
Unchecked may rise, and climb from art to art;   40
But when his own great work is but begun,
What Reason weaves, by Passion is undone.

   Trace Science then, with Modesty thy guide;
First strip off all her equipage of Pride;
Deduct what is but Vanity, or Dress,   45
Or Learning's Luxury, or Idleness;
Or tricks to shew the stretch of human brain,
Mere curious pleasure, or ingenious pain;
Expunge the whole, or lop th' excrescent parts
Of all our Vices have created Arts;   50
Then see how little the remaining sum,
Which served the past, and must the times to come!

   II. Two Principles in human nature reign;
Self-love, to urge, and Reason, to restrain;
Nor this a good, nor that a bad we call,   55
Each works its end, to move or govern all:
And to their proper operation still,
Ascribe all Good; to their improper, Ill.
   Self-love, the spring of motion, acts the soul;
Reason's comparing balance rules the whole.   60
Man, but for that, no action could attend,
And but for this, were active to no end;
Fixed like a plant on his peculiar spot,
To draw nutrition, propagate, and rot;
Or, meteor-like, flame lawless thro' the void,   65
Destroying others, by himself destroyed.
   Most strength the moving principle requires;
Active its task, it prompts, impels, inspires.
Sedate and quiet the comparing lies,

------

53 ff. Pope reflects the traditional view of man's nature as a tension between
appetitive and regulatory elements. Self-love is a generic name for the
former and means not selfishness but self-fulfilment. 59. *acts:* actuates.

Formed but to check, delib'rate, and advise.   70
Self-love still stronger, as its objects nigh;
Reason's at distance, and in prospect lie:
That sees immediate good by present sense;
Reason, the future and the consequence.
Thicker than arguments, temptations throng,   75
At best more watchful this, but that more strong.
The action of the stronger to suspend,
Reason still use, to Reason still attend.
Attention, habit and experience gains;
Each strengthens Reason, and Self-love restrains.   80
    Let subtle schoolmen teach these friends to fight,
More studious to divide than to unite;
And Grace and Virtue, Sense and Reason split,
With all the rash dexterity of wit.
Wits, just like Fools, at war about a name,   85
Have full as oft no meaning, or the same.
Self-love and Reason to one end aspire,
Pain their aversion, Pleasure their desire;
But greedy That, its object would devour,
This taste the honey, and not wound the flower;   90
Pleasure, or wrong or rightly understood,
Our greatest evil, or our greatest good.
    III. Modes of Self-love the Passions we may call;
'Tis real good, or seeming, moves them all:
But since not every good we can divide,   95
And Reason bids us for our own provide;
Passions, tho' selfish, if their means be fair,
List under Reason, and deserve her care;
Those, that imparted, court a nobler aim,
Exalt their kind, and take some Virtue's name.   100
    In lazy Apathy let Stoics boast
Their Virtue fixed; 'tis fixed as in a frost;
Contracted all, retiring to the breast;
But strength of mind is Exercise, not Rest:
The rising tempest puts in act the soul,   105
Parts it may ravage, but preserves the whole.
On life's vast ocean diversely we sail,
Reason the card, but Passion is the gale;

---

98. *List:* enlist. 99. *Those . . . imparted:* i.e., the passions after reason has
become their guide. 101. *Apathy* was the Stoic's ideal passionless state.

Nor God alone in the still calm we find,
He mounts the storm, and walks upon the wind.   110
  Passions, like Elements, tho' born to fight,
Yet, mixed and softened, in his work unite:
These 'tis enough to temper and employ;
But what composes Man, can Man destroy?
Suffice that Reason keep to Nature's road,   115
Subject, compound them, follow her and God.
Love, Hope, and Joy, fair Pleasure's smiling train,
Hate, Fear, and Grief, the family of Pain,
These mixed with art, and to due bounds confined,
Make and maintain the balance of the mind: 120
The lights and shades, whose well accorded strife
Gives all the strength and colour of our life.
Pleasures are ever in our hands or eyes;
And when in act they cease, in prospect rise: *we want pleasure*
Present to grasp, and future still to find,   125
The whole employ of body and of mind.
All spread their charms, but charm not all alike;
On different senses different objects strike;
Hence different Passions more or less inflame,
As strong or weak, the organs of the frame;   130
And hence one MASTER PASSION in the breast,
Like Aaron's serpent, swallows up the rest.
  As Man, perhaps, the moment of his breath,
Receives the lurking principle of death;
The young disease, that must subdue at length,   135
Grows with his growth, and strengthens with his strength:
So, cast and mingled with his very frame,
The Mind's disease, its RULING PASSION came;
Each vital humour which should feed the whole,
Soon flows to this, in body and in soul: 140
Whatever warms the heart, or fills the head,

109-10. E.g., in the Old Testament, God appears not only in the "still small voice" of 1 Kings 19:11-12, but also on "wings of the wind" in Psalms 18:10. 132. *Aaron's serpent:* Aaron's rod, which, when he cast it down before Pharaoh, changed to a serpent which devoured the serpents that the rods of Pharaoh's magicians had been changed to (Exodus 7:10-12). Thus the ruling passion (like all the passions: cf. 111 ff.) is of divine origin. 141. *heart, head:* The "vital spirits" of the old physiology were found in the *heart;* the "animal spirits" in the *head.* They are what Pope means by *each vital humour* in 139.

As the mind opens, and its functions spread,
Imagination plies her dangerous art,
And pours it all upon the peccant part.

Nature its mother, Habit is its nurse;   145
Wit, Spirit, Faculties, but make it worse;
Reason itself but gives it edge and power;
As Heaven's blest beam turns vinegar more sour.

We, wretched subjects, tho' to lawful sway,
In this weak queen some favourite still obey: 150
Ah, if she lend not arms, as well as rules,
What can she more than tell us we are fools?
Teach us to mourn our Nature, not to mend,
A sharp accuser, but a helpless friend!
Or from a judge turn pleader, to persuade   155
The choice we make, or justify it made;
Proud of an easy conquest all along,
She but removes weak passions for the strong:
So, when small humours gather to a gout,
The doctor fancies he has driven them out.   160

Yes, Nature's road must ever be preferred;
Reason is here no guide, but still a guard:
'Tis hers to rectify, not overthrow,
And treat this passion more as friend than foe:
A mightier Power the strong direction sends,   165
And several Men impels to several ends:
Like varying winds, by other passions tost,
This drives them constant to a certain coast.
Let power or knowledge, gold or glory, please,
Or (oft more strong than all) the love of ease;   170
Thro' life 'tis followed, even at life's expense;
The merchant's toil, the sage's indolence,
The monk's humility, the hero's pride,
All, all alike, find Reason on their side.

Th' Eternal Art educing good from ill,   175
Grafts on this Passion our best principle:
'Tis thus the Mercury of Man is fixed,
Strong grows the Virtue with his nature mixed;
The dross cements what else were too refined,
And in one interest body acts with mind.   180

As fruits, ungrateful to the planter's care,

---

165 ff. I.e., ruling passions make men differ, so that the variety of the world's work can be carried on; and also, they make men constant to one objective. 175. *Eternal Art:* God's Providence: cf. I 293.

On savage stocks inserted, learn to bear;
The surest Virtues thus from Passions shoot,
Wild Nature's vigour working at the root.
What crops of wit and honesty appear   185
From spleen, from obstinacy, hate, or fear!
See anger, zeal and fortitude supply;
Even avarice, prudence; sloth, philosophy;
Lust, thro' some certain strainers well refined,
Is gentle love, and charms all womankind;   190
Envy, to which th' ignoble mind's a slave,
Is emulation in the learn'd or brave;
Nor Virtue, male or female, can we name,
But what will grow on Pride, or grow on Shame.
   Thus Nature gives us (let it check our pride)   195
The virtue nearest to our vice allied:
Reason the bias turns to good from ill,
And Nero reigns a Titus, if he will.
The fiery soul abhorred in Catiline,
In Decius charms, in Curtius is divine: 200
The same ambition can destroy or save,
And makes a patriot as it makes a knave.
   IV. This light and darkness in our chaos joined,
What shall divide? The God within the mind.
   Extremes in Nature equal ends produce,   205
In Man they join to some mysterious use;
Tho' each by turns the other's bound invade,
As, in some well-wrought picture, light and shade,
And oft so mix, the difference is too nice
Where ends the Virtue, or begins the Vice.   210
   Fools! who from hence into the notion fall,
That Vice or Virtue there is none at all.

---

195. *pride:* i.e., our Stoic-like pride in supposing that we must root out
Nature in order to attain virtue; for actually Nature has bestowed on us a
passional force that can be as readily turned into a characteristic virtue as
a characteristic vice. 198. *Titus:* the Roman emperor who is said to have
sighed when a day went by without a good deed done: cf. IV 146-8. 200.
Decius, Curtius: two legendary Romans who sacrificed themselves for the
good of the nation. 203-4. God's creating Spirit divided the light from
the darkness in Chaos (Genesis 1:4); man is to imitate this in ordering
the "chaos" of his own being: cf. II 13, 111 ff. 205. Meaning perhaps that
opposites cooperate—as dryness and rain to a good harvest; or that opposites
have similar effects—as extreme cold and extreme heat both scarify the flesh.
206. Alluding to the passional force (cf. 195 above) which can become
either a vice or a virtue—i.e., an ambitious man has both a Nero and a
Titus in him.

If white and black blend, soften, and unite
A thousand ways, is there no black or white?
Ask your own heart, and nothing is so plain;   215
'Tis to mistake them costs the time and pain.
　　V. Vice is a monster of so frightful mien,
As, to be hated, needs but to be seen;
Yet seen too oft, familiar with her face,
We first endure, then pity, then embrace.   220
But where th' Extreme of Vice, was ne'er agreed:
Ask where's the North? at York, 'tis on the Tweed;
In Scotland, at the Orcades; and there,
At Greenland, Zembla, or the Lord knows where.
No creature owns it in the first degree,   225
But thinks his neighbour further gone than he;
Even those who dwell beneath its very zone,
Or never feel the rage, or never own;
What happier natures shrink at with affright,
The hard inhabitant contends is right.   230
　　VI. Virtuous and vicious every Man must be,
Few in th' extreme, but all in the degree;
The rogue and fool by fits is fair and wise;
And even the best, by fits, what they despise.
'Tis but by parts we follow good or ill;   235
For, Vice or Virtue, Self directs it still;
Each individual seeks a several goal;
But HEAVEN's great view is One, and that the Whole.
That counter-works each folly and caprice;
That disappoints th' effect of every vice;   240
That, happy frailties to all ranks applied,
Shame to the virgin, to the matron pride,
Fear to the statesman, rashness to the chief,
To kings presumption, and to crowds belief:
That, Virtue's ends from Vanity can raise,   245
Which seeks no interest, no reward but praise;
And build on wants, and on defects of mind,
The joy, the peace, the glory of Mankind.
　　Heaven forming each on other to depend,
A master, or a servant, or a friend,   250
Bids each on other for assistance call,
Till one Man's weakness grows the strength of all.
Wants, frailties, passions, closer still ally
The common interest, or endear the tie.
To these we owe true friendship, love sincere,   255

Each home-felt joy that life inherits here;
Yet from the same we learn, in its decline,
Those joys, those loves, those interests to resign;
Taught half by Reason, half by mere decay,
To welcome death, and calmly pass away.   260
   Whate'er the Passion, knowledge, fame, or pelf,
Not one will change his neighbour with himself.
The learn'd is happy nature to explore,
The fool is happy that he knows no more;
The rich is happy in the plenty given,   265
The poor contents him with the care of Heaven.
See the blind beggar dance, the cripple sing,
The sot a hero, lunatic a king;
The starving chemist in his golden views
Supremely blest, the poet in his Muse.   270
   See some strange comfort every state attend,
And Pride bestowed on all, a common friend;
See some fit Passion every age supply,
Hope travels thro', nor quits us when we die.
   Behold the child, by Nature's kindly law,   275
Pleased with a rattle, tickled with a straw:
Some livelier play-thing gives his youth delight,
A little louder, but as empty quite:
Scarfs, garters, gold, amuse his riper stage,
And beads and prayer-books are the toys of age: 280
Pleased with this bauble still, as that before;
'Till tired he sleeps, and Life's poor play is o'er.
   Mean-while Opinion gilds with varying rays
Those painted clouds that beautify our days;
Each want of happiness by hope supplied,   285
And each vacuity of sense by Pride:
These build as fast as knowledge can destroy;
In Folly's cup still laughs the bubble, joy;
One prospect lost, another still we gain;
And not a vanity is given in vain;   290
Even mean Self-love becomes, by force divine,
The scale to measure others' wants by thine.
See! and confess, one comfort still must rise,
'Tis this, Tho' Man's a fool, yet God is WISE.

❧

269. *chemist:* alchemist. 280. *beads:* rosaries. 288. *bubble:* The secondary meaning—"dupe" or "deceptive show"—is also relevant.

Argument of Epistle III

OF THE NATURE AND STATE OF MAN, WITH RESPECT TO SOCIETY

I. The whole Universe one system of Society, v. 7, &c. Nothing made wholly for itself, nor yet wholly for another, v. 27. The happiness of Animals mutual, v. 49. II. Reason or Instinct operate alike to the good of each Individual, v. 79. Reason or Instinct operate also to Society, in all animals, v. 109. III. How far Society carried by Instinct, v. 115. How much farther by Reason, v. 128. IV. Of that which is called the State of Nature, v. 144. Reason instructed by Instinct in the invention of Arts, v. 166, and in the Forms of Society, v. 176. V. Origin of Political Societies, v. 196. Origin of Monarchy, v. 207. Patriarchal government, v. 212. VI. Origin of true Religion and Government, from the same principle, of Love, v. 231, &c. Origin of Superstition and Tyranny, from the same principle, of Fear, v. 237, &c. The Influence of Self-love operating to the social and public Good, v. 266. Restoration of true Religion and Government on their first principle, v. 285. Mixt Government, v. 288. Various Forms of each, and the true end of all, v. 300, &c.

EPISTLE III

*H*ere then we rest: "The Universal Cause
Acts to one end, but acts by various laws."
In all the madness of superfluous health,
The trim of pride, the impudence of wealth,
Let this great truth be present night and day;   5
But most be present, if we preach or pray.
  I. Look round our World; behold the chain of Love
Combining all below and all above.
See plastic Nature working to this end,

---

2. *End:* the general good: cf. 14, below. 7. *chain of love:* a conception of the universe as a chain-like unity held together by the power of divine love (the force which originally brought order out of chaos) as reflected and refracted in the love of each order of created beings for the orders below and above it. Thus the notion of the universe as a chain of beings (Epistle I) merges here with the notion of it as a chain of relationships or chain of love. 9. *plastic nature:* the informing and forming power of God as manifested in the creativity of nature.

The single atoms each to other tend,   10
Attract, attracted to, the next in place
Formed and impelled its neighbor to embrace.
See Matter next, with various life endued,
Press to one centre still, the general Good.
See dying vegetables life sustain,   15
See life dissolving vegetate again:
All forms that perish other forms supply,
(By turns we catch the vital breath, and die,)
Like bubbles on the sea of Matter born,
They rise, they break, and to that sea return.   20
Nothing is foreign: Parts relate to whole;
One all-extending, all-preserving Soul
Connects each being, greatest with the least;
Made Beast in aid of Man, and Man of Beast;
All served, all serving: nothing stands alone;   25
The chain holds on, and where it ends, unknown.
    Has God, thou fool! worked solely for thy good,
Thy joy, thy pastime, thy attire, thy food?
Who for thy table feeds the wanton fawn,
For him as kindly spread the flowery lawn: 30
Is it for thee the lark ascends and sings?
Joy tunes his voice, joy elevates his wings.
Is it for thee the linnet pours his throat?
Loves of his own and raptures swell the note.
The bounding steed you pompously bestride,   35
Shares with his lord the pleasure and the pride.
Is thine alone the seed that strews the plain?
The birds of heaven shall vindicate their grain.
Thine the full harvest of the golden year?
Part pays, and justly, the deserving steer: 40
The hog, that ploughs not nor obeys thy call,
Lives on the labours of this lord of all.
    Know, Nature's children all divide her care;
The fur that warms a monarch, warmed a bear.
While Man exclaims, "See all things for my use!"   45
"See man for mine!" replies a pampered goose:

---

12. *embrace:* a term emphasizing unity through 'love,' even at the inanimate level. 27 ff. In opposition to a common view that lower creatures were exclusively made for man's delight, Pope argues that man was also made for the animals' delight and that animals are made in part for their own delight. 30. *lawn:* punning on its meaning as (table) 'linen.'

And just as short of reason he must fall,
Who thinks all made for one, not one for all.
  Grant that the powerful still the weak controul;
Be Man the Wit and Tyrant of the whole: 50
Nature that Tyrant checks; he only knows,
And helps, another creature's wants and woes.
Say, will the falcon, stooping from above,
Smit with her varying plumage, spare the dove?
Admires the jay the insect's gilded wings?   55
Or hears the hawk when Philomela sings?
Man cares for all: to birds he gives his woods,
To beasts his pastures, and to fish his floods;
For some his Interest prompts him to provide,
For more his pleasure, yet for more his pride: 60
All feed on one vain Patron, and enjoy
Th' extensive blessing of his luxury.
That very life his learnèd hunger craves,
He saves from famine, from the savage saves;
Nay, feasts the animal he dooms his feast,   65
And, 'till he ends the being, makes it blest;
Which sees no more the stroke, or feels the pain,
Than favoured Man by touch ethereal slain.
The creature had his feast of life before;
Thou too must perish, when thy feast is o'er!   70
  To each unthinking being Heaven, a friend,
Gives not the useless knowledge of its end:
To Man imparts it; but with such a view
As, while he dreads it, makes him hope it too:
The hour concealed, and so remote the fear,   75
Death still draws nearer, never seeming near.
Great standing miracle! that Heaven assigned
Its only thinking thing this turn of mind.
II. Whether with Reason, or with Instinct blest,
Know, all enjoy that power which suits them best;   80
To bliss alike by that direction tend,
And find the means proportioned to their end.
Say, where full Instinct is th' unerring guide,
What Pope or Council can they need beside?

---

50. *Wit:* the only intellectual being on earth. 51-2. It was a traditional belief that man alone (of all earthly creatures) knew compassion. 53-6. It was
also a belief that man alone had sense of beauty. 56. *Philomela:* the nightin-
gale. 59. *Interest:* self-interest. 68. *favoured:* Among some peoples, persons
killed by lightning were held sacred. 79 ff. The relative merits of human
reason and animal instinct. As part of the poem's general assault on man's
pride, Pope minimizes the former. 84. *Council:* alluding to the Roman

Reason, however able, cool at best,   85
Cares not for service, or but serves when prest,
Stays 'till we call, and then not often near;
But honest Instinct comes a volunteer,
Sure never to o'er-shoot, but just to hit;
While still too wide or short is human Wit;   90
Sure by quick Nature happiness to gain,
Which heavier Reason labours at in vain,
This too serves always, Reason never long;
One must go right, the other may go wrong.
See then the acting and comparing powers   95
One in their nature, which are two in ours;
And Reason raise o'er Instinct as you can,
In this 'tis God directs, in that 'tis Man.
    Who taught the nations of the field and wood
To shun their poison, and to choose their food?   100
Prescient, the tides or tempests to withstand,
Build on the wave, or arch beneath the sand?
Who made the spider parallels design,
Sure as Demoivre, without rule or line?
Who bid the stork, Columbus-like, explore   105
Heavens not his own, and worlds unknown before?
Who calls the council, states the certain day,
Who forms the phalanx, and who points the way?
    III. God in the nature of each being founds
Its proper bliss, and sets its proper bounds: 110
But as he framed a Whole, the Whole to bless,
On mutual Wants built mutual Happiness:
So from the first, eternal ORDER ran,
And creature linked to creature, man to man.
Whate'er of life all-quickening æther keeps,   115
Or breathes thro' air, or shoots beneath the deeps,
Or pours profuse on earth, one nature feeds
The vital flame, and swells the genial seeds.

Catholic council, which claims infallibility. 99 ff. The "who" formula is perhaps calculated to recall God's speaking from the whirlwind to Job and Job's abasement before Him. 102. Referring to the supposed nesting habits (*on the wave*) of the bird anciently called the halycon and the real nesting habits (*beneath the sand*) of the kingfisher, with which the halycon is usually identified today. 104. A notable French mathematician (1667-1754) who had settled in London. 109 ff. The poem now discusses the origins of all society in animal instinct (109-30) and the consolidation of human society through human reason (131-46). 115. *aether:* thought of in Pope's day and earlier as the divine breath informing the universe and generating all living things—in the *air*, the *deeps*, the *earth.* 118. *genial:* procreative.

Not Man alone, but all that roam the wood,
Or wing the sky, or roll along the flood,   120
Each loves itself, but not itself alone,
Each sex desires alike, 'till two are one.
Nor ends the pleasure with the fierce embrace;
They love themselves, a third time, in their race.
Thus beast and bird their common charge attend,   125
The mothers nurse it, and the sires defend;
The young dismissed to wander earth or air,
There stops the Instinct, and there ends the care;
The link dissolves, each seeks a fresh embrace,
Another love succeeds, another race.   130
A longer care Man's helpless kind demands;
That longer care contracts more lasting bands:
Reflection, Reason, still the ties improve,
At once extend the interest, and the love;
With choice we fix, with sympathy we burn;   135
Each Virtue in each Passion takes its turn;
And still new needs, new helps, new habits rise,
That graft benevolence on charities.
Still as one brood, and as another rose,
These natural love maintained, habitual those: 140
The last, scarce ripened into perfect Man,
Saw helpless him from whom their life began:
Memory and fore-cast just returns engage,
That pointed back to youth, this on to age;
While pleasure, gratitude, and hope, combined,   145
Still spread the interest, and preserved the kind.
    IV. Nor think, in NATURE'S STATE they blindly trod;
The state of Nature was the reign of God:

121-4. The rooting of all forms of love in self-love is often misconstrued as
an eccentric notion of Pope's age. Actually the idea goes back through
Aquinas and Augustine to Aristotle, and is strongly represented in the
Christian exhortation, Love thy neighbor as thyself. 133. *Reflection:* cf. I,
225n. Reflection is here the ability to look back and acknowledge obliga-
tion; reason, the ability to look forward and recognize that someday oneself
will be old and in need of aid. 135-6. i.e., marriage ramifies into all the
characteristic human relationships, affections, and therefore virtues: cf. *Par.
Lost* iv 754-7. 138. *benevolence on charities:* i.e., a general virtuous habit of
mind on concrete natural affections. 143. *Memory and forecast:* cf. 133n.,
above. 147 ff. Pope's poem opposes the Hobbesian view that man's original
'natural' state was a war of all on all, and now offers a vision of the age of
innocence that is carefully 'philosophical' rather than 'theological'—i.e.,
based on Pythagorean conceptions about the Golden Age rather than Christian traditions about Eden.

Self-love and Social at her birth began,
Union the bond of all things, and of Man.
Pride then was not; nor Arts, that Pride to aid;   150
Man walked with beast, joint tenant of the shade;
The same his table, and the same his bed;
No murder clothed him, and no murder fed.
In the same temple, the resounding wood,
All vocal beings hymned their equal God: ·   155
The shrine with gore unstained, with gold undrest,
Unbribed, unbloody, stood the blameless priest:
Heaven's attribute was Universal Care,
And Man's prerogative to rule, but spare.   160
Ah! how unlike the man of times to come!
Of half that live the butcher and the tomb;
Who, foe to Nature, hears the general groan,
Murders their species, and betrays his own.
But just disease to luxury succeeds,   165
And every death its own avenger breeds;
The Fury-passions from that blood began,
And turned on Man a fiercer savage, Man.
  See him from Nature rising slow to Art!
To copy Instinct then was Reason's part;   170
Thus then to Man the voice of Nature spake—
"Go, from the Creatures thy instructions take:
Learn from the birds what food the thickets yield;
Learn from the beasts the physic of the field;
Thy arts of building from the bee receive;   175
Learn of the mole to plough, the worm to weave;
Learn of the little Nautilus to sail,
Spread the thin oar, and catch the driving gale.
Here too all forms of social union find,
And hence let Reason, late, instruct Mankind: 180

---

150. *Union,* i.e., love (cf. the *chain of love*). 157-8. *Unbribed, unbloody:*
alluding to animal sacrifice, which in the Golden Age had not begun. 161-8.
It was a long-standing tradition (reflected in *Par. Lost*) that man became
a carnivore only after the Fall and that his slaughter of animals led to the
slaughter of his fellows. 169 ff. Pope's point (again part of the attack on
Pride) is that the very arts on account of which man presumes himself superior to 'nature' and the other creatures spring from nature. 173. Mariners
on a strange shore often decided what fruits and berries were fit to eat by
watching birds. 174. i.e., by using the herbs animals seek out when ill. 175.
The bee is traditionally famous for the architectural skill evidenced in its
hive. 176. *worm:* the silk worm. 177. *Nautilus:* the 'Paper Nautilus,' formerly thought to sail by spreading a membrane between its two dorsal arms.

Here subterranean works and cities see;
There towns aerial on the waving tree.
Learn each small People's genius, policies,
The Ant's republic, and the realm of Bees;
How those in common all their wealth bestow,   185
And Anarchy without confusion know;
And these for ever, tho' a Monarch reign,
Their separate cells and properties maintain.
Mark what unvaried laws preserve each state,
Laws wise as Nature, and as fixed as Fate.   190
In vain thy Reason finer webs shall draw,
Entangle Justice in her net of Law,
And right, too rigid, harden into wrong;
Still for the strong too weak, the weak too strong.
Yet go! and thus o'er all the creatures sway,   195
Thus let the wiser make the rest obey;
And, for those Arts mere Instinct could afford,
Be crowned as Monarchs, or as Gods adored."

    V. Great Nature spoke; observant Men obeyed;
Cities were built, Societies were made: 200
Here rose one little state; another near
Grew by like means, and joined, thro' love or fear.
Did here the trees with ruddier burdens bend,
And there the streams in purer rills descend?
What War could ravish, Commerce could bestow,   205
And he returned a friend, who came a foe.
Converse and Love mankind might strongly draw,
When Love was Liberty, and Nature Law.
Thus States were formed; the name of King unknown,
'Till common interest placed the sway in one.   210
'Twas VIRTUE ONLY (or in arts or arms,
Diffusing blessings, or averting harms)
The same which in a Sire the Sons obeyed,
A Prince the Father of a People made.

    VI. 'Till then, by Nature crowned, each Patriarch sate, 215
King, priest, and parent of his growing state;
On him, their second Providence, they hung,

---

184. Ant-societies were traditionally thought to be democratical (in fact socialist: 185) and those of bees monarchical. 198. It was customary to account for the origin of the pagan gods by supposing them deified men. 199 ff. Through 'natural' family societies, men now move into 'political' ones.

Their law his eye, their oracle his tongue.
He from the wondering furrow called the food,
Taught to command the fire, control the flood,   220
Draw forth the monsters of th' abyss profound,
Or fetch th' aerial eagle to the ground.
'Till drooping, sickening, dying they began
Whom they revered as God to mourn as Man:
Then, looking up from sire to sire, explored   225
One great first Father, and that first adored.
Or plain tradition that this All begun,
Conveyed unbroken faith from sire to son;
The worker from the work distinct was known,
And simple Reason never sought but one: 230
Ere Wit oblique had broke that steady light,
Man, like his Maker, saw that all was right;
To Virtue, in the paths of Pleasure, trod,
And owned a Father when he owned a God.
LOVE all the faith, and all th' allegiance then;   235
For Nature knew no right divine in Men,
No ill could fear in God; and understood
A sovereign being but a sovereign good.
True faith, true policy, united ran,
This was but love of God, and this of Man.   240
    Who first taught souls enslaved, and realms undone,
Th' enormous faith of many made for one;
That proud exception to all Nature's laws,
T' invert the world, and counter-work its Cause?
Force first made Conquest, and that conquest, Law;   245
'Till Superstition taught the tyrant awe,
Then shared the Tyranny, then lent it aid,
And Gods of Conquerors, Slaves of Subjects made:
She 'midst the lightning's blaze, and thunder's sound,

225-8. The two usual explanations of the origin of divine worship: either
that a tradition of God's existence descended from the first man, or that it
was an inevitable inference by the natural light of reason. 229. i.e., the
religion was not pantheistic. 231. *light:* i.e., of reason. 233. I.e., as described
above, III, 135 ff. 235 ff. In traditional political theory, tyranny was associated with fear, proper monarchy with love; and right government on
earth with a right understanding of God's government. 242. *enormous:*
abnormal. 244. Because in reality all creatures are made for all, the tyrant's
assumption *inverts the world* and opposes its Creator. 245. *and . . . law:*
i.e., conquest brought law into being, as explained below in 271 ff. 249. *She:*
superstition.

When rocked the mountains, and when groaned the ground,   250
She taught the weak to bend, the proud to pray,
To Power unseen, and mightier far than they:
She, from the rending earth and bursting skies,
Saw Gods descend, and fiends infernal rise:
Here fixed the dreadful, there the blest abodes;   255
Fear made her Devils, and weak Hope her Gods;
Gods partial, changeful, passionate, unjust,
Whose attributes were Rage, Revenge, or Lust;
Such as the souls of cowards might conceive,
And, formed like tyrants, tyrants would believe.   260
Zeal then, not charity, became the guide;
And hell was built on spite, and heaven on pride,
Then sacred seemed th' ethereal vault no more;
Altars grew marble then, and reeked with gore:
Then first the Flamen tasted living food;   265
Next his grim idol smeared with human blood;
With Heaven's own thunders shook the world below,
And played the God an engine on his foe.

  So drives Self-love, thro' just and thro' unjust,
To one Man's power, ambition, lucre, lust: 270
The same Self-love, in all, becomes the cause
Of what restrains him, Government and Laws.
For, what one likes if others like as well,
What serves one will, when many wills rebel?
How shall he keep, what, sleeping or awake,   275
A weaker may surprise, a stronger take?
His safety must his liberty restrain:
All join to guard what each desires to gain.
Forced into virtue thus by Self-defence,
Even Kings learned justice and benevolence: 280
Self-love forsook the path it first pursued,
And found the private in the public good.

  'Twas then, the studious head or generous mind,
Follower of God or friend of human-kind,
Poet or Patriot, rose but to restore   285
The Faith and Moral Nature gave before;

---

256. *weak Hope:* i.e., lack of faith in the ultimate rightness of the divine
plan. 261. *zeal:* sectarian passion. 262. *hell . . . spite:* i.e., so as to damn
all who disagreed. 263. *vault:* sky. 265. I.e., animal sacrifice began. 268.
I.e., used God as if he were one's own personal minister of vengeance.
283 ff. Pope refers to 'restorations' like those associated with Lycurgus,
Solon, etc.

Re-lumed her ancient light, not kindled new;
If not God's image, yet his shadow drew:
Taught Power's due use to People and to Kings,
Taught not to slack, nor strain its tender strings,   290
The less, or greater, set so justly true,
That touching one must strike the other too;
'Till jarring interests, of themselves create
Th' according music of a well-mixed State.
Such is the World's great harmony, that springs   295
From Order, Union, full Consent of things:
Where small and great, where weak and mighty, made
To serve, not suffer, strengthen, not invade;
More powerful each as needful to the rest,
And, in proportion as it blesses, blest;   300
Draw to one point, and to one centre bring
Beast, Man, or Angel, Servant, Lord, or King.
    For Forms of Government let fools contest;
Whate'er is best administered is best:
For Modes of Faith let graceless zealots fight;   305
His can't be wrong whose life is in the right:
In Faith and Hope the world will disagree,
But all Mankind's concern is Charity:
All must be false that thwart this One great End;
And all of God, that bless Mankind or mend.   310
    Man, like the generous vine, supported lives;
The strength he gains is from th' embrace he gives.
On their own Axis as the Planets run,
Yet make at once their circle round the Sun;
So two consistent motions act the Soul;   315
And one regards Itself, and one the Whole.
    Thus God and Nature linked the general frame,
And bade Self-love and Social be the same.

---

289 ff. The oldest of political metaphors: the state as a musical harmony
matching the harmony of the cosmos. 304. I.e., honest and merciful administration can redeem the worst form of government, as its opposite can spoil
the best form. 305. *graceless:* with a pun on its theological sense. 307-8. Cf.
I Corinthians 13:13: "And now abideth faith, hope, charity, these three; but
the greatest of these is charity." 311 ff. The epistle closes (cf. its beginning)
with two images relating to the love that binds the universe together. The
love of the vine and the elm was traditionally instanced in this connection;
so, in Pope's time, was the Newtonian principle of 'attraction' or gravitation.
As usual in the poem the tension of social and self-regarding 'motions' prescribed for man reflects a similar tension in the macrocosmos. 315. *act:*
actuate.

Argument of Epistle IV

OF THE NATURE AND STATE OF MAN WITH RESPECT TO HAPPINESS

I. FALSE Notions of Happiness, Philosophical and Popular, answered from v. 19 to 77. II. It is the End of all Men, and attainable by all, v. 29. God intends Happiness to be equal; and to be so, it must be social, since all particular happiness depends on general, and since he governs by general, not particular Laws, v. 35. As it is necessary for Order, and the peace and welfare of Society, that external goods should be unequal, Happiness is not made to consist in these, v. 49. But, notwithstanding that inequality, the balance of Happiness among Mankind is kept even by Providence, by the two Passions of Hope and Fear, v. 67. III. What the Happiness of Individuals is, as far as is consistent with the constitution of this world; and that the good Man has here the advantage, v. 77. The error of imputing to Virtue what are only the calamities of Nature, or of Fortune, v. 93. IV. The folly of expecting that God should alter his general Laws in favour of particulars, v. 111. V. That we are not judges who are good; but that, whoever they are, they must be happiest, v. 131, &c. VI. That external goods are not the proper rewards, but often inconsistent with, or destructive of Virtue, v. 167. That even these can make no Man happy without Virtue: Instanced in Riches, v. 185. Honours, v. 193. Nobility, v. 205. Greatness, v. 217. Fame, v. 237. Superior Talents, v. 259, &c. With pictures of human Infelicity in Men possessed of them all, v. 269, &c. VII. That Virtue only constitutes a Happiness, whose object is universal, and whose prospect eternal, v. 309, &c. That the perfection of Virtue and Happiness consists in a conformity to the ORDER of PROVIDENCE here, and a Resignation to it here and hereafter, v. 327, &c.

EPISTLE IV

OH HAPPINESS! our being's end and aim!
Good, Pleasure, Ease, Content! whate'er thy name:
That something still which prompts th' eternal sigh,
For which we bear to live, or dare to die,
Which still so near us, yet beyond us lies,   5
O'er-looked, seen double, by the fool, and wise.

Plant of celestial seed! if dropt below,
Say, in what mortal soil thou deign'st to grow?
Fair opening to some Court's propitious shine,
Or deep with diamonds in the flaming mine?   10
Twined with the wreaths Parnassian laurels yield,
Or reaped in iron harvests of the field?
Where grows?—where grows it not? If vain our toil,
We ought to blame the culture, not the soil:
Fixed to no spot is Happiness sincere,   15
'Tis nowhere to be found, or everywhere;
'Tis never to be bought, but always free,
And fled from monarchs, ST. JOHN! dwells with thee.
    I. Ask of the Learn'd the way? The Learn'd are blind;
This bids to serve, and that to shun mankind;   20
Some place the bliss in action, some in ease,
Those call it Pleasure, and Contentment these;
Some sunk to Beasts, find pleasure end in pain;
Some swelled to Gods, confess ev'n Virtue vain;
Or indolent, to each extreme they fall,   25
To trust in every thing, or doubt of all.
    Who thus define it, say they more or less
Than this, that Happiness is Happiness?
    II. Take Nature's path, and mad Opinion's leave;
All states can reach it, and all heads conceive;   30
Obvious her goods, in no extreme they dwell;
There needs but thinking right, and meaning well;
And mourn our various portions as we please,
Equal is Common Sense, and Common Ease.
    Remember, Man, "the Universal Cause   35
Acts not by partial, but by general laws;"
And makes what Happiness we justly call
Subsist not in the good of one, but all.
There's not a blessing Individuals find,
But some way leans and hearkens to the kind: 40
No Bandit fierce, no Tyrant mad with pride,
No caverned Hermit, rests self-satisfied:
Who most to shun or hate Mankind pretend,
Seek an admirer, or would fix a friend:
Abstract what others feel, what others think,   45
All pleasures sicken, and all glories sink:

---

15. *sincere:* pure. 20-6. The alternative programs are those of the Stoic and Epicurean philosophies respectively, with a glance at the Skeptics in 25-6.

Each has his share; and who would more obtain,
Shall find, the pleasure pays not half the pain.
ORDER is Heaven's first law; and this confest,
Some are, and must be, greater than the rest, 50
More rich, more wise; but who infers from hence
That such are happier, shocks all common sense.
Heaven to Mankind impartial we confess,
If all are equal in their Happiness:
But mutual wants this Happiness increase; 55
All Nature's difference keeps all Nature's peace.
Condition, circumstance is not the thing;
Bliss is the same in subject or in king,
In who obtain defence, or who defend,
In him who is, or him who finds a friend: 60
Heaven breathes thro' every member of the whole
One common blessing, as one common soul.
But Fortune's gifts if each alike possest,
And each were equal, must not all contest?
If then to all Men Happiness was meant, 65
God in Externals could not place Content.

Fortune her gifts may variously dispose,
And these be happy called, unhappy those;
But Heaven's just balance equal will appear,
While those are placed in Hope, and these in Fear: 70
Nor present good or ill, the joy or curse,
But future views of better, or of worse.

Oh sons of earth! attempt ye still to rise,
By mountains piled on mountains, to the skies?
Heaven still with laughter the vain toil surveys, 75
And buries madmen in the heaps they raise.

III. Know, all the good that individuals find,
Or God and Nature meant to mere Mankind,
Reason's whole pleasure, all the joys of Sense,
Lie in three words, Health, Peace, and Competence. 80
But Health consists with Temperance alone;
And Peace, oh Virtue! Peace is all thy own.

73-6. I.e., those who heap up worldly goods become spiritually *buried* in them at last, as the Titans who sought to reach heaven by piling Mt. Ossa on Mt. Pelion in their rebellion against Zeus were buried *in the heaps they raised*. Pope thus associates with rebellion against God the pride of ethical materialism, as he has earlier associated with it pride of anthropocentrism (Epistle I), pride of hyper-intellectualism (Epistle II), pride of self-sufficiency. 80. *Competence:* the competency of goods required to support life.

The good or bad the gifts of Fortune gain;
But these less taste them, as they worse obtain.
Say, in pursuit of profit or delight,   85
Who risk the most, that take wrong means, or right?
Of Vice or Virtue, whether blest or curst,
Which meets contempt, or which compassion first?
Count all th' advantage prosperous Vice attains,
'Tis but what Virtue flies from and disdains: 90
And grant the bad what happiness they would,
One they must want, which is, to pass for good.
    Oh blind to Truth, and God's whole scheme below,
Who fancy Bliss to Vice, to Virtue Woe!
Who sees and follows that great scheme the best,   95
Best knows the blessing, and will most be blest.
But fools the Good alone unhappy call,
For ills or accidents that chance to all.
See FALKLAND dies, the virtuous and the just!
See god-like TURENNE prostrate on the dust!   100
See SIDNEY bleeds amid the martial strife!
Was this their Virtue, or Contempt of Life?
Say, was it Virtue, more tho' Heaven ne'er gave,
Lamented DIGBY! sunk thee to the grave?
Tell me, if Virtue made the Son expire,   105
Why, full of days and honour, lives the Sire?
Why drew Marseille's good bishop purer breath,
When Nature sickened, and each gale was death?
Or why so long (in life if long can be)
Lent Heaven a parent to the poor and me?   110
    IV. What makes all physical or moral ill?
There deviates Nature, and here wanders Will.
God sends not ill; if rightly understood,
Or partial Ill is universal Good,

---

84. I.e., the worse the means by which men obtain worldly goods, the less
they can enjoy them. 87. *whether . . . curst:* whether blest with worldly
success or not. 94. I.e., that happiness goes with vice and unhappiness with
virtue. 99-101. Three instances of virtuous men who were subject to the
ills or accidents that chance to all in battle: Lucius Cary, Viscount Falkland,
killed in 1643 in the English civil wars; Turenne, Louis XIV's great general,
killed at Sassbach in 1675; and Sir Philip Sidney, killed at Zutphen in 1586.
103-10. Four instances which argue specifically that there is no correlation
between virtue and length of life: the younger Digby, who died aged 40;
the elder Digby, who was still alive aged 74; Bishop Belsunce, who had
tended the dying throughout the plague at Marseilles without contracting
the disease; and Pope's mother, who had just died aged 91.

Or Change admits, or Nature lets it fall;   115
Short, and but rare, till Man improved it all.
We just as wisely might of Heaven complain
That righteous Abel was destroyed by Cain,
As that the virtuous son is ill at ease
When his lewd father gave the dire disease.   120
Think we, like some weak Prince, th' Eternal Cause
Prone for his favorites to reverse his laws?
    Shall burning Ætna, if a sage requires,
Forget to thunder, and recall her fires?
On air or sea new motions be imprest,   125
Oh blameless Bethel! to relieve thy breast?
When the loose mountain trembles from on high,
Shall gravitation cease, if you go by?
Or some old temple, nodding to its fall,
For Chartres' head reserve the hanging wall?   130
    V. But still this world (so fitted for the knave)
Contents us not. A better shall we have?
A kingdom of the Just then let it be:
But first consider how those Just agree.
The good must merit God's peculiar care;   135
But who, but God, can tell us who they are?
One thinks on Calvin Heaven's own spirit fell;
Another deems him instrument of hell;
If Calvin feel Heaven's blessing, or its rod,
This cries there is, and that, there is no God.   140
What shocks one part will edify the rest,
Nor with one system can they all be blest.
The very best will variously incline,
And what rewards your Virtue, punish mine.
WHATEVER IS, IS RIGHT.—This world, 'tis true,   145
Was made for Cæsar—but for Titus too:
And which more blest? who chained his country, say,
Or he whose Virtue sighed to lose a day?
    "But sometimes Virtue starves, while Vice is fed."
What then? Is the reward of Virtue bread?   150
That, Vice may merit, 'tis the price of toil;

---

115. *Change:* Cf. I 151n. 123-4. The Greek philosopher Empedocles was
reputed to have been killed while studying an eruption of Aetna. 126.
Bethel: Hugh Bethel, an intimate friend of Pope's, much troubled by
asthma. 130. *Chartres:* Francis Chartres, one of the greatest scoundrels of
the age. 148. Cf. II 198n.

The knave deserves it, when he tills the soil,
The knave deserves it, when he tempts the main,
Where Folly fights for kings, or dives for gain.
The good man may be weak, be indolent;   155
Nor is his claim to be plenty, but content.
But grant him Riches, your demand is o'er?
"No—shall the good want Health, the good want Power?"
Add Health, and Power, and every earthly thing,
"Why bounded Power? why private? why no king?"   160
Nay, why external for internal given?
Why is not Man a God, and Earth a Heaven?
Who ask and reason thus, will scarce conceive
God gives enough, while he has more to give:
Immense the power, immense were the demand;   165
Say, at what part of nature will they stand?
  VI. What nothing earthly gives, or can destroy,
The soul's calm sunshine, and the heart-felt joy,
Is Virtue's prize: A better would you fix?
Then give humility a coach and six,   170
Justice a Conqueror's sword, or Truth a gown,
Or Public Spirit its great cure, a Crown.
Weak, foolish man! will Heaven reward us there
With the same trash mad mortals wish for here?
The Boy and Man an individual makes,   175
Yet sigh'st thou now for apples and for cakes?
Go, like the Indian, in another life
Expect thy dog, thy bottle, and thy wife:
As well as dream such trifles are assigned,
As toys and empires, for a god-like mind.   180
Rewards, that either would to Virtue bring
No joy, or be destructive of the thing:
How oft by these at sixty are undone
The Virtues of a saint at twenty-one!
To whom can Riches give Repute, or Trust,   185
Content, or Pleasure, but the Good and Just?
Judges and Senates have been bought for gold,
Esteem and Love were never to be sold.
Oh fool! to think God hates the worthy mind,
The lover and the love of human-kind,   190
Whose life is healthful, and whose conscience clear,
Because he wants a thousand pounds a year.

---

171. *gown:* a clerical gown (cf. l. 198) or possibly an academic one. 177-8. Cf. I 99 ff.

Honour and shame from no Condition rise;
Act well your part, there all the honour lies.
Fortune in Men has some small difference made,   195
One flaunts in rags, one flutters in brocade;
The cobbler aproned, and the parson gowned,
The friar hooded, and the monarch crowned.
"What differ more (you cry) than crown and cowl?"
I'll tell you, friend! a wise man and a Fool.   200
You'll find, if once the monarch acts the monk,
Or, cobbler-like, the parson will be drunk,
Worth makes the man, and want of it, the fellow;
The rest is all but leather or prunella.

Stuck o'er with titles and hung round with strings,   205
That thou may'st be by kings, or whores of kings.
Boast the pure blood of an illustrious race,
In quiet flow from Lucrece to Lucrece:
But by your fathers' worth if yours you rate,
Count me those only who were good and great.   210
Go! if your ancient, but ignoble blood
Has crept thro' scoundrels ever since the flood,
Go! and pretend your family is young;
Nor own, your fathers have been fools so long.
What can ennoble sots, or slaves, or cowards?   215
Alas! not all the blood of all the HOWARDS.

Look next on Greatness; say where Greatness lies?
"Where, but among the Heroes and the wise?"
Heroes are much the same, the point's agreed,
From Macedonia's madman to the Swede;   220
The whole strange purpose of their lives, to find
Or make, an enemy of all mankind!
Not one looks backward, onward still he goes,
Yet ne'er looks forward farther than his nose.
No less alike the Politic and Wise;   225
All sly slow things, with circumspective eyes:
Men in their loose unguarded hours they take,
Not that themselves are wise, but others weak.
But grant that those can conquer, these can cheat;
'Tis phrase absurd to call a Villain great: 230

---

193. *Condition:* class. 204. I.e., dress: the cobbler's apron of leather, the
clergyman's gown of prunella. 208. *Lucrece:* the Roman Lucretia, type of
the chaste matron. 220. *Macedonia's madman* is Alexander the Great; *the
Swede* is Charles XII, who had died in 1718 after a dazzling career of military conquest.

Who wickedly is wise, or madly brave,
Is but the more a fool, the more a knave.
Who noble ends by noble means obtains,
Or failing, smiles in exile or in chains,
Like good Aurelius let him reign, or bleed   235
Like Socrates, that Man is great indeed.
    What's Fame? a fancied life in others' breath,
A thing beyond us, even before our death.
Just what you hear, you have, and what's unknown
The same (my Lord) if Tully's, or your own,   240
All that we feel of it begins and ends
In the small circle of our foes or friends;
To all beside as much an empty shade
An Eugene living, as a Cæsar dead;
Alike or when, or where, they shone, or shine,   245
Or on the Rubicon, or on the Rhine.
A Wit's a feather, and a Chief a rod;
An honest Man's the noblest work of God.
Fame but from death a villain's name can save,
As Justice tears his body from the grave;   250
When what t' oblivion better were resigned,
Is hung on high, to poison half mankind.
All fame is foreign, but of true desert;
Plays round the head, but comes not to the heart:
One self-approving hour whole years out-weighs   255
Of stupid starers, and of loud huzzas;
And more true joy Marcellus exiled feels,
Than Cæsar with a senate at his heels.
    In Parts superior what advantage lies?
Tell (for You can) what is it to be wise?   260
'Tis but to know how little can be known;
To see all others' faults, and feel our own:
Condemned in business or in arts to drudge,
Without a second, or without a judge:
Truths would you teach, or save a sinking land,   265
All fear, none aid you, and few understand.

---

235. *Aurelius:* Marcus Aurelius Antoninus, Roman emperor and author of a volume of stoical meditations which many readers have placed among the noblest moral documents of the ancient world. 240. *Tully's:* Cicero's. 244. *Eugene:* Prince Eugene of Savoy, one of the great eighteenth-century generals, still commanding in the field at this time, though over seventy. 257-8. *Marcellus* was banished from Rome by Caesar for his loyalty to Pompey. 260. *You:* Bolingbroke.

Painful pre-eminence! yourself to view
Above life's weakness, and its comforts too.
  Bring then these blessings to a strict account;
Make fair deductions; see to what they mount: 270
How much of other each is sure to cost;
How each for other oft is wholly lost;
How inconsistent greater goods with these;
How sometimes life is risked, and always ease:
Think, and if still the things thy envy call,   275
Say, would'st thou be the Man to whom they fall?
To sigh for ribbands if thou art so silly,
Mark how they grace Lord Umbra, or Sir Billy:
Is yellow dirt the passion of thy life?
Look but on Gripus or on Gripus' wife: 280
If Parts allure thee, think how Bacon shined,
The wisest, brightest, meanest of mankind:
Or ravished with the whistling of a Name,
See Cromwell, damned to everlasting fame!
If all, united, thy ambition call,   285
From ancient story learn to scorn them all.
There, in the rich, the honoured, famed, and great,
See the false scale of Happiness complete!
In hearts of Kings, or arms of Queens who lay,
How happy! those to ruin, these betray.   290
Mark by what wretched steps their glory grows,
From dirt and sea-weed as proud Venice rose;
In each how guilt and greatness equal ran,
And all that raised the Hero, sunk the Man:
Now Europe's laurels on their brows behold,   295
But stained with blood, or ill exchanged for gold:
Then see them broke with toils, or sunk in ease,
Or infamous for plundered provinces.
Oh wealth ill-fated! which no act of fame
E'er taught to shine, or sanctified from shame!   300
What greater bliss attends their close of life?
Some greedy minion, or imperious wife.

---

278. *Lord Umbra* means "Lord Shadow," "Lord Empty"; *Sir Billy* is any silly nobleman of minor rank. 280. *Gripus:* "Gripe," i.e., Miser. 282. *meanest:* alluding to Bacon's dismissal from the Chancellorship on the charge of corruption. 284. *damned . . . fame:* i.e., as a rebel against his lawful sovereign, Charles I. 290. I.e., their happiness consisted in ruining the kings who trusted them and betraying the queens who loved them.

The trophied arches, storied halls invade
And haunt their slumbers in the pompous shade.
Alas! not dazzled with their noon-tide ray, 305
Compute the morn and evening to the day;
The whole amount of that enormous fame,
A Tale, that blends their glory with their shame!
   VII. Know then this truth (enough for Man to know)
"Virtue alone is Happiness below." 310
The only point where human bliss stands still,
And tastes the good without the fall to ill,
Where only Merit constant pay receives,
Is blest in what it takes, and what it gives;
The joy unequalled, if its end it gain, 315
And if it lose, attended with no pain:
Without satiety, tho' e'er so blessed,
And but more relished as the more distressed:
The broadest mirth unfeeling Folly wears,
Less pleasing far than Virtue's very tears: 320
Good, from each object, from each place acquired,
For ever exercised, yet never tired;
Never elated, while one man's oppressed;
Never dejected, while another's blessed;
And where no wants, no wishes can remain, 325
Since but to wish more Virtue, is to gain.
   See the sole bliss Heaven could on all bestow!
Which who but feels can taste, but thinks can know:
Yet poor with fortune, and with learning blind,
The bad must miss; the good, untaught, will find; 330
Slave to no sect, who takes no private road,
But looks thro' Nature up to Nature's God;
Pursues that Chain which links th' immense design,
Joins heaven and earth, and mortal and divine;
Sees, that no Being any bliss can know, 335
But touches some above, and some below;
Learns, from this union of the rising Whole,
The first, last purpose of the human soul;
And knows, where Faith, Law, Morals, all began,
All end, in LOVE OF GOD, and LOVE OF MAN. 340

---

310. The *Virtue* that Pope usually has in mind in this epistle is Charity—i.e., love. 311. Cf. St. Paul's statement that whereas everything else is transient, "Charity never faileth" (1 Corinthians 13:8). 315. *end:* i.e., eternal life in heaven.

For him alone, Hope leads from goal to goal,
And opens still, and opens on his soul;
'Till lengthened on to Faith, and unconfined,
It pours the bliss that fills up all the mind.
He sees, why Nature plants in Man alone   345
Hope of known bliss, and Faith in bliss unknown:
(Nature, whose dictates to no other kind
Are given in vain, but what they seek they find;)
Wise is her present; she connects in this
His greatest Virtue with his greatest Bliss;   350
At once his own bright prospect to be blest,
And strongest motive to assist the rest.
    Self-love thus pushed to social, to divine,
Gives thee to make thy neighbour's blessing thine.
Is this too little for the boundless heart?   355
Extend it, let thy enemies have part:
Grasp the whole worlds of Reason, Life, and Sense,
In one close system of Benevolence:
Happier as kinder, in whate'er degree,
And height of Bliss but height of Charity.   360
    God loves from Whole to Parts: but human soul
Must rise from Individual to the Whole.
Self-love but serves the virtuous mind to wake,
As the small pebble stirs the peaceful lake;
The centre moved, a circle straight succeeds,   365
Another still, and still another spreads;
Friend, parent, neighbour, first it will embrace;
His country next; and next all human race;
Wide and more wide, th' o'erflowings of the mind
Take every creature in, of every kind;   370
Earth smiles around, with boundless bounty blest,
And Heaven beholds its image in his breast.
    Come then, my Friend! my Genius! come along;
Oh master of the poet, and the song!
And while the Muse now stoops, or now ascends,   375
To Man's low passions, or their glorious ends,
Teach me, like thee, in various nature wise,
To fall with dignity, with temper rise;
Formed by thy converse, happily to steer
From grave to gay, from lively to severe;   380

---

373. *Genius:* guardian-spirit (i.e., Bolingbroke).

Correct with spirit, eloquent with ease,
Intent to reason, or polite to please.
Oh! while along the stream of Time thy name
Expanded flies, and gathers all its fame,
Say, shall my little bark attendant sail,   385
Pursue the triumph, and partake the gale?
When statesmen, heroes, kings, in dust repose,
Whose sons shall blush their fathers were thy foes,
Shall then this verse to future age pretend
Thou wert my guide, philosopher, and friend?   390
That urged by thee, I turned the tuneful art
From sounds to things, from fancy to the heart;
For Wit's false mirror held up Nature's light;
Shewed erring Pride, WHATEVER IS, IS RIGHT;
That REASON, PASSION, answer one great aim;   395
That true SELF-LOVE and SOCIAL are the same;
That VIRTUE only makes our Bliss below;
And all our Knowledge is, OURSELVES TO KNOW.

❧

Epistle to a Lady

Of the Characters of Women

(1735)

NOTHING so true as what you once let fall,
"Most Women have no Characters at all."
Matter too soft a lasting mark to bear,
And best distinguished by black, brown, or fair.
    How many pictures of one Nymph we view,   5
All how unlike each other, all how true!
Arcadia's Countess, here, in ermined pride,
Is, there, Pastora by a fountain side.

---

388. *foes:* Bolingbroke was at this time a leader of the Opposition party
which was seeking to unseat Walpole.

EPISTLE TO A LADY: 7-14. Alluding to the various poses, or rôles, in which
a single fashionable lady might be painted. The names suggest that the
titles of the rôles might be: "The Great Lady," "The Innocent Shepherdess,"
"The Knowing Matron," "The Beautiful Adulteress," "The Penitent Sinner,"
"The Saint."

Here Fannia, leering on her own good man,
And there, a naked Leda with a Swan.   10
Let then the Fair one beautifully cry,
In Magdalen's loose hair, and lifted eye,
Or drest in smiles of sweet Cecilia shine,
With simpering Angels, Palms, and Harps divine;
Whether the Charmer sinner it, or saint it,   15
If Folly grow romantic, I must paint it.
  Come then, the colours and the ground prepare!
Dip in the Rainbow, trick her off in Air;   *moon*
Choose a firm Cloud, before it fall, and in it
Catch, ere she change, the Cynthia of this minute.   20
  Rufa, whose eye quick-glancing o'er the Park,
Attracts each light gay meteor of a Spark,
Agrees as ill with Rufa studying Locke,
As Sappho's diamonds with her dirty smock;
Or Sappho at her toilet's greasy task,   25
With Sappho fragrant at an evening Masque:
So morning Insects that in muck begun,
Shine, buzz, and fly-blow in the setting-sun.
  How soft is Silia! fearful to offend;
The Frail one's advocate, the Weak one's friend: 30
To her, Calista proved her conduct nice;
And good Simplicius asks of her advice.
Sudden, she storms! she raves! You tip the wink,
But spare your censure; Silia does not drink.
All eyes may see from what the change arose,   35
All eyes may see—a Pimple on her nose.
  Papillia, wedded to her amorous spark,
Sighs for the shades—"How charming is a Park!"
A Park is purchased, but the Fair he sees
All bathed in tears—"Oh odious, odious Trees!"   40
  Ladies, like variegated Tulips, show;
'Tis to their Changes half their charms we owe;

---

17. *ground:* i.e., background. 18. *trick:* (1) adorn, (2) sketch in outline. 20. *Cynthia:* cf. the Introduction, page 30. 21. *Rufa:* i.e., "Redhead." 22. *Spark:* beau. 23. *Locke:* John Locke, author of an *Essay Concerning Human Understanding* (1690), and other philosophical works. 24-6. *Sappho:* This may refer to any slovenly poetess (but see the *Ep. to Arbuthnot,* 101n., 305 ff n., 369n. 26. *Masque:* masquerade. 31. *Calista:* evidently (as the innuendo of the line suggests) Pope's variant spelling for Callisto, an attendant of Diana who became secretly pregnant by Zeus. *nice:* proper. 32. *Simplicius:* I.e., "Simple-mind." 37. *Papillia:* i.e., "Butterfly."

Fine by defect, and delicately weak,
Their happy Spots the nice admirer take:
'Twas thus Calypso once each heart alarmed,   45
Awed without Virtue, without Beauty charmed;
Her Tongue bewitched as oddly as her Eyes,
Less Wit than Mimic, more a Wit than wise;
Strange graces still, and stranger flights she had,
Was just not ugly, and was just not mad;   50
Yet ne'er so sure our passion to create,
As when she touched the brink of all we hate.
    Narcissa's nature, tolerably mild,
To make a wash, would hardly stew a child;
Has even been proved to grant a Lover's prayer,   55
And paid a Tradesman once to make him stare;
Gave alms at Easter, in a Christian trim,
And made a Widow happy, for a whim.
Why then declare Good-nature is her scorn,
When 'tis by that alone she can be borne?   60
Why pique all mortals, yet affect a name?
A fool to Pleasure, yet a slave to Fame:
Now deep in Taylor and the Book of Martyrs,
Now drinking citron with his Grace and Chartres:
Now Conscience chills her, and now Passion burns;   65
And Atheism and Religion take their turns;
A very Heathen in the carnal part,
Yet still a sad, good Christian at her heart.
    See Sin in State, majestically drunk;
Proud as a Peeress, prouder as a Punk;   70
Chaste to her Husband, frank to all beside,
A teeming Mistress, but a barren Bride.
What then? let Blood and Body bear the fault,
Her Head's untouched, that noble Seat of Thought:
Such this day's doctrine—in another fit   75
She sins with Poets thro' pure Love of Wit.

they just don't make sense [handwritten annotation]

---

45. *Calypso:* The name is that of the nymph on whose island Odysseus was
shipwrecked and detained seven years. It means literally "one who conceals
something." 53. *Narcissa:* i.e., "Self-love" (with reference to the Greek
youth Narcissus, who fell in love with his own image). 54. *wash:* lotion.
63. I.e., deep in religious reading—e.g., Jeremy Taylor's *Holy Living* (1650)
and *Holy Dying* (1651), and Foxe's *Actes and Monuments,* popularly called
the *Book of Martyrs* (Latin ed. 1559, English ed. 1563). 64. *his Grace:*
i.e., any duke. *Chartres:* a notorious contemporary rake.

What has not fired her bosom or her brain?
Cæsar and Tall-boy, Charles and Charlemagne.
As Helluo, late Dictator of the Feast,
The Nose of Hautgoût, and the Tip of Taste,   80
Critiqued your wine, and analysed your meat,
Yet on plain Pudding deigned at home to eat;
So Philomedé, lecturing all mankind
On the soft Passion, and the Taste refined,
Th' Address, the Delicacy—stoops at once,   85
And makes her hearty meal upon a Dunce.

Flavia's a Wit, has too much sense to Pray;
To Toast our wants and wishes, is her way;
Nor asks of God, but of her Stars, to give
The mighty blessing, "while we live, to live."   90
Then all for Death, that Opiate of the soul!
Lucretia's dagger, Rosamonda's bowl.
Say, what can cause such impotence of mind?
A Spark too fickle, or a Spouse too kind.
Wise Wretch! with Pleasures too refined to please;   95
With too much Spirit to be e'er at ease;
With too much Quickness ever to be taught;
With too much Thinking to have common Thought:
You purchase Pain with all that Joy can give,
And die of nothing but a Rage to live.   100

Turn then from Wits; and look on Simo's Mate,
No Ass so meek, no Ass so obstinate.
Or her, that owns her Faults, but never mends,
Because she's honest, and the best of Friends.
Or her, whose life the Church and Scandal share,   105
For ever in a Passion, or a Prayer.
Or her, who laughs at Hell, but (like her Grace)
Cries, "Ah! how charming, if there's no such place!"
Or who in sweet vicissitude appears
Of Mirth and Opium, Ratafie and Tears,   110

---

78. *Tall-boy* is a low comedy character in Richard Brome's *Jovial Crew* (1641); Charles is generic for "servant." 79. *Helluo:* i.e., "Glutton." 80. *Hautgout:* anything with a strong taste or odor. 83. *Philomedé:* i.e., "Laughter-lover." 87. *Flavia:* i.e., "Blonde." 92. *Lucretia, Rosamonda:* i.e., the Roman wife who killed herself after being raped by Tarquin, and the mistress of Henry II of England, whose queen forced her (according to legend) to swallow poison. 101. *Simo:* here roughly equivalent to "Old Man"—from an elderly character of this name in Terence's *Andria* and Plautus's *Mostellaria.* 107. *her Grace:* an unnamed duchess. 110. *Ratafie:* ratafia, a

The daily Anodyne, and nightly Draught,
To kill those foes to Fair ones, Time and Thought.
Women and Fool are two hard things to hit;
For true No-meaning puzzles more than Wit.
    But what are these to great <u>Atossa's</u> mind?   115
Scarce once herself, by turns all Womankind!
Who, with herself, or others, from her birth
Finds all her life one warfare upon earth:
Shines in exposing Knaves, and painting Fools,
Yet is, whate'er she hates and ridicules.   120
No Thought advances, but her Eddy Brain
Whisks it about, and down it goes again.
Full sixty years the World has been her Trade,
The wisest Fool much Time has ever made.
From loveless youth to unrespected age,   125
No Passion gratified except her Rage.
So much the Fury still out-ran the Wit,
The Pleasure missed her, and the Scandal hit.
Who breaks with her, provokes Revenge from Hell,
But he's a bolder man who dares be well.   130
Her every turn with Violence pursued,
Nor more a storm her Hate than Gratitude:
To that each Passion turns, or soon or late;
Love, if it makes her yield, must make her hate:
Superiors? death! and Equals? what a curse!   135
But an Inferior not dependent? worse.
Offend her, and she knows not to forgive;
Oblige her, and she'll hate you while you live:
But die, and she'll adore you—Then the Bust
And Temple rise—then fall again to dust.   140
Last night, her Lord was all that's good and great;
A Knave this morning, and his Will a Cheat.
Strange! by the Means defeated of the Ends,
By Spirit robbed of Power, by Warmth of Friends,
By Wealth of Followers! without one distress   145
Sick of herself thro' very selfishness!
Atossa, cursed with every granted prayer,
Childless with all her Children, wants an Heir.
To Heirs unknown descends th' unguarded store,
Or wanders, Heaven-directed, to the Poor.   150

---

liqueur. 115. *Atossa:* The name of a tempestuous Persian Queen, wife to
Cambyses and then to Darius. 130. *well:* i.e., on good terms with her. 133.
that: i.e., hate.

Pictures like these, dear Madam, to design,
Asks no firm hand, and no unerring line;
Some wandering touches, some reflected light,
Some flying stroke alone can hit 'em right:
For how should equal Colours do the knack?   155
Chameleons, who can paint in white and black?

"Yet Chloe sure was formed without a spot"—
Nature in her then erred not, but forgot.
"With every pleasing, every prudent part,
Say, what can Chloe want?"—She wants a Heart.   160
She speaks, behaves, and acts just as she ought;
But never, never, reached one generous Thought.
Virtue she finds too painful an endeavour,
Content to dwell in Decencies for ever.
So very reasonable, so unmoved,   165
As never yet to love, or to be loved.
She, while her Lover pants upon her breast,
Can mark the figures on an Indian chest;
And when she sees her Friend in deep despair,
Observes how much a Chintz exceeds Mohair.   170
Forbid it Heaven, a Favour or a Debt
She e'er should cancel—but she may forget.
Safe is your Secret still in Chloe's ear;
But none of Chloe's shall you ever hear.
Of all her Dears she never slandered one,   175
But cares not if a thousand are undone.
Would Chloe know if you're alive or dead?
She bids her Footman put it in her head.
Chloe is prudent—Would you too be wise?
Then never break your heart when Chloe dies.   180

One certain Portrait may (I grant) be seen,
Which Heaven has varnished out, and made a *Queen*:
THE SAME FOR EVER! and described by all
With Truth and Goodness, as with Crown and Ball.
Poets heap Virtues, Painters Gems at will,   185
And shew their zeal, and hide their want of skill.
'Tis well—but, Artists! who can paint or write,
To draw the Naked is your true delight.
That robe of Quality so struts and swells,
None see what Parts of Nature it conceals: 190
Th' exactest traits of Body or of Mind,
We owe to models of an humble kind.

---

155. *equal:* even, uniform. *knack:* trick. 164. *Decencies:* proprieties. 182. *Queen:* i.e., Queen Caroline, wife of George II.

If QUEENSBURY to strip there's no compelling,
'Tis from a Handmaid we must take a Helen,
From Peer or Bishop 'tis no easy thing   195
To draw the man who loves his God, or King:
Alas! I copy (or my draught would fail)
From honest Mah'met, or plain Parson Hale.

But grant, in Public Men sometimes are shown,
A Woman's seen in Private life alone: 200
Our bolder Talents in full light displayed;
Your virtues open fairest in the shade.
Bred to disguise, in Public 'tis you hide;
There, none distinguish 'twixt your Shame or Pride,
Weakness or Delicacy; all so nice,   205
That each may seem a Virtue, or a Vice.

In Men, we various Ruling Passions find;
In Women, two almost divide the kind;
Those, only fixed, they first or last obey,
The Love of Pleasure, and the Love of Sway.   210
    That, Nature gives; and where the lesson taught
Is but to please, can Pleasure seem a fault?
Experience, this; by Man's oppression curst,
They seek the second not to lose the first.

Men, some to Business, some to Pleasure take;   215
But every Woman is at heart a Rake:
Men, some to Quiet, some to public Strife;
But every Lady would be Queen for life.

Yet mark the fate of a whole Sex of Queens!
Power all their end, but Beauty all the means: 220
In Youth they conquer, with so wild a rage,
As leaves them scarce a subject in their Age:
For foreign glory, foreign joy, they roam;
No thought of peace or happiness at home.
But Wisdom's triumph is well-timed Retreat,   225
As hard a science to the Fair as Great!
Beauties, like Tyrants, old and friendless grown,
Yet hate repose, and dread to be alone,
Worn out in public, weary every eye,
Nor leave one sigh behind them when they die.   230

---

193. *Queensbury:* "Kitty" Hyde, Duchess of Queensbury, one of the great beauties of Pope's age. 198. *Mah'met:* A Turk named Mahomet, servant to George I. *Parson Hale:* Dr. Stephen Hales (1677-1761), clergyman and physiologist. 205. *nice:* finely, delicately discriminated. 211, 213: *That, this:* i.e., love of pleasure, love of sway. 219. *Queens:* with a play on "queans," meaning women of easy virtue.

Pleasures the sex, as children Birds, pursue,
Still out of reach, yet never out of view;
Sure, if they catch, to spoil the Toy at most,
To covet flying, and regret when lost:
At last, to follies Youth could scarce defend,   235
It grows their Age's prudence to pretend;
Ashamed to own they gave delight before,
Reduced to feign it, when they give no more:
As Hags hold Sabbaths, less for joy than spite,
So these their merry, miserable Night;   240
Still round and round the Ghosts of Beauty glide,
And haunt the places where their Honour died.
  See how the World its Veterans rewards!
A Youth of Frolics, an old Age of Cards;
Fair to no purpose, artful to no end,   245
Young without Lovers, old without a Friend;
A Fop their Passion, but their Prize a Sot;
Alive, ridiculous, and dead, forgot!
  Ah! Friend! to dazzle let the Vain design;
To raise the Thought, and touch the Heart be thine!   250
That Charm shall grow, while what fatigues the Ring
Flaunts and goes down, an unregarded thing:
So when the Sun's broad beam has tired the sight,
All mild ascends the Moon's more sober light,
Serene in Virgin Modesty she shines,   255
And unobserved the glaring Orb declines.
  Oh! blest with Temper, whose unclouded ray
Can make to-morrow cheerful as to-day;
She, who can love a Sister's charms, or hear
Sighs for a daughter with unwounded ear;   260
She, who ne'er answers till a Husband cools,
Or if she rules him never shews she rules;
Charms by accepting, by submitting sways,
Yet has her humour most, when she obeys;
Let Fops or Fortune fly which way they will;   265
Disdains all loss of Tickets, or Codille:
Spleen, Vapours, or Small-pox, above them all,
And Mistress of herself, tho' China fall.
  And yet, believe me, good as well as ill,
Woman's at best a Contradiction still.   270

---

251. *Ring*: cf. *Rape of the Lock*, I 44n. 266. *Codille*: cf. *Rape of the Lock*,
III 92n.

Heaven, when it strives to polish all it can
Its last best work, but forms a softer Man;
Picks from each sex, to make the Favourite blest,
Your love of Pleasure, our desire of Rest:
Blends, in exception to all general rules,   275
Your Taste of Follies, with our Scorn of Fools:
Reserve with Frankness, Art with Truth allied,
Courage with Softness, Modesty with Pride;
Fixed Principles, with Fancy ever new;
Shakes all together, and produces—You.   280
 Be this a Woman's Fame: with this unblest,
Toasts live a scorn, and Queens may die a jest.
This Phœbus promised (I forget the year)
When those blue eyes first opened on the sphere;
Ascendant Phœbus watched that hour with care,   285
Averted half your Parents' simple Prayer;
And gave you Beauty, but denied the Pelf
That buys your sex a Tyrant o'er itself.
The generous God, who Wit and Gold refines,
And ripens Spirits as he ripens Mines,   290
Kept Dross for Duchesses, the world shall know it,
To you gave Sense, Good-humour, and a Poet.

✌

Epistle to Dr. Arbuthnot

(1734)

Sʜᴜᴛ, shut the door, good John! fatigued, I said,
Tie up the knocker, say I'm sick, I'm dead.
The Dog-star rages! nay 'tis past a doubt,
All Bedlam, or Parnassus, is let out:
Fire in each eye, and papers in each hand,   5
They rave, recite, and madden round the land.
 What walls can guard me, or what shade can hide?
They pierce my thickets, thro' my Grot they glide;

---

288. *Tyrant:* i.e., husband. 289. *God:* Apollo, god of the sun (which in the old theory caused metals to grow) and god of wit—i.e., poetry.

ᴇᴘɪsᴛʟᴇ ᴛᴏ ᴅʀ. ᴀʀʙᴜᴛʜɴᴏᴛ: 1. *John:* John Searl, Pope's servant. 3. *Dog-star:* the star Sirius, traditionally identified with midsummer madness. 4. *Bedlam:* Bethlehem Hospital for the insane. 8. *Grot:* Pope's grotto.

By land, by water, they renew the charge;
They stop the chariot, and they board the barge.   10
No place is sacred, not the Church is free;
Even Sunday shines no Sabbath-day to me;
Then from the Mint walks forth the Man of rhyme,
Happy to catch me just at Dinner-time.

    Is there a Parson, much bemused in beer,   15
A maudlin Poetess, a rhyming Peer,
A Clerk, foredoomed his father's soul to cross,
Who pens a Stanza, when he should *engross*?
Is there, who locked from ink and paper, scrawls
With desperate charcoal round his darkened walls?   20
All fly to TWIT'NAM, and in humble strain
Apply to me, to keep them mad or vain.
Arthur, whose giddy son neglects the Laws,
Imputes to me and my damned works the cause:
Poor Cornus sees his frantic wife elope,   25
And curses Wit, and Poetry, and Pope.

    Friend to my Life! (which did not you prolong,
The world had wanted many an idle song)
What *Drop* or *Nostrum* can this plague remove?
Or which must end me, a Fool's wrath or love?   30
A dire dilemma! either way I'm sped,
If foes, they write, if friends, they read me dead.
Seized and tied down to judge, how wretched I!
Who can't be silent, and who will not lie.
To laugh, were want of goodness and of grace,   35
And to be grave, exceeds all Power of face.
I sit with sad civility, I read
With honest anguish, and an aching head;
And drop at last, but in unwilling ears,
This saving counsel, "Keep your piece nine years."   40

    "Nine years!" cries he, who high in Drury-lane,
Lulled by soft Zephyrs thro' the broken pane,
Rhymes ere he wakes, and prints before *Term* ends,

---

10. *barge:* In Pope's time one could be rowed up and down the Thames by watermen. 13. *Mint:* a hide-away for debtors, who on Sunday were free from fear of arrest. 18. *engross:* copy (accounts) in a fair large hand. 21. *Twit'nam:* Twickenham (near London), where Pope lived. 25. *Cornus:* from the Latin for *horn:* hence any wearer of horns, i.e., cuckold. 29. *Drop:* "Ward's drop"—a quack medicine. 40. *Keep . . . years:* Horace's advice to poets (in his *Ars Poetica* 386 ff.) 43. *Term:* The law-court "terms" were the best time to publish, since more people were then in town.

Obliged by hunger, and request of friends:
"The piece, you think, is incorrect? why, take it,   45
I'm all submission, what you'd have it, make it."
    Three things another's modest wishes bound,
My Friendship, and a Prologue, and ten pound.
    Pitholeon sends to me: "You know his Grace,
I want a Patron; ask him for a Place."   50
'Pitholeon libelled me,'—"but here's a letter
Informs you, Sir, 'twas when he knew no better.
Dare you refuse him? Curll invites to dine,
He'll write a *Journal,* or he'll turn Divine."
    Bless me! a packet.—" 'Tis a stranger sues,   55
A Virgin Tragedy, an Orphan Muse."
If I dislike it, "Furies, death and rage!"
If I approve, "Commend it to the Stage."
There (thank my stars) my whole Commission ends,
The Players and I are, luckily, no friends,   60
Fired that the house reject him, " 'Sdeath I'll print it,
And shame the fools——Your Interest, Sir, with Lintot!"
'Lintot, dull rogue! will think your price too much:'
"Not, Sir, if you revise it, and retouch."
All my demurs but double his Attacks;   65
At last he whispers, "Do; and we go snacks."
Glad of a quarrel, straight I clap the door,
"Sir, let me see your works and you no more."
    'Tis sung, when Midas' Ears began to spring,
(Midas, a sacred person and a king)   70
His very Minister who spied them first,
(Some say his Queen) was forced to speak, or burst.
And is not mine, my friend, a sorer case,
When every coxcomb perks them in my face?
    "Good friend, forbear! you deal in dangerous things.   75
I'd never name Queens, Ministers, or Kings;
Keep close to Ears, and those let asses prick;
'Tis nothing—" Nothing? if they bite and kick?
Out with it, Dunciad! let the secret pass,
That secret to each fool, that he's an Ass: 80

---

48. *Prologue:* i.e., to a play. 49. *Pitholeon:* type-name for a bad poet, like
Codrus in 85, *Bavius* in 99 and 250, and *Balbus* in 276. 53. *Curll:* Edmund
Curll, a disreputable publisher, who would like to persuade "Pitholeon" to
another libel. 54. *write a Journal:* i.e., become a journalist in the pay of the
Walpole government. 62. *Lintot:* Bernard Lintot, another publisher. 80.
that . . . Ass: i.e., that his folly (ass's ears) is visible.

The truth once told (and wherefore should we lie?)
The Queen of Midas slept, and so may I.
　　You think this cruel? take it for a rule,
No creature smarts so little as a fool.
Let peals of laughter, Codrus! round thee break,   85
Thou unconcerned canst hear the mighty crack:
Pit, Box, and gallery in convulsions hurled,
Thou stand'st unshook amidst a bursting world.
Who shames a Scribbler? break one cobweb thro',
He spins the slight, self-pleasing thread anew: 90
Destroy his fib or sophistry, in vain,
The creature's at his dirty work again,
Throned in the centre of his thin designs,
Proud of a vast extent of flimsy lines!
Whom have I hurt? has Poet yet, or Peer,   95
Lost the arched eye-brow, or Parnassian sneer?
And has not Colley still his Lord, and whore?
His Butchers Henley, his free-masons Moore?
Does not one table Bavius still admit?
Still to one Bishop Philips seem a wit?   100
Still Sappho—"Hold! for God's sake—you'll offend,
No Names!—be calm!—learn prudence of a friend!
I too could write, and I am twice as tall;
But foes like these—" One Flatterer's worse than all.
Of all mad creatures, if the learn'd are right,   105
It is the slaver kills, and not the bite.
A fool quite angry is quite innocent:
Alas! 'tis ten times worse when they *repent*.
　　One dedicates in high heroic prose,
And ridicules beyond a hundred foes: 110
One from all Grubstreet will my fame defend,
And more abusive, calls himself my friend.
This prints my *Letters,* that expects a bribe,
And others roar aloud, "Subscribe, subscribe."

---

97. *Colley:* Cf. 22n. 98. *Henley, Moore:* Henley was an eccentric open-air preacher, who in one of his sermons had celebrated the butcher's trade; Moore was a plagiarizing poetaster involved in free-masonry. 100. *Bishop:* Hugh Boulter, Archbishop of Armagh, was for some years patron to Ambrose Philips (179-80n.). 101. *Sappho:* any female writer of poetry, though perhaps here identifiable with Lady Mary Wortley Montagu. 111. *all Grubstreet:* i.e., all penurious writers—so-called from the section of London where they lived.

There are, who to my person pay their court: 115
I cough like *Horace,* and, tho' lean, am short,
Ammon's great son one shoulder had too high,
Such *Ovid's* nose, and "Sir! you have an Eye"—
Go on, obliging creatures, make me see
All that disgraced my Betters, met in me.   120
Say for my comfort, languishing in bed,
"Just so immortal *Maro* held his head:"
And when I die, be sure you let me know
Great *Homer* died three thousand years ago.

   Why did I write? what sin to me unknown   125
Dipt me in ink, my parents', or my own?
As yet a child, nor yet a fool to fame,
I lisped in numbers, for the numbers came.
I left no calling for this idle trade,
No duty broke, no father disobeyed.   130
The Muse but served to ease some friend, not Wife,
To help me thro' this long disease, my Life,
To second, ARBUTHNOT! thy Art and Care,
And teach the Being you preserved, to bear.

   But why then publish? *Granville* the polite,   135
And knowing *Walsh,* would tell me I could write;
Well-natured *Garth* inflamed with early praise;
And *Congreve* loved, and *Swift* endured my lays;
The courtly *Talbot, Somers, Sheffield,* read;
Even mitred *Rochester* would nod the head,   140
And *St. John's* self (great *Dryden's* friends before)
With open arms received one Poet more.
Happy my studies, when by these approved!
Happier their author, when by these beloved!
From these the world will judge of men and books,   145
Not from the *Burnets, Oldmixons,* and *Cookes.*

   Soft were my numbers; who could take offence,
While pure Description held the place of Sense?
Like gentle *Fanny's* was my flowery theme,
A painted mistress, or a purling stream.   150

---

117. *Ammon's . . . son:* Alexander the Great. 122. *Maro:* Virgil. 125-6. John 9:2: ". . . who did sin, this man or his parents, that he was born blind?" 128. *numbers:* verses. 135 ff. With the well-known writers, critics, and peers who had approved his writings, Pope contrasts the hack authors who had attacked them. 149. *Fanny:* often identified as Lord Hervey (for whom, see 305 ff.), but applicable to any insipid poet.

Yet then did *Gildon* draw his venal quill;—
I wished the man a dinner, and sat still.
Yet then did *Dennis* rave in furious fret;
I never answered,—I was not in debt.
If want provoked, or madness made them print,   155
I waged no war with *Bedlam* or the *Mint*.
  Did some more sober Critic come abroad;
If wrong, I smiled; if right, I kissed the rod.
Pains, reading, study, are their just pretence,
And all they want is spirit, taste, and sense.   160
Commas and points they set exactly right,
And 'twere a sin to rob them of their mite.
Yet ne'er one sprig of laurel graced these ribalds,
From slashing *Bentley* down to pidling *Tibalds:*
Each wight, who reads not, and but scans and spells,   165
Each Word-catcher, that lives on syllables,
Even such small Critics some regard may claim,
Preserved in *Milton's* or in *Shakespeare's* name.
Pretty! in amber to observe the forms
Of hairs, or straws, or dirt, or grubs, or worms!   170
The things, we know, are neither rich nor rare,
But wonder how the devil they got there.
  Were others angry: I excused them too;
Well might they rage, I gave them but their due.
A man's true merit 'tis not hard to find;   175
But each man's secret standard in his mind,
That Casting-weight pride adds to emptiness,
This, who can gratify? for who can *guess?*
The Bard whom pilfered Pastorals renown,
Who turns a Persian tale for half a Crown,   180
Just writes to make his barrenness appear,
And strains, from hard-bound brains, eight lines a year;

151-72. Though Pope had personal scores against all four of the individuals
named here, they are used in the poem primarily as types: Charles Gildon
and John Dennis as irresponsible critics whose views of literary merit were
determined (so Pope believed) in the one case by money and in the other
by personal resentment; Richard Bentley and Louis Theobald as pedantic
scholars with plenty of *pains, reading, study,* but not enough *spirit, taste,
and sense.* Bentley (though a very great classical scholar) had recently
played havoc with the text of *Paradise Lost, slashing* it to suit himself, and
Theobald—with some very memorable exceptions—had brought more learning than light to the text of Shakespeare's plays. 179-80. Ambrose Philips
(cf. 100), author of some derivative pastorals and a translation called *Persian Tales* (as well as a few respectable poems).

He, who still wanting, tho' he lives on theft,
Steals much, spends little, yet has nothing left:
And He, who now to sense, now nonsense leaning,   185
Means not, but blunders round about a meaning:
And He, whose fustian's so sublimely bad,
It is not Poetry, but prose run mad:
All these, my modest Satire bade *translate,*
And owned that nine such Poets made a *Tate.*   190
How did they fume, and stamp, and roar, and chafe!
And swear, not ADDISON himself was safe.

   Peace to all such! but were there One whose fires
True Genius kindles, and fair Fame inspires;
Blest with each talent and each art to please,   195
And born to write, converse, and live with ease:
Should such a man, too fond to rule alone,
Bear, like the Turk, no brother near the throne.
View him with scornful, yet with jealous eyes,
And hate for arts that caused himself to rise;   200
Damn with faint praise, assent with civil leer,
And without sneering, teach the rest to sneer;
Willing to wound, and yet afraid to strike,
Just hint a fault, and hesitate dislike;
Alike reserved to blame, or to commend,   205
A timorous foe, and a suspicious friend;
Dreading even fools, by Flatterers besieged,
And so obliging, that he ne'er obliged;
Like *Cato,* give his little Senate laws,
And sit attentive to his own applause;   210
While Wits and Templars every sentence raise,
And wonder with a foolish face of praise:——
Who but must laugh, if such a man there be?
Who would not weep, if ATTICUS were he?

   What tho' my Name stood rubric on the walls   215
Or plaistered posts, with claps in capitals?
Or smoking forth, a hundred hawkers' load,

---

183. The reference in *He,* here and in 185 and 187, is general.   190. *Tate:*
Nahum Tate, named here as the type of poet without talent.   198. Alluding to the Sultans' alleged habit of doing away with kinsmen lest they
try to usurp the throne.   209. Addison had written a play about Cato the
Elder, leader of the Roman Senate.   211. *Templars:* i.e., barristers (who were
often amateurs of literature) occupying law chambers in the Inner or Middle Temple.   *raise:* exalt.   215. *rubric:* i.e., advertised in red.   216. Booksellers plastered their door-posts with advertising placards (*claps*).

On wings of winds came flying all abroad?
I sought no homage from the Race that write;
I kept, like *Asian* Monarchs, from their sight: 220
Poems I heeded (now be-rhymed so long)
No more than thou, great GEORGE! a birth-day song.
I ne'er with wits or witlings passed my days,
To spread about the itch of verse and praise;
Nor like a puppy daggled thro' the town,   225
To fetch and carry sing-song up and down;
Nor at Rehearsals sweat, and mouthed, and cried,
With handkerchief and orange at my side;
But sick of fops, and poetry, and prate,
To *Bufo* left the whole *Castalian* state.   230
     Proud as *Apollo* on his forkèd hill,
Sat full-blown *Bufo,* puffed by every quill;
Fed with soft Dedication all day long,
Horace and he went hand in hand in song.
His Library (where busts of Poets dead   235
And a true *Pindar* stood without a head,)
Received of wits an undistinguished race,
Who first his judgment asked, and then a place:
Much they extolled his pictures, much his seat,
And flattered every day, and some days eat: 240
Till grown more frugal in his riper days,
He paid some bards with port, and some with praise;
To some a dry rehearsal was assigned,
And others (harder still) he paid in kind.
Dryden alone (what wonder?) came not nigh,   245
Dryden alone escaped this judging eye:
But still the *Great* have kindness in reserve,
He helped to bury whom he helped to starve.
     May some choice patron bless each gray goose quill!
May every *Bavius* have his *Bufo* still!   250
So, when a Statesman wants a day's defence,
Or Envy holds a whole week's war with Sense,
Or simple pride for flattery makes demands,
May dunce by dunce be whistled off my hands!

---

222. *George:* George II, whose birthday odes by the Poet Laureate, Colley
Cibber, were too bad to be *heeded,* and who was too unliterary to heed
them even if they had been good. 225. *daggled:* The word implies both
slovenly movement and dirtying oneself in mud. 230. *Castalian state:* i.e.,
literature (so-called from the Castalian spring on Mt. Parnassus). 231 ff.
The type of the literary patron. 244. *in kind:* with his own literary efforts.

Blest be the *Great!* for those they take away,   255
And those they left me; for they left me GAY;
Left me to see neglected Genius bloom,
Neglected die, and tell it on his tomb:
Of all thy blameless life the sole return
My Verse, and QUEENSBURY weeping o'er thy urn.   260
   Oh let me live my own, and die so too!
(To live and die is all I have to do:)
Maintain a Poet's dignity and ease,
And see what friends, and read what books I please;
Above a Patron, tho' I condescend   265
Sometimes to call a minister my friend.
I was not born for Courts or great affairs;
I pay my debts, believe, and say my prayers;
Can sleep without a Poem in my head;
Nor know, if *Dennis* be alive or dead.   270
   Why am I asked what next shall see the light?
Heavens! was I born for nothing but to write?
Has Life no joys for me? or (to be grave)
Have I no friend to serve, no soul to save?
"I found him close with *Swift*"—'Indeed? no doubt,   275
(Cries prating *Balbus*) 'something will come out.'
'Tis all in vain, deny it as I will.
'No, such a Genius never can lie still;'
And then for mine obligingly mistakes
The first Lampoon Sir *Will.* or *Bubo* makes.   280
Poor guiltless I! and can I choose but smile,
When every Coxcomb knows me by my *Style*?
   Curst be the verse, how well soe'er it flow,
That tends to make one worthy man my foe,
Give Virtue scandal, Innocence a fear,   285
Or from the soft-eyed Virgin steal a tear.
But he who hurts a harmless neighbour's peace,
Insults fall'n worth, or Beauty in distress,

255-6. I.e., blest be the great lords for the dunces they patronize and so rid
me of, and also for the writers of real talent like John Gay whom they
had not enough sense (Gay had died the year before) to patronize. Pope
mockingly echoes the words with which Job accepts the decisions of *his*
Lord: "The Lord gave, and the Lord hath taken away; blessed be the name
of the Lord." 260. The Duke of *Queensbury* had befriended Gay, and Pope
had written Gay's epitaph. 280. *Sir Will., Bubo:* Identifiable as Sir William
Yonge and Bubb Dodington, but more generally any titled poetaster and
any pretentious fool (*Bubo* is the Latin name for owl, and also suggests
"booby").

Who loves a Lie, lame Slander helps about,
Who writes a Libel, or who copies out: 290
That Fop whose pride affects a patron's name,
Yet absent, wounds an author's honest fame:
Who can your merit *selfishly* approve,
And show the *sense* of it without the *love;*
Who has the vanity to call you friend,   295
Yet wants the honour, injured, to defend;
Who tells whate'er you think, whate'er you say,
And, if he lie not, must at least betray:
Who to the *Dean,* and *silver bell* can swear,
And sees at *Canons* what was never there;   300
Who reads, but with a lust to misapply,
Make Satire a Lampoon, and Fiction, Lie:
A lash like mine no honest man shall dread,
But all such babbling blockheads in his stead.

Let *Sporus* tremble—"What? that thing of silk,   305
Sporus, that mere white curd of Ass's milk?
Satire or sense, alas! can *Sporus* feel?
Who breaks a butterfly upon a wheel?"
Yet let me flap this bug with gilded wings,
This painted child of dirt, that stinks and stings;   310
Whose buzz the witty and the fair annoys,
Yet wit ne'er tastes, and beauty ne'er enjoys:
So well-bred spaniels civilly delight
In mumbling of the game they dare not bite.
Eternal smiles his emptiness betray,   315
As shallow streams run dimpling all the way.
Whether in florid impotence he speaks,
And, as the prompter breathes, the puppet squeaks;
Or at the ear of *Eve,* familiar Toad,

299-300. Alluding to satirical references in Pope's earlier poetry which certain readers had undertaken to "pin down" to particular persons and places. 305. *Sporus:* A homosexual of Nero's court. The contemporary application is usually taken to be to Lord Hervey, (Vice Chamberlain of George II's court and confidant to Queen Caroline) who, with Lady Mary Wortley Montagu, had written a savage attack on Pope's appearance, personality, family, and works. Of Hervey a contemporary wrote: "He has certainly parts and wit, but is the most wretched profligate man that ever was born, besides ridiculous; a painted face, and not a tooth in his head" (cf. 310 ff.); and another contemporary, describing him as "a circulator of tittle-tatle," "a stationed spy," (cf. 319 ff.) declared that he was "such a nice composition of the two sexes that it is difficult to distinguish which is the most predominant" (cf. 324 ff.) 319. Cf. *Par. Lost,* IV 800.

Half froth, half venom, spits himself abroad, 320
In puns, or politics, or tales, or lies,
Or spite, or smut, or rhymes, or blasphemies.
His wit all see-saw, between *that* and *this,*
Now high, now low, now Master up, now Miss,
And he himself one vile Antithesis. 325
Amphibious thing! that acting either part.
The trifling head or the corrupted heart,
Fop at the toilet, flatterer at the board,
Now trips a Lady, and now struts a Lord.
Eve's tempter thus the Rabbins have exprest, 330
A Cherub's face, a reptile all the rest;
Beauty that shocks you, parts that none will trust;
Wit that can creep, and pride that licks the dust.

Not Fortune's worshipper, nor fashion's fool,
Not Lucre's madman, nor Ambition's tool, 335
Not proud, or servile—be one Poet's praise
That, if he pleased, he pleased by manly ways:
That Flattery, even to Kings, he held a shame,
And thought a Lie in verse or prose the same.
That not in Fancy's maze he wandered long, 340
But stooped to Truth, and moralized his song:
That not for Fame, but Virtue's better end,
He stood the furious foe, the timid friend,
The damning critic, half approving wit,
The coxcomb hit, or fearing to be hit; 345
Laughed at the loss of friends he never had,
The dull, the proud, the wicked, and the mad;
The distant threats of vengeance on his head,
The blow unfelt, the tear he never shed;
The tale revived, the lie so oft o'erthrown, 350
Th' imputed trash, and dulness not his own;
The morals blackened when the writings scape,
The libelled person, and the pictured shape;
Abuse, on all he loved, or loved him, spread,
A friend in exile, or a father dead; 355
The whisper, that to greatness still too near,
Perhaps yet vibrates on his SOVEREIGN's ear:
Welcome for thee, fair *Virtue!* all the past;

---

349 ff. Pope alludes to reports (mostly slanders) circulated by his enemies.
But it is only fair to observe that by pillorying bad writers in the *Dunciad*
he had invited this kind of attack. 357. Cf. 319.

For thee, fair Virtue! welcome even the *last!*
   "But why insult the poor, affront the great?"   360
A knave's a knave, to me, in every state:
Alike my scorn, if he succeed or fail,
Sporus at court, or *Japhet* in a jail,
A hireling scribbler, or a hireling peer,
Knight of the post corrupt, or of the shire;   365
If on a Pillory, or near a Throne,
He gain his Prince's ear, or lose his own.
    Yet soft by nature, more a dupe than wit,
Sappho can tell you how this man was bit;
This dreaded Satirist *Dennis* will confess   370
Foe to his pride, but friend to his distress:
So humble, he has knocked at *Tibbald's* door,
Has drunk with *Cibber,* nay has rhymed for *Moore.*
Full ten years slandered, did he once reply?
Three thousand suns went down on *Welsted's* lie.   375
To please a Mistress one aspersed his life;
He lashed him not, but let her be his wife.
Let *Budgel* charge low *Grubstreet* on his quill,
And write whate'er he pleased, except his Will;
Let the two *Curlls* of Town and Court, abuse   380
His father, mother, body, soul, and muse.
Yet why? that Father held it for a rule,
It was a sin to call our neighbour fool:
That harmless Mother thought no wife a whore:
Hear this, and spare his family, *James Moore!*   385
Unspotted names, and memorable long!
If there be force in Virtue, or in Song.

---

363. *Japhet:* Japhet Crook, a notorious forger. 365. *Knight . . . post:* a falsifying witness. 369. *Sappho:* Pope probably means that he was betrayed by Lady Mary (cf. 101n., 305n.), with whom he had once been friendly and perhaps in love. 371. *friend:* In Dennis's poverty-stricken old age, Pope wrote a prologue for a play to be performed for his benefit, and may have used influence on his behalf in other ways. 373. *Moore:* Cf. 98n. The allusion is to some lines Moore plagiarized from Pope. 375. *Welsted:* Leonard Welsted, who had circulated many slanders about Pope. 378-9. *Eustace Budgel,* a hack author, accused Pope of conducting a gossipy newspaper called the *Grubstreet Journal.* Pope says he has let Budgel write whatever slander he pleased, but would not want Budgel to write his will—alluding to the charge that Budgel by forging a will got himself the whole property of a friend to the exclusion of the rightful heirs. 380. two *Curlls:* i.e., the publisher (l. 53) and Hervey.

Of gentle blood (part shed in Honour's cause,
While yet in *Britain* Honour had applause)
Each parent sprung—"What fortune, pray?"—Their own,   390
And better got, than *Bestia's* from the throne.
Born to no Pride, inheriting no Strife,
Nor marrying Discord in a noble wife,
Stranger to civil and religious rage,
The good man walked innoxious thro' his age.   395
No Courts he saw, no suits would ever try,
Nor dared an Oath, nor hazarded a Lie.
Un-learn'd, he knew no schoolman's subtle art,
No language, but the language of the heart.
By Nature honest, by Experience wise,   400
Healthy by temperance, and by exercise;
His life, tho' long, to sickness passed unknown,
His death was instant, and without a groan.
O grant me, thus to live, and thus to die!
Who sprung from Kings shall know less joy than I.   405
    O Friend! may each domestic bliss be thine!
Be no unpleasing Melancholy mine:
Me, let the tender office long engage,
To rock the cradle of reposing Age,
With lenient arts extend a Mother's breath,   410
Make Langour smile, and smooth the bed of Death,
Explore the thought, explain the asking eye,
And keep a while one parent from the sky!
On cares like these if length of days attend,
May Heaven, to bless those days, preserve my friend,   415
Preserve him social, cheerful, and serene,
And just as rich as when he served a QUEEN.
    "Whether that blessing be denied or given,
Thus far was right, the rest belongs to Heaven."

❧

391. *Bestia:* type name for a receiver of bribes. 395. *innoxious:* innocent.
406. *Friend:* i.e., Arbuthnot. 408 ff. Pope's tender care of his aged mother
is well known. 417. Arbuthnot had been physician to Queen Anne.

Epilogue to the Satires

In Two Dialogues

DIALOGUE I

(1738)

Fr. Not twice a twelve-month you appear in Print,
And when it comes, the Court see nothing in't
You grow *correct,* that once with Rapture writ,
And are, besides, too *moral* for a Writ.
Decay of Parts, alas! we all must feel—   5
Why now, this moment, don't I see you steal?
'Tis all from Horace; Horace long before ye
Said, "Tories called him Whig, and Whigs a Tory;"
And taught his Romans, in much better metre,
"To laugh at Fools who put their trust in Peter."   10
  But Horace, Sir, was delicate, was nice;
Bubo observes, he lashed no sort of *Vice:*
Horace would say, Sir Billy *served the Crown,*
Blunt could *do Business,* H—ggins *knew the Town;*
In Sappho touch the *Failings of the Sex,*   15
In reverend Bishops note some *small Neglects,*
And own, the Spaniard did a *waggish thing,*
Who cropt our Ears, and sent them to the King.
His sly, polite, insinuating style
Could please at Court, and make Augustus smile: 20
An artful Manager, that crept between
His Friend and Shame, and was a kind of *Screen.*
But 'faith your very Friends will soon be sore;

---

1. *Fr.:* i.e., friend (but no one in particular). 3. *correct:* cool, punctilious. 5. *Parts:* talents. 10. *Peter:* Peter Walter, a rapacious money-lender. 11 ff. *Horace* (the friend says) would have found inoffensive names for people's vices. 12-3. *Bubo, Sir Billy:* Cf. *Ep. to Arbuthnot,* 280n. 14. *Blunt, H—ggins:* Sir John Blunt and John Huggins, both convicted of breach of trust with public funds. 15. *Sappho:* Cf. *Ep. to Arbuthnot,* 101n., 305n., 369n. 17-18. Alluding to the story that a Spanish sea captain had cut off the ears of an English sea captain (named Jenkins) and told him to take them to his king. This incident, which supposedly occurred in 1731, was still rankling in 1737-8 and helped bring on the ensuing war with Spain, sometimes called the War of Jenkins' Ear. 20. *Augustus:* The Roman emperor (but the name had also been—ironically—applied to George II). 22. See the Introduction, pp. 32-3.

Patriots there are, who wish you'd jest no more—
And where's the Glory? 'twill be only thought   25
The Great man never offered you a groat.
Go see Sir ROBERT—
               P. See Sir ROBERT!—hum—
And never laugh—for all my life to come?
Seen him I have, but in his happier hour
Of Social Pleasure, ill-exchanged for Power;   30
Seen him, uncumbered with the Venal tribe,
Smile without Art, and win without a Bribe.
Would he oblige me? let me only find,
He does not think me what he thinks mankind.
Come, come, at all I laugh he laughs, no doubt;   35
The only difference is I dare laugh out.
   F. Why yes: with *Scripture* still you may be free;
A Horse-laugh, if you please, at *Honesty;*
A Joke on JEKYL, or some odd Old Whig
Who never changed his Principle, or Wig: 40
A Patriot is a Fool in every age,
Whom all Lord Chamberlains allow the Stage:
These nothing hurts; they keep their Fashion still,
And wear their strange old Virtue, as they will.
If any ask you, "Who's the Man, so near   45
"His Prince, that writes in Verse, and has his ear?"
Why, answer LYTTLETON, and I'll engage
The worthy Youth shall ne'er be in a rage;
But were his Verses vile, his Whisper base,
You'd quickly find him in Lord *Fanny's* case.   50
Sejanus, Wolsey, hurt not honest FLEURY,
But well may put some Statesmen in a fury.

---

24. *Patriots:* i.e., even men on your side politically. *Patriots* was the name
taken by members of the Opposition party, to which many of Pope's friends
belonged. 26. *The Great Man:* Sir Robert Walpole. 34. Alluding to Walpole's supposed statement that every man has his price: see the Introduction,
page 17. 39. *Jekyl:* Sir Joseph Jekyl, a man of principle, who though a loyal
Whig opposed Walpole whenever he thought him wrong. 42. Since the
previous year (1737), government censorship had been applied to all plays.
47. *Lyttleton:* George Lyttleton, minor poet and miscellaneous writer, secretary at this time to the Prince of Wales, and highly respected among the
Opposition "Patriots." 50. *Fanny:* Lord Hervey (cf. the *Ep. to Arbuthnot,*
305 ff, esp. 319, 356-7). 51. I.e., calling a good man names will not disturb
him. *Fleury,* one of France's ablest statesmen, was compared by his enemies to the intriguing ministers of Tiberius (Sejanus) and Henry VIII
(Wolsey). 52. *some Statesmen:* e.g., Walpole, who also had been compared
to Sejanus and Wolsey.

Laugh then at any, but at Fools or Foes;
These you but anger, and you mend not those.
Laugh at your friends, and, if your Friends are sore,   55
So much the better, you may laugh the more.
To Vice and Folly to confine the jest,
Sets half the world, God knows, against the rest;
Did not the Sneer of more impartial men
At Sense and Virtue, balance all again.   60
Judicious Wits spread wide the Ridicule,
And charitably comfort Knave and Fool.
    P. Dear Sir, forgive the Prejudice of Youth:
Adieu Distinction, Satire, Warmth, and Truth!
Come, harmless Characters, that no one hit;   65
Come, Henley's Oratory, Osborne's Wit!
The Honey dropping from Favonio's tongue,
The Flow'rs of Bubo, and the Flow of Y—ng!
The gracious Dew of Pulpit Eloquence,
And all the well-whipt Cream of Courtly Sense,   70
That First was H—vy's, F—'s next, and then
The S—te's, and then H—vy's once again.
O come, that easy Ciceronian style,
So Latin, yet so English all the while,
As, tho' the Pride of Middleton and Bland,   75
All Boys may read, and Girls may understand!
Then might I sing, without the least offence,
And all I sung should be the *Nation's Sense,*
Or teach the melancholy Muse to mourn,
Hang the sad Verse on CAROLINA's Urn,   80
And hail her passage to the Realms of Rest,

---

65 ff. Pope now invokes the insipid characteristics of writers in and for the court. 66. *Henley, Osborne:* Henley was called "Orator" Henley because in his open-air pulpits he taught elocution: cf. *Ep. to Arbuthnot,* 98n. Osborne was the pen name of James Pitt, a party writer for the Walpole government; Pope believed Henley also to be in government pay. 67. *Favonio:* "The Favorer." 68. *Y—ng:* Sir William Yonge: cf. 13, and *Ep. to Arbuthnot,* 280n. 69. *gracious:* with a pun on grace. 71-2. Pope refers to a formal resolution of condolence to George II on the death of Queen Caroline in 1737. It was proposed by Henry *Fox,* adopted by parliament (the *Senate*), had been written originally (so Pope evidently believed) by Lord *Hervey,* and the gist of it became *Hervey's once again* in a Latin epitaph on the queen which he presented to the king. 75. *Middleton and Bland:* distinguished Latinists, who (Pope suggests) probably wrote Hervey's epitaph for him. 78. *Nation's Sense:* contemporary political cant term.

All Parts performed, and *all* her Children blest!
So—Satire is no more—I feel it die—
No *Gazetteer* more innocent than I—
And let, a God's-name, every Fool and Knave   85
Be graced thro' Life, and flattered in his Grave.
  F. Why so? if Satire knows its Time and Place,
You still may lash the greatest—in Disgrace:
For Merit will by turns forsake them all:
Would you know when? exactly when they fall.   90
But let all Satire in all Changes spare
Immortal S—k, and grave De—re.
Silent and soft, as Saints remove to Heaven,
All Ties dissolved and every Sin forgiven,
These may some gentle ministerial Wing   95
Receive, and place for ever near a King!
There, where no Passion, Pride, or Shame transport,
Lulled with the sweet Nepenthe of a Court;
There, where no Father's, Brother's, Friend's disgrace
Once break their rest, or stir them from their Place: 100
But past the Sense of human Miseries,
All Tears are wiped for ever from all eyes;
No cheek is known to blush, no heart to throb,
Save when they lose a Question, or a Job.
  P. Good Heaven forbid, that I should blast their glory,   105
Who know how like Whig Ministers to Tory,
And, when three Sovereigns died, could scarce be vext,
Considering what a *gracious Prince* was next.
Have I, in silent wonder, seen such things
As Pride in Slaves, and Avarice in Kings;   110
And at a Peer, or Peeress, shall I fret,
Who starves a Sister, or forswears a debt?

---

82. Pope is probably right in hinting that the queen died without taking the last sacrament, and without being reconciled with the Prince of Wales. 84. *Gazetteer:* any journalist in government pay. 92. *S—k, De—re:* Charles Douglas, Earl of Selkirk, and John West, Earl De Le Warr. Selkirk had survived a series of monarchs (as far back as James II), and hence is *immortal;* De La Warr was sparing, i.e., *grave,* as treasurer of the king's household. The passage suggests that both men were time-servers without principles. 98. *Nepenthe:* a legendary drug inducing forgetfulness. 102. Revelation 21 : 4: "And God shall wipe all tears from their eyes." 104. *Question:* parliamentary motion. *Job:* A public trust turned to private advantage. 107-8. *And . . . Prince:* An ironic allusion to George II (the fourth ruler of Pope's lifetime), and a complimentary allusion to the Prince of Wales, on whom the men of the Opposition pinned their hopes.

Virtue, I grant you, is an empty boast;
But shall the Dignity of *Vice* be lost?
Ye Gods! shall Cibber's Son, without rebuke,   115
Swear like a Lord, or Rich out-whore a Duke?
A Favourite's Porter with his Master vie,
Be bribed as often, and as often lie?
Shall Ward draw Contracts with a Statesman's skill?
Or Japhet pocket, like his Grace, a Will?   120
Is it for Bond, or Peter, (Paltry things)
To pay their Debts, or keep their Faith, like Kings?
If Blount despatched himself, he played the man,
And so may'st thou, illustrious Passeran!
But shall a Printer, weary of his life,   125
Learn, from their books, to hang himself and Wife?
This, this, my friend, I cannot, must not bear;
Vice thus abused, demands a Nation's care;
This calls the Church to deprecate our Sin,
And hurls the Thunder of the Laws on *Gin.*   130

  Let modest FOSTER, if he will, excel
Ten Metropolitans in preaching well:
A simple Quaker, or a Quaker's Wife,
Out-do Llandaff in Doctrine,—yea in Life:
Let humble ALLEN, with an awkward Shame,   135
Do good by stealth, and blush to find it Fame.
Virtue may choose the high or low Degree,
'Tis just alike to Virtue, and to me;
Dwell in a Monk, or light upon a King,
She's still the same, beloved, contented thing.   140
Vice is undone, if she forgets her Birth,
And stoops from Angels to the Dregs of Earth:

---

115. *Cibber's Son:* Colley Cibber's son, Theophilus. 116. *Rich:* John Rich,
an eighteenth-century actor, theatre owner, producer. 119. *Ward:* a forger.
120. *Japhet:* Japhet Crook, another forger. 121. *Bond, Peter:* Denis Bond
was an embezzler; on Peter, see 10n. 123. *Blount:* Charles Blount,
a deistic writer of some reputation, who had committed suicide as the result of a love affair. 124. *Passeran:* Alberto Radicati, Count of Passerano,
author of a book arguing that suicide is not sinful. 125-6. An actual incident; the printer's name was Richard Smith. 129. *deprecate:* (1) disap-
prove, (2) pray for deliverance from. 130. *Gin:* the drink of the lower
classes, against their exorbitant use of which an act had been passed in 1736.
131. *Foster:* James Foster, Anabaptist minister. 132. *Metropolitans:* Arch-
bishops. 134. *Llandaff:* the Bishop of Llandaff (in Wales). 135. *Allen:*
Ralph Allen, an exceptionally charitable man, the model for Squire All-
worthy in Fielding's *Tom Jones.* 142. *Angels:* i.e., Satan and the angels
who fell.

But 'tis the *Fall* degrades her to a Whore;
Let *Greatness* own her, and she's mean no more;
Her Birth, her Beauty, Crowds and Courts confess;   145
Chaste Matrons praise her, and grave Bishops bless;
In golden Chains the willing World she draws,
And hers the Gospel is, and hers the Laws,
Mounts the Tribunal, lifts her scarlet head,
And sees pale Virtue carted in her stead.   150
Lo! at the wheels of her Triumphal Car,
Old England's Genius, rough with many a Scar,
Dragged in the dust! his arms hang idly round,
His Flag inverted trails along the ground!
Our Youth, all liveried o'er with foreign Gold,   155
Before her dance: behind her crawl the Old!
See thronging Millions to the Pagod run,
And offer Country, Parent, Wife, or Son!
Hear her black Trumpet thro' the Land proclaim,
That NOT TO BE CORRUPTED IS THE SHAME.   160
In Soldier, Churchman, Patriot, Man in Power,
'Tis Avarice all, Ambition is no more!
See, all our Nobles begging to be Slaves!
See, all our Fools aspiring to be Knaves!
The Wit of Cheats, the Courage of a Whore,   165
Are what ten thousand envy and adore;
All, all look up, with reverential Awe,
At Crimes that 'scape, or triumph o'er the Law;
While Truth, Worth, Wisdom, daily they decry—
"Nothing is Sacred now but Villainy."   170
   Yet may this Verse (if such a Verse remain)
Shew there was one who held it in disdain.

❧

150. *carted:* exhibited from a cart (as a prostitute). 157. *Pagod:* idol—in this case, money and/or Walpole.

Biographical and Bibliographical References

JOHN DRYDEN

LIFE: Born 1631 or 1632—the traditional date, 9 August 1631, is unreliable —to Erasmus and Mary Pickering Dryden at Aldwinkle in Northampton-shire. Brought up under Puritan influences, both the Drydens and the Pickerings being Parliamentary sympathizers during the Civil Wars, which began when Dryden was ten or eleven and lasted till he was nineteen or twenty. Educated at Westminster School, under its famous headmaster Dr. Richard Busby, from ca. 1644 to 1650; and at Trinity College, Cambridge, from 1650 to ca. 1654. Married in 1663 to Lady Elizabeth Howard, eldest daughter of the Earl of Berkshire, by whom he had three sons. Appointed Poet Laureate and Historiographer Royal under Charles II, in 1670; and to a post in the Customs under James II, in 1683. Dismissed from all his offices at the Revolution in 1688, when he refused to renounce the Roman Catholicism to which he had become a convert in 1686. Owing to these reverses, Dryden's final years were spent in comparative poverty. He died 1 May 1700, and was buried in Westminster Abbey, close to Chaucer.

LITERARY CAREER: Dryden won eminence in original poetry, transla-tion, drama, literary criticism. Among his critical writings, those most interesting today are *An Essay of Dramatic Poesy* (1668), and his preface to the *Fables* (1700), which contains an admirable appreciation of Chaucer, some of whose *Canterbury Tales* Dryden had been "translating" into mod-ern English. As a translator of the classical poets, Dryden produced— besides many vigorous renderings of parts of Homer, Lucretius, Ovid, Persius, Juvenal—a masterpiece in his translation of Virgil's *Aeneid*. As a dramatist, he achieved a further masterpiece in *All for Love,* a tragedy based on the story of Antony and Cleopatra. Dryden's most important non-dramatic original poems, apart from those contained in this volume, are his two odes, *To the Pious Memory of Mrs. Anne Killigrew* (1685), and *Alexander's Feast* (1697); his defense of the Church of England, entitled *Religio Laici* (1683), and his defense (following his conversion in 1687) of the Church of Rome, entitled *The Hind and the Panther;* his poems of compliment like the lines *To the Memory of Mr. Oldham,* and *Eleonora;* and his racy prologues and epilogues to plays.

BIOGRAPHY AND CRITICISM: BIOGRAPHIES: Samuel Johnson's life of Dryden in his *Lives of the English Poets* (1779-81); Walter Scott's, in his edition of Dryden's *Works* (1808); and George Saintsbury's, in the *Eng-lish Men of Letters* series (1881). Much information on particular points is contained in J. M. Osborn's *John Dryden: Some Biographical Facts and*

Problems (1940). CRITICISM: M. Van Doren, *John Dryden: A Study of His Poetry* (1922: 3d ed., 1946); A. Nicoll, *Dryden and His Poetry* (1923); T. S. Eliot, *John Dryden: the Poet, the Dramatist, the Critic* (1932); B. Dobrée, "Milton and Dryden," in *Journ. of Engl. Lit. Hist.*, iii (1936). The nature and evolution of Dryden's thought is helpfully studied in L. I. Bredvold, *Intellectual Milieu of John Dryden* (1934). SPECIFIC WORKS: *Absalom and Achitophel*: See W. Raleigh, "Dryden and Political Satire," in his *Some Authors* (1923); R. Wallerstein, "To Madness Near Allied," in *Huntington Libr. Quart.*, vi (1942-3).

JOHN GAY

LIFE: Born, 30 June 1685, at Barnstaple in Devonshire, the youngest child of William Gay. His mother and father died by the time he was ten, and he was cared for thereafter by a paternal uncle in Barnstaple, who provided him with an excellent education in the local grammar school. On his uncle's death in 1702, he sought his fortunes in London, and after serving half an apprenticeship to a silk merchant (1702-6), found employment as a secretary, first (1708-11) to Aaron Hill, an affluent former school-fellow who had come up to London to dabble at poetry and plays, and then (1712-14) in the household of the Duchess of Monmouth. After 1714 Gay had no regular employments. His literary reputation was now beginning to be established, and between the profits of his later writings (which were occasionally appreciable), the benefactions of his wealthy friends the Duke and Duchess of Queensberry, and a small stipend which he received (1722-31) from a sinecure commissionership of lotteries, he managed to eke out, with a gaiety that endeared him to all who knew him, a life of comfortable improvidence. He died quite suddenly of a fever, 4 December 1732, and was buried in Westminster Abbey, close to Chaucer and to Dryden.

LITERARY CAREER. Though he wrote and collaborated in the writing of a number of plays and operas, Gay's best work (apart from *The Beggar's Opera*) was done in non-dramatic forms. His *Fables* (1727), a series of short poems which adapt and sophisticate the Aesopic fable, became immensely popular with eighteenth- and nineteenth-century readers, and had run by 1890 through 350 editions. For the twentieth century, his most attractive writings after the *Opera* are his *Shepherd's Week* (1714), a series of six pastoral poems (one for each weekday) which parody the elegantly unreal world of ordinary pastoral poetry by creating out of studied inelegances one that is equally unreal; and his *Trivia* (1715), a mock-heroic poem whose theme is the vigorous concreteness of the rough and tumble life of London streets as seen against and through the abstract classic grandeurs implicit in the epic formulae.

BIOGRAPHY AND CRITICISM. BIOGRAPHY: W. H. Irving's *John Gay, Favorite of the Wits* is by far the best biography. CRITICISM: For a recent critical appraisal of Gay, see James Sutherland's "John Gay," in *Pope and His*

Contemporaries, ed. Clifford and Landa, (1949). SPECIFIC WORKS: On *The Beggar's Opera,* see William Empson's essay in his *Some Versions of Pastoral,* (1935; reprinted as *English Pastoral Poetry,* 1938); and B. H. Bronson's "The Beggar's Opera," in *Studies in the Comic* (Publ. of the Calif. Dept. of Eng., viii, 1941).

ALEXANDER POPE

LIFE: Born 21 May 1688, in London, to the Roman Catholic family of Alexander Pope, a retired linen merchant, and his second wife Editha Turner Pope. Educated largely at home, owing to the restrictions on Roman Catholics, which also occasioned, in 1700, the family's removal to Binfield in Windsor Forest, to comply with a regulation forbidding papists to reside within ten miles of London. After his father's death, Pope settled in 1718 with his mother at Twickenham, a small village near London beyond the ten-mile limit. There he spent the remainder of his life, occupied with his writings and literary affairs in the city, with the care of his mother, who lived until 1733, with the landscaping of his small grounds, and with ill health—for he was always a fragile person, four and a half feet tall at his tallest, and afflicted, in later life especially, with recurrent headaches as well as tubercular curvature of the spine. He died 30 May 1744, and was buried in Twickenham Church.

LITERARY CAREER: Pope's best work was done as original poet and as translator of Homer. Through his translations of the *Iliad* (1715-20) and *Odyssey* (1725-6), he achieved financial independence and became the first English poet to make his living by his pen. His translation of the *Odyssey* is equaled and in some respects surpassed by Chapman's Elizabethan translation, but his translation of the *Iliad* is unmatched. Apart from his translations, most of Pope's poetry is satiric. Important poems not included in this volume are *Eloisa to Abelard* (1717); the third and fourth *Moral Essays* (1733, 1731) entitled *Of the Use of Riches;* and his specific "imitations" of Horace, notably the imitation addressed to George II and usually called the *Epistle to Augustus* (1737).

BIOGRAPHY AND CRITICISM: BIOGRAPHIES: W. J. Courthope's life of Pope in the Elwin-Courthope edition of Pope's *Works,* vol. v (1889); Edith Sitwell, *Alexander Pope* (1930); George Sherburn, *The Early Career of Alexander Pope* (1934). CRITICISM: F. R. Leavis, "Pope," in his *Revaluation* (1936); G. Tillotson, *The Poetry of Pope* (1938), and "Alexander Pope," in his *Essays in Criticism and Research* (1942); R. K. Root, *The Poetical Career of Alexander Pope* (1938); A. Warren, "The Mask of Pope," in his *Rage for Order* (1948); W. K. Wimsatt, Jr., "One Relation of Rhyme to Reason: Alexander Pope," in *Mod. Lang. Quart.,* v (1944), and "Rhetoric and Poems: The Example of Pope," in *English Institute Essays* (1949). SPECIFIC WORKS: *The Rape of the Lock:* See G. Tillotson's introduction to the poem in the Twickenham Edition of *The Poems of Alexander Pope,* vol. ii (1942); and Cleanth Brooks, "The Case of Miss Arabella Fermor," in *The Well Wrought Urn* (1947). *An Essay on Man:* See the introduction to the poem in the Twickenham Edition of *The Poems of Alexander Pope,* vol. iii, pt. 1 (1950).

JONATHAN SWIFT

LIFE: Born of English parents—Jonathan Swift and Abigail Erick Swift—in Dublin, 30 November 1667. Educated (with William Congreve, who became his life-long friend) at Kilkenny Grammar School (1673-81); and then at Trinity College, Dublin (1681-8; A.B. 1686). Employed (1689-99) as secretary in the household of Sir William Temple, a retired diplomat and amateur of literature; but with an interlude (1694-6) in which he took orders and held the prebend of Kilroot in Ireland. Returned to Ireland on Temple's death in 1699, this time with a prebend at the cathedral of St. Patrick in Dublin, of which in 1713 he was made Dean. In the interval (from 1708 on) he had become widely known in England as a political and ecclesiastical controversialist, had put his pen at the service of the Tory ministry which came to power in 1710, and had joined a group of young friends (chiefly Pope, Arbuthnot, and Gay) in the famous Scriblerus Club, whose conversations and unformed jottings were to take shape eventually in *Gulliver's Travels, The Beggar's Opera,* and *The Dunciad.* When on Queen Anne's death in 1714 the Tory ministry fell, to be followed by the long Whig rule of Robert Walpole, Swift's chances of further preferment were destroyed. He returned reluctantly to Ireland, and except for visits to England in 1726 and 1727 spent the rest of his life there, occupying himself increasingly with the miserable condition of the Irish poor and with efforts to alleviate it (like the "expedients" mentioned in his *Modest Proposal*) or to force attention to it (like the *Proposal* itself). The indifference which met most of his efforts to help the Irish, his keen sense of exile from the life of literary and social brilliance that he had known in England, the frustration of his own personal ambitions, and (after 1738) the worsening of a chronic malady (a kind of vertigo), combined to embitter him as he grew older, and there were long periods toward the close of his life when he was actually insane. He died, 19 October 1745, and was buried in St. Patrick's, where his tomb bears the inscription he composed: *Ubi saeva indignatio ulterius cor lacerare nequit* (Where savage indignation no longer lacerates the heart).

LITERARY CAREER: Though Swift is author of a large amount of poetry, some of it excellent, his distinction lies in prose—the medium in which he achieved an imaginative as well as logical precision that perhaps no other English writer has quite matched. His writings in prose embrace a wide variety of subject-matters (English and Irish politics, religion and the church, ancient and modern history, economics, literature, quack astrologers, broomsticks, and many more) and are difficult to classify, except into non-satirical and satirical. Swift's most important satirical writings, apart from those included in this volume, are *A Tale of a Tub* (1704), which is a richer, but less concentrated, assault on human self-deceptions than *Gulliver; The Battle of the Books* (1704), a mock-heroic treatment of the perennial theme of tradition and the individual talent; *The Drapier's Letters:* a group of letters written in the *persona* of a Dublin cloth merchant (and with a plain man's simple eloquence) to protest the attempt of a certain William Wood, backed by the English government, to impose on Ireland an inferior copper coinage; and *Polite Conversation* (1738), a parody of polite *clichés* and cant.

BIOGRAPHY AND CRITICISM: BIOGRAPHIES: Though there are now many studies of aspects of Swift's biography, the best factual account of his life as a whole is still that by H. Craik (1882). More recent studies include C. Van Doren, *Swift* (1930), S. Gwynn, *The Life and Friendships of Dean Swift* (1933), B. Newman, *Jonathan Swift* (1937); and R. Quintana offers an excellent introduction to his literary career in *The Mind and Art of Jonathan Swift* (1936). CRITICISM: E. Pons, *Swift: les années de jeunesse et le 'Conte du Tonneau';* M. M. Rossi and J. M. Hone, *Swift: or the Egotist* (1934); W. B. C. Watkins, *Perilous Balance: The Tragic Genius of Swift, Johnson, and Sterne* (1939); J. F. Ross, *Swift and Defoe (Univ. of Calif. Publ. in Engl.,* xi, 1947); Herbert Davis, *The Satire of Jonathan Swift* (1947). SPECIFIC WORKS: *A Modest Proposal:* For an excellent account of the economic backgrounds of this satire, see L. A. Landa, "A Modest Proposal and Populousness," in *Mod. Philol.,* xl (1942). *Gulliver's Travels:* See J. B. Moore, "The Role of Gulliver," in *Mod. Philol.* xxx (1928); J. F. Ross, "The Final Comedy of Lemuel Gulliver," in *Studies in the Comic* (Publ. of the Calif. Dept. of Engl., viii, 1941); J. Horrell, "What Gulliver Knew," in *Sewanee Review,* li (1943); S. Kliger, "The Unity of Gulliver's Travels," in *Mod. Lang. Quart.* vi (1945); A. E. Case, *Four Essays on Gulliver's Travels* (1945).